D0959795

✳ BODIES OF WORK ✳

BODY, COMMODITY, TEXT

Studies of Objectifying Practice

A series edited by

ARJUN APPADURAI,

JEAN COMAROFF, and

JUDITH FARQUHAR

EDWARD SLAVISHAK

✳ **BODIES OF WORK** ✳

CIVIC DISPLAY AND LABOR IN

INDUSTRIAL PITTSBURGH

DUKE UNIVERSITY PRESS   DURHAM AND LONDON   2008

© 2008 Duke University Press

All rights reserved

Printed in the United States of America

on acid-free paper ∞

Designed by C. H. Westmoreland

Typeset in Warnock Light by

Keystone Typesetting, Inc.

Library of Congress Cataloging-in-Publication

Data appear on the last printed

page of this book.

TO MY MOTHER

CONTENTS

ILLUSTRATIONS

ACKNOWLEDGMENTS

I wish to thank the people who work the stacks—the staffs of the Archives of the Historical Society of Western Pennsylvania, the University of Pittsburgh's Archives Service Center, Frick Fine Arts Library, and Special Collections Library, the Pennsylvania Department and Science/ Technology Department of the Carnegie Library of Pittsburgh, the Albert and Shirley Small Special Collections Library at the University of Virginia, the Saint Vincent College Library, and the interlibrary loan departments of the University of North Carolina's Davis Library and Susquehanna University's Blough-Weis Library. I gratefully acknowledge research and travel funding from the Department of History of the University of North Carolina at Chapel Hill, Susquehanna University's School of Arts, Humanities, and Communications, and an Albert Beveridge Research Grant from the American Historical Association.

The book has benefited greatly from critiques by Peter Filene, Leon Fink, Jerma Jackson, and Judith Farquhar. Portions of this work have appeared previously in the *Journal of Social History,* the *Pennsylvania Magazine of History and Biography,* and the *Journal of the Gilded Age and Progressive Era.* The respective editors, Peter Stearns, Tamara Miller, and Alan Lessof, offered great patience and guidance, along with the helpful suggestions of anonymous reviewers. I also thank colleagues with whom I have discussed my work at conferences of the Pennsylvania Historical Association, the Popular/American Culture Association, Interdisciplinary Nineteenth-Century Studies organization, and the Mining History Association. My editor Ken Wissoker and anonymous readers for Duke University Press have helped improve this work substantially. Two special notes of thanks: the late Eugene Levy taught me how to be a historian when I was an undergraduate at Carnegie Mellon University. This book's story could not have emerged until I understood his innovative research on the aesthetics of power lines and industrial landscapes. My biggest debt is to John Kasson, who casually mentioned artificial limbs one day as a potential dissertation topic. That insight, his encouragement to focus on Pittsburgh, and his generous commentary on my writing made my ideas flourish.

Finally, I wish to thank my mother, Patricia Slavishak, for being my number one cheerleader. She has always joked that she will step in and write for me if I am too busy. I have not taken her up on the offer . . . yet. My greatest thanks go to my wife, Stacy, and son, Neil. Stacy read early drafts to make sure that I wrote a book that actually meant something. Neil has shown me that books are best enjoyed while being chewed or submerged in water. In their own ways, they never allow me to take myself too seriously.

NOTE ON USAGE

Two spelling variations—Pittsburgh and Pittsburg—appear in this book. Before 1891 and since 1911, the city's name has been spelled Pittsburgh. Between 1891 and 1911, however, the *h* was dropped from official spellings, following regulations of the U.S. Geographic Board of Names to standardize the spelling of various "burgs" in the United States. Throughout the book, I use the full form of the name but retain the shortened form in direct quotations and in the titles of books, pamphlets, and articles published between 1891 and 1911.

When sensational newspapers are short on their line of goods, they love to picture Pittsburg as a volcano vomiting forth sensations.

—*Bulletin*, 11 March 1905

INTRODUCTION

✶ "Strenuous America is the place for work—hard work and lots of it." So declared the *Bulletin*, a magazine of Pittsburgh arts and society, in 1905. The notion that the United States was the proper home for hard work at the turn of the century found voice in many places beyond the humming city of industry in southwestern Pennsylvania. Popular writers, clergymen, and politicians all stressed the importance of work to the global success of American business and culture. The traditional work ethic that had guided the American middle class through the nineteenth century held that devotion to hard work strengthened one's character, improved one's social standing, and guaranteed the survival of the nuclear family. Hard work was home in the "strenuous" America of the late nineteenth century and early twentieth because American men consciously worked to make it so, battling specters of feminization and modern softness through sermons on industriousness, popular sporting activities, and campaigns for hardened primitiveness. The fact that a Pittsburgh journal declared work to be an American possession would have surprised no one in 1905. If the United States cultivated a love of hard work at the turn of the century, then Pittsburgh perfected it. Pittsburgh seemed a particularly fitting place in which to prove that hard work gave meaning to the nation, for the city had propelled itself into the national consciousness several decades earlier with its symbols of constant work— its smoky shroud, towering mills, record output, and hard bodies.[1]

Yet by 1900, the logic and promise of the work ethic faced serious challenges from recent technological, demographic, and economic changes. As work itself was remade by machine technology, mass immigration, and the emergence of an urban office culture, many intellectuals worried that work in America no longer contained the very features that had made it so vital to the nation's future. If, as many critics believed, American labor had been subdivided by management, "saved" by new machinery, invaded by unskilled foreigners, and made impotent by white-collar occupations, then its ability to orchestrate American life had been severely compromised. Accordingly, both blue-collar and white-collar workers looked beyond the workplace for new forms of independence and physical ability that would function in ways similar to the old. The historian Keith Gandal identified three sets of popular sites and figures of the "movement for strenuousness" at the turn of the century: war and the soldier, the American West and the cowboy, and the urban slum and the investigative reporter. To this collection of symbolic stages upon which American men rehearsed their roles as rugged, manly men, I add the industrial workplace and the worker who occupied it. Even as work lost much of its ability to arm men with a sense of mastery, it remained an arena in which imagined narratives of strength thrived. The strength of the industrial workplace in Pittsburgh relied on the worker's body as an expression of masculine force, coordination, and control.[2]

During the Progressive era, the human form often expressed the power and character of the nation's cities as well. From Carl Sandburg's description of Chicago as the city of "the Big Shoulders" to Henry James's efforts to read the "faces" of New York and Washington, the overlapping of bodies and cities proliferated as a way of thinking about urban America during this time. Just as cities appeared to possess physical features of human bodies, so, too, did individual bodies appear to take on the characteristics of the cities in which they lived; with this two-way symbolic traffic commentators represented cities and bodies as one and the same and created a convenient metaphor for those who were invested in the success of Pittsburgh's industries. The dance historian Linda Tomko noted that American culture between 1880 and 1920 exhibited a particularly keen campaign to "capture the body; to make the body stable for a moment; to address its (knowable) needs." In Pittsburgh, the body of the industrial worker was captured time and again, held motionless while those who wished to understand Pittsburgh (or those who wished *others* to understand Pittsburgh) charted its strengths and weaknesses. In doing so, boosters, reformers, labor leaders, and a host of other actors who scrutinized the worker's body also held in the spotlight ideas about work and the city that fostered it. The working body frequently appeared in public moments of celebration, criticism, and commiseration as a way to focus attention on the quotidian aspects of city life that, in the service of various economic and political agendas, became representative of the city as a whole.[3]

The displays, narratives, and performances studied in *Bodies of Work* targeted both internal and external audiences. Boosters defined their dual role as educating locals and enticing outsiders. D. C. Ripley, a glass manufacturer and civic promoter, argued that white-collar Pittsburghers reflected on local wonders only "when an acquaintance comes to our city and expresses a desire to see our industries; then we take a day off and are often more interested than the stranger." The city's boosters disseminated statistics and symbols as if locals knew little about the region. Labor reformers also tried to teach residents of the city something about their state of affairs, while simultaneously using scenes of Pittsburgh work to launch arguments against American industrial practices as a whole. Both groups implied that they knew the real face of local industry and that their counterparts missed (or deliberately misconstrued) something crucial about work and the city.[4]

CHANGE AND CHANGING SYMBOLS

How did the image of the Pittsburgh body of work change during this time of mechanization and immigration? This book considers what happened to the symbolic confluence of work, the city, and the body when work was radically remade. Those who wielded the body as a metaphor attempted to persuade themselves and others about the present state of Pittsburgh by invoking narratives of the past and images of the future. Nostalgia certainly permeated city boosters' vision of the working body, yet their images were only several of many. The figure of the body at work was part of a shared visual vocabulary that served as both an anchor and a propeller, slowing the course of change to focus the public's attention on traditional visions of men at work, yet also pressing forward into new understandings of how industrial change affected life and limb. If the visual vocabulary of working figures was shared, it was also subject to different inflections. There were multiple ways to read industrial workers' bodies in turn-of-the-century Pittsburgh; this book charts these interpretations. The fact that workers' bodies became surrogates for competing ideas about work and the city suggests a fugitive quality to such representations, belying any notion of fixed meaning. Representations of Pittsburgh workers did not necessarily determine the way in which target audiences understood their world. On the contrary, such representations gambled frequently with their own authority, leaving the door open for conflicting interpretations and revealing the many obstacles encountered in the act of presenting the work processes of an industrial city.[5]

The Man of Steel figure illustrates the way in which, as the historian William Sewell Jr. suggests, "every act of symbolic attribution puts the symbols at risk." Since the mid–nineteenth century the image of a strong, confident, capable worker appealed to labor unions as a portable symbol of manual skill and political rights. Historians have shown that industrial workers in Pittsburgh and elsewhere used images of broad-shouldered, muscular men to connote labor's social and economic contributions. Elizabeth Faue found numerous examples of massive male bodies in union cartoons supporting organizing efforts in Minneapolis during the Great Depression. Working-class veneration of prizefighters since the mid–nineteenth century likewise emphasized coordination, power, and domination. Finally, workers' comportment in parades in the 1880s and 1890s endorsed a formal vision of labor as disciplined, solid, and physically developed. Such symbolizing involved real risks, however. The same figure used to represent working people could be readily adapted for other projects as well. In Pittsburgh, boosters put forward a parallel image of working-class health and vitality to promote the city as a place in which one needed only a hardy work ethic to achieve economic independence and physical mastery. Boosters' representations implied that a will to succeed did more to improve workers' well-being than any proposed labor reforms, redistributions of wealth, or municipal improvements. The Pittsburgh Chamber of Commerce used imagery of tireless workers to present Pittsburgh as a place in which workers had nothing to complain about.[6]

The implications of such risk are profound. At stake in turn-of-the-century Pittsburgh was the power to determine the public face of physical tasks and routines hidden from view. In a sense, it was a public relations war, but a public relations war related to the nonsymbolic aspects of immigration policy, allocation of resources, and, literally, lives and limbs. Rivals in the struggle to capture the essence of Pittsburgh through its industrial work vied for a hegemonic position—a position of domination that functioned without overt coercion and with the passive approval of the dominated. They fought to define reality for others. Particularly helpful on this point are Sewell's observations on authority and cultural coherence. "Centrally placed" actors' typical method to achieve stability, he notes, "is not so much to establish uniformity as it is to organize difference. They are constantly engaged in efforts not only to normalize or homogenize but also to hierarchize, encapsulate, exclude, criminalize, hegemonize, or marginalize practices and populations that diverge from the sanctioned ideal. By such means, authoritative actors attempt, with varying degrees of success, to impose a certain coherence onto the field of cultural practice."[7]

To achieve such a position of coherence, however temporary or partial, groups have to present an account of the world that resonates by seeming inevitable, natural, or even beneficial. In Pittsburgh, this meant producing representations that were relevant to governmental practices, manufacturing concerns, and cultural discourses. In order to create symbols of work, distribute them broadly, and gain enough acceptance so that a critical mass of observers thought in a similar way about the city, symbol makers had to target multiple audiences via flattery, wonder, and shame. Establishing that work in the city was a positive, creative experience for workers encouraged further investment in a harmonious, productive region and potentially weakened any attempt to alter local labor arrangements in significant ways. Establishing that the same types of work were punishing exercises in danger and tedium, on the other hand, pressured government to regulate the worst aspects of industry and could make it much more difficult for capitalists to maintain the status quo. Local political contests in the era of muckraking depended in part on angering or disgusting middle-class voters to the extent that they would compel officials to take action. Lincoln Steffens's survey of political corruption, "Pittsburg: A City Ashamed" (1903), chronicled Pittsburghers' muted exasperation at the state of their government in order to "sound for the civic pride of an apparently shameless citizenship." Steffens tried to awaken readers by chiding them for either not knowing what they should have known or not caring enough to act upon what they knew. An emphasis on discovery and consequent action pervaded work iconography in Pittsburgh; boosters, workers, reformers, painters, journalists, and entrepreneurs all agreed that they could reveal something remarkable about industrial labor that would inspire celebration, class solidarity, legal revision, mass education, tourism, or a purchase.[8]

This is not to suggest that industrial workers would have maintained the political and economic power they enjoyed before the 1880s if they had only created provocative images of themselves for public consumption. Neither is it to argue that if boosters had successfully promoted a positive view of Pittsburgh industrial labor as reality they would have wielded unchecked power within the city. With the anthropologist James Scott, I argue that hegemony is much more difficult to achieve than it might appear. Scott cautions that what scholars see as the unrivaled cultural leadership of hegemony must often be qualified by the nature of the sources used to measure it: "Short of the total declaration of war that one does occasionally find in the midst of a revolutionary crisis, most protests and challenges—even quite violent ones—are made in the realistic expectation that the central features of the form of domination will remain intact. So long as that expectation prevails, it is impossible to know from the public transcript alone how much of the appeal to hegemonic values is prudence and formula and how much is ethical submission."[9]

In the Pittsburgh of this period agreement across classes and groups, then, was not only as difficult to achieve as Sewell suggests but was constantly undermined by the existence of Scott's "hidden transcripts"— unguarded, "backstage" thoughts expressed when people were no longer in the presence of rivals. This "paper-thin" model of hegemony allows the historian to account for the obvious advantages of resources and distribution enjoyed by the civic elite while recognizing that vast areas of workers' daily experience remain beyond scholarly view. This is especially true of a study based on the interpretation of public events and texts; my sources are not only public transcripts, but highly formalized ones as well. The people featured in *Bodies of Work* were joined in the effort to make sense of Pittsburgh at a time when the city seemed to herald something new. I am involved in the same effort, yet my sources of observation are either texts or mediated through texts. This mediation deserves attention not as a mea culpa but as an explanation of the book's method. I cannot state with any certainty what the vast majority of Pittsburghers or non-Pittsburghers thought of industrial work between 1880 and 1915. I instead look at the ways in which a small sample of individuals and institutions decided what those audiences *should* think about industrial work. They made these decisions with an eye toward their own interests—literal and figurative investments—and their sense of audience expectations. The publics at the other end of these public displays, then, had a role to play in defining the general terms in which one could describe Pittsburgh: prosperous, healthy, chaotic, brutal, powerful, depressing. This symbolic contest offers evidence of neither candor nor outright domination, but it may help to explain why Pittsburgh became known as a bellwether of American labor fragmentation and impotence and commercial fortunes. It may also explain why Pittsburgh has remained the Steel City long after its economy ceased revolving around the production of steel.[10]

Sewell, in reconciling the stasis of ethnographic thick description with cultural change, observes that interpretations of the past move between the modes of history and the historical. History chronicles change over time. The historical suspends time to immerse the reader in the context of a particular past by connecting texts, events, actions, and beliefs with some "common but now foreign logic." This model is especially apt for a work that studies the means by which past actors confronted change in their lifetimes. *Bodies of Work* argues that a three-and-a-half-decade period spanning the beginning of the twentieth century featured specific forms of technological and social change that produced multiple attempts to "brand" Pittsburgh symbolically in the service of economic and professional goals. In history mode, I recount the events and texts through which a variety of actors narrated transformations and responded to each other's version of Pittsburgh's tale. In historical mode, I explain how the privilege of defining work, skill, manhood, and power became the focus of a contest between the economic elite, those who worked for them, and those who aspired to engineer society according to their own assumptions about science, government, or culture. The cohesive logic of the era held that workers' bodies were suitable devices by which to assess the costs and benefits of industrial capitalism. Discord sprang not from the method of measurement but from the sample measured. The media of bodily representation examined here—prose, poetry, commercial illustration, painting, sculpture, photography, performance, pageantry, and statistical survey—allowed for both complimentary and critical conclusions. Yet they also produced moments of unintentional convergence. For instance, when workers reaffirmed flattering images of industrial labor to declare their craft pride, they subscribed to a pleasing civic narrative that could work against their demands for reform. Likewise, when boosters highlighted mechanical marvels at the expense of human imagery, they reproduced elements of a Progressive argument about the fate of workers in mechanized industry. Finally, when social researchers analyzed case studies, specimens, and types of workers in order to construct narratives about work in Pittsburgh, they adopted the same rationalized understanding of human beings that they found so despicable when glimpsed in the decisions of owners and managers.

Bodies of Work describes a dialogue about workers and their jobs that was untidy and seemingly cyclical. The efforts of Pittsburghers and outsiders to represent the city seem to float off into the air without having any tangible effects on the ground. Without vast caches of reception data to divulge how people experienced these "bodies of work," the historian seeking such effects might despair that the symbols never actually *did* anything. The remedy is to see the dialogue itself as an "interaction between order and its contestatory 'others,' " to use the historian Dominick LaCapra's phrase. This means understanding how past actors challenged one another for significance, in this case, through the manipulation of signs. Sewell stresses that synchronic snapshots of cultures can, in fact, accommodate change. If culture is understood as both a "model of" and "model for" reality, then gaps between what people expect from the world and what they experience in the world create moments of innovation—in addition to moments of "conflict, communication, rivalry, or exchange." The method I have adopted is to move frequently between past trends, routines, and events and the accounts created to announce, discount, and make sense of them. "Because the world is always far more manifold than our representations of it," Sewell writes, "the representations are always potentially susceptible to change." This understanding of historical change places contingency in the foreground and looks for what LaCapra characterized as the "unrealized or even resisted possibilities of the past."[11]

Bodies of Work focuses on the space between the world as it was and the world as it was imagined. Just as it would make little sense to speak of a coherent Pittsburgh culture at the turn of the century—a period during which residents' multiple identities and practices separated the local population into isolated, wary enclaves—it would also be misleading to posit a unified culture of work iconography in the city at this time. The work iconography exhibited in Pittsburgh during this era was never a stable, comprehensive system of representation, but instead a contradictory and piecemeal affair adapted to address changes in work and population. One way of seeing Pittsburgh through the worker's body did not simply triumph over and replace another. Furthermore, each set of representations alternated between modes of intimacy and distance, welcoming the reader/viewer into a seemingly close relationship with the Pittsburgh workingman but ultimately providing few clues about his life.

INDUSTRIAL PITTSBURGH

Two vivid images of Pittsburgh were central to nineteenth-century popular accounts of the city: the Smoky City and the Great Workshop. Moreover, the local business elite made conspicuous efforts to maintain an image of Pittsburgh in the twentieth century as an advanced and vigorous place "where the clang of hammers, the rattle and crash of machinery, the roar of traffic and the hum of myriad industries create[d] a more than Wagnerian symphony." The core of this image was an idealized version of the male industrial worker, an able body meant to exude the confidence of a growing city whose leaders hoped to rub civic elbows with the likes of New York and Chicago. The city's boosters first attempted to wield the worker's body as a useful symbol in the 1880s and 1890s, when Pittsburgh appeared regularly in the national press as a city on the rise. Early in their campaign to create an image for the city, boosters seized upon the worker's body as a useful, recognizable vehicle of civic pride. At a time when most American cities were symbolized by female allegorical figures, they associated the Steel City with the contours of the male body.[12]

Advocates and national writers presented Pittsburgh as a city devoted to the type of manhood defined by rough work. As Elizabeth Beardsley Butler, the secretary of New Jersey's Consumer League, noted of Pittsburgh in 1909, "Workshop this city is, but a workshop which calls for the labor of men." The three main industries examined here, steel, glass, and coal, were almost exclusively male, certainly so in areas of production that involved the manual movement of massive quantities of materials. By studying the heaviest labor that took place in the city's heavy industries, I focus on physical tasks that epitomized Pittsburgh work. I am just as interested in the process by which observers came to see these tasks as characteristic of the city as I am in the technical changes that engineers brought into the workplace after the 1870s. The two were closely linked. In 1901, the journalist Waldon Fawcett wrote that Pittsburgh was the city "where above all other places a realization of the majesty of manual labor burns itself into the brain." Yet those who saw majesty in Pittsburgh's manual work were joined by those who saw mostly suffering and danger. As production shifted from batch processes that relied upon individual strength and judgment to continuous flow processes that employed machinery to remove much of the strength and judgment required to do a job, critics of capital warned that the majesty of a body at work had become a grim joke. New threats of monotony, pace, and physical hazards characterized the steel, glass, and coal industries in the late nineteenth century and early twentieth. Friction between those who built Pittsburgh's industries and those who called for their overhaul produced an intermittent public dialogue that allied individuals and groups who would have found very little in common otherwise.[13]

Work in Pittsburgh iron manufacturing and window glass production required varying levels of skill, strength, and endurance. Among the work tasks featured in these industries, two positions—iron puddling and window glass blowing—emerged by the 1880s as the most visually spectacular and most frequently described in print. Puddlers, who stirred molten metal to improve its chemical properties, were not the best-paid workers in Pittsburgh's iron mills; rollers and heaters generally earned more than puddlers for their supervisory roles. Yet puddling became the most chronicled and the most widely displayed job in the metals industry because it was a clear example of the type of difficult skilled work that those who championed the city found most compelling. Window glass blowers were only one of many types of laborers in the city's glass industry, yet they, too, performed a heavy, skilled task that resembled puddling in its archetypal triumph of man over fire and molten material. A third task typical of work done in Pittsburgh industry, the mining of bituminous coal, failed to generate the same sort of celebratory scrutiny; its relative absence in the iconography of Pittsburgh work highlights the qualities of skill, creativity, and performance that made a work task either an ideal spectacle or unnoticed toil. Moreover, the puddling of iron and the blowing of window glass emerged as recognizable spectacles of idealized Pittsburgh work at the very time industrialists marginalized them in favor of more efficient, continuous systems of making metal and glass. This was no coincidence. Boosters' tales of modern industrial Pittsburgh were rooted in a historical argument about what the city had offered to the nation and its residents in the second half of the nineteenth century.[14]

Though a central assumption of this book—that celebratory work iconography emerged when it did just as city boosters were trying to compensate for the changes they witnessed in Pittsburgh labor—posits a decline in the visual quality of industrial work, I recognize that new machinery made many workdays less strenuous. The window glass blower who became a machine tender may have had fewer physical demands placed on him in the course of his workday, but the unskilled glassworker tasked with loading furnaces and moving materials may have had to shovel, lift, and carry more than ever. This book thus focuses on both the skilled worker, who carried boosters' civic pride at the turn of the century, and the unskilled worker, who emerged in the public discourse of Pittsburgh work in a more negative fashion. The labor historian David Montgomery commented two decades ago that scholars tended to ignore the work experiences of the common laborer, a figure who defied the "celebration of incessant change and of mechanical power" that captured much scholarly interest. Boosters, too, ignored the unskilled worker in favor of men who performed spectacular tasks. Yet city backers focused on the puddler and the glassblower not for their signification of change, but for their claims to continuity; here were men who performed seemingly impossible work tasks that endured because they were indispensable to modern American life. Before (and especially after) these tasks became obsolete, the idea that the city's work remained essential to modern civilization appealed to those who identified with the business of Pittsburgh industry.[15]

Scholarly studies of the effects of changes in manufacturing processes have explored ways in which new technologies and production strategies altered the nature of industrial work. Harry Braverman's *Work and Monopoly Capital: The Degradation of Work in the Twentieth Century* (1974), a Marxist analysis of management's organization and control of the industrial work floor, amplified an ongoing debate about the labor process. As the subtitle suggests, Braverman set the tone by showing a decline in traditional work processes and skills under industrial capitalism, arguing that workers' alienation from their jobs and a growing chasm of skill between laborers and management characterized American work in the twentieth century. Some historians have followed Braverman's lead, describing the process through which established skills and ways of working were "persistently diluted or erased." Others have reassessed his thesis, questioning whether Braverman romanticized the craft worker and overstated the industrial worker's powerlessness within a mechanized system. Michael Nuwer's and David Jardini's studies of metals manufacturing represented the push to demonstrate that continuous production processes offered some workers strategic positions within the workforce. Both scholars contrasted evidence of deskilling in turn-of-the-century industry with signs of workers' new strategic importance in continuous manufacturing processes. Although machine tending was certainly monotonous and required less training than crafts, workers in charge of key segments of production could maintain or disrupt the flow of materials through the workplace. Certain machine tenders, then, gained new leverage with their employers even as their old monopoly on skill diminished. Finally, the economists Claudia Goldin and Lawrence Katz argue that the employment of skilled workers in any given industry after mechanization depended on "whether the machine-maintenance demand for skilled labor [was] offset by the production-process demand for unskilled labor." Skilled workers after mechanization performed tasks that were different from those of their premechanical counterparts, installing and regulating the machines that unskilled or semiskilled workers operated. Machinists and mechanics certainly produced, but their creation was a *system*, not a tangible object like an iron bar or a pane of glass. Underlying all historical models of skill transformation is the unexplored point that as work changed, its appearance changed as well. This visual transformation becomes significant when one asks how people within and peripheral to industry used the idea of work to make claims about men, the city of Pittsburgh, and modernity.[16]

The following chapters examine changes in the city's work and reveal the variety of reactions they elicited from those who lived in Pittsburgh or those who scrutinized it from without. The first chapter examines the effects of technology and new immigration patterns on the spectacle of work in the three industries. Mechanization of manufacturing and mass immigration from southern and eastern Europe produced an industrial order in which observers depicted machines doing work and humans either passively guiding machines or toiling within unskilled gangs. The results were less than picturesque. Chapter 2 delves further into disagreeable imagery by exploring written accounts of the Carnegie Steel Company's lockout of 1892 at its massive works in the town of Homestead and the violent clash that ensued between Pinkerton guards and people of the Pittsburgh region. I focus on writers' attention to the bodies "at war" in Homestead to suggest just how negative industrial and civic images could be when narrators read ethnic difference and lack of skill in the physiques before them. In its unpredictability and bedlam, the so-called Battle of Homestead served as a counterpoint to the staged performances and ordered spectacles that boosters mounted in the city.

Chapter 3 marks a shift from the unpleasant to the consciously triumphant. Pittsburgh's Chamber of Commerce, in conjunction with the city's establishment press, designed an image for the city that was rooted in the physical artistry of the skilled industrial worker. The mayor's declaration in 1892 that "here, if anywhere, man has learned to believe that 'next to faith in God is faith in labor'" illustrated a guiding tenet of economic and cultural elites, who believed that Pittsburgh's future lay in the marriage of manufacturing power and intellectual stimulation. Theirs was a Pittsburgh of technological supremacy, aesthetic beauty, and dramatic work praised in public art, pageants, and guidebooks. A different kind of drama steers the analysis of chapter 4, where I examine the social science of the Pittsburgh Survey to explain how labor reformers entered into a symbolic debate with boosters, confronting inspiring imagery with signs of injury and weakness. Progressive efforts to redesign society along lines of ordered efficiency used workers' bodies as sites where local and national knowledge met. This understanding of the vulnerable body and its connection to macroeconomic trends came after decades of local reporting of industrial accidents and international research on exhaustion in the workplace. The writers of the survey adopted representations of working bodies and arguments of causation that demonstrated the need for the very kind of expertise and engineering the survey writers could provide.[17]

Chapter 5 refocuses on the gendered aspects of Pittsburgh work spectacles by considering how labor reformers approached the presence of women in the industrial workforce. I argue that the Pittsburgh Survey's critique of female labor centered on an inability to find any redeeming visual cues in the sight of a woman at work. City advocates highlighted heavy, spectacular work tasks as typical of spirited labor, denying women the privilege of representing the glorious city. Social researchers presented a bleak view of women's work to prove their incompatibility with industry. Unlike men, then, women did not function for Progressive writers as appropriate vehicles for implementing material changes in the workplace—because, the argument went, women did not belong there in the first place.

Chapter 6 describes three institutional efforts to address the most glaring problem raised by this exchange of representations and narratives centered on the worker's body. The introduction of workplace safety and medical procedures, the development of a statewide workmen's compensation system, and the marketing of artificial limbs were capitalists' and legislators' solutions to the economic and social crisis of bodies destroyed by work. Combined, these efforts promised not just a solution, but a resolution, namely, the assurance that workers, industries, and cities could withstand the moment of catastrophe, put it behind them, and recover dependable narratives of beneficial, character-building work. The schemes' visibility bolstered the image of the tireless, triumphant man of steel.

The machine age, writes the historian Randolph Bergstrom, brought progress "only at a cost assessed in flesh." The problem for the historian is to imagine this period of deskilling and injury as something other than capital's complete domination of the industrial worker. Workers resisted the onslaught of mechanization and accidents, just as they countered the prevailing images of themselves through their own illustrations and narratives. The official images of Pittsburgh workers that adorned city streets and graced magazine pages suggested the business elite's undisputed control of the idea of work—a degree of control that was buttressed by popular consent won through public participation in the pleasant diversions of civic festivals and ornaments. But if industry's control of the idea of work mirrored its control of work itself, then workers mitigated the effects of such symbolic mastery, in much the same way they asserted some degree of autonomy in the workplace. Scientists and social reformers may have zeroed in on workers' bodies for evidence of social waste, yet workers themselves were able to address their bodies' needs and deficiencies by adopting strategies of physical management and self-representation. If middle-class representations of workers rendered them passive and voiceless, then workers' self-representations played upon equal measures of strength and weakness to convince themselves that their contribution to American society was still valuable, if undervalued. These self-made images of work and life in industrial Pittsburgh rarely reached beyond the bounds of workers' own journals and communities. The worker at the turn of the century was represented by others—artists, journalists, social reformers, employers— for public consumption; through these representations his role as a worker became mere acting, his body standing in for his subjectivity. This book examines the decades-long effort to explain Pittsburgh to itself and the nation, a dialogue in which industrial work became a shadowy performance and the industrial worker became simply a body of work.[18]

Make a study of the men who you see there . . . invariably you
will be able to distinguish a mechanic from a laborer.

—PETER M. KLING,

Why a Boy Should Learn a Trade (1906)

1

THE MAGIC OF THE NINETEENTH CENTURY

INDUSTRIAL CHANGE AND WORK

IN PITTSBURGH

✳   In the late nineteenth century and early twentieth, a lively debate
sprang up in the pages of the national press, centering on a thorny issue:
the proper nickname for the city of Pittsburgh. Choosing the right name
for the southwestern Pennsylvania manufacturing center was a matter of
choosing the industrial product that best represented the business that
took place there. In an edition of the *Magazine of Western History* from
1885, the writer Seelye Willson claimed that the association of the city
with its metal products was so strong that the words *Pittsburgh* and *iron*
were, in fact, synonymous. The Iron City produced metal for the world,
creating the very foundation of modern civilization. Willson's historical
sketch of the city's development confirmed what he believed was a widely
held mental association: Pittsburgh as a city founded on iron, bursting
with iron, named for iron. By the first decade of the twentieth century,
however, when the local steel magnate William Scaife announced to the
nation the arrival of a "new great city," he wrote of iron production in

Pittsburgh as a thing of the past, a relic of the last century. Scaife praised the "growth and wealth of the Steel City" as the new story of interest for American readers. Iron had seen its best days; steel was ascendant. *Harper's Weekly* went even further, declaring in 1903 that the Steel City was a more appropriate title for Pittsburgh than the Iron City because "if Iron is King, the steel throne of His Industrial Highness is in Pittsburgh." Moreover, it was important for *Harper's* readers to take note of the Steel City because, the writer announced, "the Steel Age is upon us." Ultimately, however, the anonymous writer concluded that such royal analogies had no place in a city where "human labor is our King." Steel epitomized turn-of-the-century Pittsburgh, but it was the effort of workers that epitomized steel.[1]

This flurry of name calling underscores the intense national scrutiny Pittsburgh received in the second half of the nineteenth century. The popular press, technical journals, trade groups, and writers and artists all looked closely at Pittsburgh in an attempt to explain the new brand of industrial life exhibited there. In 1850, Pittsburgh was well known as the nation's Iron City. Between 1880 and 1920, however, the city came to be much better known throughout the United States as the Steel City. This minor change in appellation denoted several significant transformations in industrial technology that led to iron's displacement by steel as the nation's most demanded structural and manufacturing metal. Mechanization of metal production, epitomized by the introduction of the Bessemer and open-hearth processes in the 1870s and 1880s, made steel cheaper and faster to produce than iron. New processes also required fewer highly skilled workers to fashion molten metal into finished products. Whereas mills of the Iron City were filled with skilled workmen controlling discrete segments of the production process, the Steel City's mills were filled with greater numbers of semiskilled and unskilled workers operating machines and moving raw materials. The shift from iron to steel incorporated multiple changes in the social and economic relations of industrial work in Pittsburgh. As steel plants grew in size and number throughout the Pittsburgh district, the steel workforce expanded in proportions that dwarfed the earlier ranks of ironworkers. In the process, skilled workers lost much of their power to hire assistants and apprentices. The craft pride and relatively high wages associated with skilled work in Pittsburgh's iron mills gave way to the routine tasks and meager wages offered by lower-status jobs. Despite diminishing prospects for steelworkers in a city that pushed production records and trampled unions, Pittsburgh attracted increasing numbers of new immigrant groups to its mills and factories after 1880. The city grew as the steel industry grew.[2]

Although it provided a fitting rubric for this series of developments in the metals industry, the symbolic shift from the Iron City to the Steel City failed to describe the evolution of two other leading industries that employed hundreds of thousands and made Pittsburgh the third most productive manufacturing city in the nation at the turn of the century. Pittsburgh during these years was also a national center for the glass and bituminous coal industries. Similar shifts occurred in these sectors as well, as both the manufacture of glass and the mining of coal were mechanized between 1880 and 1905 and transformed by an influx of immigrant workers from southern and eastern Europe. Iron and steel may have stolen much of the national attention fixed on Pittsburgh during this time, but it was the glass and coal trades that first put the city on the manufacturing map. Pittsburgh's glassworks met a raging domestic demand for tableware, bottles, and lamp chimneys and made possible the extensive use of window glass in retail establishments in the late nineteenth century. Coal from the region's mines and its refined counterpart, coke, fueled every major industry in the city as well as the burgeoning national railroad network. The extensive industrialization of the glass and coal industries, along with the startling expansion of the regional steel industry, remodeled Pittsburgh as a vision of American industrial life.[3]

As the Steel City emerged from the remnants of the Iron City, a new world emerged with it—an unfamiliar order of industrial organization and labor for those who worked in Pittsburgh and those who worked to popularize their efforts. First, the physical demands of the workday changed as local capitalists orchestrated an era of labor-saving machinery that collected, transported, refined, and shaped raw materials with little human assistance. Mechanical engineers and machinists replicated key segments of the manufacture of steel and glass and the extraction of coal, increasing production without relying on a commensurate amount of exertion from workers. Simultaneously, the increasing pace and scope of industrial establishments meant that work became less strenuous for certain workers and more onerous for others. The individual skilled worker who manipulated massive quantities of raw materials at a pace he determined, a common sight in the premechanized mill or mine, gave way to teams of lesser-skilled workers hauling much greater quantities of raw materials at a pace determined by both machines and a centralized production plan. By the early 1900s machines did much of the lifting, picking, and hammering, but in large mills and mines much was still demanded of the hands, arms, and backs of laborers.

Second, workers' repertoire of tasks and manual techniques changed as well. Several well-known manual work tasks of the late nineteenth century either became obsolete or no longer featured the very physical acts that made them the object of such interest to those who visited area workplaces before 1900. As puddling vanished from Pittsburgh, the sight of an individual worker shaping incredible quantities of metal at the door of a furnace vanished. Glassblowing machinery eliminated the vast majority of skilled workers who stood before melting pots and fashioned window glass cylinders with the help of their upper-body strength and gravity. The miner's daily task of removing coal with picks, shovels, and hammers became less common in the new era of mining machinery. Each of these work spectacles was replaced by new regimes in which compressed air and the metal surfaces of machines interacted with raw materials and finished goods, removing workers' bodies further from the work process. Compared to the traditional means of working in Pittsburgh, the new type of work appeared to be far less exotic to the contemporary writers and illustrators who represented the daily toil and sweat of the city's laboring classes.

Finally, the implementation of massive machinery meant that workers faced greater physical threats to their well-being, whether from accidental injury, occupational disease, or gradual exhaustion. After 1800 the heaviest work may have been done by machines, but the mechanical speed and mass needed to do the work of many laborers precluded any sense of repose for employees. When functioning well, machines placed great demands of pace and repetition on those who worked with them. Machines that collapsed, exploded, or otherwise malfunctioned created serious conditions for workers. The physical effects of industrial work—the way it conditioned, strained, and focused attention on the body—changed as machinery began doing the work that thousands of men in Pittsburgh had used previously to define themselves as vigorous, masculine individuals. Critics of industry focused on the bodily dangers inherent in mechanized industrial work as a primary characteristic of modern life in American cities, but the implications of mechanized industrial work went beyond the crisis of injuries and death. Even those working-men whose strenuous lives were arguably improved by the advent of labor-saving machinery experienced an ambiguous change as work be-came more a matter of mechanical power than human power.

PITTSBURGH'S INDUSTRIAL PROMINENCE

When he toured the mills and mines of southwestern Pennsylvania in the early 1890s, James Kitson, a representative of the British Iron and Steel Institute, touted the inevitability of Pittsburgh's expansion in size and industrial output at the end of the nineteenth century. Indeed, Kitson noted that Pittsburgh "could not help becoming a great industrial cen-tre," such was its advantage in natural resources and location. Kitson's theory was simple: owing to its prime location at the confluence of three rivers and atop a rich vein of bituminous coal, Pittsburgh had trans-formed itself from a nondescript commercial town to an industrial giant that defied description. Coal and coke fueled manufacturing establish-ments in the city. Rivers and railroads expedited the transport of mate-rials to Pittsburgh's mills and the distribution of finished products to the rest of the world. By achieving new feats in the production of iron, steel, glass, and coal, the city claimed the lofty position that geological and geographical fortune had determined for it. City boosters agreed with this assessment; the souvenir city guide created by the Pittsburgh Com-mittees of Reception for Kitson's visit informed him that the city's "pur-pose in history has been manifest from the first; it has always been a city of manufactures." Congressman John Dalzell echoed this tale of Pitts-burgh's success at a Chamber of Commerce banquet in 1902: "Nature designed her [Pittsburgh] for the center of industrial enterprise. Situated in the midst of raw materials of unbounded wealth, she has all the facili-ties for manufacture. Situated at the headwaters of the Ohio, with the Monongahela on the one side and the Allegheny on the other, she has all the facilities for distribution." Kitson and Dalzell removed humans from the process of economic growth and made the city's location and to-pography the agent of profit.[4]

The tale of Pittsburgh's inevitable rise to industrial glory overlooked the key role that mechanization played in the growth and commercial record breaking of the 1880s and 1890s. Pittsburgh industrialists did not build their empires on the strength of coal and river transportation alone. Instead, national figures such as Andrew Carnegie and national conglomerates such as the U.S. Steel Corporation built themselves upon a foundation of gears, pistons, and power. The writer Lillian Betts recognized this when she observed in 1901 that "the whir and throb of machinery have silenced the songs of birds" in Pittsburgh. Yet Betts, too, separated the transformation from the people who engineered it, noting that "the magic of the nineteenth century [had] wrought her marvelous changes." If the city's production machinery was captivating by the turn of the century, it was also profitable. Mechanization of production and increasing numbers of plants and residents went hand in hand—swift, mechanized production allowed greater scales of production, which demanded newer, larger establishments and greater workforces. Industry in Pittsburgh between 1880 and 1900 was a pageant of change, witnessing an unprecedented growth that can be seen in both the increasing number of manufactories in the city and the rising population figures for the city and the surrounding Allegheny County.[5]

Publishers of Pittsburgh's business directories struggled in the 1880s and 1890s to keep apace of annual industrial additions. The number of blast furnaces dotting the city's landscape increased from 15 in 1880 to 44 in 1908. The size of blast furnaces grew during this period as well, allowing a standard furnace in 1900 to do the work of two or three from 1880. The number of iron- and steelworks that spewed forth finished products rose steadily during these years—from 10 in 1880 to 27 in 1890 to 50 in 1900. In 1910, the state's factory inspector reported 313 iron- and steelworks in the Pittsburgh inspection region. The size of the average mill grew threefold during this period, culminating in mile-long mills stretching to the horizon. In the early 1880s, the average workforce of an iron or steel mill in Pittsburgh was 350. Although smaller steelworks remained throughout the city after 1900, several immense mills employed thousands of men each. Large steel workforces became more common in Pittsburgh, not because there were simply more workers in the area, but because continuous processes replaced traditional batch-production techniques that did not benefit from large numbers of workers. After mechanization, the increased scale and pace of production made hiring of more workers economically rational.[6]

In the Pittsburgh glass industry, the late nineteenth century witnessed the specialization of production, as companies stopped making several forms of glass in individual factories and instead erected factories that produced single product lines. At the end of the 1870s, there were 61 glasshouses in the Pittsburgh district, roughly a third of the national total. Of these, 24 produced only window glass and employed 1,200 workers. In 1890, the Committees of Reception counted 29 window glass works in Pittsburgh. By the turn of the century, 115 glassworks spread throughout the city's manufacturing region, not counting 62 establishments within 80 miles of Pittsburgh in West Virginia and Ohio. Approximately 20 of these factories produced window glass. The number of window glass works in Pittsburgh actually declined after 1890, as machinery allowed firms to produce more glass with fewer glasshouses. The total number of glassworks in the area increased, however, as industrialists built more tableware and bottle factories along the rivers. The relatively early mechanization of pressing and bottle blowing created a boom in those branches of the industry in the last two decades of the nineteenth century.[7]

The number of coal-mining operations in the Pittsburgh district increased as well. In 1880, there were fewer than 700 mining operations in the bituminous region. By the turn of the century, there were well over 1,000 mines, most deeper and more extensive than the mines of twenty years earlier. The infrastructure of the regional industry, combining railroads, water transportation, riverside storage yards, and outdoor mechanized sorting systems, matured into a relatively seamless network that brought coal to the city. The vast Pittsburgh deposit to the south and east of the city fueled massive activity along the Monongahela and Youghiogheny rivers, creating the infamous southwestern Pennsylvania mining towns that received intense scrutiny during the Progressive era.[8]

Much of the increase in size and production came as industrialists moved their operations farther up and down Pittsburgh's three rivers. The surrounding hills and valleys allowed for little industrial expansion within the city's central triangle, making a move to an adjacent area or neighboring county a necessity for expansion. Moreover, relocation to more remote areas allowed employers to establish greater control over their workers' economic and living conditions. Miners were not the only ones in the Pittsburgh region who lived in towns owned and operated by the companies for whom they worked. Towns like Homestead, Braddock, and McKeesport, several miles upriver from the downtown area, grew tremendously as owners constructed larger steel mills and glass-works beyond the city's limits. As one writer noted, the physical growth of the Pittsburgh region seemed relentless in the last decades of the nineteenth century, as "town after town made steel" and "one mill bred another." Pittsburgh spilled over its borders repeatedly, erasing the boundaries between the central industrial area and rural areas.[9]

A final measure of Pittsburgh's growth was the increasing number of people who made it their home. The city's population doubled in the twenty years between 1880 and 1900, and by 1910 was more than three times its 1880 level, rising to over half a million people. The population of Allegheny County doubled as well in the last two decades of the century, as industrialists filled in the surrounding gaps with mills and mines. By 1910, a county of 355,000 people thirty years earlier now held over 1 million. The influx of people to the Pittsburgh region crowded established towns and created new ones with incredible speed. A town like Homestead, crucial to the manufacture of Bessemer and open-hearth steel in the 1890s, grew rapidly around its steelworks. Between 1880 and 1910, the town's population grew to thirty times its original size (from 592 to 18,713 people). Another steel town in Pittsburgh's orbit, Monessen, grew between 1893 and 1910 from a village of eight farmhouses, two barns, and one school to a town that boasted almost 12,000 people, several tin and steel plants, and a foundry.[10]

The by-products of Pittsburgh's increasing scale of production were more places to work and more workers; the increase in population corresponded with similar increases in the size of the workforce in the city's three main industries. Although it is difficult to gauge the exact size of Pittsburgh's industrial workforce during this period, several sets of figures suggest a staggering increase in the number of workers. Census figures, which account for only those workers living within the city limits, show the iron and steel workforce doubling in the 1880s (increasing from 6,125 workers in 1880 to 12,379 in 1890). By 1910, the Census Bureau calculated the iron and steel workforce of the Pittsburgh Metropolitan District, including the city itself and adjacent towns in surrounding counties, as being just over 61,000 workers. The Pittsburgh Chamber of Commerce's set of figures, designed to sell the power of the city in terms of its incredible size, listed 39,000 men in iron and steel in 1890 and 85,000 in 1907. According to the state factory inspector's reports, there were 69,000 workers in the city's iron and steel industry in 1904 and almost 120,000 six years later.[11]

The workforce in Pittsburgh's glass industry increased more modestly before and after the turn of the century. The Census Bureau counted roughly 6,000 glassworkers living in Allegheny County in 1880. By 1910, the number was 7,300, a meager increase when compared to steel statistics. However, the addition of 1,300 workers over thirty years came during a period when the local glass industry was contracting in size while expanding production. Unlike steel's displacement of iron, the mechanization of tableware, bottle, lamp chimney, and window glass manufacturing did not introduce processes that required a much greater scale than traditional means of production. Instead, glass entrepreneurs replicated the handblown method of manufacturing with machinery, allowing them to boost production figures without building vast factories to accommodate new processes. When manufacturers did build new glasshouses, they needed fewer workers to operate them. The number of workers needed to produce window glass, for example, actually declined after the turn of the century. The slight increase in the glass workforce, then, says less about the stagnation of the local industry than it does about the new economy of glass production in the machine age.[12]

Employment figures for the regional coal industry are somewhat misleading, for they represent the number of miners in the entire bituminous mining industry of Pennsylvania. Although Pittsburgh was the industrial heart of the state's bituminous coalfields, which extended from the Ohio border to the Allegheny Mountains, men working as far as one hundred miles from Pittsburgh were included in the figures. Much of the bituminous region in Pennsylvania consisted of the Pittsburgh deposit, a fourteen-thousand-square-mile vein of coal that brought the highest concentration of workers to counties immediately surrounding the city. Thus, although the increase in the number of bituminous miners working in Pennsylvania overstates the number of workers who considered themselves economically connected to Pittsburgh, it still sheds light on the growth of the city's coal industry after 1880. In the Pennsylvania bituminous region as a whole in 1880 there were over 33,000 coal miners. By century's end, there were over 100,000 miners. Ten years later, that number had almost doubled.[13]

The astounding growth in the number of industrial establishments, jobs, and people would have meant little had capitalists not harnessed the expanded scope of industry with more efficient methods of production. Kitson's model of organic industrial growth explained Pittsburgh's rise in terms of rivers and resources, omitting the key element of mechanization as a catalyst for larger manufacturing plants, faster production paces, higher production quotas, and burgeoning workforces. The pinnacle of "American Commercial Genius," a civic quality boasted of in glowing journalistic reports from the city, was Pittsburgh industrialists' ability to recognize the commercial power of steelmaking, glassblowing, and coal-cutting machinery. In each case, the introduction of machinery led to momentous transformations in the ways men worked. If Pittsburgh's history was "so romantic and so unique" in the late nineteenth century, its intrigue and novelty derived from the systematic application of machinery to traditional production processes that turned a common commercial town into a "solid, substantial, wide-awake city" by the turn of the century.[14]

MECHANIZATION IN METALS

The most instrumental industrial change in Pittsburgh between 1880 and 1900 was steel's emergence as an inexpensive competitor of iron. The Iron City and the Steel City had much in common, but the prevalence of mechanized work processes characterized the latter as a distinct departure from traditional forms of local industry. Machinery allowed capitalists to bypass slow, labor-intensive work tasks that had predicated production on the speed and judgment of individual workingmen. Scaife, writing in 1905, explained why steel had replaced iron in the preceding twenty years: "Principally, the cheapness and great productivity of the processes of soft-steel manufacture and the small number of men required for a large output. . . . Moreover, one of the greatest aids to the introduction of the Bessemer process in the Pittsburg district was the desire on the part of iron-masters to get rid of puddling, which was the cause of more labor troubles than all the other departments of their works."[15]

In Scaife's explanation, the phrase "labor troubles" meant strikes and work stoppages, but it could just as well have been used to denote manufacturers' problem of relying exclusively on the heavy labor of skilled puddlers. Puddling was necessary to convert brittle pig iron into wrought iron, a malleable metal containing less carbon and fewer impurities. For most of the nineteenth century, puddling epitomized the type of work done in iron mills in Pittsburgh—heavy work that required an equal measure of knowledge and energy. Described as "laborious, crude, and unsatisfactory" at a meeting of the American Institute of Mining Engineers in February 1880, puddling relied on the mastery of individual workers and could not be performed by just anyone with the requisite strength. Apprentice puddlers learned their craft over several years, assisting established puddlers and observing the correct technique of movement, force, and decision making. Owners attempted throughout the late nineteenth century to mechanize the puddling process, but no one could successfully replicate the motion and judgment that went into this "enormous amount of labour." For decades, puddling's resistance to mechanization protected puddlers' position, but it was also the "fatal weakness" that brought wrought iron production to a steady decline in Pittsburgh.[16]

Pittsburgh puddlers in the 1880s worked five heats per ten-hour workday, handling approximately three thousand pounds of molten pig iron and almost four thousand pounds of coal or coke in the process. If the iron was not puddled correctly during the heats, it often broke during the next stage of manufacturing, when it was squeezed through rollers into its initial bloom shape. Iron that broke during squeezing was returned to the puddling furnace for further work. The puddler's judgment was thus a crucial element in wrought iron manufacture—he had to decide when enough carbon had burned off, how to adjust and maintain temperature, and how to divide the entire batch into thirds. The expertise of the puddler also brought an element of uncertainty to the economic planning of iron manufacturers.[17]

When the daily rhythms of iron production ground to a halt in mills throughout the city, owners and managers blamed their workers. Production bottlenecks typical of metal manufacturing in 1880, located primarily at blast and puddling furnaces, were a result of manufacturers' dependence on individual human labor. Although mechanizing the blast furnace helped employers greatly, the heart of the mechanical revolution in metal making was manufacturers' sudden ability to bypass puddling by producing steel. The metallurgical basis for this transition was simple: steel was just as malleable, yet stronger than wrought iron. Steel could withstand heavier loads than wrought iron, making it both a superior and cheaper metal. As Scaife observed, iron initially gave way in Pittsburgh after 1880 because its production could not be mechanized to the extent that steel manufacturing could. Puddlers resisted employers' attempts to increase managerial control and institute faster paces or more heats per day, declaring their right as men to defend themselves from forced submission. The manual puddling process was not replaced by machinery, then, but suffered a decline in Pittsburgh as iron manufacturers decided to invest in the production of a metal that was highly conducive to mechanization. The Bessemer and open-hearth processes made steel production standardized, efficient, and cheaper than iron production. The transition was swift; city directories show that the number of steel mills in the city surpassed the number of iron mills in the 1890s. Whereas there were thirty-one iron mills and nine steel mills in Pittsburgh in 1880, by 1900 there were thirty iron mills and forty-seven steel mills. Pittsburgh's iron king now sat firmly upon a steel throne.[18]

The Pittsburgh debut of the Bessemer process occurred at Carnegie Steel's Edgar Thomson Steel Works in Braddock in 1875. The Homestead Works, another mill employing Bessemer production, opened five years later. The success of the two steelworks proved the advantages of new techniques over traditional practices. Before the introduction of the Bessemer process, steel was made as an extension of wrought iron production. After puddlers removed excess carbon from pig iron to make wrought iron, steelworkers reintroduced a small quantity of the carbon in a charcoal furnace. The result, blister steel, was then melted in small crucibles to form a completely uniform product known as crucible steel. Crucible steel's advantage over wrought iron was its combination of increased malleability and strength, but its production still depended on the unmechanized work of the puddler. The success of the Bessemer process, as one industry commentator observed in the 1880s, was due to the "wonderful power and perfection of the machinery" that made the process continuous and relatively independent of human labor.[19]

The open-hearth process followed quickly on the heels of the Bessemer process as an alternative way to mechanize steel production. The economic historian Peter Temin explained the open-hearth process as the "logical development of the puddling process," a mechanical adaptation that made steel continuously but with the same principles used for making wrought iron. The open-hearth process secured steel's place at the top of the metals market in the 1880s and 1890s. Although introduced in Pittsburgh several years after the Bessemer process, it soon became the leading steelmaking method. The open-hearth furnace was essentially a massive puddling furnace that could accommodate greater heat and thus required no puddler. The main technical obstacle to the widespread use of the open-hearth process was the inability of conventional furnaces to sustain the temperature required to refine pig iron into molten steel. Regenerative furnaces, such as those used in the Siemens-Martin open-hearth process, solved this problem by passing air through a series of extremely hot firebricks before it came into contact with the metal. The intense heat of the open-hearth furnace converted increasingly larger quantities of pig iron into steel.

In 1908, for the first time, the United States produced more steel with the open-hearth process than with the Bessemer process. By 1910, there were 15 Bessemer converters and 117 open-hearth furnaces in Pittsburgh. Although the open-hearth process was much slower than the Bessemer process, it allowed manufacturers to hold melted steel indefinitely while workers took samples to measure the quality of the metal. Steel tapped from a Bessemer converter was always a rough approximation of the desired product, whereas the final product of an open-hearth furnace was a steel "purer, more homogenous, and tougher" than Bessemer steel. One writer announced as early as 1903 that the Bessemer process seemed "to have run its course." The importance of the two processes cannot be overstated, however. Both presented metal manufacturers with a long-awaited solution to problems associated with relying on skilled workers in a noncontinuous production process. Both made steel production an economically rational and profitable endeavor for local ironmasters. Finally, both reduced puddling to the status of a dying craft, as Scaife noted in 1905 when he wrote of it as an ancient practice from the dark days of the city's history.[20]

What did these work tasks actually look like? A tour of the iron- and steelmaking processes in Pittsburgh before and after the mechanical transformation shows how workers' bodies became less relevant to the spectacle of industrial work. The first stage in making both iron and steel was the production of pig iron in blast furnaces. Before mechanization work in the city's blast furnaces was hot, strenuous, and deafening. Laborers loaded furnaces by hand, shoveling tons of iron ore, limestone, and coke into elevators that dumped the raw materials at the top of the elongated, barrel-shaped structure through a hole at the top. Most blast furnaces in Pittsburgh at the turn of the century were fifty to one hundred feet in height, the "giant offspring of very feeble ancestors." When the furnace was in operation, blasts of one-thousand-degree compressed air were shot through the melted mixture to refine it into pig iron. The noise produced by the chemical reaction within was enough to shake the foundations of even the largest plant. The heat from the furnace and the blasts of air were severe. After the blast had eliminated most of the impurities from the molten mixture, workers then tapped the furnace with long iron poles. Liquid pig iron poured from the base of the furnace, filling floor-level molds and cooling into solid blocks. When the iron cooled, workers broke the "pigs" from their molds and lifted them into wheeled cars. The daily experience of blast furnace workers, then, was the repetitive motion of shoveling and lifting raw materials. Added to this basic task were the jobs of relining furnaces with chemical mixtures and keeping the work floor clear of obstructions.[21]

Mechanization in the blast furnace industry did not alter the pig iron process significantly until the 1890s. Before this time, major advances in blast furnace design were due to increases in the size of furnaces rather than to mechanized production processes. Pittsburgh boasted some of the largest blast furnaces in the world by 1890, a fact the Chamber of Commerce broadcast repeatedly. Having achieved such impressive capacities, industrialists in the 1890s focused on the ways in which raw materials moved to and from the great receptacles. By the turn of the century, the most advanced blast furnaces in Pittsburgh were loaded by mechanical cars, eliminating the "severe labor of many men" that slowed production paces in the 1880s. Machinery brought raw materials to the furnace, guided by one or more workers moving levers and pulling chains. Visitors to one Pittsburgh blast furnace were surprised by the "few workmen necessary for feeding these insatiable monsters," at a pace of ten tons every minute. By 1908 teams of workmen manually loaded blast furnaces in only two of Pittsburgh's mills. Machinery eliminated the need for men stationed at the base of the furnace pushing piles upon piles of ore, limestone, and coke. Tapping the furnace after mechanization meant using machinery to release pig iron from the furnace. In the city's modern steel plants after the turn of the century, pig iron never cooled from its molten state. Instead, mechanized cupolas and trains carried a stream of molten metal directly from the blast furnace to a large heating mixer, where it awaited the next stage of production.[22]

When machinery came to the blast furnace, the work demanded of employees shifted from a monotonous day of loading and tapping the furnace to an equally routine schedule of operating and maintaining machinery. The most demanding of blast furnace tasks, carrying tons of materials, was taken over by cranes, hoists, and cars. The historian David Brody has shown that as the mechanization of blast furnace work progressed, employers did not require workers to keep apace of machinery because the process essentially ran itself. However, unskilled workers in outdoor stockyards who were charged with filling mechanical cars with raw materials could expect few breaks from their daily toil. Machinery displaced the strain of blast furnace work from the periphery of the furnace to more remote areas of the plant. If visitors to the mills could find no workers involved in the mechanized production of pig iron, they were looking in the wrong place. Employers reduced the heavy drudgery and expense of manual loading, but pig iron production was fundamentally the same in 1910 as it had been in 1880.[23]

Whereas mechanization of the blast furnace meant only less shoveling for certain workers, changes in what happened to the metal after it was removed from the blast furnace signaled the very revolution that brought steel to the foreground. Once pig iron was produced, the next stage in iron manufacture was puddling, the traditional, small-batch refining technique used to produce a consistent metal. To begin the process, the puddler and his assistant loaded a furnace with pig iron and bituminous coal or coke. Puddling furnaces were relatively small structures, measuring roughly seven feet high and seven feet wide. The amount of pig iron that workers loaded per heat was typically six hundred pounds, eventually divided into three balls weighing two hundred pounds each. As much as eight hundred pounds of coal or coke was used per heat. When the pig iron reached an adequate temperature after thirty minutes of melting, the puddler's assistant stirred the molten batch with an iron rod, or rabble, measuring five feet in length and weighing up to twenty-five pounds. Within the puddling furnace, iron was separated from the burning fuel by a low wall, allowing the iron to be manipulated fully without removing it from the heat. Workers maintained their furnaces at an intense heat—"as hot as coal could make it," according to one—making the task of puddling a physical strain in more ways than one. After the initial work by his assistant, the puddler took charge, stirring the iron through ports in the furnace wall, working it into a uniform mass, bringing it in constant contact with the air, and burning off carbon. The most dramatic stage of the puddling process was the boil, the point at which carbon gas forcibly ejected itself from the molten mass. As the boiling metal, "hot as the fiery lake in Hades," sent showers of sparks and gas throughout the furnace, visitors to iron mills were astonished that men could work in such proximity to hazardous reactions. With the carbon removed, the remaining iron began congealing, or "coming to nature," and the puddler stirred the sticky mixture for another thirty minutes. The difficulty of puddling after the boil was to keep the pure iron constantly in motion to prevent it from oxidizing on top and chilling on bottom. When the pasty glob of refined iron was ready to be worked further into iron bars, the puddler used a long paddle and a hook to form it into three balls, which he removed from the furnace with the rabble. Balling the iron took approximately fifteen minutes, a time during which the puddler held hundreds of pounds on the end of the rabble, turning it slowly to form an even sphere. Once they removed the glowing balls from the furnace, puddlers transferred them quickly to another worker in the mill. They used long-handled tongs to carry the molten balls away from the furnaces. Visitors to Pittsburgh iron mills remarked that the speed with which puddlers ran their balls of iron to the next stage of production seemed impossible.[24]

The Bessemer process, described by a writer for *Harper's Weekly* as "simply titanic," replaced the individual ironworker with a mechanical converter that refined pig iron in large quantities. With the aid of hoisting machinery, workers tipped the pear-shaped converter, the "indispensable mammoth of steel manufacture" four to five times as high as it was wide, into a horizontal position. After loading it with molten pig iron, often coming directly from the blast furnace in movable cupolas, operating workers raised the converter into a vertical position. Men who controlled the workings of the converter stood on a raised platform nearby, manipulating a row of levers. Blasts of compressed air were then shot by mechanical means through the metal. When carbon in the pig iron began to burn, a violent reaction of fire and sparks occurred, usually lasting for several minutes. As air passed through and around the molten iron, the oxygen-carbon reaction burned off much of the carbon impurities that made

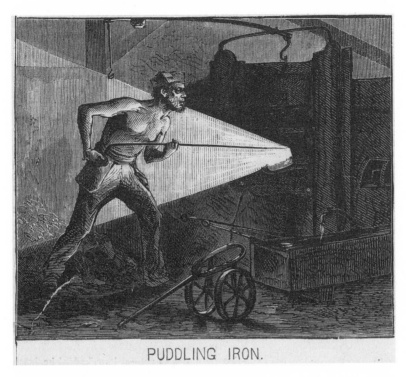

PUDDLING IRON.

1. Puddling iron, from *Harper's Weekly*, 18 February 1871.

pig iron unsuitable for manufacturing. When the refined iron cooled slightly into a more viscous state, the converter was tipped to a horizontal position again, and its molten metal poured into hydraulic ladles. The "titanic bowing and curtseying" of the Bessemer converter stunned journalists and other visitors, who could not believe that such massive machinery could move so effortlessly and without the aid of human muscle. An operator then positioned an overhead crane to move the ladles of molten steel above empty molds, dumping the liquid in small batches to produce rough beam shapes. By 1905, the Bessemer process took only twenty minutes from charging to tapping. The amount of Bessemer steel made by a single converter in one day dwarfed the amount of wrought iron produced by even the largest iron mill in the city.[25]

The first stage of the open-hearth process began as workers charged the large, dish-shaped furnace with pig iron. As in the Bessemer process, employers soon eliminated the manual loading of pig iron by transporting molten pig iron directly from the blast furnace. In the early 1890s, workers at the Homestead and Braddock works still loaded furnaces by hand; by the first decade of the twentieth century, pig iron used in most open-hearth departments in Pittsburgh never cooled from its liquid state. In the manual method of charging, three men—one melter and two helpers—worked each furnace. The melter, described by a fellow worker as a "boy at the levers," operated machines that charged the furnace with reactive chemicals. *Harper's Weekly* noted that the melter at the American Iron and Steel Works merely "look[ed] into the furnace from time to time" from his perch atop mechanical cranes and hoists while his helpers scurried below. Helpers did the dirty work of the open-hearth process, first using long shovels to load the furnace with twenty-five to thirty tons of pig iron and finally tapping it with long iron bars after it had reached its desired chemical composition. After mechanized loading became widely used in Pittsburgh, the helpers' job was reduced to adding small quantities of materials to the mixture and tapping. One heat in an open-hearth furnace took eight hours and produced as much metal as twelve puddlers.[26]

Mechanization in metal manufacturing did not stop at the base of the Bessemer converter or at the doors of the open-hearth furnace. The shaping of metals with rolling machines also underwent a drastic transformation in the last decades of the nineteenth century. Rolling in Pittsburgh's iron mills hinged upon the ability of many men to wrestle heavy pieces of red-hot metal through rolls quickly and evenly. After the puddler's balls of wrought iron went through the squeezing machine to give them an oblong shape (a bloom), they entered the realm of the roller. Apart from the puddler, the roller occupied the most respected position on the work floor. Whereas the puddler supervised the work of his assistant, the roller was in charge of dozens of workers who made up his rolling crew. Skilled iron rollers were valued in the mill for their judgment, their management abilities, and their determination not to break the rolls. Any slight error in the way in which the bloom passed through or the temperature at which it entered could crack the rolls, requiring a lengthy and expensive procedure to replace the rolls. The roller's work was thus mainly managerial, as the other members of the rolling crew performed the strenuous task of guiding the glowing iron through the rolls. To do this, workers used iron hooks, bars, and tongs. As the two-hundred-pound bloom made multiple passes back and forth through the rolls, workers shoved it on one end and caught it on the other.[27]

The rolling process in Pittsburgh's steel mills became a matter of mechanics by the turn of the century. Skilled rollers still supervised laborers' work, but the number of men needed to assist in mechanized steel rolling decreased from over twenty to only two. A crane carried slabs of hot steel from heating furnaces and placed them on a "roadway of steel travellers" that moved them into the rolls. Machinery passed the steel back and forth through the rollers until the desired shape and thickness was reached. A "vast carrier" then took the beams to the finishing rolls. The roller stood above the action, hands upon levers that controlled the space between the rolls and the motion of the steel. The rest of the rolling crew consisted of two men who stood next to the roller and operated the engine of the rolls. The job of the roller and his crew was to operate machinery correctly, using care to allow hoists and cranes to handle the steel without damaging the metal or fellow workers. Electric machinery took care of the heaviest work, leaving skilled workers to monitor and coordinate the process.[28]

Within blast furnace, Bessemer, open-hearth, and rolling departments of Pittsburgh's major steel mills, electricity revolutionized the way in which manufacturers transported materials from one stage of production to another. Through electrification, Temin noted, "people disappeared from the mills." Electric trolleys, cranes, and mechanical ladle cars replaced workers who had previously hauled iron ore, limestone, coke, and finished pig iron. John Fitch of the Pittsburgh Survey stressed that mills that had been "alive with men" in the 1880s seemed to hide their workers by the first decade of the twentieth century. To spy skilled workers in electrified mills, observers had to look away from the action, scanning the ceiling for the control platforms and cabins from which small numbers of individuals guided the production of tons of metal daily. The technology writer Waldon Fawcett claimed in 1901 that a visitor to a Pittsburgh steel mill would "be surprised by the seemingly meager force of men that people the immense structure. Standing at one end of the building, he can scarcely distinguish any of the objects [from] the other, but under his gaze comes only a vast vista of machinery. The mechanical workers rise from the floor, reach out from the walls, cling to the ceiling."[29]

As the historian Daniel Nelson has concluded, "The Bessemer process required less physical force than puddling, and the open-hearth process required even less." Proponents of mechanization touted its ability to reduce unnecessary strain. In this vision, mechanization did not eliminate the skilled workman from the mill but reduced "the laborious work of the early stages of the heat, which require[d] brute force rather than experience." Yet puddling was a practice in which force and experience could not be separated; a successful puddler relied on the interplay of the two. If skill characterized puddling, it was skill hard won through years of working with tools and materials. By eliminating the work of the puddler, one engineer boasted, mechanization of the metal-making process eliminated the "weary toil of so many thousands." Scaife argued that by doing away with puddling, steelmakers had actually helped the puddler, who was now able to "exchange his former laborious task for the less strenuous steel processes." Beyond the elimination of puddling, mechanization made loading a blast furnace and rolling steel much easier tasks for skilled workmen, who began running machinery instead of hauling metal. The engineer Henry Howe boasted that visitors to Pittsburgh would "find no signs of unwholesome exhaustion" in the city's Bessemer works but would instead notice "the cheery tunes, the passing jest which . . . predict no early decay" in steelworkers' health and vitality. Although skilled work in steel mills certainly became less backbreaking than it had been in unmechanized iron mills, the daily lot of the unskilled worker did not improve in equal fashion. As long as men were needed to move raw materials in the spaces between mechanized carrying systems, common laborers continued to fill the majority of positions on steel manufacturers' payrolls. Unskilled labor was both crucial and relentless by the turn of the century, when the city's major mills were making steel twenty-four hours a day.[30]

During the 1890s, steel manufacturers in Pittsburgh began to dismantle iron mills and puddling furnaces in order to expand their steel production facilities. Newspaper reports of puddlers being dismissed from area mills appeared frequently throughout the decade. In the spring of 1892 alone, the Jones and Laughlin Company closed thirty-five puddling furnaces and fired all puddlers from its American Iron and Steel Works, and the Carnegie Steel Company fired two hundred puddlers from its Upper Union Mill. Smaller iron companies in Pittsburgh continued to use puddlers well into the twentieth century, suggesting that the eclipse of puddling by the Bessemer and open-hearth processes was never as complete as it seemed before 1900. Fitch estimated that two thousand puddlers still worked in Allegheny County in 1908. By that time, puddling was no longer the central task in Pittsburgh metal making, but it had not vanished completely from local industry. It endured as a reminder of local work history, a "suggestion of the older days" when human labor moved large amounts of metal with little or no help from machinery. The puddler became a tragic figure, the subject of labor poems that declared,

We urged that human machine, yet
We found he was too slow
His output, tho' he did his best
Was in the bottom row.
We crushed him till no youngster would
Acquire his tiresome trade
While death kept slyly picking off
Old timers years had made.[31]

Mechanization in the city's steel mills was impressive by the turn of the century, even to those who felt personally the economic threat of machinery. In his testimony before Congress in 1899, Mahlon Garland, the president of the Amalgamated Association of Iron and Steel Workers, declared that he could "hardly explain the great changes in that direction, because they [were] so constantly occurring." By 1900, it seemed to Garland and to many that "machinery [was] doing the work that everybody thought utterly impossible eight or ten years ago." Garland's words were notable for the way they explained the changes in Pittsburgh steelwork—after mechanization, *machinery* did the work of steelmaking, not workers. A gulf had formed between workers' bodies and the routines, tasks, and motions that they had once performed. This gulf was first seen in Pittsburgh in the steel industry, but a similar transformation took place elsewhere. If steel was the most extensively mechanized local industry at this time, window glass was soon to follow.[32]

MECHANIZATION IN GLASS

Pittsburgh's glass industry was one of the oldest manufacturing endeavors in western Pennsylvania in the late nineteenth century. The first glasshouse was built in the region in 1797, four years after the erection of the first iron foundry. Operated by Craig and O'Hara, the works produced both bottles and window glass during the first half of the century.

From that small beginning, the Pittsburgh glass industry grew into a commercial behemoth. Local inventors and machinists received many nineteenth-century patents for innovations in glass composition, product design, and machinery. Manufacturers in the area boasted that only the Pittsburgh glassworker could "rival the Venetian and excel the Bohemian workmen" in artistic vision and technical skill. In the 1870s, Pittsburgh's glassworkers produced annually about half of all glass made in the United States. By the last two decades of the century, "Pittsburgh glass was everywhere."[33]

Although local workers were praised for their high levels of skill and artistry, glass manufacturers increased glass production not through the efforts of their workers, but by incorporating machinery into processes that made tableware, bottles, lamps, and windows. In all but the window glass industry, production was partially mechanized before 1880. Virtually all tableware and bottles were produced with pressing and molding machinery by the 1860s. The manufacture of window glass remained the only sector of the local industry that resisted the extensive use of machinery to shape and handle glass. The size and weight of window glass cylinders made a mechanized production process impossible until after the turn of the century, when mechanics developed self-adjusting machinery that did not break molten glass regularly. Until then, window glass production continued as a manual, labor-intensive craft. The Pittsburgh window glass blower enjoyed a lofty status, one similar to that of the iron puddler in the 1870s. The blower's continued reliance on his physical ability made the production of cylinders a unique work task in the late nineteenth-century glass industry.[34]

Until 1900, American manufacturers produced window glass through handblowing, and the primary tool of the skilled worker was thus the blowpipe. The Pittsburgh *Bulletin* lamented the fact that the glassblower of 1893 was the same as the glassblower of 1793: "a strong-lunged man, a straight iron pipe, and trained muscles." The major breakthrough industrialists sought in the 1890s was a machine to replace the skilled blower who made windows. In 1880, the prospect of mechanizing the blowing process seemed impossible to skeptical industry observers and an inevitable culmination to others. On the one hand, the local manufacturer Robert Schwartz noted that no machines could be invented to replace the window glass blower, such was the delicate and intrinsically *human* nature of his work. A journalist described the skilled work of the window glass blower as the "most marvelous part of the fascinating series of transformations witnessed in the glass-house." Machinery, however advanced and intricate, could not achieve similar results. On the other hand, the trade journal *American Pottery and Glassware Reporter* predicted in 1879 that within ten years, window glass works would operate "without the employment of a single skilled worker." Such optimistic industry views proved wrong, for skilled window glass workers continued to command the work of glass factories after 1890. In fact, by the end of the nineteenth century, blowers enjoyed what was perhaps their most secure position in the production process. After the Civil War, Pittsburgh window glass blowers consolidated their positions by delegating peripheral tasks to helpers and concentrating on blowing more cylinders per day. Earlier in the century, blowers had gathered, blown, cracked, flattened, and cut glass themselves. As late as 1860, window glass blowers performed both gathering and blowing duties in most Pittsburgh glasshouses. By the 1880s, however, blowers had succeeded in limiting their daily tasks to the single act of working molten cylinders on the ends of blowpipes. Their ability to work heavy masses of glass separated skilled blowers from the majority of laborers who made up the workforce of a typical Pittsburgh glassworks. By giving most of their ancillary jobs to others, blowers limited the number of men in the city who had the experience and ability to perform this central task. The blower's job became more monotonous as he concentrated on producing cylinders, but he traded a varied workday for the respect and wages associated with blowing.[35]

Production of double-thick glass required a level of strength and stamina that not all blowers could muster. The historian Richard O'Connor estimates that only a quarter of blowers could make double-thick cylinders, and for their effort they received two and a half times the wages of their single-thickness counterparts. During their busy workdays, double-thick blowers wielded up to seventy pounds of glass and iron pipe ten feet above their heads for eight and a half hours each day, with little time to rest between successive cylinders. The heat and noise of the glasshouse also contributed to the physical strain. A woman who toured the city's glassworks as a child remembered "roaring ovens full of sound and fury" surrounding men as they worked. Melting furnaces routinely reached over two thousand degrees, making the typical glasshouse an uncomfortable place even on the coldest days and a veritable inferno on the hottest.

Blowers and gatherers protected themselves from the heat of the furnace by covering themselves in leather and wearing masks over their faces, but few could leave the glassworks at the end of the day without feeling the effects of such an environment.[36]

Until the method by which manufacturers melted glass was continuous, mechanization of blowing could not fulfill its promise of efficiency. The continuous tank furnace thus became the central focus of the Pittsburgh glass industry in the 1890s. Traditional melting pots used throughout the nineteenth century limited glass production to a single-batch process similar to that used in the puddling of wrought iron. By 1900, manufacturers melted about 60 percent of American window glass in continuous tank furnaces instead of single-batch pots. In combination with the introduction of natural gas in the 1880s and 1890s, the continuous tank became the centerpiece of production. A constant supply of molten glass made mechanization an even more enticing prospect for manufacturers.[37]

The arrival of this mechanical promised land was much delayed. As late as 1899, the mechanization of cylinder blowing seemed out of reach for the Pittsburgh glass industry. James Campbell, Pennsylvania's chief factory inspector, informed the federal Industrial Commission that year that machines had made remarkable inroads in the melting and flattening stages of production but not in blowing. Manufacturers' experiments with machinery in the 1890s could not mimic the flexibility displayed in the handblown process, wherein blowers constantly monitored the temperature and thickness of the glass and adjusted their movements accordingly. It was not until 1903 that an automatic blowing machine, the Lubbers machine, became commercially viable. The introduction of this device for blowing glass cylinders mechanized the gatherer's and blower's work, creating cylinders that were forty feet long and twice the diameter of the handblown variety. By 1915, only a third of U.S. window glass was still handblown. One glass industry trade journal exclaimed that no invention in the industry had been "more far-reaching, more radical in its departure from century-old methods, or more revolutionary in its effect."[38]

Comparing the performances demanded by manual and mechanical techniques again shows how workers' bodies became passive parts of the industrial display. Unskilled workers used shovels to load a melting pot with the appropriate mixture of silica, soda, and lime and heated it into a thick, molten state. Loading pot furnaces was back-straining work involving thousands of pounds of raw materials per pot. Workers who loaded furnaces were the first to arrive at the glasshouse each morning, working for several hours before the rest of the crew began its day. The continuous tank method of melting glass changed this time-consuming configuration by allowing manufacturers to feed raw materials steadily into one end of the furnace while workers withdrew molten glass at the other end. Producers first implemented the continuous tank in western Pennsylvania in 1888 and soon integrated it into mechanical systems that conveyed raw materials from outdoor stockyards. Laborers unloaded materials from railroad cars with shovels and carts and carried them to sorting bins. From there, machines transported materials to automatic mixers and, finally, to the feeding end of the continuous tank furnace. Workers operated machinery and coordinated the transfer process.[39]

The handblown cylinder method of manufacturing window glass began when a worker known as a gatherer used a five-foot wrought iron pipe to gather a ball of molten glass from a melting furnace. For single-thickness glass, the gatherer dipped his pipe into the furnace three times, adding successive layers to reach the necessary mass, a "lump of cherry-red shapeless stickiness." If the window glass was to be doubled in thickness (usually for industrial or commercial uses), the worker gathered glass four or five times. A standard ball of glass weighed from fifteen to twenty pounds, whereas a ball for double-thickness glass typically weighed between thirty and forty-five pounds. When the gatherer finished collecting glass on the pipe, he turned the heavy molten ball in a wooden mold to produce a rudimentary sphere. The gatherer's work typically took several minutes per cylinder.[40]

At this stage, the blower came into the process. The blower took the pipe with the molten sphere on the end and began to blow it into a large globe. He often returned the globe to the pot furnace for reheating and for gathering more glass. When he had gathered the correct amount of glass and blown it into a small sphere, the worker then swung the globe above his head to allow the molten glass to settle further on the blowpipe. By swinging the blowpipe above his head and below his feet in a pendulum motion, he gradually elongated the globe into a cylindrical shape. In the early nineteenth century, blowers mounted foot benches built high above the workshop floor to allow a downward swing of the blowpipe. By midcentury glass manufacturers in Pittsburgh built swing pits into workshop floors to allow a full swing of the pipe. If the glass cooled too rapidly or stretched unevenly, the blower had to reheat the cylinder and repeat the swinging process. A writer from *Scientific American* noted that because the fifteen- to forty-pound tube was five feet long and between fifteen and eighteen inches in diameter, it dawned on the observer that the blower's "apparently playful toss" of the cylinder was actually a feat requiring "great skill and a large amount of muscle." In the span of a few minutes, the blower turned a large glob of sticky glass into a long, uniform cylinder that was then flattened and transformed into a window. Working in such a system, each pair of gatherers and blowers could produce up to eighty cylinders of window glass per day.[41]

To begin the mechanical Lubbers process that replaced the manual method, a ladling crew transferred eight hundred pounds of molten glass from a continuous tank to the intake pot at the base of the machine. When the ladling crew had filled the pot, a machine operator lowered a cast-iron cylinder directly above the pot, dipping its hollow head into the surface of the molten glass. The circular head of the Lubbers machine drew a small amount of the glass up into it, connecting the batch of glass with the apparatus that pulled it upward. After the glass had cooled within the machine's cylinder, the operator turned on motors to lift the pipe, drawing the glass with it and blowing it into a cylinder with a motorized fan. Increasing air pressure supplied by the fan prevented the glass from collapsing in on itself as the cylinder moved steadily toward the ceiling of the glassworks. The operator, who stood near the base of the machine, quickened the pace of the ascent as the cylinder neared its required height, causing the glass to thin toward the bottom. When the cylinder was complete, a worker cracked the thin portion of the glass with a cold iron pipe. A cable and pulley system suspended from the ceiling allowed workers to lower the cylinder to wooden tables, where it was cut into smaller pieces and moved to the next stage of production.[42]

The work of the blower became the work of the machine operator; it was his task to operate the lifting and blowing motors of the Lubbers machine. This duty required a quick hand and a deep understanding of the properties of glass, but it involved none of the physical exertion of handblowing. The mechanical blower stood at his bank of levers, watching the cylinder rise above him. The gatherer's work also changed drastically under the Lubbers process. The mechanized equivalent of the gatherer's task transferred to the ladling crew, a group of four or five men

Window glass blowing, from *Harper's*, July 1889.

who used cranes and rolling ladles to move the molten batch from the tank to the intake pot. Whereas the gatherer had collected glass directly, members of the ladling crew never hoisted the mass of glass themselves.[43]

When the cylinders were completed, crews took them to another part of the glassworks, where a worker known as a flattener cracked them lengthwise and placed them in a flattening oven. Using the heat of the oven to melt the glass slightly, the flattener pressed upon the top of the cylinder with heavy wooden boards on the ends of iron pipes. Guided by the pressure of the flattener, the sides of the cracked cylinder unfolded and collapsed to form flat sheets of glass. Finally, a cutter took the sheets of glass and cut them into the required sizes, paying careful attention to minimize the amount of glass left as scrap. Machines eliminated the need for manual gatherers and blowers, but flatteners and cutters remained key figures in the manufacture of window glass well into the twentieth century. Flatteners and cutters worked at the pace and output of the blower, in much the same working relationship as rollers and puddlers in premechanized metal production. Because all workers in this process earned wages based on the amount of glass they produced per day, flatteners and cutters had much invested in the blower's pace and ability.[44]

The two most common types of work remaining after the mechanization of window glass works were machine tending and materials moving. At one Pittsburgh district window glass works in 1900, only two unskilled workers shoveled a twelve-hour-shift's worth of raw materials into different bins. The conveyor systems that moved materials and products were sophisticated enough to require workers' strength only at the point of juncture in the stockyard. Everywhere else in the process, machinery and compressed air moved and shaped glass, commanded by the guidance, not the force, of workers. Blowers stopped interacting directly with globs and cylinders of glass and began manipulating them from a distance with machinery. Missing from mechanized glass production was the spectacle of a skilled worker battling the weight of a swinging glass cylinder, the "intricate ballet of hand production" that dazzled national journalists and Pittsburghers alike. The cylinder-blowing method gained fame in Pittsburgh in the nineteenth century because it displayed a combination of creativity and might that could be glimpsed in few other aspects of life. The sight of glassblowers in action was a powerful symbol of the type of work that, in the logic of Pittsburgh's celebrants, had driven the city's growth. It was a symbol that retained its visual potency even as its actual contribution to production was threatened by the persistent call for, and eventual success of, a mechanical replacement. A third industry that supplied less vivid images, the bituminous coal industry, followed the pattern of mechanization in the glass industry in the much different work context of the underground mine.[45]

MECHANIZATION IN BITUMINOUS COAL

In the early 1870s, *Every Saturday* proclaimed that Pittsburgh had become the "great metal manufactory of the United States because of its surrounding coal-fields, and because of them alone." The often-told tale of Pittsburgh's growth in the national press positioned southwestern Pennsylvanian coal as the building block upon which nearly every other industry in the area had developed. The coal trade remained little more than a catalyst to many visitors to Pittsburgh, certainly not an industrial pursuit as powerful as steel or as glamorous as glass. Local steel and glass garnered international attention, whereas the industry that made such success possible remained relatively unheralded throughout the late nineteenth century. Visitors described the hills surrounding the city as "immense coal cellars" whose single purpose was the feeding and driving of Pittsburgh industries. Bituminous coal, softer and containing more carbon than the anthracite coal of eastern Pennsylvania, was a suitable fuel for iron and glass manufacture in the days before coke became the most widespread choice. As steel and glass production expanded rapidly in the last decades of the nineteenth century, local demand for bituminous coal expanded with it. The profits of the coal industry received more attention than the work of the coal industry.[46]

Unlike steel- and glassworkers, coal miners did not create a durable product that was fashioned from raw materials. The coal they brought out of the ground of southwestern Pennsylvania *was* raw material, meant to be consumed in homes and businesses throughout the region and nation. Because their working lives were devoted to extraction rather than production, coal miners were never accorded the same level of awestruck scrutiny and description that other workers in the Pittsburgh area did. City boosters, proud of local business but wary of the city's increasingly smoky public image, championed natural gas as the answer to the dilemma of coal's griminess. However, even after the much-celebrated discovery of large natural gas fields near Pittsburgh in the 1870s and 1880s, coal continued to drive the city's industrial growth. Civic reformers may have announced the end of the coal age in the late 1880s, but the transition to natural gas was intermittent by century's end. When the natural gas supply was threatened periodically in the 1890s, the *Bulletin* predicted manufacturers' lamentable return to dirtier, less appealing coal. In contrast to the standard model of development that made Pittsburgh's rise a function of its coal resources, the *Bulletin* argued that the increase in population and industry occurred after 1880 because "a cheaper and better fuel than coal [was] available for the mills." Pittsburgh's success, according to the *Bulletin*, was "based on her consumption of gas and her discarding of coal." This was little more than wishful thinking, though, for the continued use of coal in industry made natural gas a supplemental, not a replacement, fuel.[47]

Coal companies focused primarily on the way in which workers removed coal from the walls of mine chambers, introducing machinery to increase the amount of coal a single worker could extract. At the same time, mechanized systems of cars, cranes, and hoppers optimized the transport of coal after it had been removed from the mine. In the days when miners were "compelled to excavate by hand," the daily output of a coal mine was determined by the physical stamina and financial incentive of individual workers. Miners paid by the ton balanced their need for a wage with their ability to withstand a fast work pace over a period of years and decades. The traditional means of mining bituminous coal in southwestern Pennsylvania required picks and hammers. When companies integrated machinery into the mining process, they introduced a new regimen that replaced these simple tools for breaking rock with devices that supplied power themselves.[48]

After touring the mines of southwestern Pennsylvania in the 1870s, James M'Killop noted that "all the physical energy of the workmen [was] strained to its utmost, they being in the mine as early as one o'clock in the morning, and remaining as late as eight at night." Bituminous miners kept long hours in order to maximize the amount of coal they mined; the more they extracted, the more they were paid when managers weighed it at the surface. Nevertheless, long working hours did not always lead to increased output. Numerous ancillary tasks—clearing the floor of the coal chamber, supporting the chamber roof with wooden timbers, and removing the timbers when a chamber was mined completely—occupied much of the day. Miners referred to these duties that did not contribute directly to their daily tonnage as "dead work." The work of a miner was varied before the era of mechanization, involving most stages of production and jobs that required strength, stamina, skill, and judgment. Even into the twentieth century, workers in mines were responsible for multiple tasks; it was not uncommon for a single miner to undercut, drill, blast, load, and sort coal. The introduction of machinery brought with it divisions in miners' daily tasks.[49]

The 1890s witnessed the first sustained mechanization of Pittsburgh coal. It came mainly in the form of machines for cutting coal from the seam and hauling it from the mine. Early cutting machines were not in the same league as the massive machines that made steel or blew window glass. Instead, cutting machines were essentially small mechanical devices wielded by workers to facilitate the undercutting process. With a machine in use, it took four workers to mine a single coal chamber—the first, the runner, undercut the rock with a machine; the second, the shooter, set and fired the explosive charge; the third, the loader, broke up larger pieces of coal and loaded it into cars; and the fourth, the scraper, kept the floor clear and attended to workers' lamps. When undercutting machines mechanized one of the most time-consuming manual tasks of bituminous coal mining, loading coal with shovels became the most characteristic task demanded of miners. Shooters and scrapers moved from chamber to chamber as they were needed, but loaders remained in a single chamber until it was cleared. Although undercutting machines could technically clear thirty tons of coal in a nine-hour workday, loaders could not keep up with such a pace. Loaders in the Pennsylvania bituminous region averaged fourteen tons of coal daily at the turn of the century.[50]

A description of undercutting with and without machinery suggests the effects of mechanization on the visuals of mine work. Until the 1890s, undercutting began when a miner took a sharp-pointed pick and cut a horizontal groove along the face of the mine chamber to a depth of three to six feet. The undercut groove was the key to removing large quantities from a coal face; by removing the rock's support at its base, workers could then break it or blast it from above. The groove for undercutting was often close to the base of the coal face, forcing the miner to lie on the floor of the chamber as he worked. The miner positioned himself on his side with his arms free for swinging the pick. The confined space of the mine chamber allowed little room for movement, making strong forearms and wrists a requisite for working in a mine. The skill of undercutting was judging the correct depth and length of the groove. If he undercut the coal face too deeply, he could bring the entire wall down during the next stage of extraction. If the miner did not undercut deeply or widely enough, he left behind coal that could have contributed to his total output. Undercutting took up to three hours, depending on the length of the coal face. During these hours, the miner moved himself along the floor inch by inch and swung his pick thousands of times.

Mechanization brought miners the relative luxury of being able to sit upright. The first type of machines used compressed air to drive a steel bit repeatedly into the coal, chipping away a groove in a fashion similar to the hand method of undercutting. The cutting machine, described as "small but powerful" by one contemporary writer, resembled a horizontal jackhammer placed on a wheeled, inclined platform in front of the coal face. The wheels of the platform allowed the operator, or runner, to push the machine into the rock as he cut the groove. The runner sat on the wooden platform behind the machine, working it back and forth along the face and gauging the depth of the undercut groove. The angle of the inclined plane dulled the recoil of the machine, keeping the cutting bit against the coal face without taxing the runner. The second type of machine resembled a large chainsaw on wheels that a runner pushed into the coal face to cut a continuous groove. Mine visitors in the 1890s noted that runners seemed to have little to do while operating these machines beyond manipulating and shifting them every now and then.[51]

Until the use of explosives became widespread in the late nineteenth century, miners broke the coal from the chamber wall with picks, using the undercut groove as both a guide and a fracture line. Pick mining took long hours of strenuous swinging, prying, and scraping. Workers had to impart enough force to chip into the coal on every swing but also had to brace themselves for the jarring impact of pick on rock. An effective pick was one that was heavy enough to force coal from the face; therefore, the weight of the pick and the repetition of the miner's movements made pick mining one of the most exhausting jobs in southwestern Pennsylvania. By the 1880s and 1890s, though, area miners broke most coal faces with explosive charges rather than picks. To set an explosive charge in the coal face, a worker drilled several holes by hand with an auger and filled them with blasting powder and a fuse. After clearing the room, the miner lit the fuse and blasted the coal face outward and downward. The undercut groove allowed the coal to break and settle evenly, although even the best undercutting could not prevent hurtling debris and dangerous mine collapses. When miners returned to the chamber, they found scattered piles of splintered coal and other rocks. If the charge had been set correctly, the miners' next task was loading the coal.[52]

Removing coal from the mine required shovels. Although machines cut coal from the earth before the turn of the century, workers continued to load it by hand well into the 1920s and 1930s. Technical impasses and limited space made it difficult for coal companies to implement conveyor belt systems or automatic loading machines that would have made hand loading obsolete. Loading was long, strenuous work, requiring workers to separate coal from slate and rock before dumping it in cars. Miners paid by the ton were not credited for the weight of waste rock, making sorting a crucial part of the loading process. Loading might have been drudgery, but it was not a task that workers could immediately master. The low ceilings of bituminous mines and the high rims of coal cars

3. Mechanized undercutting, from *Transactions of the American Institute of Mining Engineers*, 1899.

meant that miners had to develop a loading rhythm that brought their full shovels high enough to clear the car and low enough to avoid banging them against the ceiling.[53]

When mechanization was completed in any given mine, the nature of work within changed significantly for some workers and remained the same for others. Manual undercutting was by no means glamorous work, but it did involve the miner's judgment and the strength needed to dig a groove while lying on his side. The use of machines took much of the exertion out of undercutting, transferring the bulk of the labor in a mine to loaders, who had to cope with increased cutting and blasting capabilities. Runners sat behind their machines and guided them to each side, rather than dragging themselves along the chamber floor and cutting rock by hand. After mechanization, unskilled workers did what they had always done, shoveling, scraping, hammering, and lifting coal from the ground into cars. Jett Lauck, investigating for the Immigration Commission in 1910, noted that the use of machines in southwestern Pennsylvania had "reduced the occupation of a miner to that of an unskilled laborer, engaged in loading and clearing away." The work done in mines offered nothing characteristic or visually stunning to give it the same appeal as distinct tasks like puddling and glassblowing. Furthermore, machinery used to cut coal was not on the grand scale of steel- and glass-making machines. If neither the work nor the machines captured the imagination of contemporary commentators, the cool, murky atmosphere of mines did attract visitors who found novelty in the hive of activity deep beneath the earth's surface. The work done there was of little interest because it was so mundane, so ubiquitous in the Pittsburgh region.[54]

IMMIGRATION IN THE STEEL CITY

The prevalence of nondescript, unheralded, and unskilled work in Pittsburgh's three main industries in the late nineteenth century coincided with the movement of millions of people from southern and eastern Europe to the United States in search of employment. The final destination for many of those immigrants was that "new great city" whose reputation as both producer and employer grew rapidly. Many immigrants who came to Pittsburgh planned on staying temporarily to earn enough money to return to their homelands. Others made Pittsburgh a permanent residence, forming thriving ethnic enclaves in the city's hilly neighborhoods that retained their distinctiveness well into the twentieth century. Much has been written about the lives and experiences of immigrants in Pittsburgh, but a significant chapter of their story has gone unexplored. Immigrants from southern and eastern Europe came at the time when the Iron City gave way to the Steel City, and work in the city's three main industries underwent profound changes. Mechanization changed the way in which industrial laborers worked in Pittsburgh after 1880, but the demographic shift that occurred during the same time period changed the nature of the workforce itself. The imagery of labor in the Steel City was thus much different from that of the Iron City because the writers, illustrators, tourists, and city boosters who produced most of Pittsburgh's civic narratives held strong assumptions about the abilities and meanings of foreign working bodies. Immigration patterns during this period reveal the considerable extent to which the face of the industrial workforce changed in the decades after 1880 (see also chapter 3).[55]

The major immigrant groups that came to Pittsburgh before the 1880s were Irish and German. Irish residents of Pittsburgh at midcentury accounted for over 20 percent of the city's population, and another 15 percent was composed of German immigrants. Welsh and Scottish residents formed smaller, but equally cohesive communities in the city after the Civil War. All groups took advantage of the city's labor market, and the regional workforce reflected the pattern of west European immigration in the mid-nineteenth century. In 1880, the most predominant groups in the iron industry were native-born Americans, Irishmen, Englishmen, and Germans. Pittsburgh's skilled glassworkers were a more select group, many brought to the United States by particular manufacturers. Most highly skilled glassworkers in Pittsburgh were German, French, or Belgian. Skilled window glass workers in 1880 were primarily native-born and immigrant Germans. Finally, before the 1880s, the region's coal miners were overwhelmingly native-born Americans or English, Welsh, Irish, and German men whose families had moved to Pittsburgh during the 1840s and 1850s. In each industry, a handful of nationalities held all but a few of the jobs.[56]

Foreign-born residents of Pittsburgh and Allegheny City in 1880 were 27 percent of the total population, a percentage that remained virtually the same through the 1910s. The change in population in Pittsburgh was not so much an increase in foreigners, then, but a shift in points of origin. Southern and eastern Europe began sending men, women, and children to the city in place of the west Europeans who had built the local population before 1880. Pittsburgh was certainly not unique in this respect; cities like New York, Chicago, and Cleveland attracted millions during the "new immigration" of the late nineteenth century and early twentieth. Among the many factors that pushed and pulled immigrants from southern and eastern Europe, industrial wage labor available in cities like Pittsburgh became the most common. Once new residents had formed information networks with their families and friends to advise them about traveling expenses and job opportunities, the pace of immigration quickened. Pittsburgh became a city known for both its industry and "the score of nationalities assembled there, hodge-podge."[57]

The ethnic diversity of the steel and coal workforces after several decades of the new immigration suggests the efficiency with which immigrants found industrial employment. The coke and coal regions south and east of the city were the first to attract new immigrant groups to southwestern Pennsylvania in the late 1870s and early 1880s, but in the two decades that followed Pittsburgh and its adjacent mill towns became popular destinations. By 1910 six of every ten steelworkers in the Pittsburgh district had been born in the nations of southern and eastern Europe. Factoring in the second generation of immigrants reveals even higher proportions. A full 80 percent of men in the Carnegie Steel Company's Pittsburgh workforce in 1907 were either born in or could trace their families back to southern and eastern Europe. Towns that sprang up around steel mills beyond the Pittsburgh city limits after 1880 featured high concentrations of new immigrants. In 1910, 47 percent of Duquesne residents, 44 percent of Braddock residents, and 41 percent of Homestead residents were natives of southern and eastern Europe. Mining towns in southwestern Pennsylvania also held large populations of Croatians, Italians, Hungarians, Poles, and Slovaks by 1900. Over three-quarters of bituminous coal miners in the Pittsburgh district were foreign born in the first decade of the twentieth century.[58]

Custodians of Pittsburgh's civic image met this influx with ambivalence. On the one hand, the city's growth in population fit well with efforts to sell Pittsburgh as the center of American industrial power, financial power, and manpower. City boosters boasted of the ever-expanding "army of skilled workmen" that made Pittsburgh their home because of its incomparable work opportunities. Apparently the city attracted the best of the world's workers and put them to work in the world's most important pursuits. Local business leaders reasoned that Pittsburgh's industrial products were universally useful, and thus it was fitting that the world should offer some of its people to aid in the effort. Although this glowing view of immigration was expressed infrequently and was usually limited to the opening paragraphs of city guides and newspaper commemorations of Labor Day, the idea of an international army of workers had a certain appeal to those who believed that the size of the city and an aura of limitless growth were keys to future commercial success.

On the other hand, those who wanted Pittsburgh to become an industrial and cultural capital shied away from the fact that most immigrants arriving after 1880 were unskilled and therefore seemingly less civilized than the skilled workers who had established their families and careers in Pittsburgh earlier. Although the Chamber of Commerce noted in 1876 that the area had a population "noted for intelligence and sagacity," this vision depended upon craft enterprises. The skilled army of workmen was a rather small proportion of the city's workforce by 1910. Even as their work produced the "bones and sinews of civilization" for the world, unskilled immigrants failed to capture the imagination of the city's cultural elite, an audience that promoted only work with physical exertion *and* nobility. The terms that fellow workers and middle-class Pittsburghers used to denote new immigrants' lack of skill—*Hunky, peasant, Polack*—served as broad slurs that placed more emphasis on the type of work performed than on their origins. Though employed in production and manufacturing, these men from southern and eastern Europe were marked as inherently unproductive and unruly, a drain on industry's ability to operate continuously and efficiently. The local writer H. C. Stiefel narrated the disorder among new immigrants: "With the Dago and the Hunky and the Polack, it's a jab here and stab there, with a knife, an old pointed file, or a coke fork. And that ends chapter one. Then the relatives come into the story, and jab and stab a little on their side, a couple more dead Hunkys, end of chapter two, and all is hunky-dory."[59]

One decade into the new immigration, the city's society journal, the *Bulletin*, demanded that the "Old World . . . keep its human refuse on the other side of the Atlantic." What denied such immigrants social value? Editors of the *Bulletin* made it clear that workers arriving after 1880 were those who could not survive in their homelands, let alone in the mechanized and highly technical work environment of Pittsburgh, because they could not work as well as the laboring men who had made the Steel City great. The persistence of Hunkies and Polacks might have suggested otherwise, but the *Bulletin*'s criticisms underscored the central role that notions of skill played in arousing animosity toward new foreigners. Migratory craftsmen were one thing, but waves of unskilled laborers were another. By 1911 the Chamber of Commerce worried that native-born, English, and German residents of Pittsburgh were "piled up in front of the foreign wave," almost crowded out of the city they had made successful. Chamber of Commerce members exalted "that pioneer race, whose descendants throughout all the generations have kept the virtues that conquered the savage wilderness—courage, honesty, thrift, the grit that belongs to the maker of steel." These qualities produced the "hardy manhood" of a bygone era.[60]

Critics of the new immigration had little trouble grouping immigrants from all countries of southern and eastern Europe into a single ethnic group, usually referred to as either Slavs or Hungarians. The federal Immigration Commission defined a Slav in 1911 as a member of the race or language group that inhabited "the greater part of Russia and the Balkans." The commission explained that "physically and perhaps temperamentally" Slav immigrants were far more "Asiatic" than people from western Europe. Their geographic proximity to the Orient mirrored their cultural and physical otherness in the milieu of industrial America. Novelists who imagined that new immigrants carried with them "the tang and odor of the ground" of eastern Europe similarly argued that these workers were soiled by their geographic origin in noncultural ways. Both government and popular criteria marked Slavs—Lithuanians, Hungarians, Croats, Poles, Serbs, and Slovaks among them—as a single breed apart from the nationalities that had previously established themselves in the city. The category originated as a designation of a language group. In the context of industrial Pittsburgh, however, the label soon became a marker of skill and physical difference. As the *Bulletin* declared in 1905, "It does not take long to convert soiled rags into white paper, but it is going to take a century or two to convert the ragged and physically and morally degenerate immigrants that are now coming here into a fine quality American citizen."[61]

Organized labor was no less leery of new immigrant groups. Fueled more by concern about the contours of the labor market than about the purity of Pittsburgh's image, unions alerted their members to the problems of the new immigration. The *Commoner and American Glass Worker*, a paper representing several craft unions in Pittsburgh and the Ohio Valley, argued that workers throughout the region should "insist that none but natural desirable emigrants" be allowed to enter Pittsburgh's labor market. Immigrants had to be both natural and desirable, though the terms meant essentially the same thing. The *Commoner's* editors deemed a foreign worker natural and desirable if he came from a country that had traditionally supplied Pittsburgh's workforce. Only through vigilance and political pressure could skilled workers stave off the "undesirableness of Italians, Hungarians and Pollack" immigration. In the early 1880s, William Weihe, the president of the Amalgamated Association of Iron and Steel Workers (AAISW), informed a Senate committee that workers arriving in Pittsburgh from southern and eastern Europe were of "bad quality" because "good workingmen," he believed, would not "let themselves be imported." Men who allowed themselves to be used in such a way were those who did not care if they lowered wages for their fellow workers, forced out experienced workers, and crowded the local labor market.[62]

By the early 1890s, native and second-generation Pittsburghers distanced themselves from new immigrant groups at the workplace. The division reflected language and cultural barriers, but it also illustrated the postmechanization rift between skilled, semiskilled, and unskilled positions. William Roberts, a steelworker at the Homestead Works, observed in 1892 that visitors to his mill would not find the "Americans or the people from parts of Europe that speak the English language down among the laborers any more." Employers instilled a hierarchy within mills and mines between two broad groups—Slavs on the bottom and "natural desirable" on top. When Fitch toured the city's blast furnaces in 1906 and 1907, he found that employers gave supervisory positions only to native-born and west European workers. The rest of the workforce was made up "almost entirely of Hungarians and Slavs." Bituminous coal mining underwent a similar reorganization, as men from southern and eastern Europe composed the majority of loaders and scrapers after the turn of the century, and native-born and English, German, and Irish workers controlled machine-operating jobs. The stigma of unskilled jobs, incomprehensible languages and cultural practices, and poverty allowed skilled workers to define themselves against the new immigrants. A Homestead steelmaker who referred to a fellow worker in 1912 as "only a hunky" noted that "no decent American would have anything to do with him."[63]

As one trade journal described it, employers and managers assigned workers to particular jobs in Pittsburgh's industries by criteria that were "largely racial." One explanation for the ethnic division of the labor force was that workers from different countries gravitated to certain jobs. Certainly, information networks of chain migration brought workers across the Atlantic to seek employment in particular industries. Workers wrote to friends, neighbors, and family members in Europe about their working experiences in Pittsburgh and, if possible, used their positions to find employment for new immigrants in the same mill or mine. Necessity also limited new immigrants' options. *Iron Age* claimed that unskilled work in the Steel City was "largely specialized, in the sense that certain races only are disposed to accept employment in it." New immigrants were willing to accept the worst jobs because they could often find nothing else. Steelworkers recognized the fact that new immigrant employees always began and usually remained in unskilled labor gangs that accounted for much of the steel workforce. The coal industry also introduced immigrants from southern and eastern Europe at the lowest level of the employment hierarchy and kept them there. With only unskilled positions open to them in the mines, the average annual wage of foreign-born coal miners in the first decade of the twentieth century was $160 less than that of native-born miners.[64]

A better explanation for ethnic division in the workplace was employers' assumption that certain races were inherently better at certain types of work than others owing to the physical differences that defined racial and ethnic categories. After discussing such differences within the city's industrial workforce with several steel mill managers at the turn of the century, the writer Thomas Nevin reported that Poles and Slavs recently arrived in Pittsburgh were "hard-working, sturdy people . . . especially well-fitted to do the arduous manual work." Well-fitted workers had bodies that were accustomed to the demands of shoveling, hammering, lifting, and pulling. As the historian Josephine Wtulich has explained, the term *Hunky* contained specific somatic references that went beyond notions of class. Hunkies were unskilled, but they were also imagined as physically strong, insensitive to pain, and submissive to visible displays of power. Employers believed that the prized combination of strength, endurance, and docility could be found much more readily in immigrants from southern and eastern Europe than in western Europeans and native-born Americans. New immigrants, with their "splendid physiques and powers of endurance," were "apparently insensible to the rigors of January" and could withstand the summer heat as well. The Immigration Commission explained that in the Pennsylvania bituminous coal industry, racial characteristics emerged quickly as new immigrant groups filled the ranks of unskilled laborers: "In industriousness and attentiveness, the Slovaks and Poles are perhaps the best of the recent immigrant races, with the Northern Italians, Lithuanians, Russians, and Magyars about equal in desirability, and the Southern Italians and Croatians less so. . . . The races of recent immigration, particularly the Slavic races, are much more submissive."[65]

Although employers earmarked certain types of immigrants as ideal for certain jobs, they deplored what they perceived as a gradual decline in immigrants' physical ability once they had lived in Pittsburgh's working-class neighborhoods for an extended period of time. Steel managers and hiring agents believed that new immigrants came to the city in the best physical condition possible, fresh from the healthy work of Europe's countryside. After a year or two of the "unsanitary conditions of life, the ignorance of hygienic measures," and excessive alcohol consumption, their "vitality and physical stamina" had sunk below that of the native Pittsburgher. Employers did not blame the work itself, but the way in which workers lived when they were away from work. The problem, according to bosses, was the cultural practices brought from southern and eastern Europe: immigrants' tendency to live crowded together, eat poorly, not wash properly, and distrust the medical establishment.[66]

For their part, immigrants understood that the power and appearance of their bodies was the key to finding employment. When immigrant workers in Pittsburgh wrote home to their relatives in eastern Europe, some of them advised prospective travelers to guard their health and conserve their strength. Leon Mioduski, a Polish immigrant living in Pittsburgh, asked his brother in 1890 if he was "strong enough to cope with such strenuous American labor." If his brother moved to Pittsburgh, he would have to prove his physical worth to his employer immediately by being able to withstand the long hours of heavy labor without injury or complaint. Another immigrant worker wrote his family that coal hiring agents selected workers "just as they pick out beasts at the market in the old country," choosing only those who seemed "strong, young, healthy, and industrious." When immigrant workers wrote of "American labor," they meant the kind of highly mechanized, subdivided, standardized, and onerous work that proliferated in Pittsburgh after 1880. Mechanization and the new immigration produced new forms of work.[67]

MECHANIZATION, IMMIGRATION, AND THE STORY OF WORK

In 1880, it was not a stretch of a journalist's imagination to declare that "were Pittsburgh not the Iron City, she certainly should be the Coal City, and did she deserve neither appellation, assuredly she would be the Glass City." One way of thinking about the connection between industries and cities in the nineteenth century defined Pittsburgh by its products. The city's worth and meaning revolved around that which it produced for the world, and its historical development had been an inevitable path toward industrial supremacy. An increasingly prevalent way of thinking after 1880, however, defined Pittsburgh by the work that made the products and, more important, the bodies that performed the work. Visiting journalists and residents of the city studied labor taking place in the midst of grand change. Certain types of work were disappearing from the city's workplaces, while other types took their place and redefined the ways in which workingmen made their living. Machinery also became a substantial part of the industrial workday. By the turn of the century, the standard Pittsburgh travelogue published in the nation's newspapers and magazines mentioned not only the smokiness of the city ("a cloud by day"), but also the "roar of charging machinery" that filled the air for many miles and seemed to punctuate the lives of Pittsburghers. Signs of machinery were everywhere, blast furnaces and cranes lining the rivers, railroad cars filled with coal and molten steel hurtling over bridges, and elaborate furnaces glowing at night. If, as a contemporary wrote, "mechanical power multiplies laborers, and machines multiply brains," then Pittsburgh seemed to multiply everything associated with industrial America.[68]

Accounts of new, mechanized work processes focused on the awesome sights and sounds of machinery in action. One writer described a Bessemer converter he encountered in the city's American Iron and Steel Works as the "most spectacular manufacturing thing in the world." Breathless descriptions of flames erupting from blast furnaces and Bessemer converters accompanied detailed chronicles of every rumble, clang, and hiss that escaped from cranes and rollers. The action in these accounts took place by itself, with no need for human intervention. Writers described the "snorts and roars" of furnaces, the "fireworks" and "pinwheels" of blasts, and rolling machines that "mauled and pummeled" steel ingots. Glassblowing machinery produced a similar effect, making massive glass cylinders that seemed to float in the air above the work floor. The frenzied atmosphere of mechanized coal mines, with cutting machinery blasting away at the coal face and mine cars screeching under their heavy loads, frightened and delighted the few writers who made it underground in southwestern Pennsylvania. In these descriptions workers were often invisible or, at best, passive figures who watched the process along with the visitor but rarely exerted themselves. In a sense, writers suggested that the industrial worker had become more observer than laborer, more removed from the process than involved in it.[69]

For skilled workers, machinery became the site of work. Scaife noted that the first time steelworkers made contact with any form of the metal was at the very end of Bessemer production, when the ends of cooled steel rails were straightened and drilled. Until then, skilled workers operated levers and cranks to move metal through to the finished product. Similarly, the creation of a window glass cylinder under the Lubbers process brought skilled workers into direct contact with glass only toward the end, to flatten and cut a blown cylinder. Coal runners worked in closer proximity to their raw materials than skilled steel- and glassworkers, but still, they watched a machine chip away at coal while they sat behind it, five to ten feet from the coal face. Naturally, machine tending had its advantages and disadvantages. In each industry, the traditional measure of a day's work—so many heats of iron, so many cylinders of glass, so many tons of coal—became obsolete as machinery allowed workers to eclipse former standards.[70]

Writers of the era often remarked that the details of traditional work processes were well known to their readers. Fitch considered puddling the "oldest, the most picturesque and most self-assertive" of Pittsburgh industrial tasks, one that had been described in detail so many times over the past decades that little more could be said about it. Ironworkers, too, considered puddling a self-assertive task that was the most physically taxing labor process available to a workingman in the city. In 1903, a writer for *Harper's Weekly* glossed over the method by which workers blew cylinders of window glass, explaining that it was "known to all." The sight of workers blowing glass by hand was "beautiful and instructive" because it displayed both the limits of human strength and the delicate nature of artistic creation. These were the most celebrated work processes, evidence of the city's grand accomplishments. Coal mining, literally buried deep beneath the surface of southwestern Pennsylvania, came into focus less frequently and never displayed a comparable aura of creation. But like the skilled work done in metal and glass, manual undercutting still appeared more like *work* than its mechanized counterpart. Although the three industries experienced their technological shifts to varying degrees and at different times, few Pittsburgh residents and visitors could ignore the fact that in each the physical act (and visual spectacle) of work changed forever by the turn of the century. The daily tasks of men employed in steel, glass, and coal lost their ability to surprise and delight the observer. Instead of seeing men in direct contact with raw materials—shaping them, heating them, hammering them, breaking

them—visitors to Pittsburgh's industrial establishments saw men standing apart from the actual work being done. Fitch's description of a worker
rolling steel—"a man, high up on a raised platform, moves a lever and the
three-ton block rumbles forward"—epitomized the sense of mundane
detachment that pervaded highly skilled work after mechanization. The
writer James Oppenheim described the differences between work in the
iron and steel industries at the start of the new century: "The men in the
iron mills have work as creative as that of a carpenter; the product
depends on their skill. In the steel mills often they do one little thing over
and over again; they stand in one position all day long." Earlier processes
had been "picturesque," not an important characteristic for production
but crucial to the way in which work symbolized the city.[71]

Brody's summary, that steelworkers who had been the "manipulators of
raw materials and molten metal" soon became the "tenders of machines,"
describes the plight of those whose skill, experience, and ethnic identity
kept them above the ranks of common laborers. For unskilled workers,
whose labor had never been picturesque and had inspired few commen-
taries about the significance of Pittsburgh in the late nineteenth century,
mechanization escalated the demands placed on them. The number of
yard workers in the metals, glass, and coal industries increased greatly as
mechanization allowed manufacturers to implement continuous processes. Unskilled laborers crowded coal yards along Pittsburgh's rivers,
loading railroad cars that transported coal from thousands of mines.
Teams of workers packed the stockyards of blast furnaces, steel mills, and
glasshouses, moving materials from railroad cars to carts, trucks, and
hoppers. Men who "kept the scrap off the floor," to quote one McKeesport worker, received none of the credit in the written and visual accounts
of Pittsburgh work. The fact that most of those workers were members of
new immigrant groups further devalued their contributions.[72]

Many contemporary social critics viewed the mechanization of work
and the prevalence of unskilled immigrants as a degradation of the very
characteristics that had made traditional crafts so important to American society in the first half of the nineteenth century. Like middle-class
intellectuals who studied changes in work nationwide, local labor's objec-
tion to new immigrants stemmed from more than fear of reduced wages;
it also involved the coincidence of immigration and mechanization. The
great increase in the proportion of jobs in Pittsburgh's leading industries
considered unskilled occurred simultaneously with a great increase in

the number of immigrants from southern and eastern Europe who occupied those positions. The labor press stressed that the widespread
hiring of unskilled immigrants promised to "lower the moral standard"
of Pittsburgh's industrial trades. Skilled workers had established this
moral standard in the Iron City's plebeian days, when their mastery and
strength had made them bearers of the city's industrial images. By the
turn of the century, however, skilled machine tending and unskilled materials moving were the most prevalent industrial spectacles. The historian Antoine Joseph has argued that technological homogenization of
work produced fissures within the industrial workforce that weakened
"effective means of resistance." These means included the ability to project images of solidarity across ethnic and racial divides. For local labor
unions the sudden plethora of new immigrant workers was part of the
same phenomenon that had stripped work tasks of the very features that
had been defended so vigorously throughout the nineteenth century.[73]

Immigration played a central role in the reconceptualization of how
work was done in Pittsburgh. Middle-class preoccupation with the city's
immigrants at the turn of the century was focused not on the immigrant
resident of Pittsburgh, but on the "immigrant worker in the mill," notes
the historian Nora Faires. The model male immigrant of the Steel City
could not be removed from the mill or mine in which he worked. He
lived in the workplace, belonged in the workplace, and had come from
Europe for no other reason than to labor in the workplace. Those who
wrote about Pittsburgh imagined masses of immigrant bodies engaged in
heavy, unskilled labor. The constructed term *Slav* joined people with a
variety of cultures, languages, and histories into a convenient group—
convenient because the group or mass of immigrants, not the individual
immigrant worker, was considered the menace to Pittsburgh. That most
Slavs worked in labor gangs in steel mills, glass factories, and bituminous
mines only reinforced the image of groups of immigrant workers in
Pittsburgh. The most common adjectives used to describe these groups—
swarthy, dark, brutish—reveal the means by which new immigrants were
associated physically with the non-Western world. Descriptions of the
city's industrial workforce after 1880 contrasted the whiteness of old
immigrants (the ironworker's skin that was so fair it burned before the
puddling furnace; the glassblower's pale arms reflecting the light of the
blow furnace; the coal miner who washed the blackness from his skin
each evening) with the darkness of the new. As many scholars have

argued, whiteness has tended to be formulated as a relational category in the United States, defined more by the colors relegated to its outer boundaries than by its own hue. Pittsburgh narrators branded the paleness of old immigrants as normal and the new immigrant's ethnicity as a marker of an alien physique. The "barbarian-featured" Hungarians who came to Pittsburgh beginning in the 1880s evoked the ire of the city's upper crust for their crowded neighborhoods and low standard of living, but they voiced their displeasure as a critique of bodies in the industrial context. As Steel City labor became a matter of machinery and unskilled masses, writers and illustrators attributed a marked bodily image to this increasingly visible aspect of industry. Distinct from that attributed to old immigrants, the new bodily image was not used to boast of the city's accomplishments in the nineteenth century. New immigrants and their bodies were too novel and too alien to speak for Pittsburgh's history.[74]

Writing in 1905, Scaife noted that the history of the Steel City connected two eras of American history, spanning "from the time when the laborer was a beast of burden to the present age of mechanical appliances, when the workers direct the forces of nature for the benefit of man." Neither of the two poles seemed particularly ideal to Pittsburgh's boosters. The premechanization beast of burden suffered for his wage, bringing nothing to the work beyond his muscles. The worker who directed machinery exhibited little to suggest he was truly working (in the traditional sense of creation through exertion). Somewhere between the two historical bookends of the Steel City lay the skilled worker before mechanization. Straining and sweating, yet also creating and taming, the puddler and the glassblower were ideal vehicles for boosters' deification of work. In the late nineteenth century, that idol was threatened. The worker who despaired for "the human machine that roasts his brain before the fiery furnace and strains his muscle before the rumbling rolls" acknowledged the confluence of man and machine that characterized modern industry. How could one explain the work done in a modern steel mill or coal mine? Increasingly, boosters' answer was to focus on the body (detached from the work process) or the machine (where work occurred). Workers' bodies and machines came to the foreground of promotional efforts to explain industrial Pittsburgh because the work itself became more awkward to narrate and illustrate. Yet advertising was not the only spirit in which people wrote about the Steel City. They also approached it in the guise of crafting news stories, explaining technical innovations, and translating sensations. A Homestead steelworker described himself in the 1890s as "a creature who seems to be made by the work, and not for it." As industrialists changed the nature of Pittsburgh work, many in the city agreed that they created new "creature[s]" as well. When these new types of men asserted or assembled themselves collectively, they offered important opportunities for writers who made their living by discovering the atypical or the alarming. The summer of 1892 was a particularly eventful one in the Pittsburgh region, demonstrating just how alarming observers could find the new world of work.[75]

Ethnologists of the future will have little trouble

tracing origins here.—*Bulletin*, 4 March 1905

2

WORKING-CLASS

MUSCLE IN THE BATTLE OF HOMESTEAD

✳ In his diary entry from the evening of 6 July 1892, Robert Cornell recorded the news of the violence that had occurred earlier that day in Homestead, a mill town six miles upriver from Pittsburgh and home to the Carnegie Steel Company's massive works: "They are having a very searious [*sic*] riot at Homestead. There is a great many killed and wounded on both sides and it will continue until the state troops put it down." Even before the regional and national press made the events at Homestead a drama between labor and capital, Pittsburghers like Cornell recognized their significance. The former coal worker offered two ways to capture the day's meaning: as a breakdown of civic order and as a tally of the damage done to bodies. By describing the clash between steelworkers and employees of the Pinkerton National Detective Agency as a riot that would cease only when National Guard troops enforced order, Cornell assumed that workers had broken free of the constraints that normally held them in check. Industrial discipline, craft pride, and regular wages no longer channeled the power of Homestead's thirty-eight hundred workers into the production of steel. Instead, workers now exhibited that power on the streets through acts of violent unity. Furthermore, in noting the physical toll of the day's fighting, Cornell situated 6 July 1892 as a day of battling bodies that could be understood in terms of injury and death. Combined, Cornell's dual explanations represented a striking interpretation of the meaning of Homestead, one that was echoed throughout the nation in the establishment press. The events at Homestead became the first sustained media focus on the bodies of Pittsburgh workers in the era of mechanization and mass immigration. Images of workers' bodies at war that emanated from the coverage of Homestead raised troubling questions about the essence of Pittsburgh industry, questions that took years to address.[1]

The Homestead steel lockout claims a powerful place in the history of American labor. Historians have viewed the lockout as a contest over definitions of rights and responsibilities, a stunning setback for a dominant labor union, and a Gilded Age triumph of employers over workers. The historian Paul Krause has called the story of Homestead a "quasi-mythical epic" that became entrenched in American folklore through images of riot and bloodshed. By viewing the so-called Battle of Homestead through contemporary written accounts that emphasized workers' bodies in modes of spectacle, horror, and suffering, I focus not on the event itself, but on observers' attempts to use the event to explain such industrial by-products as demographic change and the division of labor. Although the violence at Homestead erupted quickly and unexpectedly, it did not go unseen by spectators. A plethora of journalists had descended on the mill town in the weeks before the fighting to report on the war of words between the union and the company. The result was a publishing frenzy that sold the story of labor strife to the city and the nation. Arthur Burgoyne's *Homestead* and Myron Stowell's *"Fort Frick,"* both book-length accounts of the lockout published in 1893, presented themselves as eyewitness chronicles written by local reporters who understood the essence of Pittsburgh's industry. Burgoyne's and Stowell's accounts arrived relatively late, however. Joining the two writers in Homestead on that turbulent morning were dozens of reporters from newspapers in Pittsburgh, journalists from major newspapers throughout the nation, Associated and United Press correspondents, and even a representative of the *London Times.* By mid-July, Homestead's *Local News* reported that at least 135 journalists from all corners of the globe had passed through the town to gather information for their stories. The American establishment press, as opposed to publications by labor organizations, socialist groups, or other entities sympathetic to the workers' cause, narrated industrial growth and conflict to a primarily middle-class audience that was unfamiliar with the world of mechanized industry. Journalists aimed their vocabulary and rhetorical techniques toward the exotic, troubling elements of the Pittsburgh workforce.[2]

For professional observers—reporters, novelists, and social critics who narrated the violence—Homestead epitomized the startling physical struggle of industrial workers who challenged the governing laws of mechanized industry. Although it was not yet common in the early 1890s to read newspaper and magazine articles about the strains and dangers that workers faced each day on the job, written accounts of turbulent strikes in the United States appeared regularly. Before the turn of the century, workers' physiques came into public focus most clearly when labor conflicts suspended mill operations. In their descriptions of battles between labor and capital, writers devoted considerable space to depicting the spectacle of working-class men amassed to argue their position against their employers. Workers' physical strength and bodily movements during disputes with their bosses became a symbolic shorthand that suggested the demographic shifts occurring in local industry. Journalists interpreted these physiques as a menacing index of work's degradation in the late nineteenth century. Press coverage of Homestead reveals the centrality of the body in attempts to explain the effects of mass immigration to the United States in the 1880s and 1890s.

The physical nature of the clash in Homestead meant that the bodies of the town's steelworkers became key items of interest for those attempting to make sense of the hostility. By emphasizing the display of thousands of workers engaged in common defense and describing in detail their physical sacrifices and feats of strength, contemporary Homestead narratives reveal a tension between several descriptive strategies used to capture the essence of the battle. The tension stemmed as much from perceived physical differences in the ranks of steelworkers (the pale, wiry, English-speaking worker and the dark, bulky worker from southern and eastern Europe) as from the skill and job divisions that separated them during the workday. Two sets of images emerged from Homestead accounts. First, reporters were struck by the spectacle of large groups of working-class people moving in and around Homestead. Attempts to describe the scene of the lockout focused repeatedly on the sight of a dark mass of workers as it took command of the town. A great number of laborers' bodies moving together in a common purpose impressed and clearly threatened observers, who equated this physical type of social disorder with a breakdown of American industrial progress. Owing to the large number of unskilled immigrants in the Homestead workforce, descriptions of the gathered workers relied on terms that stressed the savage, animal nature of the group. Second, reporters waded through the mass to find scenes of individual strength, bravery, and suffering taking place during and after the battle. When observers turned their attention to individual actions, they produced a taxonomy of bodily types and abilities that divided the mass of workers further along lines of skill and ethnicity. For most observers who wrote about the events at Homestead, the individual and the mass represented different factions of the Pittsburgh working class—one that had elevated the city to industrial prominence and one that threatened to topple it. In the summer of 1892, workers' bodies appeared to be anything but the passive partners of mechanized production. Here was industrial labor embodied as an alien force, a physical and social threat to the industrial city. Here, too, was a striking illustration of the ways in which writers depicted labor for middle-class audiences.

WALLS AND FENCES

The bitter conflict in Homestead began when skilled workers interpreted an announced wage cut as an assault on their most prized privileges. In mid-June, the Carnegie Steel Company announced that the minimum wage paid to its "tonnage men" under the sliding scale system would be lowered from twenty-five dollars to twenty-two dollars per ton of steel billets produced. The tonnage men were members of the AAISW, unlike the rest of the Homestead workforce, which consisted of nonunionized mechanics and laborers who were paid by the day. Homestead's tonnage men were overwhelmingly native-born workers and members of old immigration groups that had established themselves in Pittsburgh by midcentury. When eight local AAISW lodges refused to accept the wage reduction, Carnegie Steel's chief of operations, Henry Frick, responded by ending the company's recognition of the union and locking workers out of the steelworks on the banks of the Monongahela River. If workers wanted to reclaim their jobs, they had to do so under the company's terms and as individuals, not as members of a labor organization.[3]

The week preceding the conflict afforded journalists their first opportunity to present readers with stories focusing on the ways in which workmen in Homestead carried themselves. As locked-out workers held meetings and waited for further action from their employer, journalists emphasized the order that seemed to hold skilled and unskilled workers together. This order was epitomized by the lack of physical menace on the streets—no workers committed violent acts, stumbled around drunkenly, or tried to intimidate others. As opposed to scenes they wrote about a week later, the writers initially described a strict code of conduct in Homestead, where "men acted like trained soldiers" in following the orders of the AAISW Advisory Committee. The reportage began with images of stillness; local writers noted the absence of the usual noises of steel production in the town, replaced by "the thunder of an awful silence." Workers' bodies complemented this silence as they remained at rest and received only cursory press attention. Although work had ceased in Homestead, the discipline of the industrial workplace held the workers in check. Skilled workers—the "deep-chested champions of organized labor"—reproduced their positions of authority within the steel mill and convinced the unskilled to heed their call for calm. The press duly noted the physical restraint of which Carnegie's best workers were capable, reiterating the claims to respectable manhood that historians have identified in labor discourses in the mid- to late nineteenth century. Whereas unions used the mantle of respectable manhood as a strategy to give skilled workers the social respect as men that they were denied as workers, the press used the concept to explain the actions of men who led lives of physical conditioning and coordination. Unionized workers asserted their civic legitimacy by displaying both physical strength and the moral character to contain it.[4]

The emphasis on the order that the steelworker demanded of himself and his fellow workers echoed journalistic treatments of the steelworks before the disputes of July 1892. Reporters stressed the clockwork rhythms of mechanized production as the system of work became more noteworthy than workers within the system. A *Pittsburgh Times* article by Harry Latton illustrated the local approach to explaining the daily operations at the mill. Surveying the mill in the spring of 1892, Latton marveled at the technological achievements and hard work that formed the "genius, skill, and experience" needed to make the best steel. Latton stressed the combination of processes, machines, and men that produced the "perfect system." Although many actions took place simultaneously under the rooftops of the mill, there was never chaos on the work floor. Instead, management and labor had worked together with the "utmost care" to make every function contribute to the master plan. Employees, Latton noted, appeared content within a system that demanded instruction, coordination, and constant regulation. This idealized vision of life in Carnegie's mill presented workers as the willing partners in a management-machine-labor relationship; workingmen accepted the necessity of their own compliance and accommodated their bodies to the larger system designed by the mill's architects. Reporters depicted the gathered workers in the week before the battle with the Pinkertons as an extension of this belief in order, now transplanted beyond the confines of the workplace. Although divisions were clear between the union and nonunion workers, they managed, at least initially, to control themselves as a single group.[5]

As rumors circulated throughout Homestead after 1 July about groups of outside workers or soldiers approaching the closed mill, journalists sought signs of increasing tension within the general scene of composure. Frick called upon James McCleary, the Allegheny County sheriff, to provide a force of men to protect the mill's management from locked-out workers. A group of deputy sheriffs traveled by rail to Homestead on 5 July to issue a proclamation prohibiting assemblies outside the mill gates. Both Frick and McCleary were concerned about the ability of a large group of workers to control mill activities from the streets. Reporters amplified this apprehension, gradually presenting gathering workers not as a well-drilled group of soldiers accustomed to discipline, but as a crowd on the edge of physical disorder. Workers' bodies began attracting more journalistic scrutiny when they became disturbing, that is, when they became tools against the power of employers and the state.

When sheriff's deputies arrived at Homestead, an estimated two thousand workers met them at the station. Here was the first crowd scene reported in Homestead that summer, a "solid wall of surging humanity" that filled the streets of the town on 5 July and threatened sheriff's representatives. The *Pittsburgh Dispatch* described an unnamed AAISW leader urging his fellow members to stay calm in order to protect the deputies from the wanton power of the "unthinking mob." The distinction between the restraint of the union and the unruliness of nonunion workers continued throughout the weeks of reportage from Homestead. Although union workers themselves were at the center of the dispute, reporters focused on nonunion, mostly south and east European workers as the driving force behind the violence of 6 July. The majority of immigrant workers in Homestead were Slovaks who had come to town since the mill opened in 1881. In previous major disputes between workers and Carnegie's company in 1882 and 1889, south and east Europeans had joined with British, Irish, and native-born workers who composed the bulk of the AAISW at Homestead. When the union official spoke on 5 July of the "unthinking mob" in the town, reporters interpreted this as a warning of the potential violence emanating from uncontrollable immigrant workers.[6]

The spectacle of 5 July revealed a mass of workers becoming a cordon for city officials. As AAISW officials escorted the sheriff's deputies to union headquarters, they moved slowly between two "walls of swaying humanity." The *Dispatch* article introduced readers to the spectacle of a working-class crowd that moved as a single body, with its own sense of coordination and its own pulse. The crowd surged and swayed, carried along not by rational thought but by the certainty of its physical power. Workers formed human walls in the streets of Homestead, creating a new architecture with the collective use of their bodies. These *moving* walls, however, always threatened to engulf the deputies. Journalists impressed upon their readers the image of officers of the law sent to Homestead to secure access to the closed steel mill and being forced to make their way between men who clearly had the physical power to determine who could travel where. Though this was only the first of several times that week that workers amassed to control the streets of the town, "walls" of workers on 5 July troubled observers as the first public exhibit of the laboring classes' united power.[7]

The crowd on 5 July provided journalists with a model of bodily power and menace that they used to a much greater degree in their narratives of the following day. In what Krause has called a "fetishization of the physical violence" at Homestead, observers focused time and again on several key scenes used to encapsulate the day's struggle. Journalists like a St. Louis writer who cautioned that "the story of this battle is hard to tell," used these events to make sense of the often chaotic action that began in the early morning hours of 6 July. The complexity of narrating Homestead stemmed from both contradictory sources of information available to reporters (workers, company officials, townspeople, Pinkerton guards, other reporters) and linguistic obstacles placed in their path. How could one describe a monthlong struggle between a company and its workers that amounted to a lengthy stalemate punctuated by tumultuous episodes of bodily violence? What vocabulary offered a sufficient representation of the sight of a workforce arrayed against the efforts of its employer? Specific physical feats mitigated the narrative difficulty by focusing the tale of Homestead on its extraordinary plot of workers' bodies used to exert workers' will. Accounts of the day of fighting generally began with the town being woken by the whistles of lookouts who had detected the approach of barges from Pittsburgh and quickly moved to breathless depictions of workers in action.[8]

Homestead residents were already on alert after a week of rumors about invasion, and the alarm of that morning only confirmed widely held fears. Frick was known in town as the man who had crushed immigrant workers' strikes at his western Pennsylvania coke fields the decade before. A local minister, J. J. McIlyer, spoke of Frick as the man who was "less respected by the laboring people than any other employer in the country." The call that came around 2:30 a.m. thus was met with a swift reply; townspeople left their homes quickly and moved toward the steelworks. The *New York Herald* reporter could discern "no method, no leadership apparent" in workers' quick reaction. There was not enough time to organize a response through the official channels of the AAISW, so workers moved against what they viewed as a potential attack. Stowell described Homestead's streets between three and four o'clock as "one surging, congested mass of human beings." The mob of the previous day—powerful and threatening but arrayed in distinct forms—had now lost its organization. Workers no longer formed avenues in the streets of the town but instead filled those streets as they rushed to the works.[9]

The first specific action to receive news correspondents' rapt attention was the dismantling of a wooden fence surrounding the company's property. Frick had erected the eleven-foot structure in the last week of June as a stopgap measure to secure the works. One of Homestead's local papers promptly christened the mill Fort Frick and warned that workers loathed the fence because it blocked both their view of and access to the mill. Knights of Labor leader Terence Powderly later defined the fence as a direct threat to the livelihood of Homestead workingmen, an attempt to keep them from their rightful place as wage earners and steelmakers. When it became clear that the barges moving up the Monongahela would land at the mill, workers destroyed the fence to gain access. Burgoyne described a mass of "strong men" who tore the fence down "with a roar of anger" and pushed it aside on their way to the riverbank. The *New York Times* reporter noted how the heavy fence of planks and barbed wire "fell like a paper wall" under the workmen's power. Another New York paper questioned the decision to erect the fence in the first place, arguing that it stood as nothing but a physical challenge to men who responded vehemently to tasks that required muscle. Who could have truly believed, asked the writer, that such a fence could "keep out the mob when its blood was up?"[10]

The fall of the perimeter fence represented the first time that week that workers' bodies actually made violent contact with Carnegie's property. This fact was not lost on observers who chronicled the approaching confrontation. Until this point, the display of workers' physical power had been purely spectacle. The sight of thousands of bodies grouped together had frightened Frick, muted sheriff's deputies, and awed correspondents. The working-class mass had transformed the town of Homestead through its visual potential, its suggestion of what industrial workers' bodies *could* do. When the fence fell under the exertions of Burgoyne's "strong men," however, the potential of the mass had translated into actual power. If there was no question in the mind of the *New York Herald* writer that the fence would fall, it was because the spectacle of steelworkers' bodies had been so unnerving the day before. After all, how could a fence of wood hope to stop men who wrestled with steel six days a week?

If the trampled security fence was the first overt physical act of the lockout, reporters also interpreted it as the last blow to workers' self-restraint. As they moved past the fence, workers appeared to journalists as if they had broken free of the bounds of civilization itself. The St. Louis reporter watched as "on the maddened mass rushed." The men began "swarming around cupolas" as they entered the massive yard of the works, "wild with warlike delight over their easy victory." The emphasis on wildness, along with the reference to the workers' blood being up as they demolished the fence, correlated closely to a theory of the biological process of labor strikes popular among American social critics in the

1890s. After two decades of strike activity in the United States, writers who addressed the "labor problem" began describing patterns in the evolution of strikes. In an article titled "The Methods of the Rioting Striker as Evidence of Degeneration," James Weir summarized late nineteenth-century efforts to detect signs of savagery in labor conflicts. Weir investigated striking workers' "strange desire to revert to the customs, habits, and beliefs of our barbarous progenitors." Elsewhere, popular historians illustrated their accounts of labor conflicts in the Gilded Age with photographs of strikers presented in the style of police mug shots. The rhetorical device of such "striking specimens" attempted to link workers' physical appearance with their supposed moral and cultural deficiencies. The savage practices Weir emphasized amounted to the liberal use of workers' size and strength to injure and intimidate their opponents. In this model of workers' action, the striking group was composed mostly of immigrants and sons of immigrants, men who differed in startling fashion from "normal man," who, Weir implied, was either native-born or an English-speaking European immigrant. The savage element was even more dangerous because of its power over its civilized Anglo-Saxon brethren—as Weir noted, "The fear of bodily harm or the fear of being considered a coward have made many a law-abiding man a criminal."[11]

When a reporter for the *World* followed workers as they "ran like wild men" over the downed fence and into the yard, he participated in the larger narrative tradition of chronicling the descent into savagery that accompanied violent clashes between workers and their employers. One reporter went so far as to compare the noise of the building crowd to the "charging cry of the black fanatics of the Sudanese desert." In the pages of the national press writers transformed Homestead steelworkers into objects of fear and wonder, human beings who threatened to become something less than human while also displaying extreme physical ability. Work in mechanized industry had produced hardened bodies, but the strength that lay within them was not governed by "normal" intellect. Reporters in Homestead defined what was normal for American workers by presenting the boundaries of normalcy as they were toppled along with the fence. In that sense, a model of the civilized citizen-worker of the Pittsburgh region came into being only when workers committed an act that could be fit easily into the pattern of savage, degenerate labor troubles.[12]

As the steel yard filled with over three thousand workers and townspeople, reporters in Homestead set the scene for the confrontation of two distinct forces. The first was as yet unseen, moving silently upriver under the cover of darkness. The second was omnipresent, in constant motion as it occupied the steelworks. The tension of the scene was heightened by the darkness of early morning, as the barges landed at the mill around 4:30 a.m. At this point, Burgoyne switched his mode of presentation and attempted to place his readers inside the Pinkerton barges, looking out onto a riverbank full of men and women, "some of them half-dressed . . . some with stones or clubs in their hands." The scene before them, noted Burgoyne, "was one to appall the bravest." According to the *New York Herald*, the riverbank at the steelworks was filled with a "dark, angry mass of men."[13]

The darkness of the mass signified more than the hour of the morning. Burgoyne's technique of bringing the reader into the mind of a Pinkerton guard as he approached a howling crowd carrying primitive weapons simulated late nineteenth-century travel narratives that recorded explorers' first contact with the indigenous people of exotic locales. In the narrative of savage regression that characterized the reportage of the morning hours of 6 July, it made sense to observers like Burgoyne to imagine themselves not in the streets of Homestead, but advancing toward those streets, as if exploring the Monongahela River for the first time. This technique made the Pinkertons' discovery of the Homestead workforce a surrogate for reporters' discovery of the day's physical spectacle. Although reporters encountered the workers before the arriving Pinkertons did, they replayed the scene of first contact to stress the terror that took shape before them. The popularity of tales of exotic adventure depended on several popular concerns at the turn of the century. Social critics seized upon theories of Darwinism and recapitulation to reinforce claims to Anglo-American advancement. Under recapitulation theory, the growth of individuals and the growth of racial and ethnic groups were conflated to such an extent that they mirrored each other. If cultures, like species, evolved over time into more sophisticated forms, then those who lived in an advanced culture and rejected it—immigrants who were slow to respond to Americanization—offered a glimpse of biological primitivism that demanded the public's attention. The voyage to alien shores became a form of scientific inquiry as well as travel. The influx of immigrants to the United States in the 1880s challenged the assumption that vast ethnic and cultural difference could be found only in distant lands. Indeed, much turn-of-the-century anthropology in the United States considered the exotic as it existed at home, in the form of Appalachian hillbillies, natives of the American West, and the foreign-born of mill towns. Moreover, the dramatic climax in exotic adventure tales was the first glimpse of the tribe, when all questions were still unanswered and all responses, friendly or otherwise, were still possible. Burgoyne's sympathy for Pinkerton guards at this point in the narrative was more than an idle device to depict workers. Burgoyne dared readers to assume the viewpoint of men who were about to face this crowd of steelworkers. The glut of description that preceded this scene established tension and compelled the reader to expect the worst from Homestead's labor force. Given the fact that the workers had made quick work of the fence, what would the reader do if faced by this mob?[14]

As the barges arrived at the riverbank, workers moved forward to meet them. William Foy, an English-born worker, walked to the head of the crowd to address the Pinkertons as they landed just below the mill. When a gangplank lowered from one of the barges, Foy stepped forward and stood at its end. The showdown at the gangplank appeared in most accounts of 6 July, but the details of what occurred there differed slightly from version to version. The *New York Herald* reported that Foy bellowed to the Pinkertons, "Come on, and if you come you'll come over my carcass!" Stowell recalled Foy's declaration as, "Before you enter those mills you will trample over the dead bodies of 3,000 honest workingmen!" Burgoyne feared for Foy's safety, sensing that if the Pinkertons insisted on securing the steelworks, "they would have done so over his body." Reports presented Foy's body or multiple workers' bodies, dead or alive, as the chief obstacle to the disembarking Pinkertons. Workers had used their bodies to destroy the fence; they would use them now to defend their mill.[15]

The significance of Foy's "piece of bravado" at the gangplank lies in its individual agency. His solitary action was the first that writers mentioned, the first they isolated from the chaotic movements of the mob. Foy, a middle-aged man who reportedly wished to "grapple with the powers of darkness in bodily form," was the first worker to stand out amid a crowd that reporters depicted as dark and bloodthirsty. Foy illustrated the precarious position that writers created for the Anglo-American worker in Pittsburgh industry. He was determined to fight the darkness present in Homestead, but whether the darkness was in the form of Pinkerton guards or immigrant masses was left up to the reader to decide. Writers stressed the physical difference between Foy and the mass of unskilled workers, but they also suggested the transcendence of such difference. Foy stood for the rest of the crowd, leading it in defense of the steelworks; he also stood apart from the crowd, acting as a bright focal point distinct from the mass that was too dark to be scrutinized thoroughly. Whether the Pinkertons had to trample over his body alone or the bodies of all three thousand "honest workingmen," the laborers' anger was expressed coherently through the initial sacrifice of a white body. Foy was the first to be hit by a bullet that morning as gunfire volleyed between the two sides, seconds after he offered his somatic challenge to the arriving Pinkertons.[16]

Once the hail of bullets had begun, Stowell quoted a worker as saying, "There are but two weeks between civilization and barbarism, and I believe it will take only two days of this work to make the change." To reporters, the transformation had already been made. The actual armed battle at Homestead lasted throughout the morning and afternoon, ending with the Pinkertons' full surrender after four o'clock. For over ten hours, workers and guards fired intermittently at each other, while workers sought cover behind piles of metal in the mill yard and guards barricaded themselves in their barges. The press at Homestead presented the events leading up to this battle as clear moments in which workers wielded their bodies as weapons against the invasion of an external police force. In the press narrative, though, the armed struggle that followed was a step removed from the level of flesh and blood. The battle was chaotic and confusing for journalists, who sought cover from the gunfire at varying distances from the mill yard. Only when workers suffered gruesome injuries or took actions beyond the monotony of firing bullets did their bodies come back into focus.[17]

The chaos of the day's fight meant that observers strove to focus on fragments of the action instead of on the entire dizzying scene. At one point in the morning, Stowell's focal point became the "tall, brawny workman" who led his comrades in throwing sticks of dynamite toward the barges after it was clear that simply shooting at Pinkertons would not lead to a definite conclusion. This "Herculean workman" was one of many who heaved explosives rhythmically "until every muscle showed like a whipcord" on their bodies. Stowell captured this snapshot of workers' muscles in action as the number of injured people on land and in the barges mounted. Before the direct physical contact between workers and guards that accompanied surrender, signs of violence on the riverbank were fleeting and haphazard. Workers fell suddenly, struck in their knees, shoulders, and chests by unseen bullets. Injuries from bullets occurred so quickly that the press only observed their results, as men fell and clutched their wounded bodies. Smoke from discharged weapons and fires obscured the scene on the riverbank from many reporters, making the suffering of injured workers a highly personal experience.[18]

Of the deaths that occurred during the battle, Silas Wain's attracted the most attention from correspondents. While workers devised methods to assault the barges, several men on the north bank of the Monongahela River, opposite the steelworks, produced a cannon that belonged to a local post of the Grand Army of the Republic. Their intention was to demolish the Pinkerton barges one shot at a time, but they missed their mark. A shell struck Wain, a young worker standing in the yard of the works. His injuries were massive; as the *World* reported, "His flesh was horribly lacerated and he presented an awful appearance as he lay bleeding on the ground." According to the *New York Herald*, his body was reduced to a "mangled mass of bloody flesh." That Wain was struck with a shell fired by his fellow townspeople was less important to the press than the fact that his ruined body illustrated the ultimate vulnerability of the strong working-class physique. The bodies of Foy and the other workers who had been shot showed little of the gore caused by artillery. Instead, they displayed the impact of the fight through other means—writhing in the dirt, falling from perches, suddenly lying still. Wain's dying body, on the other hand, was not "eloquent with the effects of battle." Instead, it brought correspondents' reports to an abrupt halt, as if signaling a moment that defied simple description. A decade later, Pittsburgh Survey researchers highlighted the appearance of damaged and spent working bodies, yet such a technique did not prevail in the early 1890s. Damaged working bodies were not yet a regular feature of Steel City narratives; descriptions of Wain's body, turned inside out, stressed the extraordinary nature of a spectacle that was only tenuously connected to industry but remained a testament to the extremes of bodily violence.[19]

Those who were less injured than Wain sought cover from the Pinkertons' view. Stowell described injured workers "dragging their bodies like snakes along the ground" to find safe places to wait for aid. In a yard littered with stacks of scrap and pig iron, workers lay alongside the materials with which they normally worked. During the exchange of gunfire workers formed less of a threatening mass, scattering to all corners of the mill yard. Stowell's description of the workers as slithering snakes suggests a marked diminution of their physical scale. Workers who had seemed larger than life in the early hours of the morning now attempted to make themselves as small as possible. A man who was shot a few feet from the *World*'s correspondent "was carried into the mill, his wounds roughly dressed, and loving hands bore him to his home." Injuries turned men into feeble shadows of the Herculean figures who could overpower city officials. The exposed weaknesses and ultimate mortality of Homestead workers emerged most in the media coverage of these middle hours. Before and after the gun battle, reporters glimpsed few signs of frailty in the town's steelworkers.[20]

The dozens of injured workers were only a small portion of the "maddened men" who fought Pinkertons on 6 July. Though scattered by gunfire, the uninjured workers showed a unity at this point that seemed unbreakable to the press. The reporter for the *New York Herald* surveyed the crowd, from the "smooth faced boys" to the "huge mustached old steel workers," and found them all determined to crush the Pinkerton advance. When workers tried to destroy the Pinkertons' barges, whether with dynamite or flaming rafts, reporters presented them as moving with a single mind. Having such a sense of purpose, it seemed as if the promise of destruction had provided workers with the organizational scheme they had lacked earlier in the morning. To the *Harper's Weekly* reporter, the unity was apparent as the "mob took out a hand engine and . . . pumped oil into the river." Injury and death might have been isolating experiences for unlucky workers, but those who remained unscathed by the fighting were further joined together by the flurry of action and the insult of injury.[21]

Reporters also chronicled the efforts of several union officials who counseled physical restraint during the hours of bloodshed. When white handkerchiefs began waving from barges in the afternoon, William Weihe, the president of the AAISW, used his influence among the workers to encourage them to accept a surrender. The *New York Times* reporter watched as "President Weihe loomed up, and heavy as his voice was, he was almost unable to be heard" above the crowd. As more union men attempted to restore some sense of order in the mill yard during the stalemate, Stowell reflected on the ambiguous nature of steelworkers who alternated between bloodlust and calm. These men "were not savages, but men of families who, perhaps a few hours before, had held infants on their knees or kissed their wives farewell. They were good, strong men, wrought up by the sight of blood." Stowell, for one, could not quite determine whether workers had descended completely to a state of unmanageable savagery. The experience of physical violence, with its threats to and demands on the body, had abridged the "two weeks" that separated civilization and barbarism but did not turn the world upside down. Underlying Stowell's observation was the belief that the moment's savagery was caused directly by the horrors of battle and could be ended only by an equally spectacular conclusion. Peaceful surrender, it seemed, would not be enough.[22]

When the workers accepted the Pinkertons' surrender in the late afternoon, they forced the guards to exit their barges through the crowd of workers, townspeople, and, according to Burgoyne, "thousands of outsiders—some of them millmen from South Pittsburgh, some roughs and toughs . . . some Anarchists." The gauntlet scene as presented by reporters at Homestead was the full culmination of the mob scene from the day before. Whereas the 5 July mob had simply wielded its collective power through a tangible sense of menace, the mob on 6 July struck out at surrendered Pinkertons with fists and clubs. The creation of the gauntlet was the first instance in many hours in which steelworkers and others in the yard had organized themselves again as a mass of bodies in order to control their enemy. As Krause notes, the sight of bloodied Pinkertons stumbling through the gauntlet became the most widely used image to symbolize Homestead workers' temporary victory. The scene also became shorthand for working-class savagery; the House Committee that investigated the Homestead affair concluded that the physical violence of the gauntlet was not only disgraceful to Homestead, "but to civilization as well."[23]

The *World* adopted Burgoyne's device of placing the reader in the shoes of the Pinkertons as they made their way from the besieged barges. After a day spent in smoky, cramped quarters, the guards entered a terrifying setting: "At the top of the bank, they found themselves in a narrow passageway between two huge piles of rusty pig-iron. When they emerged, it was to enter a lane formed by two long lines of infuriated men who did not act like human beings. They were frenzied by the long day of fighting and bloodshed." Again, Homestead's architecture came alive in the pages of newspapers and magazines as workers formed themselves into walls that served the same purpose as the pig iron surrounding them—to funnel Pinkertons into a narrow space of violent retribution. The press hinted that the impersonal violence that accompanied the day's crossfire had not been enough to calm Homestead's frenzy. Stowell's "good, strong men" had not yet decided to go back to their wives and children. Reporters expressed their horror in recounting the scene as guards were "led like lambs to the slaughter" and fell to the "pack of wolves" awaiting them. In order to identify the enemy, workers forced Pinkertons to remove their hats. Guards' bare heads, noted one journalist, "offered an easy mark to their half-crazed assailants." The press focused on such details of violence to illustrate the combination of method and mayhem that correspondents experienced in the hour after the Pinkerton surrender. *Harper's Weekly* described the gauntlet as "cruel and cowardly business" that epitomized workers' approach to solving disputes with employers.[24]

Tales of adventure in the American West had popularized the gauntlet in the late nineteenth century as a brutal Native American torture device. In the biographies of Daniel Boone and other frontiersmen, native tribes used the gauntlet to weaken and demoralize a captive before his ultimate execution. In such a context, the gauntlet was a tool of the savage, a relic from the late eighteenth century and early nineteenth that retained a vivid sense of brutality in 1892. Just three years earlier, Theodore Roosevelt had published the first two volumes of his *The Winning of the West*, in which he detailed the experiences of the captive Simon Kenton. Roosevelt's description of the gauntlet stressed its size and menace: "Next morning he was led out to run the gauntlet. A row of men, women, and boys, a quarter of a mile long, was formed, each with a tomahawk, switch, or club." Kenton suffered terribly as the Indians "beat him lustily with their ramrods, at the same time showering on him epithets." White traders eventually negotiated Kenton's release, but not before he was forced to run the gauntlet eight times. His "battered, wounded body" required weeks of healing. If men like Kenton and Boone were the "favorite heroes of frontier story" in the 1890s, it was because they had managed to face Indians' primitive ferocity and survived to tell about it. The historian Sherry Smith notes that the end of the nineteenth century was an ambiguous turning point for white America's understanding of American Indians. The 1890s witnessed new attempts to refute the stereotypes attached to Indians, but it was also a decade in which the image of the ignoble savage persisted in popular and scientific works. The tale of the gauntlet, along with tales of scalpings, deaths at the stake, and cannibalism reinforced easy, automatic images of savagery.[25]

In this context, observers' focus on the gauntlet was both a convenient translation device for a readership assumed to be well versed in adventure tales and a means of increasing the narrative's emotional stakes. Placing the Pinkertons on the path of such primitive cruelty, Burgoyne noted that "if the experience before them was not destined to be almost as trying as that attributed to the victims of the gauntlet torture in the tales of Indian life, it was not because the mob did not show all signs of thirsting for a fierce carnival of revenge." When a writer for the *Army and Navy Register* noted in 1892 that the defeat of the "red savage" meant that the chief domestic concern for the nation's military was now "white savages growing more numerous and dangerous," his argument rested on the same equation of strikers and Native Americans with which Burgoyne explained the "fierce carnival of revenge." According to a narrative tradition in which those who used the gauntlet on their captives were savages, the press fit townspeople easily into such sinister roles.[26]

The tension of the gauntlet did not subside once all of the guards had passed through it. As union leaders escorted guards from the mill and through the streets of Homestead, workers and others continued to harass their foes. A local paper chronicled the continuing violence as "this great restless throng arrived in front of the unpainted walls of the headquarters, then . . . halted and spread out until the neighboring streets and lanes were filled to overflowing." At this stage, the press suggested, the center of the lockout returned once again to the streets surrounding the mill. Having successfully stopped the invasion, the workers now refilled Homestead's avenues with their bodies and took over the town. As the Pinkertons finally reached the haven of the skating rink in which they were held, the physical action of the lockout ended. The town returned once more to a state of expectation and pondered the consequences of the day's battle.[27]

The captured Pinkertons left Homestead by train that night, their departure bringing an end to the narrative, but not to the narration, of 6 July. Two weeks after the violence, the *Bulletin* reported that Pittsburghers were still talking about the drama of the gauntlet and the wider implications of worker violence. Reporters in town turned their attention to scenes of bitterness, vigilance, and mourning. The press juxtaposed the physical weakness of men killed and injured during the fight with the persistent power of their unscathed fellow workers. Although a number of men had suffered because of it, the battle of Homestead gave workers temporary control of the town. Neither the sheriff and his deputies nor Frick and his managers could disperse the crowd. Until eight thousand troops of the National Guard arrived on 12 July, workers occupied both the streets and the journalists' attention.[28]

As opposed to threatening mob images that had appeared in reports from 5 and 6 July, journalists framed the gathering in Homestead after the battle as an embodiment of the union. In their narrative, the AAISW had lost its hold over unskilled workers on the day of the contest. During the gun battle and amid the violence of the gauntlet, union leaders had called for restraint, stressing that the workers' goal should be not to injure Pinkertons but to drive them from Homestead. The press presented the days after the fighting as the resumption of union control. The *New York Times* interpreted throngs of workers in the streets as "the Amalgamated men standing shoulder to shoulder" to keep nonunion workers from stealing their jobs. The mass of workers' bodies in this sense had political and economic meanings that were absent a few days earlier. Now, workers huddled in mass to preserve their opportunity to make steel. Union leaders organized small groups of men—"the best representatives of brawn and muscle," according to the *St. Louis Dispatch*— to maintain order in the streets of Homestead between 7 and 12 July. The press clarified that order was threatened by anyone whose motives differed from the union's—anarchists, the intemperate, but also nonunion workers who might be unable to control their animosities. The AAISW now used its brawn to keep Homestead workers in line.[29]

The notion of bodies subdued in the days following the sixth was also noted in the reportage of dead workers' funerals. In mourning their dead, workers appeared in a drastically different fashion than when engaged in violence. At the funeral for Joseph Sotak, a Slovak-American steelworker who died from a gunshot wound in the knee, Stowell found the mass of mourners filled with "typical Hungarians—stoical, morose, and silent." The crowd was mostly steelworkers, with only "eight women among three hundred brawny men." Workers' brawn complicated the scene of reflection and sorrow, as memories of muscles in violent action clashed, for Stowell, with empathy for the mourners. Their brawn was muted, turned impotent before Sotak's body. On a subsequent day, funeral processions for John Morris, a native-born AAISW member, and Peter Faris, an unskilled Slovak-American worker, met as they approached Homestead's cemetery. A reporter from the *World* watched as three hundred union men, marching four abreast, and five hundred nonunion men joined in "stern silence" to walk around the cemetery. The difference between a procession and a mob, noted the reporter, became clear through this "labor of love." The religious purpose of the procession gave it a legitimacy not displayed by the mob's strength-in-numbers.[30]

The most lasting effects of the lockout were the physical demands placed on workers and their families when they no longer collected wages. Burgoyne found men "almost worn-out with fatigue and hunger" on the day of the battle, harbingers of the difficult days ahead. Burgoyne concluded that the strain of the day's fighting had been "enough to tax sorely the most robust physique." Fighting weakened the workers' bodies, but poverty did as well. The ephemeral victory of 6 July came to an abrupt halt. As early as 11 July, the *New York Times* reported that the people of Homestead were "hollow-eyed" from lack of sleep and "gaunt from the irregularity of their habits." The physical consequences of taking on Carnegie Steel were seen even more clearly several months later. With Christmas approaching, the *Pittsburgh Press* turned its attention on 9 December to the workers who had been refused rehiring at the steelworks and their families. The mill, run by replacement workers since August and regular workers since mid-November, was a "lost paradise to the hungry men" standing outside the gates. To journalists who lingered in Homestead, the result of the lockout was the worker's body suppressed once more—in death, in hunger, or in the production of steel.[31]

When the writer Hamlin Garland toured Homestead in the fall of 1893, his visit was the culmination of a recent literary tour of hopelessness. Garland's short story collection *Main-Travelled Roads* (1891) presented readers with dozens of examples of what William Dean Howells called "those haunted, grim, sordid, pathetic, ferocious figures . . . whose blind groping for fairer conditions is so grotesque to the newspapers and so menacing to the politicians." The writer's tales of debt, grueling work, and inequity in the Midwest provided a template for his reaction to the world of southwestern Pennsylvania steel. Garland found in Homestead a town on the verge of collapse. In the streets, "groups of pale, lean men slouched in faded garments" toward destinations unknown. The town's residents struck Garland as "the discouraged and sullen type to be found everywhere labor passes into the brutalizing stage of severity." The workers in the mill appeared "lean, pale, and grimy," while those without work stumbled around outside. Garland's parting thought about Homestead was that "the town and its industries lay like a cancer on the breast of a human body." If the steel town was a cancer that marred the Pittsburgh region, then the effects of the fight against capital still plagued workers' bodies as well.[32]

Garland's article on Homestead, written for *McClure's* magazine and published in 1894, challenged readers to see a link between these seemingly despondent townspeople and the characters of his rural short stories. The specific plights of each could be generalized to encompass the ordeal of people caught in an economic vise. Although Garland had declared to an editor several years earlier that he designed everything he wrote to "bring beauty and comfort and intelligence into the common American home," the ugliness of a town that was "as squalid and unlovely as could well be imagined" offered little to cheer readers. If his project was to instruct readers on the lessons of Homestead, however, he found plenty of material in the scene before him. The physical effects of the lockout played out in the bodies of Homesteaders and in the town itself. Garland noted, "Such towns are sown thickly over the hill-lands of Pennsylvania, but this was my first descent into one of them. They are American only in the sense in which they represent the American idea of business." Garland found it impossible to separate the unsightliness of a grim and muddy river town from the social injustices wrought there by industry in 1892. This was perhaps the most damning form of Homestead narrative for those interested in maintaining a positive view of the Pittsburgh region because it bridged the distance between minute physical description (the pallor, greasy clothing, and slumped posture of the workers) and grand social commentary (widespread despair created by greed). Garland insisted that one could see the problem with industrial capitalism merely by looking at the people toiling in a place like Homestead. This was a technique that the writers of the Pittsburgh Survey used extensively a decade later, when they urged readers to discern economic and political facts by interpreting bodies.[33]

Making sense of the flurry of representation that ended with Garland's dark account is like counting bullets on the bank of the Monongahela— one may be able to determine the side from which they were fired but must strain to discern their specific targets and larger meanings. The press narrated the events with an eye toward the physical stakes of labor's challenge to capital. Headlines alerting readers to a bloody battle or to fallen victims introduced stories meant to explain in part how such spectacular violence could occur in an American industrial center (and what it looked like when it did). The Pittsburgh area was no stranger to working-class violence. Fifteen years earlier, during the railroad strikes of 1877, workers and their sympathizers had burned large sections of the city and freight cars of the Pennsylvania Railroad. A regiment of National Guard troops took over Pittsburgh in much the same way their counterparts did in Homestead fifteen years later. The plot of 1892, however, surpassed that of 1877 in its dramatic simplicity—a single battle on a single battlefield with a distinct pair of combatants and an unmistakable story line. Although chaotic and confusing at times, the battle of Homestead allowed for a narrative focus that the earlier citywide confrontation precluded. That focus fell on the contours, feats, and limits of the working body at war.

One legacy of the reportage of Homestead was the lasting image of two sets of industrial workers in Pittsburgh, one in control of its physical power, one running wild within a mob. Three years after the lockout, James Martin published a novel about the life and struggles of an industrial town titled *Which Way, Sirs, the Better?: A Story of Our Toilers.* Martin's story was inspired by events at Homestead and set in the fictional Beldendale, a town in the "iron regions of Pennsylvania." Throughout the novel, conventions established in journalists' impressions and images of the summer of 1892 informed Martin's method of presenting the Beldendale workforce. His description of an assembled group of workers echoed the press coverage: "Some are respectably and cleanly dressed; others are in shirt sleeves, and without evidence of change of garments from the workshop; some are washed and shaven; others are as grim and sooted as when they left the mills and forges; some are grave, sober, and thoughtful; others are flushed, excited, and even boisterous; some bear evidence of no mean order of intelligence, scholarship, and refinement; others are brutish, ignorant, and uncouth." Brutish, uncouth, flushed, and boisterous workers also out-bulked the washed and thoughtful ones. The *New York Times* offered a model of the "average striker" in Homestead as a "healthy, broad-shouldered, dark-skinned fellow . . . with clumsy hands and knotted joints, slender waist, and clear eye." This, the writer concluded, was "a magnificent specimen of manly development." Rules of averages and types at the turn of the century held that the ethnic specimen stood for the ethnic whole—the average striker was the mob of strikers, indistinguishable from the rest unless isolated as a specimen, as if on the slide of a microscope. The average striker was dark and manly, but the eight hundred Amalgamated workers who formed the leadership of the Homestead workforce were not average strikers. Hugh O'Donnell, chairman of the AAISW Advisory Committee and a leader of the Homestead defenders throughout the day of fighting, appeared to Burgoyne as an unlikely model of leadership. O'Donnell's body, "rather slight of build" and pale, was less visually impressive than those of others in town. His slender but developed frame spoke eloquently of the decreasing physical demands required of a skilled worker—"one of the superior class of workmen"—in a mechanized steel mill. The work of a laborer, on the other hand, required long hours of constant exertion. What was hidden in the "magnificent specimen of manly development" was any sense of the drudgery and long hours that characterized the development process.[34]

The invisibility of work in Homestead in the summer of 1892 was a second significant effect of battle narratives. The art historian Rina Youngner noted that during such strikes and lockouts, workers appeared primarily as "dangerous mobs," not producers. For an industrial region that prided itself on production and the visible evidence of productivity, scores of articles describing workers' actions outside of the workplace were anomalies. Instead of enthusiastic reports on the success of the Steel City, writers and illustrators across the country presented groups of men who were notable because they were not performing their usual duties. Journalists alternated their graphic depictions between faceless members of an unruly mass and individual models of the essential American workman removed from work. In the first approach, commentators pictured thousands of workers as a single, living entity characterized by violence and physical power. The "dark" crowd existed on an animal level, lusting for Pinkerton blood. These were the "cultureless, alien be-ings" that dominated contemporary literature on labor strikes. Second, authors and reporters occasionally took readers further into this crowd to isolate individual figures who gave nuance to the ominous gathering. The individual Homestead worker described therein complicated the notion of an unthinking mass by appearing physically cultivated instead of raw and by using his body in heroic fashion to repel the hired invaders. Moreover, men who stood out to reporters were often skilled union men desperate to stop their fellow workers from taking violence too far. They represented the physical restraint that reporters saw in so few workers. In addition to the interplay between group and individual, when writers discussed workers as individuals, they divided them further into several physical types—the wiry Anglo-Saxon leader, the massive immigrant la-borer, and the weakened victim. Each figure had its moment in the spot-light during the Homestead drama, but the emphasis regularly placed on work in Pittsburgh was nowhere to be seen.[35]

In the decades before and after the lockout, both apologists and crit-ics of the Steel City made each of these representations a common arche-type for thinking about the new world of work, skill, and ethnicity that emerged in the United States. With slight modifications in context, the violent horde became the faceless industrial army (those whom the *Bulletin* would call the "hordes of ignorant, unclean and little-to-be-desired denizens of the countries of Continental Europe"). The heroic striker became the mythic Man of Steel. The Joseph Sotaks and Silas Wains of 6 July became the industrial scrap heap exposed in the first decade of the twentieth century. These local characters and groups were first used in vivid fashion in the narrative of the fight against the Pinkertons. The importance of physical display during the Homestead lockout was not simply a figment of reporters' imaginations. Indeed, workers themselves recognized the power of their spectacle. When National Guard troops arrived in town on 12 July, O'Donnell requested the opportunity to pa-rade his Homestead defenders before them. The men of the steelworks planned to show that although they would fight to the end against the interests of greed, they respected the authority of the state militia and recognized the rights of property. General Snowden of the National Guard denied O'Donnell's request and in so doing denied workers a last opportunity to define with their bodies the significance of their re-cent battle.[36]

Further denials were to follow from city boosters as well. When merchants who published the city guidebook *Pittsburgh Illustrated* turned their attention briefly to the topic of Homestead in the autumn of 1892, they presented little detail about what actually happened on 6 July. Instead, writers for the A. L. Sailor Clothing Company explained that facts regarding the physical violence of the day were "too fresh in all our memories to need any explanation." Troubling images of dark and unruly laborers streaming through town and drowning out the rational voices of skilled workers would not be forgotten, but they would be elided from official accounts of Pittsburgh. The city's civic and business associations narrated and promoted the story of local industrial life by connecting it to idealized images of Anglo-American workers' bodies. The press scrutiny of the Homestead lockout was not merely a setback for boosters' project of establishing a favorable idea of Pittsburgh; it was also an illustration of the high stakes and potential pitfalls of work iconography in an era of rapid technological and demographic change. Robert Cornell's diary entry on the "searious riot at Homestead" certainly understated the lockout's gravity for the Steel City.[37]

We foreign guests can carry away with us this lesson from
Pittsburgh, that no work is drudgery unless we make it so.
The cloud we have seen hang over your city is gilded with the
golden glow of ennobled and ennobling wealth.

—MAARTEN MAARTENS, at the dedication in 1907
of the Carnegie Institute, in *Memorial of the Celebration
of the Carnegie Institute at Pittsburgh, P.A.*

3

THE WORKING BODY AS

A CIVIC IMAGE

✳ The Homestead lockout brought national attention to Pittsburgh
workers' bodies in a way that tarnished the Steel City's image. For merchants, real estate agents, bankers, railroad executives, and a host of
other business professionals who relied upon heavy commercial traffic
in southwestern Pennsylvania, the true threat of Homestead was not a
working-class horde run amok, but the image of such disorder reproduced in cities throughout the United States by journalists and labor
critics. A city whose fortunes had been tied to raw materials and finished
goods had suddenly been thrust into the national spotlight for, of all
things, the physical menace and savagery of its workforce. In response to
the swift mechanization and immigration that formed the background of
Homestead's dark image, the region's business elite adorned the Steel
City with representations that rehabilitated the image of work and the
bodies that performed it. Boosters constructed images of Pittsburgh that
suggested that despite troubling signs of civic instability, the city was
actually thriving. The bodies they presented to the city and the nation

proved that in terms of physical health and vitality, Pittsburgh was a paragon of modern advancement.

The dissemination of work imagery in Pittsburgh was not a unique case of a civic elite with too much time and money on its hands. Towns throughout the nation displayed workers as figures to be scrutinized, respected, and associated with local achievements. The sociologist Tony Bennett has offered the concept of an "exhibitionary complex" to describe the nineteenth-century emergence of urban institutions and associations "involved in the transfer of objects and bodies from the enclosed and private domains in which they had previously been displayed . . . into progressively more open and public arenas." Turn-of-the-century Pittsburgh was home to such a complex of exhibitionary projects, projects designed to bring the worker's body (and its related idea of beneficial work) out of the privacy of the industrial workplace and into such public venues as city thoroughfares, exposition halls, bank lobbies, library courtyards, and museum foyers. Pittsburgh's boosters suffered particularly from a fear that the multiplicity and fragmentation of modern industrial society made it difficult to narrate daily life therein and that the meaning of their city could not be known without tremendous promotional effort. A local manufacturer complained a month before the Homestead lockout that beyond western Pennsylvania, the name Pittsburgh meant "the blackness of darkness, in which dwells neither sweetness not light, the house of the Philistine in which art is never a guest." The object of their promotional displays was to make the city knowable— to represent it with an easily recognizable symbol—by rendering one of its most hidden aspects visible. The male working figure would become a visual cue that both instructed middle-class residents and visitors in the transformative grandeur of hard work and assuaged Anglo-American workers' fears about their compromised position in the local labor market. Moreover, the display of working bodies followed artistic conventions that were greatly influenced by the political and economic interests of local industrialists. The idealized Pittsburgh worker was not a random figure in a mill but a highly selective creation characterized by denial and manipulation.[1]

Historians' work on American boosters has centered mainly on the efforts of western and southern business promoters to encourage commercial growth in the mid- to late nineteenth century. Scholars have identified a "booster ethos"—a view of economic growth that placed social order at the center of small towns' success. Relatively little attention has been paid to boosters' campaigns in the industrial cities of the Northeast during the era of massive industrialization. The boosterism examined here was not that of a small frontier town seeking initial waves of settlers and investors. Instead, the efforts to promote Pittsburgh took place in a city that had already made a name for itself and attracted tremendous amounts of capital and labor. Institutions like the Chamber of Commerce stressed that their efforts "for the promotion of the business interests and growth of the community" could also improve profits for individuals and firms. Local promoters focused on the cultivation of a cultural profile for their city that they hoped would add nuance to the prevailing view of Pittsburgh as a town obsessed with industrial output. Despite these differences in context, Pittsburgh's boosters likewise stressed social order as the foundation of future prosperity. The working images they offered for public consumption were thus designed to elide evidence of disorder and division caused by rampant industrial change.[2]

The organizational heart of Pittsburgh boosterism, the Chamber of Commerce, was established in 1874. Created three years before the chaos of the railroad strike of 1877 and sixteen years before the violence of the Homestead lockout, the Chamber of Commerce was guided by leaders who understood the negative power of unmanageable images of Pittsburgh's workers. A priority of the organization during its first thirty years, then, was the constant maintenance of a positive image of work in the Steel City. Throughout the 1870s and 1880s the chamber courted such organizations as the National Butter and Egg Association and the American Society of Microscopists, encouraging them to hold professional meetings in the city. Alongside the chamber were several organizations that shared its quest to present more amenable images to the public. The Committees of Reception, charged with attracting and coordinating commercial and industrial conferences in Pittsburgh, and the Western Pennsylvania Exposition Society, whose sole function was the execution of the yearly Pittsburgh Exposition, relied as much as the chamber on a civic image derived from the industrial workplace. The local establishment press also played a key role in efforts to promote the city by advertising civic events and trumpeting organizations' successes. T. J. Keenan Jr. of the *Pittsburgh Press* assured chamber members in 1892 that the local press supported their promotional ventures, "editorials, news columns, paid locals, circulation affidavits, and all." The city's papers, Keenan observed, were "ever ready to bring public opinion to [the chamber's] aid." In return, newspaper representatives received invitations to exclusive functions and membership in the city's social fraternities. The *Bulletin*, a weekly society paper, devoted itself to the cultivation of an appealing civic environment, constantly suggesting ways in which Pittsburghers could know their city and strategies by which Pittsburgh could make itself known. The *Bulletin* also served as a persistent critic of the rest of the booster community. Its chiding voice resonated for decades as the Chamber of Commerce and other organizations produced public events that were never quite ideal presentations of Pittsburgh's meaningful labor. In order to place industrial work on display, boosters were forced to make compromises that changed the work spectacle from its "natural" state in the mill or factory. The *Bulletin* lamented these compromises, pushing for a perfect form of representation that would best tell the tale of Pittsburgh.[3]

Significantly for the case of Pittsburgh, the exhibitionary complex engaged both middle-class and working-class audiences. Promoters designed displays to instruct workers about themselves while simultaneously introducing them to white-collar Pittsburghers. The image of work as a "community enterprise," rather than a site of class and ethnic conflict, depended upon presentations that took place in genial and celebratory contexts. Industrial exhibitions, public art works, and civic parades all garnered attention through a combination of booster hyperbole and the simple promise of an enjoyable show. By employing the city's middle class as an audience and workers as both audience and performers, Pittsburgh's boosters were able to create work spectacles that were seemingly incontestable representations of what went on in the workplace. The artifice behind these images was necessary to conform the realities of industrial work to middle-class expectations and skilled workers' traditional sense of artisanal identity.[4]

The display of the male working body in Pittsburgh created a masculine image for the city that echoed skilled workers' claims to respectable manhood and conformed to elite men's desire for symbols of non-threatening virility. According to the logic of these spectacles, the working bodies presented to the public were male because the city's "heavy" work environments were a masculine domain, as was the industrial capitalism that heavy work was meant to symbolize. Boosters commodified manliness as an accessible and portable physical sign, one that revealed the wonders of the city as it linked Pittsburgh's future to the economic order erected there. Matthew Riddle, a professor at the city's Western Theological Seminary, told Chamber of Commerce members in 1892, "My heart is full of Pittsburgh and I despise a man who don't want to make it more beautiful and more desirable." Riddle's intensity in improving the city's image reverberated in the halls of the chamber and beyond. As the drive for continued commercial growth and aesthetic desirability placed a positive spin on even the darkest chapters in Pittsburgh's story, the protagonist throughout was the mythic worker capable of carrying a city on his back. His image allowed the city's boosters to turn the unknowable and elusive city into an appealing spectacle.[5]

TEACHING THE ELUSIVE CITY

Selling the city was not easy. The first task was to make the city legible to a burgeoning public. Early articles on industrial Pittsburgh in the national press treated it as an exotic specimen finally coming into the national spotlight. *Harper's* presented Pittsburgh as a "black spot on the map of Pennsylvania," akin to a drop of water that, when held under the lens of a microscope, "teems with life." The journalistic focus of the 1870s and 1880s re-created the experience of seeing the city for the first time, with its hills, rivers, and glowing fires. Ralph Keeler's five-part series in the spring of 1871 presented a trip to the city as a reconnaissance mission for eastern readers who had never ventured into the wilds of southwestern Pennsylvania. The first article ended with a tantalizing glimpse of Pittsburgh; by the second installment, Keeler began to scout the city. City boosters attempted to turn in the late 1880s from depicting Pittsburgh's impressive, disorienting landscape to making a spectacle of the work that went on behind the closed doors of mills and factories. One way to accomplish this task was to bring people into the workplace to see for themselves; another was to bring the imagery of work onto a public stage. Pittsburgh's promoters used both techniques after the mid-1880s to give instruction about the meaning of Pittsburgh as it emerged as an industrial juggernaut.[6]

The need to explain the Steel City to outsiders became an obsession for those who believed that "no city in the country [was] so little understood by strangers." The local industrialist William Scaife railed in 1901 against "those who know the 'Smoky City' imperfectly, or only by reputation" as a sooty and desolate place. Another writer noted that "there are some things in nature and art that one cannot quite understand except by contact. In its modern attributes the city of Pittsburg seems to be one of these . . . there is an elusive element in its present state that cannot always be taken into account." The workplace was the ideal site for the visitor's "contact" with Pittsburgh. When the city celebrated itself with parades and pageants, observers noted that marching workers and industrial floats, while awe-inspiring in themselves, were mere referents to hidden spectacles tucked in local mills and factories. Journalists encouraged readers to use labor pageantry as the first stage of getting better acquainted with Pittsburgh's heavy labor. The *Bulletin* advised locals that the city was a "vast school that should be more appreciated by its people, young and old."[7]

Boosters in the local press urged parents to take their children on industrial tours in order to show the youth of Pittsburgh the type of work that created industrial supremacy. Similarly, guidebook writers counseled tourists to place a trip to a steel mill or glass factory at the top of their Pittsburgh itineraries. If one wanted to know the city—to know it more deeply than a city of smoke and bustle—one could grasp its significance via a well-planned tour. Here was a lesson in work ethic, physical culture, and machine culture combined in a single venue. The *Bulletin* promoted a trip to South Side glassworks and the Bessemer department of Carnegie Steel's Edgar Thomson Works as an exciting and educational lesson for children. Pedagogically, the city's backers touted the "matinee at the mills" as worth one hundred in the city's theaters. In 1907, fifteen years after it had witnessed steelworkers and Pinkerton agents killing each other, the Homestead Works of the Carnegie Steel Company became a showcase of mechanized steel production. The company produced detailed plans of potential walking routes that allowed visitors to see the most appealing segments of production. Moreover, the *Pittsburgh Sun* reported that students from the area's technical schools toured steel plants as part of their manufacturing courses. The city's education system should be focused, urged the chancellor of the University of Western Pennsylvania, Samuel McCormick, on amplifying "the industrial spirit of the community." McCormick advocated comprehensive instruction in which the "spirit of culture and character which values virtue above utility" would "touch, beautify, and perfect industrial, technical, and professional training." Pittsburgh's workplaces displayed this mix of culture, character, and industry, attracting tourists and scholars of modern industrial life.[8]

In the 1880s those who marketed Pittsburgh, the "heretofore strictly utilitarian city," recognized that the drama and spectacle of work could turn it into a "show town" for residents and visitors. A guidebook published in advance of the Allegheny County centennial in 1888 devised a five-day touring schedule, the fifth day centering around a trip to South Side steel- and glassworks. The last day of the tour was meant to allow visitors to feel the pulse of Pittsburgh, leaving them with a lasting impression of modern industry. One visitor who took the tour admitted that it was "not until one goes through one of these steel-making plants that he realizes what they mean." Meaning became apparent not through lengthy treatises on production figures or technical improvements, or through the hyperbole of Chamber of Commerce guidebooks, but through experience of the workplace. Although the modern city contained many elements that were not represented well in a tour of a mill or factory, Pittsburgh's most typical qualities—its physical resources, its mastery of difficult processes, and its labor artistry—were easily glimpsed therein. The utilitarian city reinvented itself by placing its utility on display as performed labor.[9]

Journalists who wrote of their trips to steel mills presented themselves as the first of many to make the journey. Writers encouraged readers to make trips of their own, preferably at night, when a tour became an adventure that captured the "full glory" of steel manufacturing. A night tour allowed visitors to enter the glowing mill from the surrounding murkiness, arriving at a scene of human endeavor and mechanical innovation that gave nuance to the shimmering fires dotting the Pittsburgh landscape. The editors at the *Bulletin* raved over the "weird effect produced by the brilliant, golden rays shooting heavenward from the furnaces on a winter's eve" and the surrounding "gloomy atmosphere surcharged with the spirit of unrest." The pastiche of man and machine, muscle and raw materials, made steel mills a "feast to the dullest eye." Furthermore, the "weird beauty" of the glasshouse also emerged most at night, when the heat and glare of melting furnaces and the shine of window glass cylinders stood in starkest contrast to the darkness. In the steel mill and the glasshouse, the sight of men amid sparks and smoke struck visitors as beautiful and uplifting.[10]

Yet several things were clear to both steel company executives and the booster press at the turn of the century. First, despite the frequent calls for more industrial touring, mills and factories were not filled to the rafters with visitors. By 1908, the editors of the *Pittsburgh Sun* complained that the city's schoolchildren still knew nothing about local industries, insisting that nothing was as educational as "a visit to as many local establishments as possible." Teachers and middle-class parents were charged with educating the city's youth in work spectacles, yet few seem to have accepted the duty. Second, if residents and visitors did tour mills of their own accord, they could read the scenes they saw within in strikingly different ways. The *Sun* admitted that a tour of an industrial establishment without a well-trained guide could be useless to the uninitiated, as educational as attending a lecture in a foreign language. For tourist-students to learn about Pittsburgh from viewing its work, they first had to learn a language that would allow them to appreciate what they saw and to analyze work spectacles with the tools of a connoisseur. For both the person who would not venture into mills and the person who did so without the appropriate script, city boosters created a collection of texts and a series of exhibitionary forms meant to bring the message of the spectacular workplace into public life.[11]

In the winter of 1893, Pittsburgh's Chamber of Commerce formed a committee to research and publish a souvenir guide for travelers who might stop in the city on their way to the World's Fair in Chicago. The efforts of the Committee on Advertising Pittsburgh and Western Pennsylvania at the Columbian Exposition were painstaking, for the single volume was charged with the crucial task of "properly representing and setting forth to the world at large" the meaning of Pittsburgh industry. Mayor Henry Gourley urged members to create a promotional vehicle that would "show to all nations what this great home of labor" produced for the world. The result was a slim volume that reproduced much of the content published two years earlier in J. Morton Hall's guide to the city, *America's Industrial Centre*. The souvenir guide touted the Steel City's production figures, described in great detail its historical development from a modest commercial town, and praised its sturdy workforce in the steel, glass, and coal industries. The Chamber of Commerce suggested several points of interest throughout the city, including the largest steelworks, and concluded with a common refrain, declaring that "Pittsburgh is truly a city to be proud of." The chamber placed the guide in all Pittsburgh hotels for travelers' perusal.[12]

In addition, the chamber printed a six-page city advertisement in the June 1893 issue of the *North American Review*, provided ten pages of material for the B&O Railroad's Chicago travel guide, and facilitated publication of a six-column review of the city in the *Weekly News* of Dundee, Scotland. Among other revelations, the *Weekly News* piece noted that Pittsburgh "was not nearly so black as it was reported, and that it was kept much cleaner and in better order than Chicago." Finally, the chamber sent a delegation to Chicago to promote Pittsburgh with an official exposition display. Bird's-eye views of steel mills and factories complemented statistical arrays that proved the city's value to industrial America. Despite the chamber's unprecedented effort, these promotional devices met with critical reactions from other corners of Pittsburgh's booster community. At only twenty-nine pages in length, the souvenir guide had little room in which to describe manufacturing processes in any detail. The chamber's special committee had originally envisioned fifty pages divided equally between descriptive text and visual material, until internal funding squabbles restricted the guide's scope. The *Bulletin* critiqued the World's Fair booth as "undoubtedly disappointing to those that hoped for a fitting display of the Iron City's industrial greatness." Though the booth touted the city's production figures, the editors noted that there was "no glass, no steel, no iron, no coke" to represent the city accurately. Neither was there any sign of the labor that produced such crucial components of modern society.[13]

Pride was one thing, but the successful selling of Pittsburgh was another. The perfect image for the city could not be *any* industrial worker, for Pittsburgh's boosters had more in mind than an emphasis on muscle alone. They wanted to show that the city "once symbolic only for the things which are the product of man's muscle and mechanical skill" could also stake its claim to a higher symbolism, combining muscle with brain, strength with artistic intellect. Advocates were members of the city's cultural elite, men and women who envisioned a national role for Pittsburgh in fashionable society. In addition to funding institutions that promoted the arts, boosters hoped to spread a more genteel image of the city's industry. This effort centered on the figure of the capable, creative worker. The unskilled worker was not enough, nor was the image of the skilled worker who let a machine do much of the work for him. Both of these figures, endemic to the increasingly mechanized industry of turn-of-the-century Pittsburgh, were distanced from work tasks that had traditionally appealed to social critics and popular audiences as marvelous spectacles. The best man for the job and the best image for the city was that which combined "the highest skill of the chemist, the largest courage of the capitalist and manufacturer, as well as the brawn of the highest developed form of the American working-man." The iron puddler and the glassblower demonstrated these valuable features every time they judged the quality of their batch, directed their helpers' work, and hefted heavy masses of iron and glass. Scaife stressed that the "real meaning and mission" of Pittsburgh at century's end was "the conquest of nature by intelligent energy."[14]

The spectacle of work in the coal mines of southwestern Pennsylvania never captured the imagination of visiting journalists, illustrators, and tourists as the work in the steel and glass industries did. The essence of idealized work in Pittsburgh was creation through unimaginable exertion, the worker's focused use of his body in a skilled, even artistic manner. Mining coal, in the periods both before and after the widespread use of machinery, offered none of the visual clues of creativity that made iron puddling and glassblowing appealing spectacles. In an extraordinary twist of logic, boosters imagined miners not as producers, but as machine tenders; the product of their work fueled the machines of the city. Writers imagined the men who spent their days amid the machinery, in contrast, as independent artisans whose work had little to do with mechanical aids. Mining required only physical stamina and a willingness to work underground. Puddling and blowing, on the other hand, demanded "not only different muscles of the body, but different faculties of the mind" as well. The romance of puddling emanated from both the incredible strength that puddlers displayed and their deep knowledge of the chemistry behind the "miniature volcanoes in constant eruption." Window glass blowing exhibited strength and grace as workers swung cylinders around them. Moreover, in both work processes, the worker's body was the fulcrum upon which metal and glass turned, coming into focus during its time of proximity to the glowing materials it worked. Both processes produced goods, but these were also physical ordeals to be admired. The puddler who possessed "great muscular skill like that of the heavyweight wrestler" or the blower who had to drink four gallons of water each day to replace his body's perspiration offered visions of noble sacrifice in the name of manufacturing. A *Harper's* reporter watched a window glass blower at work for a few minutes and was "puzzled which to most admire, cause or effect, workman or work." Pittsburgh's proponents intensified this dilemma in their promotional campaigns, using working bodies to stand in for the astounding tasks they performed.[15]

City boosters were not the only ones invested in images of puddlers and blowers as representatives of Pittsburgh industry. As Michael Santos has shown, puddlers and blowers themselves clung to their craft as the "one clearly identifiable source of class identity they had left." Steel triumphed over iron in late nineteenth-century Pittsburgh precisely because it could be made with machinery that did not rely on the skills of highly paid puddlers. After wages, union leverage, and self-regulation had been compromised by mechanization, the technical and physical difficulty of their occupation was workers' sole remaining claim to respect and power within the Pittsburgh labor force. The exertion required to make metal and glass in the traditional method marked the work as a distinctly masculine domain. In the late nineteenth century, as work tasks formerly monopolized by men were increasingly performed by women and even children, a reinforcement of the gendered language of certain occupations occurred. Specific groups of workingmen throughout the nation envisioned their work—whether it was lumbering in the forests of New England, cattle wrangling in the Western Plains, or tonnage work in steel and glass—as the pinnacle of new hierarchies of labor.[16]

Thus even as employers in Pittsburgh fired puddlers by the score and introduced mechanized blowing after the turn of the century, workers' symbolic currency became more valuable as a mark of working-class manhood and as an image for the city. Skilled work became less important in production, but the idea of skilled work remained essential to the elite's vision of "Pittsburgh the Powerful." When the Chamber of Commerce's Committee on Education drafted plans in 1908 for a work-themed statue to be placed at the city's Point, they envisioned the figure of Vulcan looming above the rivers' confluence. Like the mythic Vulcan, puddlers' and blowers' bodies became a convenient shorthand for an ideal form of marketable work—skilled, heavy, and artistic. The AAISW's *Amalgamated Journal* noted the conceptual generalization of the puddler's work after the turn of the century, when the label "puddler" started being used "in every sense in which man's sturdier qualities and industry are sought to be emphasized." Referring to various industrial workers as puddlers was not simply a sign of journalistic carelessness. Instead, the misappellation was a result of a pervasive way of thinking about work in Pittsburgh, fueled by boosters' two-decade effort to imagine that all of the city's workers might exhibit the same physical skill and rugged nobility that made puddlers objects of intense interest.[17]

Underlying much of the investment in the heavy work of puddlers and glassblowers were concerns about the detrimental effects of mechanical modern civilization. Throughout the nation social commentators voiced dire predictions about the fate of American health and manhood should the office replace the industrial workshop as the primary environment in which men spent their days. In 1889 William Blaikie asked the startling question, "Is American stamina declining?" The answer, for many writers who scrutinized the trends of urban life, was yes. City life, with its street-cars, administrative careers, and commercial comforts, made the urban middle class soft, unaccustomed to the physical difficulties that had hardened their pioneer ancestors. In the logic of what Gail Bederman has called a "widespread cultural concern about effeminacy, overcivilization, and racial decadence," excessive exertion of a man's mental faculties drained his body's physical power. Industrial workers offered some solace to those who envisioned the physical weakening that accompanied white-collar employment, but even work in industry seemed compromised by recent changes. Some middle-class Pittsburghers worried that labor-saving machinery had eased the strain of the skilled worker to such an extent that he was "not bodily the man his grandfather was." If the ironworker of 1860 was stronger than the steelworker of 1900 it was because the work process had asked more of his body in the era before mechanization. The skilled worker's less rigorous workday could be troubling to middle-class men who viewed their own professional or clerical careers with ambivalence. Work in the Steel City was hard, but in the era of mechanization some visitors to mills and factories wondered if it was hard enough.[18]

Intellectuals worried that not only Americans' bodies, but also the supposedly unique characteristics they contained were in danger of disappearing. The intimate connection between individual bodies and the national body came to the foreground as vocal editorialists, politicians, and clergymen cautioned about the physical abilities of the United States as the nation made its most pronounced imperialistic forays. The social critic Henry Merwin worried that the "natural impulses or instincts" that had made the United States a leading agent of civilization would be "dulled and weakened" by the nation's mechanical advances. The body's ability to respond energetically in times of crisis, to control its own irregularities, and to resist disease were all potential casualties of a society that lulled animal instincts to sleep. By extension, a weakening national body might lose its physical and military advantage over nations of the world it hoped to control. James Davis, puddler turned U.S. secretary of labor, argued that brittle bodies were like pig iron that lacked the strength and endurance of iron that had been puddled. Davis noted that only the "wrought iron races" could lead the world forward into a higher state of civilization, suggesting that the fragile state of American manhood in the 1890s and early 1900s could be repaired only through exertion.[19]

If, as the historian Richard Oestreicher has argued, skilled workers in Pittsburgh's heavy industries expressed an "assertive masculinity" built on confidence in their own "physical power and ability to overcome fatigue and danger," then changes wrought in industrial work after 1880 raised serious doubts about the survival of that type of masculine ethic in the Steel City. Work in Pittsburgh was certainly still dangerous in the midst of highly mechanized manufacturing processes, but machinery made work less strenuous for many workers who no longer had to carry the literal burden of steel, glass, or coal for a living. Concerns about the less dynamic work of the turn of the century that emerged in middle-class literature appeared in working-class popular forms as well. Pittsburgh's labor press routinely published stories involving dangerous (non-industrial) occupations, death-defying adventures, and physical violence but printed few descriptions of actual work processes. Union weeklies placed men who could wrestle wild animals and fight in hand-to-hand combat alongside the upstanding union worker as models of manhood. Industrial work lost its monopoly on assertive masculinity, but the new figures who emerged in the pages of the labor press to carry the torch of rugged manhood were designed not to compete with skilled workers. Their physical mastery was displaced from the mill to the wilds of Africa or the American West.[20]

The first step in boosters' symbolic rehabilitation of the Pittsburgh worker's body was an optimistic vision of the pace at which it worked. A swift and worrying pace governed modern life, but writers indicated that it was possible to master it. The swift pace of life in Pittsburgh struck many observers as a key ingredient of its industrial success. In 1890 the *Bulletin* noted that "the idle man . . . must feel out of place, if not positively uncomfortable in Pittsburg. There is no other city of its dimensions in the country that has as little that can be termed repose." Scaife agreed that Pittsburgh "never had a leisure class," but instead various social strata all devoted to constant industry. When explaining low attendance at Chamber of Commerce meetings, members noted that local businessmen were "a community of *workers*" who were unable to spare time for discussions when they had important work to do. The lack of rest could be a bragging point only if residents prospered in spite (or because) of it. A writer for *Harper's* claimed in 1880 that the "true Pittsburgher" reveled in the growing reputation of the city as a smoky and grimy center of difficult, relentless work. Authenticity in the Steel City, then, depended as much on a tendency to applaud hard work as on an ability to withstand it. A sesquicentennial review declared in 1908 that in Pittsburgh "everybody is always in a hurry. All within its limits work diligently; there are no idlers, and no place for such in Pittsburgh's busy life." Frequent denials of idleness served as a backhand slap against other cities in the United States that suffered from the "tramp problem" in the 1880s and 1890s. The migrant, unskilled laborer who worked seasonally until he had enough money to enjoy a few months of idleness could not exist in Pittsburgh, boosters reasoned. Work there was challenging enough to attract only those men who pursued it for both its financial prospects and its physical benefits. One writer explained that "not the prospect of ease and rest, but that of work which means independence and mastery, wins to-day the emigrant from the East." Idlers fled the city; workers remained. J. William Pope's poem "Pittsburgh," which appeared in several guidebooks and Chamber of Commerce publications in the 1880s and 1890s, epitomized the argument:

> No one need here be idle, for she calls,
> Each day for muscle, and for active brains.
> Each time the rolls go round, or hammer falls,
> The workmen and the employer count on gains.

The rhythms of the city compelled employer and employee alike to keep moving in the name of profit. Spinning rolls and the falling hammer governed the worker's actions, but he accommodated to the rhythm so much that he became one with it. Machine pace did not dull muscle and *active* brains, but invigorated and rewarded them. Boosters stressed the manliness of Pittsburgh puddlers and glassblowers based on their ability to cope with the extreme strain of their work.[21]

A second weapon in the arsenal of the city's advocates was a sympathetic vision of work that took place in close proximity to machinery. When residents and visitors to Pittsburgh followed the Chamber of Commerce's guidance and forayed into the mills and factories, they found the grandeur of new machinery and bodies of men at work combined in a single spectacle. Machinery loomed in industrial workplaces, lifting great masses of metal and belching forth fire and smoke, but city celebrants downplayed the intimidating aspects of its size and force as a means of placing the relatively small worker on more level footing. Part of puddlers' and blowers' appeal during this time was their ability to defy mechanical encroachment for much of the nineteenth century—these were men who did not need machines to help them and, seemingly, could never be replaced by them. Yet when machinery did make inroads into the Pittsburgh workplace, the city promoters accommodated their beliefs about work to the exigencies of a mechanical world. Successful promotion of the Steel City relied upon a faith that mechanization of work would not destroy the worker's body or its place in manufacturing. Instead, boosters suggested that machines accentuated men's physical abilities and allowed them to focus on demanding tasks. Reuben Miller, the president of the Bank of Pittsburgh, epitomized the theme when he spoke at a Chamber of Commerce banquet in 1892. The "manipulating machinery" found in steel mills, Miller noted, was "almost human in its work." Machines helped workers but did not rob them of the physical feats that made them extraordinary.[22]

Writers sought to correlate and synchronize the sight of men and machines at work. In their narratives, Pittsburgh's workers were masters of raw materials and difficult processes, and cranes, converters, rollers, and blowers that towered above them were mere helpers, attached to their masters with chains and levers and ready to do their bidding. The turn-of-the-century fascination with the "radical and intimate *coupling* of bodies and machines" pursued more than mechanical interventions into the human body; machines, too, could be imagined as extensions of human power and ability. Appliances that made steel and glass in Pittsburgh were not wielded in the same fashion as manual tools, yet they served the same purpose. Beginning in the 1870s, city guidebooks trumpeted the harmony in which workers and machinery coexisted in Pittsburgh, depicting them as "the various corps of a well-ordered army" that complemented each other and gave "power and endurance to the whole." The key for employers was not to make workers and machines compete but to coordinate their efforts into a single pursuit of industry. The "wonderful co-operation of ponderous perfected machinery with trained muscle" inspired some observers to reflect on workers' power to control such gigantic devices. A glassblowing machine lifted glowing cylinders to impossible heights at the beck and call of a single man. In the Homestead Steel Works, where James Bridge watched "machines endowed with the strength of a hundred giants move obedient to a touch," the pair of trolleys and cranes known as Leviathan and Behemoth responded to the skilled hands of only a few steelworkers.[23]

The congenial coupling of man and machine appeared most frequently in a common image of turn-of-the-century Pittsburgh that had little to do with the contours of local industry. The classical figure of a half-clad worker posed with his tools appeared on the pages of many guidebooks and city directories, offering writers and editors a simple way to assert an optimistic hierarchy of man over machine. Two examples from the first decade of the twentieth century illustrated this visual argument. The cover of the *Pittsburgh Leader*'s industrial review for 1901, *Pittsburg at the Dawn of the 20th Century*, featured an idealized white male worker in an ancient tunic looking back at the "busiest city in the world" as it glowed and smoldered in the starry night. The figure leaned upon a long sledge-hammer, and at his feet lay a gear, an electric battery, and other mechanical appliances. Similarly, the title page of the Union Trust Company's *Industrial Pittsburgh* (1908) featured a male figure holding a hammer and sitting on a large gear. In both images, the classical worker's body was the intended focus, placed directly above the mechanical implements that aided it without subordinating it. These images configured simple machinery as the prop upon which the worker displayed himself. For both logistical and rhetorical reasons, miniaturization became a standard technique of representation in Pittsburgh's man–machine spectacles.

Once the machine had been miniaturized and made innocuous, writers could focus their attention squarely on the worker's body. Journalists searched for words to describe workers' motions and feats, blending terminology from the animal kingdom with a linguistic equation of bodies and products of heavy industry. Writers who strained to depict

4. *Pittsburgh at the Dawn of the 20th Century* (1901). Courtesy of the Archives Service Center, University of Pittsburgh.

5. *Industrial Pittsburgh (1908).* Library and Archives Division, Historical Society of Western Pennsylvania

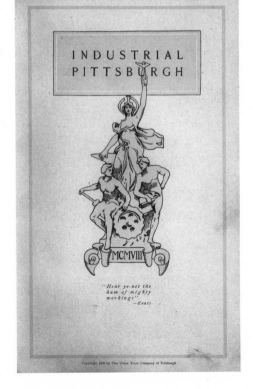

"salamander muscles" working in the glasshouse or the "tiger's action" of moving steelworkers suggested that Steel City workplaces offered a glimpse of primal manhood without the cultural savagery commonly ascribed to Native Americans or the peoples of Africa and Asia. Skilled industrial workers' animal-like physiques were tempered by their dedication to work and family and their intricate knowledge of modern manufacturing. Even Hamlin Garland, who journeyed to Homestead to expose its deficiencies as an industrial community, was exhilarated by the sight of workingmen. As Garland watched steelworkers move about the fiery mill, he "could not help admiring the swift and splendid action of their bodies." Workers moved themselves with a grace and fluidity that made them one with the process around them, and their bodies mirrored the materials with which they worked daily. Conceding to the writer's pressure to prove his strength, a steelworker offered Garland his arm to feel his muscles. The worker's arm was "like a billet of steel," his stomach, thick and firm "like a sheet of boiler iron."[24]

One visual aspect of industrial labor that escaped the notice of very few of Pittsburgh's promoters was that many workers removed their shirts to withstand the heat of the workplace. Although their assistants' work directly in front of the furnaces was overwhelmingly hot and required leather coverings, puddlers and glassblowers often wore only heavy work pants while they heaved their iron and glass around several feet away from the furnace doors. Especially during summer months, when the heat of the workplace remained above one hundred degrees each day, men tried to make themselves as comfortable as possible by taking off their dripping shirts, which would restrict their movement. Workers themselves made little of this fact, but it was crucial to the way in which boosters gave the work spectacle an added physical element. One writer noted that the "puddler's attire is beautiful in its simplicity and savors of the prehistoric." Davis described puddlers as "half-naked, soot-smeared fellows" who worked incessantly while sweat ran down their bare backs and arms. A writer for *Harper's* declared that the steelworker was "an Esquimau from his waist down [and] from his waist up a Hottentot, a Zulu, or anything innocent of clothing." The puddler's and blower's clothing (or lack thereof) gave observers access to the most primitive aspects of skilled work, suggesting the timeless quality of the crafts and their connection to a rugged past.[25]

The images of workers in Pittsburgh printed in magazines and newspapers during this period displayed men with little clothing. When the editors of the *Bulletin* printed an image of window glass blowers in 1894, they used the local artist D. B. Walkley's *The Glassblowers* as their inspiration. In Walkley's painting, three skilled blowers, stripped to the waist and with muscles rippling, worked their balls of molten glass into cylinders. The men's bodies took center stage in the painting, focusing the eye from the surrounding darkness of the glassworks to their pale backs and arms. The strain seen in the men's bodies attested to the strenuous nature of the work. Although the ball of glass in the center of the painting looked as light as the air surrounding it, the blower's body exhibited the extreme effort that was actually expended to hold the glass aloft. The blower on the left exhibited the muscles of his arm and chest, dark lines revealing where his body had been conditioned by toil. The blower in the middle showed his sturdy back to the viewer, while the blower on the right revealed powerful arms and shoulders as he bent over a swing pit, blowing into his pipe to inflate the hidden cylinder. Interestingly, a young girl watched the action of glassblowing from the left side of the raised work platform, hands clasped behind her back as if she intended to inspect the men for awhile. The girl's presence and her attention to the muscular trio's work transformed the image from a scene of work to a scene of work as spectacle; this was not simply nondescript work in a random glasshouse, but a much-heralded performance that demanded attention. The girl watched the men because their work was worth watching; it was an attractive, educational exhibit for both her and the viewer. Published in a society weekly that called since the 1880s for more public spectacles revealing the noble work done in Pittsburgh's mills, mines, and factories, Walkley's image of heavy work as bodily spectacle served as a means through which editors could present both the toil that made Pittsburgh great and the pleasure of viewing it.[26]

A convenience for the worker, the practice of stripping to the waist allowed writers to focus on torsos as barometers of the exertion required in heavy work. The son of an American Iron and Steel Works' chief engineer recalled his first trip to the mill's puddling department in the era before mechanization as an education in the adult world of industry. The scene of fiery heat and extreme strength struck him as a unique show of human physical limits, with the puddler as the main character and his work as the plot. The young visitor's reaction to the puddling spectacle centered on puddlers' exposed bodies: "From where I stood I could see

6. David Birdsey Walkley, *The Glassblowers*. Collection of The Corning
Museum of Glass, Corning, N.Y.

the puddlers bringing their hot balls of iron from all directions to the squeezers to be made into a bloom. It was a hot afternoon and most of the men were working without their shirts, and it was a sight for me to see so many big husky men running about half-naked." Half-naked bodies were impressive enough by themselves, but they were also viewed within the context of the Pittsburgh workplace, an exciting background in which to place the bodies of work. The heat of steel- and glassworks meant that workers' pants and sweating skin often steamed and smoked as they moved through cooler work areas. At times, they seemed elemental beings, half-human, half-incorporated into the raw materials and fires that surrounded them. A steelworker in Homestead described the "average mill-man" as a man who lived upon his "animal nature." Observers who marveled at the sight of working bodies agreed that there was something wild and untamable about them, but boosters' emphasis on skill tempered any threats that might be lurking in the frame of the puddler or glass-blower. In the logic of Pittsburgh boosterism, the ideal image of the city was the "brawny and brainy man upon whom fortune and beauty smiles." The city's middle class urged its sons to avoid the "paleness of intellectuality" and become the "robust, sun-burned, tough-muscled young man" who won the world's admiration. If industrial workers developed "muscled arms as big as a bookkeeper's legs," it was because they performed daily tasks that the white-collar worker could never accomplish.[27]

Although one visitor to Pittsburgh concluded that the "American working man conforms to no fixed type," the physique that city boosters promoted before the turn of the century was very much a white, Anglo-American body. When guidebooks praised the physical abilities of the "progressive, intelligent" portion of the local population, they referred to native-born and immigrant residents who had settled in Pittsburgh before the post-1880 wave of immigration from southern and eastern Europe. New immigrants' bodies were just as strong as those of established Pittsburghers (one writer noted that "they seemed to be made of iron"), but they were, to use Davis's analogy, like pig iron that had not yet been worked sufficiently into a better product. When the narrator of *Hammers of Hell*, a novel of the Pittsburgh steel industry, toured "Hunkietown," a working-class immigrant neighborhood clustered around a steel mill, he could barely draw his gaze away from the "massive, pillar-like thighs" of the men who lived there. The social reformer Edwin Bjorkman wrote that new immigrants possessed "health and strength beyond ordinary measure." The problem was not so much strength as the way in which that strength was employed; common laborers had no craft in which they could cultivate their muscles and mass into the tools of an artisan. Class and ethnicity intertwined in such a way as to make Anglo-American, skilled, working-class manhood the civic ideal and Slavic, unskilled, working-class manhood an inferior identity.[28]

Boosters' sleight of hand—praising the advantages of the machine but simultaneously implying that it had not changed the essence of work in Pittsburgh; and focusing on Anglo-American workers as representative of industries that employed great proportions of men from southern and eastern Europe—served as a convenient way to elude problems of mechanical deskilling and immigrant labor. The Bessemer, open-hearth, and Lubbers processes reduced the amount of hands-on skill required of workers, and writers in the Steel City responded to this change by virtually ignoring it. As mill tourists set foot in industrial workplaces, however, the nature of unskilled work therein could hardly escape their notice. A few visitors to Pittsburgh emphasized the importance of a strong, healthy body as the most important by-product of daily work— not as a complement, but as a substitute, for skill. A developed body became compensation for industrial work that had lost other redeeming qualities. The observations of Frank Popplewell, an Englishman who toured American steel mills after the turn of the century in order to enlighten his countrymen about their advances, demonstrate this external argument that contradicted boosters' message. According to Popplewell, skill mattered but did not preclude the advantages of strong limbs and backs. When he visited Pittsburgh in the winter of 1903, he noted that in one area mill "unskilled farm-hands from the country districts" made up a majority of the workforce. Here was a potential problem for a visitor who viewed Pittsburgh as a massive workshop filled with skilled artisans; if unskilled workers with no steel manufacturing experience filled the ranks of a mill's workforce, how could employers hope to maintain the pace and efficiency of modern industry? Popplewell discovered that, rather than being a liability to their employers, the "laboring element of fine physique" allowed the steelworks to push limits of human endurance and consistently raise production quotas. After four years of relying on the unskilled Hercules, the steelworks proved that "strong muscles and healthy frames were an asset at least equal to 'hereditary skill.'"[29]

Popplewell's observation of capable and efficient unskilled labor was a direct result of the unmanageable qualities of a mill visit. City boosters encouraged residents and visitors to tour mills and factories in order to learn about the essence of the city, but the lessons they learned there were essentially up for grabs. Skilled work tasks were only a minor part of the production processes of mechanized industrial establishments. While civic tour guides pointed to the puddler or the blower, visitors' eyes might wander to unskilled labor gangs or to the semiskilled machine tenders who shared the work floor. The problem for those championing the city, then, was one of both production and distribution. The local business elite brought more controlled images of work in Pittsburgh to the civic audience by staging work spectacles beyond the mill gates and factory doors. From the centennial celebration of Allegheny County in 1888 to the city's sesquicentennial celebration in 1908, civic promoters exhibited work in Pittsburgh as an ideal ornament for the city's public spaces.

"WORTHY SONS OF TOIL"
THE ALLEGHENY COUNTY CENTENNIAL

In the autumn of 1888, the business and civic elite in Pittsburgh orchestrated a five-day pageant of parades, speeches, and exhibits in honor of Allegheny County's one-hundredth anniversary. For four hours on the afternoon of 25 September between two hundred thousand and three hundred thousand people gathered on the city's sidewalks to watch over thirteen thousand workers and seven thousand politicians, civic leaders, and soldiers march in a lengthy procession. The AAISW, Knights of Labor, glassblowers' unions, and miners' organizations represented the bulk of the parade in both sheer numbers and symbolic intent. Local newspapers and souvenir writers heralded the great success of the centennial parade in headlines describing a "MIGHTY LABOR DISPLAY" that captured the power of "PITTSBURGH'S BRAWN." The celebration was as much a vision of the future as a history lesson for the people who lined the streets and filled the halls of the Steel City. While revering the industrial development that had occurred in the city since the late eighteenth century, boosters also used the centennial to assure the assembled populace that a promising and even more successful era of Pittsburgh industrial supremacy was to follow. The "skill acquired by its great army of mechanics" would make the county's second hundred years just as innovative and profitable as the first. The centennial offered boosters a unique opportunity to employ local history as a foundation for civic identity in a time of great change. Yet the celebration was not entirely a look backward; in the process of promoting a vision of workers, the organizers made explicit claims about present conditions of mechanized industry and possible future transformations.[30]

Just as local courthouses, bridges, and commercial buildings became sources of profound civic pride as city promoters invested their architecture with political and cultural meanings, so too did public commemorations become dramatic representations of urban productive life. The main feature of the centennial, the civic parade, embodied political, commercial, and labor organizations as marching units of varying size. Mary Ryan has described the urban parade as both the characteristic form of nineteenth-century civic ceremony in the United States and the "most general and broadly public picture that American cities presented of themselves." The centennial parade in Pittsburgh allowed city leaders and local labor to appear in highly cultivated spectacles in which every feature was designed to exalt vigorous industrial life. First, parades managed to organize the hustle and bustle of growing cities into neat compartments for public display. The organizational boundaries of nineteenth-century parades policed class and racial lines; orderly processions brought political and economic life to the foreground with little or no participation from unskilled workers and new immigrant groups. Second, parades allowed unions to present a public face that allayed middle-class fears of industrial strife and working-class rebellion. The official history of Pittsburgh—glorious, inspirational, educational—could be represented by an array of skilled workers' bodies marching in unison in front of crowds of eager onlookers.[31]

The *Pittsburgh Commercial Gazette* stressed the link between the spectacle of marching workingmen and the narrative of one hundred years of civic industrial history. After providing a before-and-after statistical overview of production figures from the early nineteenth century and the 1880s, the newspaper declared that "this brief outline of our industrial operations will enable visitors to understand how it comes that we can turn out such long lines of hardy workmen. . . . In a word, the demonstration of to-day is but one index of what may be seen more in detail within the walls of our manufacturing and business establishments." For the sight of marching workers to qualify as an index of productive power, bodily spectacles replaced work spectacles. A parade necessarily condensed industrial work into a portable symbol, stripped of the actions, equipment, and products that formed an actual production process. While workers performed a few basic crafts such as woodworking on Pittsburgh parade floats in the late nineteenth century, work in the steel and glass industries before and after mechanization relied on furnaces, which could not be rolled down the city's main streets. The civic parade of 1888 showed bodies of work as surrogates for the work itself. The *Pittsburgh Commercial Gazette* continued its praise of the labor procession, noting that marching men "exhibited more of the wealth-creating energy of the Iron City than could possibly be seen under any other circumstances, short of a personal visit to the various mills, mines, and factories in which they are employed." Again, a trip to the industrial workplace was the ideal educational junket, but the sight of marching workers was the best alternative. This logic begs a question: why did city boosters consider marching an adequate substitute for working?[32]

The answer can be found in the importance that the Chamber of Commerce and associated groups placed on the working body as a vehicle for public historical commemoration. As the historians Michael Kazin and Steven Ross have shown, labor parades in the United States have always expressed a "combination of satisfaction and discontent" as unions addressed two distinct audiences, wage earners and the general public. Parades allowed unions to display their strength and unity to nonunion workers, modeling a form of laboring solidarity in which wage earners literally and figuratively stood beside one another. Unions also used parades to prove to the general public that organized workers were respectable members of civic society—their formal clothing and disciplined marching established an image of unions as gentlemen's clubs. At the same time, marching workers used banners and songs to voice critiques of labor's place in industrializing America. Labor parades became stages for protests against long workdays, low wages, and political voicelessness. The centennial parade of 1888 was more than a labor parade, however. The march of the "sturdy workmen" was performed not for the glorification of local labor, but for the glorification of local labor history. The difference could be found less in the arrangement and movement of men in the streets than in the narratives that surrounded the parade.

Boosters actively framed the workers' march as a record of achievements of the nineteenth century.[33]

The visible presence of labor in the civic parade had a precedent in Pittsburgh that illustrated boosters' varying investment in labor parades and *civic* parades that featured labor. The Grand Labor Parade of 1882, held in the same year as the first formal Labor Day parade in New York City, was a procession organized by the AAISW, the Knights of Labor, and other local unions as a display of Pittsburgh's working solidarity. Thirty thousand workers marched on the morning of 17 June against monopoly and "wage slavery." The parade was divided into five divisions —the Knights of Labor, coal miners, glassworkers, iron molders, and assorted members of the AAISW—and was meant to amplify public support for Pittsburgh's skilled, unionized workers at a time when they were mounting a challenge to the political establishment. As Paul Krause argued, local unions organized the parade as a "major public event that would consolidate the morale of workers in Greater Pittsburgh." The spectacle of the parade was a powerful symbol of both the unity of skilled labor and visual cues that differentiated the city's working elite from protestors involved in the violent strike of July 1877. Workers displayed their muscles and numbers with a discipline and respectability that contrasted sharply with images of riot and disorder from five years earlier. Here were workers who did not need to be put down by the state. On the contrary, their ability to control themselves and unite peacefully was the central message of the spectacle. A reporter for the *Pittsburgh Telegraph* watched as "strongly built men from the mills, broad-chested men from the glass houses, and stoop-backed men from the mines" marched past in orderly, graceful procession. The labor press made much of the affair, but the city's establishment press paid little attention to it in the days before and after. Apart from a few brief articles describing what happened on that Saturday morning, city boosters treated the labor parade more as a minor news story than as a central event in the history of Pittsburgh.[34]

From the start of the planning for the 1888 celebration, on the other hand, centennial organizers framed the civic parade as a vital history lesson for the people. A year before the event, the Chamber of Commerce called upon city government to begin detailed planning. George Kelly, chairman of the chamber's Executive Committee, announced in October 1887 that the chamber would take the lead in organizing the celebration's content. One hundred years had seen work transform the city into an object of local pride, and each of those years held valuable lessons of civic achievement. The city's establishment press took every opportunity in the months leading up to the celebration to educate readers on historical anecdotes and chronologies of Pittsburgh's rise through the ranks of American cities. The *Bulletin* claimed that no American city's history had ever been "more thoroughly and systematically prepared for the instruction of the general reader" than the story of Pittsburgh in the summer of 1888. A year before the centennial, the Chamber of Commerce asked trade unions to take part in planning the celebration. The *Commoner and Labor Herald*, a newspaper that represented mainly glass and iron unions, suggested that the main goal of the centennial should be not self-congratulation, but a concerted effort "to boom the greatest city on the face of the earth." The best way to do it, according to the editors, was to focus on the increasingly national scope of the city's iron, steel, glass, and coal industries. The history lesson was one of increasing national dependence on the Steel City's work. If the parade could "let these industries be displayed and boomed as they never were before," then visitors and residents would understand how the heavy work of puddlers, blowers, and miners developed a city and a nation. Even in celebration, there was much work to be done.[35]

The *Commoner and American Glass Worker* noted in the days before the centennial that the planned festivities were the right balance of "pomp and glory and organized labor." The civic parade featured delegations of marchers followed by wagons and floats from each of the city's main industries. The centennial committee divided the city's labor force by trade, not by employer. Each group within the ranks of the labor procession was meant to display a "character representation" that encapsulated the nature of the work they performed. Such trade processions were a common feature of civic parades in nineteenth-century America and, indeed, of centuries of European celebrations. The procession of trades accentuated the civic quality of industrial labor. The displayed men, only a fraction of the total industrial workforce, were presented as workers employed by the city, not by individual firms. Their work was intended for the glory of Pittsburgh, their bodies signs of its triumph. The thirteen thousand men who marched were the unionized cream of the crop, representing the total workforce and eliding its more problematic figures.[36]

Workers were the "grand feature" of the parade, amassed to impress the observer with the size and unity of the city's labor. President Weihe of the AAISW rode a horse in front the "solid line of men" that made its way through the downtown area. Ironworkers turned in unison to salute city officials and guests seated in reviewing stands. Masters of minute physical movements, puddlers synchronized their bodies in a show of respectable unity. Glassworkers, a "fine-looking set of men," according to one observer, carried large globes and lamp chimneys with them to show the products of their work. The weight of the glass and the length of the march reproduced in a more benign form the strain of the workday. The mass of workers was so long that it took thirty minutes for the parade to pass any single point along the route. The *Pittsburgh Post* recalled that the "worthy sons of toil" were the most popular marchers in the parade, generating excitement and applause throughout the crowds that lined the streets. The *Commercial Gazette* applauded "workingmen, the mechanics, and artisans" as the "mighty bulwark of Allegheny's prosperity." The *Post* concluded that the vocal praise of the onlookers showed "the heroes of the never-ending battle of life . . . that Allegheny County's citizens appreciate the founders of Allegheny County's greatness." Along with banners and pieces of glass, marching workers also carried the burden of one hundred years of economic growth.[37]

Moving exhibits that followed the procession were meant to reveal the progress made in each industry since the late eighteenth century. Displays told a version of Pittsburgh history that focused on industrial development, as "crude furnaces and methods of first working iron ore" were followed by "the complete machinery and inventions" of 1888. Following on the heels of the thirteen thousand marching workers, the rolling machinery was dwarfed by the scale of gathered labor. Here the "sons of 1888" juxtaposed their labor and industry—the "present place of civilization" they had forged through a century of toil—with manufacturing relics of the city's earliest days. Pittsburgh was imagined as a city established solely for manufacturing, and thus the centennial parade could narrate local history with a relatively meager collection of miniature icons. The physical tasks of puddling and blowing had changed little since the early nineteenth century, but the furnaces and rollers displayed had grown in size and technical sophistication during that time. The machinery was not threatening, however; it was still compact enough to be wheeled through the streets. These were mechanical objects to look at, not to duck or dodge.[38]

The men and machines of the civic parade promoted Pittsburgh as both city boosters and union representatives had wished. As Susan Davis has noted, nineteenth-century parades that enacted the hidden world of work for general consumption "obscured the economic and political role played by the unskilled and cast the worth of labor in terms of craft knowledge." The necessity and plight of the common laborer remained invisible in the celebration carefully organized to present an ideal image of work in Pittsburgh. Recognition of the unskilled would have raised a host of troubling questions about mechanization, immigration, and the inequities of modern industrial life. The narrative of Pittsburgh's triumphant century had no room for such questions. Skilled workers appearing in the parade were encouraged by unions and organizers alike to display themselves as "respectable, classless citizens." Without the visible markers of class, their bodies could symbolize instead the history of an entire city and the credentials of an industrial century. If this was a generic and sterilized image of the Steel City, it was also one that was easy to applaud and difficult to refute.[39]

The centennial celebration was but a brief interlude in the course of late nineteenth-century Pittsburgh, yet it established a visual technique that boosters could use to complement their textual narratives of the Steel City. Although boosters glowed that the centennial was "three day's holiday earned by a hundred years of toil," work was very much a central concern of the civic parade. The image of work in Pittsburgh cultivated therein contained many elements exhibited elsewhere in Chamber of Commerce promotional campaigns—workers before machines, the skilled at the expense of the unskilled, craftsmanship above machine tending, and civic loyalties in lieu of class identity. Above all, the context of the parade framed the worker's body as a subject of public scrutiny, powerful yet rendered harmless by the conventions of marching and civic regalia. The worker's hardness, brawn, and "animal nature" were softened by his consensual act of public performance. An image of the model marching worker offered by the labor press after the turn of the century fit well with boosters' agenda:

> The man was tall and big and strong, his muscles stood like steel
> But deep within his mighty chest his heart knew how to feel.
> A smile was on his bearded lips, a tear shone in his eye
> He gently waved his massive hand as he went marching by.[40]

"ALL THAT IS INTERESTING AND ATTRACTIVE"

THE PITTSBURGH EXPOSITION, 1889–95

The civic parade of the county centennial was a fleeting event, advertised for months by energetic journalists, but over in four hours on a sunny September afternoon. Boosters presented this act of public participation as both a civic duty (displaying the Pittsburgh citizenry united in applause) and a crucial history lesson (learning why Pittsburgh was an important place in which to live). Yet the historical pretext in such celebrations also limited their ability to impress upon the general public their intended messages; not until 1908 would Pittsburgh arrive at another comparable historical milestone. After 1888, the city's boosters looked for vehicles of civic celebration that were not so tied to the calendar, civic events that focused solely on the present as a pageant of hard work and healthy physiques. The yearly Pittsburgh Exposition, first held in the autumn of 1889, continued where the Allegheny County centennial left off. Like the city's steel and glass disseminated throughout the world, the exposition was another of Pittsburgh's "exclusive products" that reflected the meaning of its creator. Bodies of work reemerged as the center of attention, this time in a representational venue that allowed for more elaboration—and more re-creation—of the world of work.[41]

When the first exposition buildings burned to the ground in 1883, local hopes for an annual display of manufactured goods to promote Pittsburgh's industries seemed to go up in smoke with them. The Pittsburgh Exposition Society (PES), founded in 1875, had purchased several small buildings on an island in the middle of the Allegheny River to exhibit "Pittsburghness" in its many manifestations to the world. The haphazard events of the late 1870s and early 1880s—dubbed the Pittsburgh Industrial Exposition—were hardly what business-minded city leaders had in mind, however. The PES struggled to hide the carnival-like atmosphere of the festivities under a veneer of high art and productive civic life. Horse races, card games, band concerts, and fireworks all tainted the first events as celebrations of working-class culture. The Chamber of Commerce supported the PES's work as a local example of the type of displays its members sent to international exhibitions in Mexico, South America, and Europe. Before the late 1880s, however, the PES failed to focus these local gatherings on the selling of Pittsburgh, allowing local vaudeville troupes and betting parlors to steer visitors to other, decidedly noncivic amusements. To those who wished to promote Pittsburgh commercially, the fire of 1883 was perhaps a fitting end to an ill-conceived endeavor.[42]

That a twenty-year run of annual exhibitions in Pittsburgh began several years later was a testament to the PES's determination to "advance Pittsburgh's industries" with a yearly show to stimulate business interest in the region. After several years of fund-raising and court battles over real estate transactions, the society erected large buildings in the heart of the city's downtown. When the first official Pittsburgh Exposition began in 1889, Francis Couvares notes, the presentation was an equal balance of Chamber of Commerce advertising and a solemn celebration of high culture. The renamed Western Pennsylvania Exposition Society (WPES) viewed the exposition as a popular venue that offered Pittsburgh visitors and residents "pleasant memories" of what made a modern industrial city tick. In this sense, the exposition fit squarely within the larger promotional project of teaching the elusive story of Pittsburgh. The WPES, funded and directed by representatives from every major manufacturer, banker, and merchant in Pittsburgh, announced itself as a "general educator of the masses," hoping for large crowds each year to prove that its pedagogical reach did the city's industries justice. Boosters who supported the WPES stressed the grand scheme into which the commercial showcase fit. One souvenir book noted that the "primary object of the Exposition is to make all who visit Pittsburg acquainted with the vast resources of the city, and to demonstrate in the most practical manner the full measure of their development. In no other way," the writer continued, "can the world be given an opportunity to form an adequate conception of the progress we have made, or the degree of perfection our artisans reached." The *Commercial Gazette* boasted that regional manufacturers and workers now enjoyed "a common bazaar" to display "all that is novel and useful, all that is interesting and attractive, all that is beautiful and artistic." Over six hundred workers and representatives of commercial firms gathered each year to exhibit their wares and services. John Dravo, of the Chamber of Commerce's special committee to oversee the exposition, boasted that the new events were "on a broader basis, wider in scope, and grander in aims" than their previous work. The exposition epitomized boosters' cultural goals, bringing together art collections, musical performances, and lectures while also placing work in the public spotlight.[43]

Amid these attractions stood the Pittsburgh worker and his "scene of fascinating strength." For its first five years, the highlight of the exposition was a glassmaking exhibit in Mechanical Hall that featured workers blowing and shaping glass for the delight of the crowd. Each night, workers moved around scaled-down versions of melting furnaces, blowing and shaping globs of molten glass into lamp chimneys. The crowds surrounding the blowing exhibit were often so large that only a fraction of the audience could actually see the work process. Visitors vied for the best positions as men gathered small batches of glass, blew them into cylindrical shapes, and carved their ends to make three-foot-long ornamental chimneys. The popularity of the glassblowers proved to the editors of the *Bulletin* that more mechanical and labor displays were needed in Mechanical Hall. As Pennsylvania's secretary of internal affairs noted, glassblowing was considered one of the "finest, most interesting, and fascinating operations" of Pittsburgh industry. The operation quickly became a popular reason for middle-class Pittsburghers to attend the exposition, generating ticket sales and press coverage for what was an otherwise typical display of mechanical devices and consumer products. Glassmaking featured aspects of physical, intellectual, moral, and aesthetic education that the WPES tried to highlight as indicative of life in industrial Pittsburgh. Mary Bakewell remembered the exposition as a "full occasion for advertisement" for the city and its industries. Exhibitors advertised an image of work in Pittsburgh along with their assortments of goods and services. The exhibit offered clues to the "real elements of Pittsburgh's industrial prowess," elements that could not be discerned in stacks of goods.[44]

The organizers of the exposition chose the production of lamp chimneys over window glass for both logistical and aesthetic reasons. Translating window glass production outside of a glasshouse would have been costly and difficult. First, furnaces required for window glass blowing were massive compared to those needed for lamp chimneys. The heat of melting furnaces made window glass factories stifling places in which to work and would have made any civic exhibit quite unenjoyable. The more diminutive furnaces employed at the exposition made a visit to Mechanical Hall hot but certainly bearable for most. Second, Pittsburgh window glass blowers of the late 1880s and early 1890s, as we have seen, were accustomed to blowing their cylinders above a swing pit cut into the floor of the glasshouse or atop platforms built above the work floor. Mechanical Hall allowed for little room to swing such cylinders, making the three-foot lamp chimney an ideal object to fashion before a crowd. Finally, blowing cylinders was only the first stage of a lengthy production process that also included flattening and cutting. Mechanical Hall was large, but it certainly could not accommodate the various stages of window manufacturing. Tableware and lamp chimneys could be made from start to finish in a relatively small area, allowing the glassmaking exhibit to occupy one central stage in the hall. Furthermore, lamp chimney manufacturing was Pittsburgh's best alternative to window glass making in terms of the worker's physical action and artistic performance. Like the reduced versions of furnaces erected for the exhibit, the making of lamp chimneys was a miniaturized version of window glass blowing, including work on the end of a blowpipe and a marvelous shape formed through skilled manipulation. Glassmaking combined features of heavy industry with the merits of the artist's workroom, adding a touch of creation to the more pragmatic displays that surrounded it. Filled with the sights and sounds of manufacturing, Mechanical Hall was meant to become a multifaceted industrial establishment. A reporter for the *Pittsburgh Commercial Gazette* marveled at the "busy hum of machinery, the whirling of wheels and flapping of great belts, with the fires from the glass-houses" that produced a "brilliant attraction" inside the exhibition hall. Manufacturers of textiles, pipe, pumps, and mechanical fans offered mechanical displays for the delight of visitors, but glassmaking provided something entirely different. The glass exhibit, "quivering with life and motion," rose above the rest of the exhibits; its stacks and furnaces stood like "monarchs of the show." Workers who "rolled and plunged and twisted the heavy tongs into the seething mass" of molten glass were masters of the display. The WPES prided itself on the "practical work" exhibited by the glassblowers, an important step beyond the presentation of products that made up the majority of the exposition. A trip to Mechanical Hall was meant to immerse visitors in an ideal vision of industry in which products were plentiful, machinery was pleasing, and even practical work was spectacular.[45]

As the historian Keith Walden has observed, industrial exhibitions in North America in the late nineteenth century were designed to "engineer consent" to a positive vision of industry as an inherent and inspirational part of modern life. Exhibitions were not mirrors of an economic and political reality, but "agents of change, creating by participation and not coercion a sense of natural order, consensus, and hierarchy." The exhibition of men working glass relied heavily not only on the display itself, but also on the public's reception of the display. The Pittsburgh Exposition transformed the notion of products and bodies as symbols of progress and city pride into a collective experience; participation in the event made the people of Pittsburgh and the city's guests part of the display's power. The first exposition in 1889 attracted 561,000 people during its five-week run. Roughly 300,000 people flocked each year to the remaining four events held before 1895. Though these crowds were composed primarily of elite and middle-class visitors, there were opportunities for working-class Pittsburghers to attend as well. Each Saturday was People's Day at the exposition, free to the masses and intended to impress upon working-class Pittsburghers the significance of their city. The dialogue of the glassmaking exhibit was thus tripartite, taking place between the performers and the middle-class audience, between the performers and the working-class audience, and between the different elements of the audience. The *Bulletin* reported that "from the time when the first glass blower takes his place, this pretty factory is surrounded by a crowd of deeply interested spectators . . . absorbed in the spectacle." To be absorbed in the spectacle, one would presumably have to be unaccustomed to the glassblowing process or enthralled by the event itself. The large crowds were crucial to the meaning of the exhibition; as visitors elbowed their way forward to see the physical art of glassmaking, they were taught a valuable lesson in the powerful appeal of working bodies. As work became a performance for a crowd, the worker's body became central to the plot, intimating all that happened behind mill and factory doors. This was not industry, which required no audience in order to function, but performance, which relied on the appreciative crowd to sanctify glassblowers' work. Here was work placed on a pedestal, roped off in a corner of Mechanical Hall for all the world to see.[46]

If the glass exhibit at the Pittsburgh Exposition remained permanent, it did so in memory only. By the mid-1890s, the wpes was desperate to cut the costs of the annual production. In addition to closing the exposition's art gallery and curtailing its musical programs, the wpes removed much of the extravagance from the displays in Mechanical Hall in the late 1890s. When the society decided to remove the glassmaking exhibit from Mechanical Hall in 1895, however, it was not because of its cost or unpopularity, but because of its excessive heat. Although glassmakers were annually the most popular performers at the exposition, the furnaces required to melt glass made Mechanical Hall too hot for some to bear. Complaints mounted from visitors and fellow manufacturing exhibitors that the hall was most uncomfortable when workers fired their batches. The authenticity of the display, with its close physical approximation of heavy industrial work, ultimately made it difficult to reproduce in an exhibitionary setting without the accompanying features that made Pittsburgh labor so strenuous. Work was hard in Pittsburgh, and it was also hard to reproduce.[47]

For the editors of the *Bulletin*, the glassmaking exhibit was a welcome glimpse of the elusive heart of Pittsburgh industry, but it also revealed the limits of transferring the city's heavy industrial work into a portable work spectacle. In a series of criticisms throughout the 1890s, the *Bulletin* encouraged the WPES to build upon the success of the exhibit with more variety and scope. If, for instance, the exposition could bring glassworkers into the public spotlight, why were ironworkers left in the shadows? Writers urged that "a showing, in miniature, of the wonderful processes going on in Pittsburg's mills" would "invest Mechanical Hall with an attribute that would make of it a reflex of the city's industries; and, as such, unique and characteristic." The argument was clear—the Pittsburgh Exposition could be representative of Pittsburgh only if it displayed work processes of its major industries, the work that had produced its wealth. Every city generated a surplus of products to display in an exposition, but only Pittsburgh had earned the right to show skilled working bodies in all their rugged grandeur. Boosters viewed skilled workers' bodies as symbols of a refined culture that appealed to higher tastes and existed above and beyond the profit motive. They used this promise of culture to suggest that the city of labor disturbances and chaotic growth was also home, in the historian Carl Smith's words, to "the very things that would hold it together against the dangerous disorder to which an excessively materialistic society was always prone." A Chamber of Commerce member, John Dravo, echoed this refrain when he urged all Pittsburghers to promote the city's "palace of art" and "display of artistic skill," lest other cities use similar advertising to become the "Pittsburgh of the Future." Performances would necessarily be smaller versions of the real thing, but the attractiveness of bodies at work would translate some of its significance in any setting. As an alternative to a visit to the industrial workplace, a "pre-eminently Pittsburg Exposition" could offer visitors a "more correct idea" of the city than they had ever imagined.[48]

A new strategy to stage work for public consumption emerged in the Steel City toward the turn of the century. Commissioned artists focused several times in the next decade on the working figure as a symbol of the city, emphasizing a subtle faith in the male body as a product of local history and an anchor in a time of flux. Decades of heavy industrial work in Pittsburgh created both products used throughout the world and muscular men with broad shoulders, solid backs, and unyielding arms. Public art brought this message to the city's edifices in an explicit way, joining patrons' desire for impressive ornament, boosters' model of work as self-promotion, and artists' belief that art could function as "a public and municipal educator." Building from the industrialist Joseph Weeks's declaration that Pittsburgh was an art center because it had mastered the art of "harnessing nature for the use of man," boosters used formal art for civic promotion in the decades after the Homestead lockout. Echoing the widespread turn-of-the-century belief that images inculcated the masses more than text, public art became an arena for further teaching about Pittsburgh. The Chamber of Commerce's Committees on Education and Municipal Art worked toward a common goal of using urban spaces as sites to convey the same arguments published in guidebooks and enacted in parades. Several prominent commissions awarded after 1895 emphasized workers' bodies as vehicles for municipal education. When the finished works were unveiled, Pittsburghers discovered that the artists, some of the nation's most renowned, had removed metalworkers from the industrial workplace to frame them in allegorical and ethereal contexts. For the representative worker to be a figure that could elicit pride in the city, his work apparently had to be elided from public view. Labor itself was beside the point because it raised questions of deskilling and exploitation that could only complicate boosters' position; thus, these works suggest the manipulative aspects of representation in Pittsburgh after mechanization.[49]

Edwin Blashfield's mural *Pittsburg Offering its Iron and Steel to the World* was the first major work of public art in Pittsburgh to glorify laborers' bodies as civic symbols. The Bank of Pittsburgh commissioned Blashfield's nine-by-nineteen-foot work for its main lobby in 1898. The centerpiece of the mural was Pittsburgh, a female allegorical figure who sat atop a throne emblazoned with the word "IRON." Her arms spread

7. Edwin Blashfield, *Pittsburg Offering its Iron and Steel to the World.*

widely, presenting a dozen male figures on either side of her who represented the city's industrial workforce. The two workers nearest the center of the mural were typical images of metalworkers, stripped to the waist, displaying arms and chests rippling with muscles, and holding long hammers in front of them. The paleness of their developed bodies was accentuated by shadows and mist in the mural's background, making their musculature and whiteness equally significant cues of their privileged status in Pittsburgh labor. In the foreground, a plaque read, "The city of Pittsburg offers its iron and steel to the commerce, industry, navigation, and agriculture of the world." Yet the only evidence of iron or steel in the painting were a few implements scattered throughout the assembled figures. Apart from the men's hammers, only a sword, a scythe, a surveyor's scope, and a plaque heralding mining machinery represented the city's contributions. The visual relationship between the central figure and the surrounding workers suggested that they, too, were part of Pittsburgh's gift to the world; both the products that kept the world's market running and the bodies of the men who produced them were made of steel.[50]

Blashfield had earned his name earlier in the decade for his work at the Chicago World's Fair and in the Library of Congress. For the World's Fair in 1893, Blashfield painted four figures at the entrance of the Manufactures and Liberal Arts Building, representing various forms of metal-working. The figures, titled "The Armourer's Craft," "The Brass-founder," "The Iron-worker," and "The Art of the Goldsmith," were each winged workers posing with tools. The art critic Pauline King described Blash-field's ironworker as a "half-clad youth" hoisting a hammer and inspiring the viewer with the visible strength of his body. He was a symbol of premechanized America, a past in which workers applied tools and skill directly to heavy materials and their bodies were integral factors of pro-duction. For the main reading room of the Library of Congress, Blashfield painted a series of twelve figures representing nations that had contrib-uted to the rise of human civilization. The final figure in the series, representing America, or "Science," was a worker in a classical, sleeveless tunic with a small dynamo at his feet. Blashfield's vision of American science placed it in an industrial context in which the worker still towered above machinery and the worker-above-machine pair symbolized the nation's gifts to the world. By 1895, when he began the mural for the Bank of Pittsburgh, he had a brief but significant history of representing the nation and its workers as muscular, heroic figures. His work struck chords in Chicago and Washington and recommended him for a project in the Steel City.[51]

Working men's bodies in Blashfield's Pittsburgh mural echoed the clas-sical figures featured in line drawings published in city histories and tour books, but they were more than referents to notions of classical beauty and physical inheritance. Blashfield urged his fellow public artists to use their interest in classical bodies to find counterparts in American culture and configure modern scenes of work that relied upon current themes. The men he painted in Pittsburgh were not Greek figures simply trans-planted into a scene of modern industry. Rather, they were Pittsburgh figures whose bodies evinced a modern work ethic and called to mind the flawless physiques of ancient art. The distinction was crucial to Blash-field; in 1913, he explained his dedication to modern working bodies as signs of American contributions to the world: "No matter how enthusi-astically we have studied the nude body, as presented in the broken fragments from Greek pediments or the marbles of Michelangelo, the muscles of Raphael's tritons and nymphs, the glowing canvases of Ven-ice, the bronzes of Donatello, we must remember that naked bodies bow themselves to dig *our* trenches and puddle *our* steel, work among *us* to-day, and are as interesting now under the American sun or in the firelight of the foundries." Worthy of the artist's scrutiny, bodies that revealed themselves in the field and in the foundry were tied to labor.[52]

Blashfield established the manliness of these half-naked bodies with visual cues of the work they performed. Their unclad bodies, their handling of heavy tools, and their contrast with the surrounding murkiness alerted viewers that these were men to admire. The workers' lack of clothing alluded to the punishing heat of the workplace, but, more important, put their physiques on display. The hammers in the mural represented a prevailing image of skilled labor in the nineteenth century. American craftsmen had long wielded the tools of their trades in public ceremonies to symbolize their monopoly of skill. The ability to use a hammer with power *and* control separated these figures from the nation's laboring masses. Finally, the striking whiteness of Blashfield's men drew the viewer's attention to them as the focal point of Pittsburgh's gift to the world. Blashfield noted that images in murals should serve as "beacons in history" to remind the people of their civic identity in times of swift change. Whiteness in the Bank of Pittsburgh mural was both a visual beacon within the composition and a plot line for local history. Anglo-American efforts were the basis of the city's contributions to civilization, boosters argued, because white identity was the one thing that connected Pittsburgh's skilled labor force to elites, professionals, and office employees.[53]

The mural's reference to physique, skill, and ethnicity appealed to the artist's commercial patrons. As a muralist of public and semipublic spaces, Blashfield believed that decorative art must harmonize with the functions of the buildings it adorned. A mural in a bank gave the artist the opportunity to connect the civic significance of financial institutions to the necessity of the Steel City's hard work. One of the Bank of Pittsburgh's rival institutions described banking as "the groundwork of civilization—the underlying principle which sways the destinies of nations and furnishes the material uplift for mankind." If Pittsburgh was the "center of the industrial world, the hub of the wheel of business," then banks supplied the financial resources that allowed the city's industries to lead the world forward. The steel magnate, the industrial worker, and the banker were thus partners, helping each other succeed in the grand project of civilization. The administrators of the Bank of Pittsburgh admired Blashfield's mural so much that they reproduced the image on their yearly reports in the late 1890s and early 1900s. They chose to represent their firm not through images of banking, but through the stripped bodies of white workingmen, offered to the world as an appealing by-product of heavy labor.[54]

A second public work of art in Pittsburgh, Daniel Chester French's *Colonel James Anderson Monument*, displayed an alternative vision of noble, physical manhood. Andrew Carnegie commissioned French's monument in honor of James Anderson, an early iron manufacturer in Pittsburgh who opened his library to workers in the 1850s and 1860s. While the Anderson sculpture was the second major work of public art commissioned at the turn of the century, it was the first to be unveiled in a grand ceremony. Dedicated in the summer of 1904 and placed in front of the Carnegie Library on the city's North Side, French's sculpture was greeted by a marching band, a parade of civic societies, and a crowd of ten thousand. The monument featured a small bust of Anderson behind a five-foot-two bronze sculpture of a worker, stripped to the waist, sitting on an anvil, and reading a book. Unlike Blashfield's workers, who stood proudly with their tools, the student-worker was both a "powerful figure of a young man" and an ambiguous view of the working world. The displayed worker turned his site of work, the anvil, into a stage for self-education, not manly toil. In Carnegie's vision and French's execution, the worker made a conscious decision to abandon work, yet never strayed far from the workplace. The sculpture, titled *Labor*, completed the patron-client relationship suggested between the capitalist who offered his books and the worker who read them. French's worker was similar in style and pose to Constantin Meunier's sculpture *The Puddler*, which became quite significant in Pittsburgh later in the decade when used as a rhetorical weapon in the Pittsburgh Survey. French produced an image of a worker whose body showed signs of strain, but whose actions revealed the possibility of transcending the working-class stereotype.[55]

Like Blashfield, French enjoyed a successful artistic career beyond his work in Pittsburgh. His *Minuteman* in Concord, Massachusetts, and his sculpture of Abraham Lincoln for the Lincoln Memorial in Washington, D.C., were both commissioned to embody the grandeur of turbulent history in heroic form. His biographer Adeline Adams noted that French's "major icons of the most important episodes in [America's] history of freedom" were designed to decorate the Revolutionary battlefield and the nation's capital with confident and capable bodies that

8. Daniel Chester French, *Colonel James Anderson Monument.* Courtesy of the Pittsburgh Photographic Library Collection of Carnegie Library of Pittsburgh.

stood for the nation's character in times of conflict. The worker's body that honored Colonel Anderson's philanthropy served a similar purpose, enacting the legend of the student-worker to whom Carnegie dedicated his altruism at the turn of the century. Although many critics of industry argued that long days of toil allowed workers few hours to visit public libraries, Carnegie envisioned the reading worker as the ultimate symbol of an ideal labor force. Here was a figure whose muscles were evident, yet they did not trump his desire for mental development. The art critic Charles Caffin claimed that French's art exhibited a peculiarly "passionless emotion" in the late nineteenth century and early twentieth. In *Labor*, the worker's emotion was hidden, lost in his downward gaze at the written word. If there was a sense of passion in the sculpture, it came less from the worker's features than from Pittsburghers' intended interpretation of the work's meaning—the civic association inherent in the combination of naked physique and opened book.[56]

The seated figure represented the educational opportunities offered to Pittsburgh workers by industrialists and other benefactors. A plaque attached to the monument added a more specific narrative: "To Colonel James Anderson, Founder of Free Libraries in Western Pennsylvania. He opened his Library to working boys and upon Saturday afternoons acted as librarian, thus dedicating not only his books but himself to the noble work. This monument is erected in grateful remembrance by Andrew Carnegie, one of the 'working boys' to whom were thus opened the precious treasures of knowledge and imagination through which youth may ascend." While the young Carnegie worked as a messenger in Pittsburgh, so the legend went, he used the knowledge offered in Anderson's library to rise through the ranks of the business world and fulfill the Steel City's destiny. The brawny worker seated on the anvil was a surrogate for Carnegie and every other businessman who had escaped manual work by recognizing the importance of literacy and self-taught knowledge. French became the "historian of local heroes," a chronicler of the care that the employer showed the worker in local industry. The fact that he was a muscular worker—not a young child or a man in a business suit—underscored the ease with which the business elite of Pittsburgh imagined their city through the figure of the industrial worker. The dedication ceremony framed the sculpture as a cherished addition to the local iconography of working physiques.[57]

Not everyone received the monument so warmly, however. The *Pittsburgh Post* reported that the sculpture came under two decidedly different forms of attack in the weeks before its debut. First, a few vocal members of Pittsburgh's middle class criticized French's worker for his lack of clothing, noting that it was unnatural to depict an industrial worker without his shirt. A library courtyard, they further argued, was no place in which to sit the stripped male figure. French defended his representation, arguing that he had often seen laborers in New England working during the summer without their shirts. Furthermore, in a comical response to the complaints of amateur art critics, a few Pittsburghers took it upon themselves to rectify the situation. On a rainy night two weeks before the monument was unveiled officially, the *Post* and *Dispatch* noted, several young "pranksters" crept up to the sculpture shortly before midnight, unwrapped its heavy canvas covering, and put a shirt on the shirtless worker before fleeing police officers. On the one hand, the complaints and the prank were typical and harmless means of incorporating new art into the local community—after all, what good was a public sculpture if would-be experts could not debate its merits and the youth of the North Side could not play with it? On the other hand, these responses revealed that local reaction to the art of work was not as ideal and manageable as city boosters and business patrons hoped. Public reception of outdoor public art at the turn of the century is notoriously difficult to gauge, but these glimpses of dissent show that boosters' ideal image of workers was never easy to maintain. If a central part of the sculpture's message was conveyed through its seminakedness, then what did it mean that even a handful of Pittsburghers complained that its seminakedness was unrealistic or inappropriate? Likewise, if the nobility of the worker's body was a testament to the dignity of hard work, then what did it mean that children ridiculed the artist's vision with a cheap shirt? Could they have responded to the statue's act of reading, a task not as rugged as hammering iron or blowing glass and thus open to such playful ridicule? Creative vandalism of this sort may have temporarily spoiled boosters' forced combination of hard work and self-improvement simply by not taking the monument seriously. The same playfulness that was common among the throngs at the exposition each year did not mix well with civic ornament. The task of the city's proponents was no less arduous in its artistic projects than in its pageants and exhibitions.[58]

Much less mischief was in the air three years later when the third major work of public art in ten years debuted in Pittsburgh. The dedication of the *Colonel James Anderson Monument* was a dress rehearsal for the most significant presentation of labor art in Pittsburgh in the first decade of the twentieth century: John White Alexander's collection of murals *The Crowning of Labor* in the main entrance of the Carnegie Institute. Alexander completed the commissioned murals for the expanded institute's dedication ceremonies in April 1907. *The Crowning of Labor* consisted of two main parts, a series of fifteen panels on the ground floor titled "Labor" and a mural on the second floor of the institute's main stairway titled "The Apotheosis of Pittsburgh." In painting the work figures for the "Labor" panels on the ground floor, Alexander remained visually vague—men were caught in the act of performing work, but the work itself was invisible, hidden in shadows and smoke. Many of the workers' torsos were at extreme angles to each other as groups of men pushed carts and pulled on chains. Visitors to the institute saw workers stretching, leaning, and bending amid a generic form of industry in which steel girders, cranes, and pulleys abounded but the actual product of the implied work was not apparent. Thirty-two of Alexander's workers were stripped to the waist, the glare of molten steel shining off their bared shoulders and backs. Their faces were mostly in shadow, although three figures stared directly at the viewer, revealing what the art critic for the *Pittsburgh Dispatch* called the archetypal "Millman face," that is, an emotionless visage absorbed in work. In the "Apotheosis of Pittsburgh" portion of the mural, Alexander represented the city as an armored knight floating through the air and receiving a crown from an angelic female figure. Around the knight young women hovered, carrying "gifts of cunning craftsmanship" from all corners of the world. The spatial relationship between the two halves of the mural suggested a sense of admirable working-class sacrifice—workers toiled below for the glory of the city above. The city itself was able to rise over the smoke and steam of its workshops to accept the world's praise for all that workers delivered. Alexander's mural thus complemented Blashfield's work: Pittsburgh and the world exchanged a bounty of iron and steel for acclaim and investment while the city's hardened workingmen kept working.[59]

At the turn of the century, Alexander was well known as one of the Steel City's most popular and perceptive sons. Having spent his childhood in Pittsburgh in the 1860s, he recalled mill scenes and used them as a template for his art. *Mentor* magazine noted that he "had a first-hand knowledge of the somber side of the great iron and steel works." An appreciation for the somber side of industry partially explained the shadows and gloom with which the artist surrounded his mill workers. Another explanation related to Alexander's goal of presenting a concept of work rather than a literal representation. The expansion of Carnegie's arts and sciences institution was meant to vault Pittsburgh to the forefront of urban cultural life. Like the Pittsburgh Exposition, the Carnegie Institute featured displays and performances designed to add genteel nuance to the "Workshop of the World." The vision of work conveyed in "Labor" accomplished this by presenting the industrial workday as an impressionistic collage of glistening bodies, individual and collective effort, and sublime ambience. Upon viewing the murals, the Dutch novelist Maarten Maartens praised Carnegie for the inspiration he had provided Alexander: "Mr. Carnegie has mixed human labor with that highest gift of the gods, imagination. He has taken the glass of pure

9. and 10. Detail from John White Alexander, *The Crowning of Labor* (1907). Carnegie Museum of Art, Pittsburgh; Gift of Haugh and Keenan Storage Company.

water—no, not pure, for it is stained with human sweat and material dregs—and suffused it with the red glow of the poet's and the painter's wine from heaven."[60]

Alexander's work was dark but not threatening because the steel men displayed were set firmly in the context of the city's renown. S. H. Church, the Institute's secretary, remarked that "out of all that riot or toil," the viewer could appreciate "the purpose and fruition of labor—Pittsburgh in its intellectual splendor." The appeal of Alexander's vigorous workers was shown clearly in dedication day reviews in the booster press. The *Dispatch* interpreted the unmistakable "striving, straining" of the men as Alexander's marvelous recognition that the work of Pittsburgh's industrial laborers was "no child's play." The *Gazette Times* applauded the "stalwart, brawny, steel-muscled men" as fitting models of the city's workers, displaying the coordination and control that the Steel City demanded of its labor force. Their bodies were placed in an appropriately chaotic environment, with "the hot glare from the furnace . . . the ring of the hammer on the anvil, the cough of the exhaust, [and] the sizzling steel and twisting iron" producing a vivid sense of hard work. Caspar Clarke of *Everybody's Magazine* equated the figures' rippling muscles to "that of the Greek athlete" and spied intelligence in the faces of the workers, suggesting both the strength and mental faculties of the ideal Pittsburgh worker. Like the finely honed steel issuing from local steel mills, workers' bodies in *The Crowning of Labor* received a high quality grade as graceful representations.[61]

The intentional obscurity of industrial work in Alexander's mural complemented critics' perception of ideal work in Pittsburgh. Rather than complaining about the shadows and clouds that cloaked the production process, the establishment press appreciated the artist's hazy vision. The *Gazette Times* interpreted Alexander's mural as the "many forms of labor—the strenuous pushing, piling, lifting, pounding, straining work that has been, and still is, the basis of all the wonderful success that is Pittsburgh." The *Dispatch* agreed that the murals depicted "not the real labor" that took place in Pittsburgh, but the "inspiration" of labor. The art critic for the *Pittsburgh Post* believed that Alexander meant his working figures to be allegorical impressions of the work that took place in Pittsburgh, ignoring the trivial details of industry that might distract. The *Dispatch* equated the vague aura of work exhibited with the city's persistent air of wonder; Pittsburgh, too, was ethereal, figurative, but strong.

The visual obscurity was thus fitting for the Steel City. Caffin reasoned that although Alexander "avoided any direct illustration of actual processes of work," his murals were still highly "suggestive of the particular kind of labor identified with the industries of Pittsburgh." Clarke explained that "Alexander's workmen are not artist models, but such men as have built up Pittsburg. Shown partly enveloped in steam, they are guiding long levers and heavy chain tackle to perform work which could formerly be accomplished by man through brute force alone."[62]

Clarke's final observation was significant, for it assumed a diminished physical ability from men painted on the walls of the institute. He praised Alexander for showing men who were *not* ideal but generalized representations of men who actually lived and worked in Pittsburgh. The artistic honesty Clarke attributed to Alexander posed a problem, however; in his interpretation, the machinery glimpsed through the smoke was not mere scenery, but the very tools which allowed workers to perform their work. Clarke read into Alexander's mural a tacit acknowledgment that "steel-muscled men" alone were not up to the tasks demanded of them. The world of mechanized work poked through the industrial steam to show that city boosters' reliance on the individual craftsman was tenuous at best. Moreover, in a mural that depicted the city as the sum of its labor, the knight-as-Pittsburgh image toward the top of the work shied away from the culminating step of embodying the city as a workman. Instead, the artist placed the spirit of the city in the form of a gallant, gentleman-warrior shrouded in the metal produced by the workers below. As the art historian Sarah Moore has noted, Alexander's knight was "removed, pictorially and ideologically, from the men toiling in the steel mills in the panels on the lower floor." Contemporary commentators argued that Alexander's method of embodying Pittsburgh as a man was bold enough. The "entirely new inventions" of turn-of-the-century male allegories were artistic adaptations to industrialization. Caffin praised Alexander's decision to "get away from the traditional device of embodying the city as a woman, recognizing that the labor of Pittsburgh is man's labor and typifying it by a man." Yet, it was not a working man, suggesting that Alexander's allegorical thinking did not identify the worker as the exclusive civic symbol. Workers' bodies could represent many of the rigorous and manly qualities of the city but could not stand alone as the city's ambassador to the world.[63]

Despite potential contradictions, the city's boosters rallied around the painted walls as vivid illustrations of the ever-elusive Steel City. News-papers encouraged Pittsburghers to visit the Carnegie Institute upon its grand opening, if for no other reason than to see the "story of Pitts-burgh" that emerged in Alexander's murals. As an educational tableau, *The Crowning of Labor* counseled civic pride based on a history of physi-cal sacrifice in the name of progress. Writers tried to judge the murals' effect upon the "mill people" who came to see them, seeking a means by which to measure the power of such public art. If the object of the murals was to "illustrate how all the toil and fatigue of the workers produced, in the end, the beauty and inspiration of life," then commentators agreed that they had succeeded. But would the city's working class come to see the work of art, let alone understand it? According to Alexander, "many sources" told him that workers in Pittsburgh cherished the images, in-cluding one man who wrote the artist a letter noting "that he had never been happy in his work until after this thought had been made plain to him by its illustration on the walls of the institute." Murals were a medium of suggestion, prompting viewers to believe in the redemptive qualities of heavy work and hard bodies. Clarke encouraged the city's "mechanics and laborers" to visit the murals at the Carnegie Institute, promising that they would "feel the dignity of their work in which each individual plays a part of almost equal importance."[64]

Although strikingly different in style and scope, the three artworks unveiled in Pittsburgh between 1898 and 1907 displayed two similar features that suggest the limits of representation for Pittsburgh work at the time. First, each of the works settled on the worker's body, not on a specific type of labor, as a symbol of industrial Pittsburgh. Blashfield's assembled iron- and steelworkers displayed their hammers, French's lone figure sat on his anvil, and Alexander's men pushed and pulled through the steam, but their allusions to production processes failed to give any record of how work was actually performed. Instead, the presence of workers' bodies was enough in each case to convey the ideals of work: muscular and mental development and a confident, competent appear-ance. The world of work in each piece was enveloped in a favorable narrative—the city offering its achievements to the world; the worker reading to improve himself morally and intellectually; the world return-ing the favor with hymns of praise—that made displayed bodies markers of civic progress and class harmony. Second, in conveying a generic sense of work, the sculpture and murals eschewed notions of the mechanical in favor of the premechanical. Blashfield's and French's images were decidedly artisanal, avoiding the machine and stressing the tools of the craftsman. Clarke's attention to the mechanical aspects of Alexander's work was insightful, yet his thoughts were not echoed by the writers and art critics in Pittsburgh who ignored the visible devices in the mural and trained their eyes on the dozens of workingmen whose strain was timeless and unaffected by motors. For boosters, detailed chronicles of the actual work taking place throughout the city did not convey noble messages of Pittsburgh's significance.

"PERFECT REPRESENTATION"

PITTSBURGH'S SESQUICENTENNIAL PARADE

The culmination of the boosters' twenty-year campaign to disseminate vital images of Pittsburgh came in the autumn of 1908, when the city celebrated its first 150 years as a frontier town turned industrial giant. The *Pittsburgh Dispatch* editorialized in the weeks before the sesquicentennial that it was essential that "the scores of thousands who will visit . . . especially on the day of the monster parade, with its floats illustrating the enormous business of this region, shall be impressed by the magnificence of the spectacle and go to their towns and homes and say that it was the greatest ever." Parades, speeches, and historical recreations reinforced the power of the working figure in a mechanical context. Displays of industry that rolled through the streets of the Steel City in 1908 brought both the worker's body and machinery to the foreground in a way that had not been attempted before. Boosters presented the industrial machine as a harmless, liberating force, demonstrating manufacturers' decision that machines and workingmen could be depicted in harmony without diminishing the appeal of the worker. The revelry of 1908 integrated the mechanical milieu into the tale of skilled workers' physical mastery with questionable results.[65]

The sesquicentennial committee dubbed Thursday, 1 October, "Greater Pittsburgh Day," "intended to celebrate the union of Allegheny with Pittsburgh and the creation of the Greater City." Taking place on the fifth day of the sesquicentennial festivities, the historical, military, and industrial parade scheduled for 1 October was to be the main attraction of the weeklong event, winding its way on a five-mile course from the North

Side across the Allegheny River and past a grand reviewing stand built in the city's Oakland neighborhood. The ceremony to honor the Chamber of Commerce's victorious campaign to annex Allegheny City after decades of legislative attempts was meant to be both "beautiful and instructive," conveying a focused narrative of regional ascendance. The Chamber of Commerce had battled for years to make Pittsburgh's official geographic identity commensurate with its mythic imagery of fires, forges, and physiques. When city residents voted for annexation in 1906, the *Pittsburgh Sun* exclaimed in verse,

> You are getting into line—Greater Pittsburgh!
> To come up big and fine—Greater Pittsburgh!
> You will now be to the fore,
> Fame will reach to foreign shores,
> Unknown you'll be no more—Greater Pittsburgh!

Proportions mattered in the organization of the parade, for the procession bore the burden of representing the city's newly brokered size. More than just marching workers and administrators, then, the parade featured eight distinct divisions and as many as thirty thousand participants. An estimated three hundred thousand people massed on the streets of Pittsburgh that morning, and dozens of the city's wealthiest residents and guests crowded into the seats on the reviewing stand (for which they had paid handsomely in the previous weeks as the organizing committee solicited contributions from the "good citizens of Pittsburgh"). The parade began with the city's police force and regiments of the National Guard, followed by divisions of politicians, civic leaders, and historical floats that presented scenes of exploration, battle, and settlement. This was apparently a mere preamble to the main attraction; the *Dispatch* stated that the "best part of the pageant, from the spectacular standpoint," were elaborate floats created for the labor and manufacturing divisions. The labor division of the parade featured thousands of workers in form and regalia similar to those of the men who had marched twenty years earlier and floats that displayed some of the city's trades. Butchers, train workers, plumbers, steamfitters, and sheet-metal workers performed work routines for onlookers from their floats. Sheet-metal workers, for example, organized a spectacle of "machinery, benches, tools, and men at work" as a representation of their trade.[66]

In the context of early twentieth-century historical and civic pageantry, the sesquicentennial committee's inclusion of a large labor contingent was a potentially volatile action for other cities to consider. William Langdon, a pageant promoter of the 1900s and 1910s, advised civic celebrations to "avoid the labor question" or run the risk of polarizing the audience into opposing groups: those who supported the rights of labor and those who supported the rights of capital. This dichotomy might have oversimplified the conflict between workers and their employers, but Langdon's concern—that a labor parade might raise difficult questions that could destroy harmony—showed that the local context of celebrations dictated whether labor was to be featured or not as an entity with its own claims to civic identity and participation. In Pittsburgh, though, labor was clearly a necessary part of the official festivities, for the same members of committees and councils that designed and funded the sesquicentennial were longtime champions of work imagery. The lack of organized Labor Day parades throughout the 1890s and the first decade of the 1900s had struck many boosters as a surprising but ultimately wise decision for the men who toiled daily in the city. The *Bulletin* longed for the "marching of the horny-handed" during these years on days that were specially "set apart for the bone and sinew of industry" but understood that workers were "too busy to bother with parades." The sesquicentennial gave workers the official sanction of the city, making it their duty to represent the physical exertion that had made "Greater" Pittsburgh by leaving their mills and factories and presenting themselves to their fellow Pittsburghers and visitors to the city.[67]

As the labor division passed by, onlookers turned to see massive floats approaching from the manufacturers' division. Fifteen companies and the city's iron and steel manufacturing committee erected twenty-foot floats pulled by horses. The *Dispatch* argued that the floats, more than mere advertising vehicles, were the "highest type" of representation of the city's industries that both "charmed and educated" the large crowds. In fact, the sesquicentennial committee urged companies participating in the parade to avoid any pretense of advertisement and instead to submit floats that showed the brilliance of the city and instructed its people. A writer for the *Dispatch* promised readers in the days before the parade that "the pageant will be an education to the average Pittsburgher, as well as to the stranger within the city's gates." The education was one of men and machinery in relation to each other, assembled on wagons to suggest that workingmen in Pittsburgh retained their stamina and supremacy in the face of mechanization. Not every float exhibited both workers and machinery, but the procession of men followed by machines, followed by men and machines together guided spectators through the history of industrial change. Three stages of this theme appeared in the most frequently discussed floats of the parade, each representing the production of steel in Pittsburgh.[68]

The float representing the city's Manufacturers Committee featured a half dozen men carrying hammers and rabbles that symbolized skilled work in the steel industry before the introduction of machinery. In each corner of the float stood ten-foot smokestacks, framing the displayed men in symbols of prosperous pollution. The center of the float was a miniaturized topography typical of southwestern Pennsylvania—a cluster of homes, churches, and mills perched on cliffs and spreading throughout valleys. The lack of machinery marked the float as a late nineteenth-century vision of steelmaking as a republican and civic pursuit. The men assembled to stand in for the Manufacturers Committee were surrounded with civic and patriotic imagery, including the city seal draped over the horses and bald eagles soaring above the upper reaches of the wagon. Workers' bodies, towering above diminutive mills and houses, were giants of industry and points of interest in this portable landscape. Sleeves rolled up and tools in hand, workers waved to the crowd as they rolled by. The work these men performed was implied by their props as manual work; they pushed, prodded, and shaped steel for a living, and their frames testified to years of animated exertion.

The other extreme of representation came on the float of the Riter-Conley Manufacturing Company, which reproduced a modern blast furnace operation on a scale that was convenient for city streets. Two blast furnaces and eight heating stoves sat in the center of the float, extending fifteen feet above the road surface and aligned neatly. The structures' crisp edges and symmetry heralded the new industrial Pittsburgh as a dazzling, machine-made landscape. The Riter-Conley float carried a single person, a man dressed in shirt and tie who stood before the rows of blast furnaces and stoves. The man's garb, distinct from the plain working clothes of men riding on other floats, implied an elevated occupational status, representative not of labor but of management. In the logic of the modern blast furnace plant, the essential employer was the man who coordinated the flow of materials into and out of the furnace. Perhaps Riter-Conley's representative exemplified a foreman or a skilled

11. Sesquicentennial float of the Manufactures Committee.

12. Sesquicentennial float of the Riter-Conley Manufacturing Company.

machine tender, positions as far removed from the heavy work of pud-dlers and glassblowers as the banker or the bookkeeper. The main spec-tacle of the float was production, cleansed of any notion that the labor of men's bodies went into it.[69]

A third float that graced the streets of Pittsburgh that day combined visual techniques of the former two displays, mixing men and machinery in an ambiguous manner. The Jones and Laughlin Steel Company float, which many commentators singled out as the most impressive display of the labor division, reproduced a Bessemer converter at the height of a chemical reaction. One end of the float featured a heaping pile of iron ore, while the opposite end housed the converter and a spray of liquid steel shooting from its opening. Jones and Laughlin positioned the mock converter on its side, aiming a stream of sparks above the workers' heads. At the workers' feet lay the products of steel manufacturing, beams, chains, and wagon wheels. The three workers riding on the float were framed by the converter, sparks, ore, and products, positioned in a small stage that encompassed the beginning and end of the work process. But what was the practical function of the workers in the middle? Here, again, the steelworkers' work was elided in favor of their bodily presence. The reporter for the *Dispatch* noted that "big muscled steelworkers were placed about" the converter, like props that accompanied the main set piece. The writer's choice of the passive voice was significant, for it implied that the men had been treated as inanimate objects, icons that by 1908 had become so utilized in Pittsburgh that their role in public pag-eantry was accepted as just that, a role. Their bodies were needed for the display, but their knowledge of industrial work was not. They were put in place to give context to the machinery, to let their bodies suggest what work in Pittsburgh meant. The visual power of the Jones and Laughlin display was its juxtaposition of steelworkers and a miniature Bessemer converter. A few media commentators could hardly believe that the company had managed to shrink the massive converter to a manageable size, yet still retain the sense of powerful technology. The drama of the display was such that the *Dispatch* feared the workmen could be in imminent danger from "five hundred tons of molten steel" that might burst forth at any minute. At the same time, the scale of workers' bodies was hardly diminished by the converter, which was presented more as a tool of the workman than an autonomous machine. The converter was small enough that it did not dominate the float. When they posed for a

13. Sesquicentennial float of the Jones and Laughlin Company.

souvenir photograph, one of the workingmen leaned against the converter with one arm, destroying the illusion of terrible heat, but also taming the machine as little more than a prop of industry. Both body and machine seemed to present a passive spectacle as the float wound through Pittsburgh's streets.[70]

Far from reading depressing signs of inactivity in the Jones and Laughlin float, however, boosters responded enthusiastically to its tale of Steel City work. The *Dispatch* writer judged the float to be a "perfect representation" of steelmaking and Pittsburgh, exhibiting the power of both man and machine. A sesquicentennial souvenir book remembered the float as "most typical of Pittsburgh, and one that few dreamed could be produced for a moving stage." Such floats "charmed and educated," teaching the assembled throngs how to think of the city. Even though the Bessemer converter was anachronistic, having been supplanted by the open-hearth furnace as the chief steelmaking vessel in Pittsburgh, the historical vision the float offered was meant to resonate with the city's middle class. By 1908, bodies and machines could appear together in public displays to impart some semblance of industrial harmony, but the results were mixed, emphasizing the fact that machinery had changed irrevocably the nature of work. In the months leading up to the parade, local newspapers had provided a fitting context for such a display. The *Chronicle-Telegraph*, for instance, published a weekly "How the Old Town Has Changed" series to juxtapose simple and sophisticated technologies of production and transportation. The installments considered buildings, machines, and processes but gave scant coverage to the ways in which people interacted with them. Pittsburgh's workers factored less in the before-and-after series than the hardware around them. The Jones and Laughlin parade float suggested that work in Pittsburgh was now as much inaction as action. If the "perfect representation" of the city's working life did not discourage parade organizers and commentators, it was because their faith in the physiques "placed about" the representation had never flagged. Pittsburgh's civic narrative still relied on bodies of work, even if work did not rely on them as much as it once had.[71]

CONCLUSION

In a souvenir booklet of Pittsburgh from 1905, the L. H. Nelson Company included with its many views of public buildings, parks, and bridges a photomontage of steel mill scenes. Although the three photos did not show any men actually at work, they nonetheless constructed a tale about work in Pittsburgh. The bottom-left image, captioned "Crew of Rollers," depicted a rolling crew posed in a dark corner of a mill, each member wielding an iron tool. The black-and-white image was a series of contrasts between workers' pale faces, arms, and chests and their dark work clothes and surroundings. What stood out most in the photograph were the workers' arms as they grasped their tools—in posing for the photographer, they (or their employer) believed their rods and pliers were an important part of the image. The photograph that showed actual steelmaking, at top, included no workers. Instead, a glowing ingot sat on a roll table several feet from rolling machinery. The photograph offered little sense of scale, and the caption "Rolling an Ingot" begged the question, *who* was rolling an ingot? Finally, the third image, at bottom-right,

14. "Scenes at the Steel Mills" (1905).

showed a group of workers posed in a stockyard, leisurely resting while "at lunch." The seeming spontaneity of the scene, undermined by the direct gaze of several workers and the obvious artifice of a group assembled in an accessible half circle, was meant to show another facet of workers' lives. Removed from the mill and their tools, workers escaped the connotations of work and became friends, citizens, Pittsburghers. Yet they were merely "at lunch," still surrounded by wagons and barrows and still resting against the backdrop of a steaming smokestack and imposing mill. The caption for the trio of photographs read, "In the great steel plants, operating day and night, are produced annually millions of tons of pig iron, steel billets, blooms, rails, rods, sheet bars, angle bars, beams, boiler, ship, and armor plate, forgings, etc. The skilled workmen share with the gigantic machinery in arousing the interest and admiration of a spectator." L. H. Nelson's caption stressed that products were made in the mill through work, although the phrase "are produced" suggested an almost magical production process not dependent upon the strain of workers *or* the force of machines. It also suggested that the three images were equally valuable as spectacles. Workers standing with tools and sitting during a lunch break were as compelling as the rolling machinery that handled millions of tons of steel each year.[72]

The "Scenes at the Steel Mills" photographs from the *Souvenir of Pittsburg* reiterated for residents and guests the series of assumptions that informed boosters' project of self-promotion between 1888 and 1908—the sight of workingmen was interesting and admirable; the display of their bodies in particular settings narrated a historical development of industry; and work should be implied but not necessarily shown. Boosters' grand theme was that Pittsburgh rewarded its workers by making their bodies objects of respect and awe. Making the body of work the unit of analysis imposed upon it severe representational burdens to offset fears of pace and mechanical chaos. Turn-of-the-century promoters of the city could project confidence while claiming that Pittsburgh "means toil inconceivable, but it also means wages and good living and comfort and luxuries for thousands and tens of thousands," because the claim appeared to be validated time and again in work spectacles and physical displays that pleased (or at least attracted) a public composed of diverse classes and ethnic groups. Images meant to promote the "bee-hive of energy"—images of "happy and cheerful, strong and healthy" workers—were products of decades of work by civic groups that tried to market industrial goods, financial investments, and the identity of a city by appealing to the extraordinary physical culture of its work.[73]

If Pittsburgh was the apotheosis of American industrial civilization for its advertisers, then the sight of the industrial worker in action was their apotheosis of Pittsburgh. Although representations of men's bodies have been noted for their ability to "deflect anxiety," it was initially the work skills for which the bodies stood, not the bodies themselves, that gave direction to a concerned Chamber of Commerce. Boosters brought workers' bodies to the foreground because they found it advantageous to present to the city's middle class and its workers an iconography that ignored the highly mechanized, strictly divided, and visually tedious work that typified industrial Pittsburgh. By 1908 the link between the bodies displayed and revelers' knowledge of the work performed by them was tenuous at best. The goal of the chamber, the *Bulletin*, and their partners in representation was to present advanced industry through a "surplus of signifiers and a dearth of signification," heightening the artifice behind the images but also allowing for more ambitious spectacles. The desire for educational displays persisted in the Steel City after 1900. The focus on an actual work process in the Pittsburgh Expositions of the 1890s and the arrangement of workers' bodies in parades and public art was not enough to appease critics of the city's self-marketing. Three weeks after the sesquicentennial the *Pittsburgh Sun* reminded its readers, "It will be a great thing for education and manufacturing, too, when our industrial expositions consist less of floats in parades or fragmentary processes on exhibition in 'machinery halls,' and more of visits to plants in actual operation." Many still believed that sporadic celebrations and artworks could never provide the same sense of Pittsburgh that one could get from seeing its work "daily exercised."[74]

A sense of nostalgia informed Pittsburgh boosters' promotional images. As work changed and the Steel City garnered fame for the results of those changes, the local business and cultural elite emphasized that which was disappearing, the highly skilled workingman whose tasks were obviated or replicated by massive machinery. The nostalgia of the city's work iconography was devoted to a bygone era that was not yet gone but seemed to be slipping away by the minute. This look back contrasted with the narratives of other cities' boosters. Carl S. Smith's analysis of "boosterature" in Chicago in the wake of the fire of 1871 revealed a "desperate kind of wishful thinking, a desire to escape the conflicts of historical experience and avoid the difficulties of the present by embracing the future, where nothing has yet happened and so the possibilities are without limit." Although Pittsburgh's boosters argued the case for an auspicious future, they did so by presenting a version of the past that allowed them to speak of the glories that lay ahead. Congressman James Francis Burke told the Chamber of Commerce in 1902, "Pittsburgh may well stand confidently upon the cornerstone of her present and look into the future with steadfast faith and hope, for back of all her noble inspirations are a people who will continue their unceasing toil until the music of the mills and the glory of her sunsets fade into mystery." Burke preached to the choir. He placed Pittsburgh's workers and work ethic at the heart of financial success in a compressed past and future. Just as the working body focused boosters' ability to spin all details positively, turning a grueling pace into a conditioned physique, a selective, usable past suggested the harmony of Pittsburgh's next century if its citizens placed their trust in the economic elite. They stressed that Pittsburghers could find evidence of their city's prospects in stylized displays of skilled craftsmen who preserved a local, hard-won definition of the work ethic. Theirs was not a denial of history but an embrace of a historical thread that conflated entrepreneurs and artisans to defuse class tensions and harmonized bodies and machines to suggest that the mechanical regime would echo the premechanical.[75]

Viewed most optimistically, male skilled workers' bodies gave a sense of history to an innovative city, a sense of cross-class affinity to an industrial district torn by social antagonisms, and a sense of white manliness to an area inundated with perceived threats from foreign arrivals. Viewed less generously, these bodily displays obscured the danger and exploitation of the workplace, reinforced physical and cultural stigmas attached to recent immigrants, and attempted to drive a symbolic wedge between the city's skilled and unskilled workforces. Boosters plied their trade by refusing to present it as a trade; their job was to educate—to "civilize"—and the body of work in their hands became one more civilizing institution. But if there was an assumed sense of control to their project, it was not hegemonic. Order, if not material comfort, was as elusive to the civic elite as it was to industrial workers. Their method of selecting and generalizing clashed with reformers' studied attempt to compile and specify. Details complicated matters, and thus promoters of turn-of-the-century Pittsburgh labored to manage those details.

When profits and not persons are made paramount, human bodies are ground into fragments, wasted with useless diseases, discarded while yet capable of the most valuable service, or even crushed, crippled and confined in childhood until the very mold of mankind is warped and deformed so that vast masses of persons are denied the opportunity to develop to anything like the full human form.

—A. M. Simons, "Wasting Human Life" (1914)

4

THE PITTSBURGH SURVEY

AND THE BODY AS EVIDENCE

✳ "Pittsburgh holds much that is menacing," the writer James Oppenheim noted ominously in 1910 after a tour of the city. "I found a feeling in many places of impending trouble." The writer struggled to define the looming threat he sensed in a city that for other observers promised the wonders of the industrial age. Articles published in the national press routinely described turn-of-the-century Pittsburgh as a dream world of technological innovation and human ability, yet Oppenheim was not the only writer to discover lurking danger. Labor reformers and social workers constructed a narrative of Pittsburgh that placed inhumane and deadly work at its very center. For industrial critics, workers' bodies were the site at which much of this "impending trouble" emerged; bodies at work thus became the subject of inspection, displayed and measured in an attempt to interpret the physical marks of frantic mechanical paces and harsh working conditions. When the writers W. E. Trautmann and Peter Hagboldt drafted their exposé novel about the local steel industry in the 1910s, they placed their workers amid "relentless machinery which crushes them, makes them unfit for work, a burden to themselves and their family." This alarming view of the industrial worker—weakened and about to succumb to the pressures of mechanized work—found new resonance as critics seized the imagery of unceasing work and straining muscles to meet their reform goals.[1]

Newspaper reports of accidents accompanied numerous warnings about the fate of the body in mechanized industry. In the last decades of the nineteenth century, intellectuals wondered whether crowding workers and machines together would result in physical/mechanical hybrids, men who had little control over their own movements and had surrendered to a machine-prescribed repertoire of simple tasks. As machinery became the "embodied action" of mechanized workplaces, some writers feared that workers' bodies lost all sense of agency. The historian James Gilbert has argued that by the beginning of the twentieth century, the work ethic "seemed to describe another era" of America's past, a time when strenuous work was morally and socially uplifting for the worker. Gilbert contrasted this image of ideal labor with the "emptiness of modern physical labor" that prevailed after 1900, when low wages, accidents, and extensive division of tasks made work less appealing to America's intellectuals. Reformers and journalists claimed that work became less safe owing to uncontrollable machinery and negligent management. Upton Sinclair attributed the "increasing recklessness of human life" to the difficulty of making profits during dour economic times. In Pittsburgh, however, accidents seemed to happen most frequently during prosperous times, when mills and mines were filled to capacity and running day and night. It was Pittsburgh employers' success, not their desperation to stay in business, that appeared to generate accidents. Industrial accidents were a national problem at the turn of the century, yet Pittsburgh seemed to many to be a particularly appropriate place in which to study their causes, their patterns, and, ultimately, their remedies.[2]

The most pronounced criticism of the ravages of modern work in Pittsburgh came in the form of the Pittsburgh Survey, a study researched between 1907 and 1908 and published during the next five years. Writing in 1912, the labor reformer Josephine Goldmark noted that until the survey findings were published, she could find no systematic investigation into the problem of American work injuries. In the decades before the publication of the survey, the public could learn of the frequency of industrial accidents and illnesses in Pittsburgh intermittently through the labor press and in the yearly reports of governmental agencies. The Engineers' Society of Western Pennsylvania even claimed that it was not until after the survey was published, during the 1910s, that the "accident situation was brought forcibly to the attention" of employers in Pittsburgh. Various efforts to announce accidents as they occurred pointed to a common argument: that as a seat of swift and heavy industrial production, Pittsburgh was an unusually dangerous place in which to work. The survey researchers built upon these attempts to quantify and explain the damage caused by work accidents in Pittsburgh. As a product of turn-of-the-century interest in statistics, physiology, and social exposé, the Pittsburgh Survey was the most forceful challenge to the Steel City's celebratory work spectacles in the decades after the Homestead lockout.[3]

The survey represented a different challenge as well: reformers' attempts to make their vision of society's ills (and cures) indispensable. Just as physiologists forged a professional field for themselves in the late nineteenth century through systematic research on the needs of bodies in motion, social researchers writing for the survey used analysis of workers' bodies as one of several tools that established their authoritative insight into the problems of industry and organization. The historian John McClymer wrote of the politics of social science: "Knowledge could be power, but only under certain circumstances. Problems had to be perceived generally as both pressing and complex. Also a consensus of expert opinion had to exist. Finally, experts had to occupy at least some of what noted sociologist C. Wright Mills called the 'command posts of power.'" Framing the working body as the site of crisis was particularly fitting for these goals. Survey writers presented statistical summaries of death and injury to argue that the day of reckoning could not be put off much longer. They borrowed from physiology, economics, legal scholarship, and engineering to make their analysis of the body multifaceted. They cited fellow practitioners of social science as often as possible to corroborate their findings. And they called for systems of regulation that required men and women educated in the same schools of thought and trained in the same skills as they had been. As McClymer notes, "Their professional careers depended upon accuracy, but they also depended upon demonstrating the necessity for social engineering." Working bodies played a central role in this project because they served well as objects of discovery and measurement, two activities the survey staff guarded closely as the hallmarks of the social survey. Pulled from the dingy interior of a mill or plucked from the proverbial scrap heap, working physiques seemed ready for the intervention of experts.[4]

UNCOVERING THE "SOMBER SIDE OF INDUSTRY"

The historian S. J. Kleinberg has shown that in 1900, Pittsburgh had the third highest mortality rate in the nation for men aged fifteen to fifty-four. The number of accidents reported through official channels increased when business was booming in the Steel City and decreased during economic recessions and work stoppages; hence, Kleinberg suggests that accident figures functioned as Pittsburgh's "macabre indication of prosperity." Few companies kept regular records of accidents in their mills, factories, and mines before the 1910s, making it difficult to assess accurately the extent of injury in the city's industries. Pennsylvania factory inspectors' reports, though incomplete and inconsistent, offer the best view of industrial injury in Pittsburgh during this period. Inspectors provided yearly tallies of accidents that were reported to them by employers, although these figures necessarily omitted many accidents which, the inspectors feared, were not reported because of careless or deceitful record keeping.[5]

Statistics compiled by M. N. Baker, the factory inspector for Allegheny County, shed some light on the dangers of industrial work in Pittsburgh. Between 1895 and 1903, when Pittsburgh claimed roughly 15 percent of the state's total number of reported accidents, the city's industries accounted for more than 26 percent of the state's reported fatal accidents. Compared to other state inspection districts, accidents in Allegheny County's mechanized mills and factories killed workers disproportionately. Baker's reports revealed the source of most accidents: between the same years of 1895 and 1903, Pittsburgh's steel industry was responsible for 65 percent of the accidents reported in the Pittsburgh region. Of 36 fatal accidents reported in Pittsburgh in 1895, for example, 32 occurred in steel mills. Baker's records during these years were far from complete, however; in 1901, when the factory inspector reported only 6 fatal accidents citywide (and official inspectors in Pennsylvania tallied only 103 statewide), the Allegheny County coroner held inquests into the accidental deaths of 112 mill workers. Between 1899 and 1915, the Allegheny

County coroner logged 2,313 accidental deaths in steel mills and 1,507 in bituminous coal mines, an average of 136 and 89 per year, respectively.[6]

Statistical summaries tell only a fraction of the tale of industrial accidents. More descriptive analyses of the way in which accidents occurred and workers were injured reveal some of the disturbingly mundane features of industrial trauma. The most prevalent type of accident in steel mills occurred when a worker was struck by falling materials, whether stray streams of molten steel, crumbling piles of scrap metal, or broken parts of overhead cranes and piping. The vertical expansion of steel mills produced cathedral-like workplaces in which falling objects were common and especially dangerous. More than one of every five accidents that occurred in an area steel mill in the 1910s involved production or structural materials hitting workers from above. Incidents in which workers crushed their arms, usually between moving cars, between other pieces of machinery, or between billets of steel, were the second-most common type of injury. The mechanized production on the grand scale achieved in Pittsburgh by the turn of the century made it very difficult for workers to keep clear of heavy, moving devices as they worked. Next in frequency came burns from hot metal; although machinery took over much of the metals-moving portion of steelmaking by the 1910s, workers still came into contact with hot metal at various stages of production. A relatively minor risk for workers (about 5 percent of all accidents) was getting caught in machinery. Unlike machinery used in textile mills, steelmaking machinery had few spinning belts that could pull workers into drive shafts. Instead, the sheer bulk of hoisting and carrying machinery made being crushed underneath them more of a concern than getting caught in pulleys. However, the rolling machinery that turned slabs of steel into plates and ingots was the main source of accidents in which men were caught in machinery. In all areas of the Pittsburgh steel mill, when machinery broke down or the production process otherwise ground to a halt, the workers sent in to fix the problem were often in the most danger of being burned, crushed, or electrocuted. The closer laborers worked to hulking machinery, the more opportunities there were for serious mishaps.[7]

The reported accidents that took place in Pittsburgh's steel mills during the month of January 1893 are exemplary. On 2 January of that year, Patrick McGee, a forty-year-old worker for the Carnegie Steel Company, fractured his collarbone when he fell into a machinery pit. Two days later, a worker at the Homestead Steel Works burned the skin off his hands and face when a crane carrying molten steel splashed him from above. On 6 January, a forty-three-year-old worker who was run over by a scrap buggy suffered a broken leg. The first fatal accident of the month occurred on 9 January, when William Leadbetter was crushed between two bulky slabs of steel at the Homestead Steel Works. On 17 January, Louis Schmidt lost two fingers at the Homestead Steel Works when a coupling pin on a hoisting crane slipped, and John Bowntski was scalded at the Oliver Iron and Steel Company when a crane exploded and sent a spray of steam and shards of metal across the work floor. The following day, Adolph Deitrich lost an arm when he slipped while climbing down from an overhead crane, and Joseph Remski was burned on his face and hands from a cinder explosion in the stockyard of the Oliver Iron and Steel Company. In the final week of the month, one worker died after fracturing his skull when caught between two scrap cars, another man lost a leg after falling under an engine, and two workers received severe cuts and burns from oil explosions. Although anecdotal descriptions of one month's reported accidents in Pittsburgh steel mills do not provide a comprehensive picture of the dangers to workers' bodies, they do give a good sense of the variety and recurrence of the perils workingmen faced while on the job. Injury from a large and varied set of causes was a daily affair in the steel industry.[8]

Physical dangers in the window glass industry were much less frequent and grim than those found in the steel industry. Government reports and the local labor press offered no evidence of recurring fatal accidents to glassworkers in the Pittsburgh area, nor did they cite severe accidental injury as a routine, defining feature of work in the glass industry (as they did for both steel and coal). The stockyards of local glassworks were just as dangerous as those found outside steel mills and coal mines, for the work men did in all three locations was almost identical and involved the same moving trains and large quantities of raw materials. Within the glass factories themselves, however, dangers to workers' lives and limbs decreased markedly. Before window glass production was mechanized in 1903, the blowing process was a relatively safe, though tiring, pursuit. Burns from molten glass and flares from furnaces were the main hazards of manual blowing, but when machines took over the process, workers had to keep an eye on the work taking place above them. In its first years of operation, the Lubbers blowing machine was infamous for its frequent failures that caused tall glass cylinders in the process of elongation to shatter and rain on workers from above. Collapsing cylinders could burn or crush workers if they fell beyond the perimeter of the machinery below. After a little experience with the Lubbers machines, glasshouse workers knew they should avoid standing underneath the rising cylinders until they were ready for hoisting and cutting. In other sectors of the glass industry, in which the amount of glass used per item was drastically less than in window glass manufacture, workers could expect little more than minor burns to their arms and legs as the daily hazard of their jobs.[9]

The most pervasive perils of work in the glass industry stemmed from the heat of the workday. According to Robert Layton, grand secretary of the Knights of Labor, local newspapers published routine reports of "five or six men having been overcome by the heat in a single day." Stripped to the waist or not, blowers and their assistants were unable at times to cope with the exceptional temperatures experienced on the work floor in front of melting furnaces. The Lubbers machine eliminated the need for blowers and gatherers to stand in raging heat, yet ladle crews that transported molten glass from tank to tank still worked in close proximity to scorching fires. The heat of the glasshouse was a day-to-day problem for workers, but it was also a persistent nuisance that could become more damaging over time. The federal Immigration Commission's report for 1911 included a dire view of the cumulative physical effects of work in the area's glasshouses: "The heat of the blowing rooms also has a tendency to break down the health of the blowers. It is stated by employers, although denied by employees, that a blower cannot earn full wages by piece-work after he reaches the age of forty years on the average, and that he is practically unfit by the time he has reached sixty." Decades of working in unrelenting heat made Pittsburgh's glassworkers casualties of industry whose scars, though less obvious to the untrained observer than dismemberment or paralysis, were just as threatening in economic and social terms.[10]

If steel and glass production posed multiple hazards to the body, so, too, did work in the region's bituminous coal industry. A Bureau of Mines bulletin from 1916 revealed the extent of accidents in southwestern Pennsylvania coal mines during the previous four decades. Between 1880 and 1914, almost 10,000 workers died from accidents in local bituminous mines, an average of over 280 workers each year. Serious disasters and idle operations made yearly totals fluctuate greatly; particularly catastrophic years such as 1904 and 1907, in both of which there were massive mine explosions, witnessed many more deaths than the average (533 and 799 deaths, respectively). The statistical average suggests that a worker died somewhere in a Pittsburgh-area coal mine almost every day. The actual distribution of fatal accidents was never so even, but the threat to miners' lives was no less grave.[11]

More than half of those killed in the mines of southwestern Pennsylvania were crushed or asphyxiated when the ceilings of their working chambers collapsed. Work in coal mines was potentially deadly for a variety of reasons, but no single cause of death rivaled the roof-fall. What one writer called "the steady, unheralded, picking-off of workers in slate falls" occurred unpredictably and with varying degrees of severity. Minor falls could break workers' limbs and trap them for minutes or hours while their fellow workers dug them out, whereas more serious collapses crushed whole groups of workers, killing them quickly. Roof-falls claimed more lives in the region, in the state, and in the nation as a whole than any other cause of mining accidents. Of 28 deaths recorded in area mines in 1880, 20 were caused by roof-falls. Between 1906 and 1910, 1 out of every 2 men killed or injured in a southwestern Pennsylvania coal mine was the victim of a roof-fall. As miners worked in their cramped quarters and stooped to avoid hitting their heads on the low ceilings of mine chambers, they were well aware that the ceilings could crumble at any minute.[12]

The dusty atmosphere of the mine produced a second hazard that affected miners' health and livelihood. Mine explosions and fires, though accounting for less than one-sixth of all mining fatalities in southwestern Pennsylvania between 1880 and 1914, often were the most shocking tragedies for mining communities. Explosions and fires were responsible for the largest single-day death tolls in Pittsburgh regional mines around the turn of the century. An explosion at the Frick Coal and Coke Company's Mammoth mine in January 1891 exemplified the carnage of severe mine explosions. Over 100 men were killed in an instant when the mine filled with flammable gas, known as fire-damp, and ignited. If the explosion itself came as a shock to both employers and employees, its physical aftermath deep beneath the ground was just as alarming. Andrew Roy described the scene as a rescue team made its way into the mine to search for possible survivors: "Dead men were encountered in all directions. . . . Some of the dead were horribly mutilated, the unfortunate victims of the explosion having been raised off their feet by the force of the blast and dashed against the pillars of the mine; others were terribly burned by the fire-damp. . . . One man, who had fallen asleep from inhaling the insidious fire-damp, had been on his knees in prayer when overcome; his hands were clasped together, his eyes upturned." Reports from such disasters underlined the fact that miners' heavy, tedious work was also a very dangerous form of labor; for miners, the workplace was a difficult trap from which to escape when things went wrong. Descriptions of miners' dead bodies after violent explosions became regular features of local reportage.[13]

Other mine hazards appeared as coal companies mechanized the extraction processes after the 1880s. Moving mine cars were as dangerous underground as their surface counterparts were in the stockyards of steel mills. Almost one in three nonfatal accidents in southwestern Pennsylvania mines between 1906 and 1910 was caused by a collision between rolling mine cars and workers.[14] Mine cars were only one of a growing number of mechanical devices underground that brought much physical risk to mining even as they increased extraction quotas. A contemporary description of a mechanized coal mine in Pennsylvania highlighted the chaos of life underground, suggesting that swiftly moving cars were the least of the miners' worries: "Machinery crashed and roared. Gongs and warning bells jarred their nerves with the apprehension of unseen danger. The floor was a network of tracks and a cobweb of cables to entrap the feet. The roof hung low enough to menace their heads. Whole trains of low mine cars that were being shifted on the switches threatened to crush the unwary."[15]

Undercutting machinery introduced in the 1890s produced three harmful effects that observers began to notice after the turn of the century. First, the noise of the cutting and punching machines made it difficult for workers to hear each other in times of emergency and caused hearing loss in many miners after years of continued exposure. Second, vibrations caused by certain undercutting machines gave runners internal injuries over time. The jarring effects of operating a punching machine were dampened somewhat by the use of inclined planes, but the runner still bore the brunt of his machine's jerks and kickbacks. Finally, the rapid punching and sawing of the cutting machines increased the amount of dust in the air, making explosions and dust-related diseases much more common than in the premechanized era. The lungs of the many men who worked in the mines for decades often became clogged and impaired. Mechanization introduced new dangers, both mundane and deadly.[16]

As early as the 1880s doctors in the region reported long-term effects of work in coal mines, but the public focus on the physical consequences of Pittsburgh work centered on the surface of the worker's body as it became scarred and broken. Reports of symptoms—"a dry hacking cough," "a dull, heavy pain across my forehead and in my temples," "a buzzing and roaring sound in my ears," or a condition in which "limbs became swollen"—suggested that the dampness and dust of mines caused an illness that, while not yet labeled as a specific condition, was nonetheless recognized as prevalent among specific groups of workers. Until the 1920s, however, medical societies, journalists, and social investigators subordinated work-related illnesses that emerged in Pittsburgh's workers after years of exposure to the more tangible problem of traumatic injury. When Pennsylvania's secretary of internal affairs presented his annual report in 1883, he included in a section on the state's mining industry an article on first aid titled "The First Bandage." Written by a European physician, the article described the help workers could provide to their colleagues when accidents and injuries occurred. The secretary considered the issue of first aid crucial "for the benefit of miners in the bituminous coal region," whom he hoped would aid each other in times of emergency. Included in the article was a drawing of injured miners with bandages, splints, and slings applied to their wounds. The image constituted a startling counterpoint to the images of healthy and vigorous workers found in public displays of Pittsburgh work spectacles. The two figures in the drawing, one kneeling and the other reclining against a rock, epitomized work injuries in an era in which statistical summaries of injuries had not yet been compiled and presented to the public. The image offered an early look at how common injuries affected coal miners' bodies in southwestern Pennsylvania. Their limbs useless and their eyes closed, the two men had only each other to commiserate with and share the experience of injury. The noticeable lack of uninjured people in the drawing—doctors, other workers, those who applied the bandages—suggested the isolation of injury, a symptom that no measure of first aid could address. Their bodies were muscular, yet broken, only the recumbent worker's right leg coming through the imagined disaster unscathed. The scene was not one of death and agony, however; the supine worker

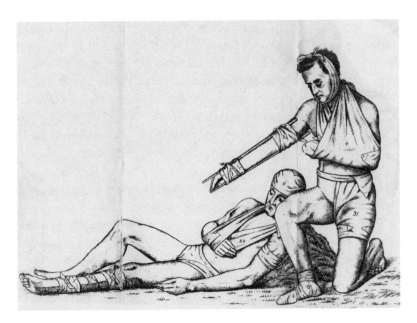

15. Injured coal miners, from the Annual Report of the Secretary of Internal Affairs of the Commonwealth of Pennsylvania (1883).

appeared to be sleeping peacefully, while the awkward position of the kneeling worker on the right seemed designed to present his body for the viewer's edification. The drawing was meant to teach miners how to apply bandages to specific wounds; the splints and wraps were numbered to lead workers step by step through the decision-making process that followed an accident. Yet while teaching the practical work of first aid, the image performed another crucial task. Though its exposure to the public was limited, the image of broken workers that the secretary of internal affairs included in his report of 1883 was one of the first to draw attention to the plight of the coal miner, an oft-neglected figure whose tale, when eventually publicized after the turn of the century, brought to the foreground more of a negative view of workers' bodies than had been held previously in Pittsburgh's public life.[17]

Beyond the damage of accidents and illness, mining stamped the worker's body with the physical effects of working in low and tight spaces. The author William Gibbons described the sight of a Pennsylvania miner in 1902: "The man's gait and appearance were those of an old man, although he was but little past thirty. There was a peculiarity in his walk which made him seem almost ape-like in his carriage. His head was bent, his shoulders drooped forward, his knees were crooked, while his hands hung so far to the front of his body that they almost touched his knee-caps. In appearance he resembled nothing so much as the man-ape of the tropical forest. . . . It is the stamp of the mine left on the body by years spent under ground in narrow veins of coal." The stamp of the mine etched its way into the worker's body, making him a walking exhibit of the effects of thousands of hours spent in tight quarters. Gibbons showed how one could read the worker's body as evidence of debilitating un-skilled work, a technique that became central to reformers' investigation of workplaces and city streets.[18]

The reportage of accidents brought a new public emphasis on immi-grant workers, especially those from southern and eastern Europe. The realities of the largely unskilled workforce that filled steel mills and coal mines by 1900 meant that more common laborers were injured than skilled workers. Language differences, lack of experience, and managerial neglect combined to place new immigrant groups directly in the line of fire when it came to the danger of industrial work. One social reformer remarked that in local industry "aliens, noted for their strength rather than their knowledge," were hired for jobs that only the most experi-enced workers could perform without frequent error. The same hiring practices that funneled particular ethnic groups to particular types of work exposed them to the brunt of accidents. A Polish steelworker for Jones and Laughlin Steel Company characterized the early 1910s as a grim time for work safety in Pittsburgh when "people died like bugs," quickly and randomly, and were instantly forgotten by management. Samuel Bloch, writing in the AAISW's *Amalgamated Journal*, accused employers of treating the immigrant worker like a "bedbug or a cock-roach or a troublesome mosquito." To the majority of industrialists, Bloch continued, workers were "so much vermin" who could be replaced with little effort and were thus expendable.[19]

Other observers resisted the urge to view immigrant workers as inno-cent victims of the city's industry, arguing that they should know enough to protect themselves and their comrades. Government investigators blamed immigrants who could not speak English for a majority of the accidents in local mills, factories, and mines. The Immigration Com-mission concluded that a direct causal link existed between the "employment of recent immigrants and the prevalence of accidents in the mines of western Pennsylvania," presumably a result of their inability to read warning signs. More egregious than injuries he inflicted on himself was the ignorant immigrant's ability to "expose the original employees to unsafe and insanitary conditions." According to the commission, "original" workers, experienced, skilled, and less ethnically exotic than recent arrivals, paid the physical price of their fellow workers' lack of ability and awareness. The immigrant worker damaged his own body, but, more important, he damaged that of the true Pittsburgher as well. If he was a victim of industrial hazards, he was also a perpetrator in a very specific sense, for he failed to learn the job properly before accepting it.[20]

The figure of the injured immigrant worker emerged around 1900 as a reminder of the serious risks involved in Pittsburgh's heavy work. The injured worker was a problem for employers and the city's boosters alike — for employers because production suffered when workers were physically unable to continue their work; for boosters because the image of physical ability and development that they had spent decades promoting as a defining symbol of Pittsburgh contrasted sharply with statistics and descriptions of workers damaged by accidents. The problem could certainly be cast in a favorable light, however. If immigrant workers constituted the largest proportion of the injured and killed workforce, then perhaps immigrant workers were especially equipped to cope with such disheartening statistics. After several decades of familiarity with people from southern and eastern Europe, doctors in Pittsburgh believed workers of the new immigration were able to recover quickly from work injuries because of the "greater vitality" they brought with them from fields and forests across the Atlantic. Such a belief was based on a faith in the working body and assumptions about the more savage, physical nature of foreigners. A doctor who contended that immigrant workers were better able to cope with the effects of accidents might have explained the phenomenon in terms of biological and cultural difference, but Pittsburgh's workforce was not as willing to leave the problem of physical integrity amid dangerous work environments up to such predetermined factors. Coping with the scars of the industrial workday was more than a matter of stamina; workers also had to adapt themselves to a culture of risk in which every minute might be their last and in which every worker's able-bodied prime preceded a future life of disability.

If reform-minded writers depicted Pittsburgh's workers as "dark figures . . . helplessly inadequate to cope with such a monster" as heavy machinery, workers, too, acknowledged that their lives, spent in mills and mines, were filled with risk and potentially debilitating circumstances. Labor responded to the strains of industrial jobs in many ways, but a major pattern evolved in the late nineteenth century and early twentieth as workers attempted to understand, mitigate, and prepare for the risks to which their bodies were subjected each time they entered the steel mill, the glassworks, or the coal mine. Agitation over what were sometimes perceived as needless elements of risk and physical decay combined with preemptive efforts to prepare themselves and their fellow workers for what were at other times seen as the inherently destructive aspects of industrial work. The same hazardous workplaces that engendered reform efforts from labor organizations inspired workers' strategies to make their bodies more capable of handling the daily grind.[21]

In other parts of the country, work cultures that valorized risk as a badge of manliness formed around manual occupations involving high speed, physical complexity, and harsh conditions. Western railroad workers' culture of risk, for instance, relied upon the experienced worker's belief that he possessed crucial skills and abilities under pressure and imminent danger that would allow him to avoid the worst accidents. Workers in such an environment wielded their bodies as finely honed tools that, if used correctly, could be carried through the most harmful situations intact. Serious injuries were to be avoided at all costs, yet less critical wounds were not necessarily a calamity for workingmen who valued risk as a source of rugged identity. In the logic of such a risk culture, workers interpreted minor injuries as signs of experience and bravery. John Williams-Searle has shown that trainmen in Iowa regarded missing fingers or scarred legs as evidence of maturity and a sense of duty in the late nineteenth century. Until a worker had been marked with a tangible sign of the danger that surrounded him, his fellow workers considered him an unreliable novice.[22]

Pittsburgh was obviously home to risky work, but did it also foster a culture of risk that defined danger as a rewarding characteristic? Little evidence exists to suggest that workers in the Steel City appreciated risk to such an extent that they viewed accidents ambivalently. Journalists' accounts of their trips to mills and factories showed that skilled workers developed a swaggering confidence based upon the ease with which they moved around dangerous machinery and materials. Risk was manly, yet workers did not interpret injuries and illnesses as the ultimate proof of physical accomplishment. The local establishment press, when it occasionally shifted out of its celebratory mode, had long lamented the fact that industrial accidents in mills and mines kept "furnishing newspaper articles and making corpses." The *Bulletin* claimed that there was "no other city in this land wherein so large a proportion of its inhabitants live in constant jeopardy of life or limb, and where the maiming and killing of men is of so frequent occurrence." The labor press, too, recognized the risks of the workday as constant reminders of the workman's mortality. The *Amalgamated Journal* railed against the randomness of accidents and illness in Pittsburgh's industries, a system of labor in which "a strong man goes to his work in the morning, rejoicing in the full flush of his strength and health. Before the day is ended he may be brought home to his family, injured or stricken down by a disease." In another criticism of negligent employers, the *Amalgamated Journal* noted that "the laborer constantly faces imminent death, and his danger increases with the progress of the age. . . . Each new speeding up of the mechanisms of industrial life, each increase in the number and size of our mighty engines, brings with it fresh human sacrifices." Layton described the life of a coal miner in southwestern Pennsylvania as a series of perils that ended only in death or retirement. Workers, Layton observed, were "constantly in danger; never out of danger; they do not know at what time a piece of 'horse flag' may fall and crush them to death." Those with intimate knowledge of Pittsburgh's workplaces described them as dismal places where the "agony of death was drowned in the bedlam thunder of the soulless hammers and whirring machines."[23]

The historian Christopher Sellers has argued that a tradition of heavy work in a few lines of production created a "a key supporting assumption" that guided both employers and employees in industrial areas like Pittsburgh in the late nineteenth century—the belief that "certain processes necessarily entailed certain hazards." The prevailing attitude of the establishment press at the time was that industries in Pittsburgh had advanced to such a scale and technological maturity that accidents were a necessary evil, a "natural but ghostly condition of everyday life." The

Bulletin summed up the city's resignation to the inevitability of injury before the turn of the century: "It could not be otherwise in a workshop so vast as is Pittsburg, and it is not a condition brought about by a disregard of human life, but of unusual opportunities for accidents of all kinds." Many "daily pursuits of life" that required men to watch out for "powerful machinery . . . gliding and twisting in all directions" were bound to maim and kill. After reviewing the city's death toll for 1909, the *Pittsburgh Sun* explained that "an increase in the number of mill fatalities was only to be expected as the result of the resumption of activity in this great industrial center."[24]

Many workers believed in the inevitability of accidents. The Homestead Steel Works' Hugh O'Donnell described steelmaking as "very healthy work" in the 1890s but noted that frequent accidents were the result of the "rush and push of a mill," not of any specific policy of his employers or culpability of fellow workers. The journalist Robert Watchorn described the official procedure after the occurrence of mining deaths in southwestern Pennsylvania: "When an untutored alien is crushed to death (which occurs so frequently as to make up an aggregate annual death list that is truly appalling), his remains are brought to the surface and a coroner's jury records its own gross ignorance and incompetence and the bare fact that the man is dead, but 'no one is held to be to blame.'" The blameless quality of accidents and the lack of an official apparatus for investigating their causes (the state's mine and factory inspectors reported more than investigated) contributed to a widespread belief that inescapable danger was just around the corner. There was little hope anyone would act to combat a problem that before 1900 few parties even attempted to understand and quantify. The sudden and unpredictable character of accidents in mills and mines made some workers fatalists. The poem "Humanity," published in the *Amalgamated Journal* in the spring of 1902, cautioned that "the one who's to-day full of vigor and health" could at any time be "lying in sickness and pain."[25]

The effects of accidents were clear, but the answers proposed to the question of causes were scattered and unfocused before the work of the Pittsburgh Survey addressed the problem in a systematic fashion. The labor press advised the city's workers from time to time that the seeming inevitability of industrial accidents was actually a result of manufacturers' financial calculations, it being less expensive to replace and pay a small benefit for a killed or injured worker than to implement proper safeguards that would prevent injury and death in the first place. Other targets of blame were, of course, immigrant workers, who were accused of knowing too little about the dangers of mills and mines to take proper precautions. Experienced workers' nonchalance could also produce harmful results. The *National Labor Tribune* explained that "by a long familiarity with a machine the sense of risk diminishes and the result is a mutilated limb, a blind eye, and a crippled man." Employers, workers, and the "rush and push of a mill" each caused their share of accidents, yet victims were not entirely helpless either.[26]

If workers viewed themselves as the sacrifices employers offered up in the name of progress, they also found ways to combat problems of injury and degradation without forfeiting their claim to manhood and citizenship. In 1887, Terence Powderly of the Knights of Labor juxtaposed the physical needs of "flesh-and-blood men" with the "iron man, who does not feel, sleep, eat, or drink, who never tires and never rests." The "iron man" ran steadily without tiring, but he was not invincible to the wear and tear of constant operations. Just as machinery needed frequent maintenance and repair, so, too, did the bodies of men who worked beside and under mechanical devices. Workers adopted informal systems of physical maintenance to keep their bodies in prime working order. By building up their bodies with food and exercise, labor leaders stressed, workers could take steps that, while not preventing accidents, would make them less damaging.[27]

The local labor press counseled workers on how to retain their health despite the exhausting conditions of industrial work. The *Amalgamated Journal* preached a program of strict bodily maintenance as a way to combat the rigors of life in mills and mines. A series of physical culture regimens appeared in the journal in the summer of 1900 to encourage workers in Pittsburgh and across the nation to look after themselves around the clock. These "rules of personal hygiene for mill men" promoted the importance of a morning routine featuring copious amounts of water (not whiskey) and a breakfast of rolled oats, eggs, ham, whole grain bread, and milk or coffee. With this start to their day, altered slightly for those who worked evening and night shifts, workers were able to enter the steel mill with an energized body as their chief weapon against injury and illness. Also crucial to these programs of physical culture were workers' efforts to ensure they got eight hours of sleep each night, practiced regular bathing routines, and engaged in popular forms of exercise, such as swimming. Exposed to a regimen of the right food, regular (nonwork) exertion, proper rest, and cleanliness, a worker's body could withstand the pressures placed on it by the production process.[28]

Workers' first step toward preserving their health involved their diet. Local coal miners testified in the 1880s to the difficulty of maintaining their physical strength without sufficient nourishment. A Westmoreland County miner informed a state investigation committee that his daily work was "extremely laborious" and that he had to "live good" in order to be able to survive in the mines each day. For most miners, living well meant getting adequate rest and eating meat regularly. A diet full of meat became the leading course of action for industrial workers who sought to maintain their energy. Workers in the labor parade in Pittsburgh in 1882 carried banners that pointed directly to the connection between the food they could afford and the work they could do. One banner depicted a skeleton speaking the words, "THIS IS ALL OF THE MAN WHO WORKS FOR NOTHING ALL DAY. ALL WE ASK IS ENOUGH TO MAKE SOME STUFFING." Meat at the dinner table (and the breakfast table as well) was presumed to build the worker's body, toughening it to withstand illnesses and accidents. Better wages afforded workers better food; better food built better bodies and produced better work. Historians have shown that a vast majority of American workers at the turn of the century, though divided in their culinary practices by the foods they were used to and could afford, valued meat as a staple of their diet. Skilled workers were better able to afford meat on a regular basis, but unskilled workers also "worshipped at the shrine of fresh beef," as one scholar has suggested. The *Amalgamated Journal*'s call for a large breakfast including meat was an attempt to influence the diet of immigrant workers from southern and eastern Europe, many of whom relied on coffee and bread in the morning and limited their meat consumption to their evening supper. Progressive food reformers counseled that breakfast was crucial to the worker's day, providing a physical advantage if planned and managed properly.[29]

In addition to advising workers to consume meat regularly, labor organizations urged their members to remain active when they were not at work. That physical activity was a key to physical success in the industrial workplace might have struck Pittsburgh's workers as an obvious, if not ridiculous, statement. Yet labor leaders had more in mind than the exertion of the workday. Although the labor press advised workers that continued exposure to hard physical labor made a man's body "more and more responsive to his will," writers cautioned that exercise beyond the workplace was just as crucial. The *Iron City Trades Journal* cited medical literature that warned against too much rest during nonwork hours. "Exercise and open air recreation," the paper declared, kept working men alive and well past the age of fifty. The editors of the *Amalgamated Journal* summarized the belief in physical cultivation outside the mill, factory, or mine when they stressed that "to have health means to live the daily life of work and play in a state of bodily ease, mental vigor, and spiritual growth. . . . mere animal health is not desirable." Both work and play could be strenuous, but they also needed to cultivate the worker's mind so that he acquired more than "animal health." Whether an attempt to distance healthy Anglo-American workers from the perceived savagery of healthy immigrants or a desire to develop the bodies and minds of *all* workers in Pittsburgh, the *Amalgamated Journal*'s call for mental vigor and spiritual growth emphasized that mere physical perfection could not protect the workingman.[30]

Two physical leisure activities promoted by local labor organizations suggest the blend of muscle and mind that such writers espoused. Leisure hours, though scarce for men who worked six days a week and ten or more hours a day, could be used to make the body more powerful and the mind nimbler. Union social gatherings in Pittsburgh often included boxing matches, and organizers encouraged members to participate in numerous amateur bouts that sprang up in mill towns throughout the year. As Elliott Gorn has shown, boxing played upon workers' frustrations with the emasculating effects of poor wages and monotonous work. Gorn argues that workers in heavy industries "turned to a more elemental concept of manhood, one they could demonstrate during their leisure hours." Boxing combined principles of strength, cunning, and honor and presented the combatant's physique as a display of perfected ability and independence. At century's end, workers' celebrations included baseball games and footraces that attracted many participants and spectators, but the annual tug-of-war was the most anticipated feature of Labor Day picnics at Kennywood Park and West View Park. The annual "fete of the toilers" revolved around the strength competition as an expression of teamwork and tactical thinking. Like boxing, the tug-of-war was not merely a physical activity, but also a contest that required strategy and coordination. Team members collaborated to throw their opponents off balance, to feign weakness, and to surprise the other team with a swift change of tactics. Boxing and tug-of-war events were not staged overtly for bodily training outside the workplace, but they were graphic examples of Pittsburgh workers' leisure culture that promoted further physical activity beyond that of industrial work. Workers in the late nineteenth century struggled to convince their employers that fewer hours at work would lead not to idleness, but to a more diverse physical life. George McNeill, the treasury secretary of the Knights of Labor in the 1880s, noted that more free time would "give more hours to the development of those muscles of the body" that never came into play in industrial work. Boxing and the tug-of-war were but two examples of physical leisure activities in which workers sought more sophisticated physical and mental development to prepare them for the trials of the workday.[31]

In the logic of the physically demanding workplace, the health and strength of a man's body became a crucial asset to both employer and employee. The *Amalgamated Journal* in 1900 asked, "What good are Mr. Rockefeller's millions to him as long as he does not possess a good, sound body?" The industrial worker, a victim of low wages and mechanical manipulation, had something that even the masters of capital did not: the impressive physical abilities to withstand a hard life of work. A good diet and leisurely exertion were meant to help the Pittsburgh worker maintain his health and stamina for a workday that could strike him down at any minute. Yet beginning in the 1890s, a new threat to the body of work emerged that could not be ameliorated by actions the worker might take during his brief time away from the mill or mine.[32]

FATIGUE AND WORK

Scrutiny of the detrimental physical effects of work captured the working body as a piece of startling evidence. Years of experiments convinced doctors and scientists that long hours of heavy work disturbed the body's tissues in a cycle of somatic distress more alarming than trauma. Whereas only a fraction of workers would ever die on the job, all workers at some time or another experienced a sensation of weariness that indicated more than a lack of sleep. Accidents attacked the body in an immediate and shocking fashion, and work-related illnesses could be understood in terms of other well-known diseases, yet critics of work in

Pittsburgh also turned to fatigue as a third and more insidious form of physical damage to workers' bodies. The discourse on fatigue in local industry arose at a time when the prevailing scientific understanding of the human body was shifting to a body-as-motor model that explained the tiring worker as a product of chemical processes within his bloodstream. Fatigue became scientists' warning about the working body's limits. Physical strain at work also became less acceptable to critics when workers' tasks lost their craft appeal. The laboring body had held a paradox in nineteenth-century Pittsburgh: in the era before mechanization, it was only through strain and physical suffering that the skilled worker learned how to accomplish his task. Exertion and fatigue were thus essential parts of the apprenticeship system in the months or years before a worker's body had adapted to work demands. After the turn of the century, however, scientific and social work communities warned that bodies *never* adapted to the fast pace of machines. Physiologists thus stripped fatigue of its connotation as an indication of a good day's work and imbued it with new meaning as a manifestation of workers' physical inadequacy.[33]

The historian Anson Rabinbach has found that a sustained discourse on fatigue emerged in European medical literature in the 1870s. Those who studied the "science of work" that grew from experiments with the chemistry of fatigue were the first to posit a causal connection between physical fatigue and accidents. Before 1900, the metaphor of the human body as motor was enticing to the rapidly expanding field of physiology, practitioners of which believed that fatigue could be studied and eventually mastered, manipulated in the same way as electrical systems. As Rabinbach shows, the discovery of fatigue as a rampant problem in industry generated "a widespread fear that the energy of mind and body was dissipating under the strain of modernity." Instead of scorning the ailing worker for his idleness, physiologists sympathized with him and his aching limbs, "evidence of the body's stubborn subversion of modernity."[34]

Physiological discourse on the fatigued working body fed off of a turn-of-the-century preoccupation with the "conversion of individuals into numbers and cases and the conversion of bodies into visual displays." The twin practices of statistics and surveillance, stressed in both social work and scientific management, focused on the "statistical person" as a unit of information gathering and knowledge creation. Once scientists rendered the individual working body an explanatory unit, they could produce vast amounts of literature about entire industries based upon experiments with only a few workers or, as was often the case, dead animals. The specialist language and complex formulas central to physiological discourse operated in tandem with innovative tools of the trade. Physiology built upon new techniques of depicting the body in motion developed in the late nineteenth century. Etienne-Jules Marey, a French scholar who experimented with time-lapse images of the human body in motion in the last decades of the nineteenth century, popularized chronophotography. Unlike Eadweard Muybridge, an English photographer who pursued artistic representations of animals and men in motion in the United States in the 1870s and 1880s, Marey focused on scientific and medical uses of the lens. Marey hoped to show with his photographs of workers in motion that highly skilled workers employed more efficient movements than those with less experience. By studying the best individuals' fluid movements, the chronophotographer and physiologist together could increase workers' endurance. Marey's work in understanding the laws of movement led to further attempts to break down human motion into discrete components. American scientific management of the early twentieth century applied these principles directly to the labor process. Frederick Winslow Taylor organized labor around the division of tasks into discrete parts, the detailed analysis of every individual part, and the coordination of various parts. Physiology, photography, and efficiency engineering were partners in a quest to discover the nature of the working body and to maximize its potential as it moved about the workplace. Professionals in each branch built their expertise around the difficulty of systematizing disorderly movements and calculating entropies.[35]

The unmanageable "human element" was the chief source of industrial error that physiologists hoped to reduce through detailed study and organization. Experiments conducted in Europe and the United States convinced physiologists that the physical and mental sensation of fatigue resulted from the circulation of waste products in the body. Blood vessels and muscles of dissected animals revealed that overexertion produced acidlike substances that were meant to be expelled quickly from the body. An individual's metabolism failed to regulate the removal of these muscular by-products when workers strained for too long. An overworked body could not expel its waste products and thus flooded its bloodstream with the toxins of exertion. One physiologist declared that "a tired person is literally and actually a poisoned person—poisoned by his own waste products." Compounding the problem within the workplace was the general environment of the Steel City. A local scientist warned that the air "on moist, dark days" in Pittsburgh was "surcharged with toxic waste products which poison the individual." The city's tired workers were drowning in fatigue.[36]

Researchers concluded that hard work was a healthy activity that tended to prolong life if performed in "an ordinary way." Too much work negated physical activity's advantages and endangered the worker. When a muscle became overworked only a "strong effort of will" could keep it functioning adequately; the mental strain needed to keep the body working produced a "brain fatigue" that accompanied muscular fatigue. The "process of slow but certain destruction" sapped the worker's brain of the energy required to think coherently about his job. When in the mill or mine long enough, "his brain slumbered, his intellect became blunted." For the industrial worker, keeping apace of machinery was "a competition of sensitive human nerve and muscle against insensitive iron." Physiologists thus defined fatigue in multiple ways, using it to refer to muscular exhaustion, a chemical state of the bloodstream, and a condition of dwindling alertness. Richard Gillespie notes that the "diversity of meaning gave industrial fatigue its power." Physiologists made the concept flexible enough to explain a range of work-related problems while also allowing themselves to apply it to an increasing array of situations that became problems only in physiological discourse.[37]

Fatigue was "an illusive phenomenon," one that crept up slowly, developing "insidiously and often without the knowledge of the worker." The sociologist Emory Bogardus argued that workers were "generally ignorant of the difference between the subjective development of fatigue and its objective correlates." Bogardus pointed to "unrelaxed tension in modern industry" and its "continuous and terrible demands on the human volitions" as the scourge of the workingman. Even worse, physiologists warned that fatigue was progressive, in the sense that it accumulated over the lifetime of a worker. The physiologist Thomas Oliver asked, "How can the poorer working men have good health . . . when they do not have in their homes and surroundings those conditions that enable them, during periods of relaxation, to sleep well, and to eliminate by their lungs and skin the waste materials formed during toil?" According to physiologists, workers' limbs, backs, and brains were slowly corroded from within. As they were worn away, they were also converted into more rigid and uncontrollable parts, divorced from natural movements and functions. Seen through the lens of physiology, overwork turned the body into a weak, mechanical shell.[38]

Fatigue was destructive in its own right, but it also led to a much larger problem when unheeded. Physiologists believed they could calculate the probability that any given worker would become fatigued to the point of exhibiting "muscular inaccuracies." The factors in this equation—"his coolness, his experience, his native quickness of reaction, his *state of being*, physical and mental"—amounted to a checklist that could hardly be tabulated for every individual. What physiologists claimed to measure, however, was the exact time at which a statistically average worker would begin to display the twitch of a finger, the slip of a foot, or the buckling of an arm that created disaster in the workplace. The certainty of this prediction was the key to physiology's promise—it secured the usefulness of the scientist by transforming the working body into a set of numerical inputs and outputs. Muscular inaccuracies caused accidents, physiologists contended, because workers who were pushed too far could not maintain the precision of movement that modern industry demanded. Bogardus noted that "the worker in the dangerous trades may suddenly through inaccurate movements find himself handicapped for life." Experts' calculations could stop these catastrophes.[39]

Physiological research attacked the Steel City notion that accidents were unavoidable. The significance of fatigue in social workers' critique of Pittsburgh's industries was that it led to accidents that injured bodies and took lives. Describing unskilled steelworkers' hot and heavy work, a Homestead worker asked, "How can any human being stand it?" The answer, he continued, was that "no one knows. They all die young." Accidents attributed to carelessness or chance could just as well be explained as a result of bodies that could no longer function properly because of fatigue. In an age of "hurry and excitement," Pittsburgh stood as an extreme example of the unending flurry of modern life. Simon Sosienski, a worker living in the mill town of Braddock, complained in the 1890s about the relentless pace of work in the steel industry. Sosienski wrote to his family about the difficulty of getting a day off from employers, who preferred to make their employees "work straight through just like the horses or oxen do back home." Sosienski's letter served as a warning to those back home that in Pittsburgh the rules governing the toil of man and beast were one and the same. Critics of local industry warned that workers who had no time in which to recuperate from persistent overwork were bound to break down physically, if not mentally. In a novel set in Pittsburgh in the first decade of the twentieth century, Trautmann and Hagboldt captured the essence of fatigue in the steel industry: "The work of the groaning men suffers no interruption. Up and down move the tired backs and the weary arms. . . . In silent agony the men stoop over the white glow of the fire. They are dazed. No sweat of relaxation appears on their bony frames. Their soul is burned out, like the skin through which the heat has drawn deep, dark-brown furrows. Here and there a sound of suffering escapes from a hollow chest."[40]

The city's labor press joined the scientific and reform communities in expressing its concern about fatigue and the pace of work. The *National Labor Tribune* declared in 1896 that "multitudes are hurried to their graves before their time, and it is haste rather than steady, continuous labor of body or mind which drives them there." The *Amalgamated Journal* reported in 1913 on experiments proving that muscles that had reached a state of fatigue needed twice as much rest as muscles that had been rested properly. Another article warned workers that twelve-hour days "fill the whole body with the poison of fatigue." Fatigue was a fact of life for Pittsburgh's workers, one that labor leaders accepted but remained vigilant about. As the *Amalgamated Journal* warned in 1908, "The fellows who were born tired are those who are apt to get punctured."[41]

The labor press presented the industrial worker's long day as a "drain on his strength and his life." The single day off that steelworkers received every two weeks, a time of "aching limbs and confused senses," allowed little recuperation. A repeated image in the labor press was that of exhausted workers trudging home after a long day of heavy work. The poem "The Poor Workingman" (1902) described the painful walk home of a common laborer:

He was only a tired workingman
Dragging along the street
So long seemed the way to his shanty
So heavy his weary feet
Each step seemed iron-laden
So stiff was the muscles' play
After 12-hours work in the hot dirty mill
At $1.25 a day.

Another poem, titled "The Slave Driver," presented a similar scene in which a worker stumbles toward the brief respite of sleep:

> It's evening: spat out from the mammoth maw
> Of Greed's grey, supine Beast, I drag my way
> A broken, sucked-out thing again to draw
> In sleep, a mending breath ere dawns the day.

Elsewhere, the *Amalgamated Journal* depicted the "stupid, listless, dwarfed, and distorted creatures with dull faces and heavy limbs creeping through the halls and up the stairways [of a boardinghouse] like strange torpid animals of an unknown species. . . . they had been made into—not machines, for machines do not feel—but adjuncts to machines, that suffer." Pittsburgh, it seemed, was filled several times each day with the walking dead, too exhausted to do anything but trudge home and collapse.[42]

An English steelworker told James Kitson in 1891 that the "stimulating atmosphere" of Pittsburgh inspired in him a greater capacity to do work than in his homeland but also wore at him physically. The worker told Kitson, "I feel that I have it in me; but I also feel and I know that it won't last. I shall be done in ten years." When "done," skilled workers often returned to the ranks of unskilled laborers. After the turn of the century, several steel companies in Pittsburgh announced they would no longer hire men who were past their prime working years. The Carnegie Steel Company stopped hiring men over forty, while the American Steel and Wire Company continued employing men over thirty-five only if they could prove their experience in steelmaking. In effecting such policies, the steel companies acknowledged tacitly the cumulative effect of fatigue by the time a worker had decades of experience. The worker's knowledge that he would no longer be physically able to work in the city's steel industry within a decade suggested a tangible, if often unheard, acknowledgment in Pittsburgh's industrial workforce that bodies were vulnerable and their abilities finite. The dual nature of the steelworker's observation is telling. He appreciated the physical difficulty as a test of his power but knew it would get the best of him. Daniel Rodgers's commentary on the persistence of the work ethic under mechanization considered such sentiments. "Even for those who chafed at labor," Rodgers noted, "the appeal of the moral centrality of work was too useful to resist." Workers admitted physical vulnerability in the face of relentless, heavy toil because that which damaged was also compelling—in terms of size, tonnage, pace, and heat, mechanized labor was astounding, if visually mundane. Though such an admission was heard only sporadically in the popular media of the Steel City at the turn of the century, between 1907 and 1910 a chorus of voices broadcast the message to the city and the nation.[43]

THE PITTSBURGH SURVEY "DISCOVERS" ACCIDENTS AND FATIGUE

As a capstone to decades of discussion about risk and fatigue, the Pittsburgh Survey focused reformers' attention on the ability of methodical research, narratives of social waste, and bodily imagery to prove the physical dangers of work (and thereby prove the necessity of professionalized social work). Whereas newspaper reporters and workers themselves previously understood industrial work as a necessarily dangerous pursuit, survey researchers pushed for changes in industrial practice that could prevent accidents. The power of the survey was not just the weight of its statistical findings, but its narrative fidelity; it was a story designed to resonate with a middle-class audience invigorated by reform movements in other cities. John McClymer persuasively described the cyclical relationship between the survey staff and the problems they defined: "They had come to Pittsburgh to investigate just those phenomena that had made their careers possible, while their careers involved just such an investigation. What they found to be true of Pittsburgh, in other words, was thereby true, in some sense, for themselves." To establish the link between danger to individual bodies and the need for universal social engineering, the survey's organizers used a new form of work imagery to take advantage of powerful visual cues that at times trumped the authority of statistics. Researchers submitted descriptions, sketches, and photographs of men at work and in states of physical suffering as an innovative type of proof that made its case in different ways than accident counts and death tolls.[44]

Oppenheim noted that although reform efforts were not new to Pittsburgh in 1907, the survey "stung the city into self-consciousness." The Chamber of Commerce described it as "an event that . . . caused more comment perhaps, on our civic conditions, than anything else that has ever happened in the history of Pittsburgh." The survey began as a broadly conceived project to expose the social ills of urban industry. Paul Kellogg, the assistant editor of *Charities and the Commons*, directed the survey for the New York Charity Organization Society (COS). When the project began, the COS had two decades of experience in reform work in northeastern cities. The historian Joan Waugh has argued that the goal of the COS throughout this period was to "bring community to an America that was increasingly rent by division and change." In Pittsburgh, the goal of community building became a project to forge a coalition of conscientious municipal and business elites, middle-class reformers, and working-class leaders. Linking them was a common belief that industrial society, like a poorly maintained machine, had broken down under its own power. Equally strong was reformers' belief in their own usefulness and the necessity of their expertise.[45]

The survey team chose Pittsburgh as the focus of the study not because it represented a startling aberration in American industry but because a small cadre of concerned welfare leaders in the city convinced them that it was entirely typical of the effects of American industrialization. One survey member defended the project from charges that it was an "invasion of vandal sociologists from the predatory wilds of Boston, Chicago, and New York" by stressing its local roots. Researchers working on the survey brought with them analytical methods to complement the desires of concerned Pittsburghers—local figures with various ties to industry. McClymer notes that reformers seeking funds for their projects had little choice but to "approach class divisions as interpreters and intermediaries," allying themselves with wealthy patrons who typically blunted any radical edges to surveys. In the project's original prospectus, Kellogg wrote that his overarching goal was "to supply unbiased reports in each field as a basis for local action and . . . for use nationally in movements for civic advance in other American cities." To Horace Deming, the chairman of the National Municipal League's executive committee, Pittsburgh represented a "conspicuous object lesson of the working of the social and economic forces that compel the birth and growth of cities." In Deming's estimation, Pittsburgh "epitomize[d] in its own history the evolution of every considerable American city." As a template for every manufacturing city, reform of the Steel City could be the start of a broad campaign to rein in runaway industry. In his study of civic reform in Pittsburgh since the turn of the century, the historian Roy Lubove argued that the central theme of the survey was the troubling discrepancy between centralized industrial planning and local government's failure to apply similar planning to the lives of its workers. Pittsburgh's social and environmental state had not kept up with its economic growth. Such thinking allowed the survey's staff to advance themselves as specialists in the science of social extrapolation. The logic that turned individual bodies into case studies of a local economic community could also turn Pittsburgh into a case study of American trends.[46]

Kellogg assembled a "flying wedge of investigators" to live in the city for one year. The researchers attempted to immerse themselves in the community and view it in terms of people who lived and worked there. Their emphasis on comprehensive research—scouring the city to explore workers' homes and neighborhood institutions, interrogating company policies and coroner's reports, and soliciting testimony—made the survey something new in the field of social work, not because it asked unprecedented questions but because it seemed to offer a method of making an immeasurable subject quantifiable. Key to the survey's innovation was the overwhelming nature of the project itself. Kellogg described fieldwork conducted "in railroad yards and mill towns, sweatshops, and great manufacturing plants; in courts, hospitals, and settlements . . . with priests and labor leaders, superintendents, claim agents and labor bosses; landlords, housewives, butchers and bakers—the workers themselves and those who live close to them." Bodies broken through years of toil or in the accidental instant marked the hinge between two conceptual halves: the industrial system that affected health and ability and the industrial system affected by compromised health and ability. Placing the body at this nexus allowed social researchers to position themselves with scientists, doctors, and other professionals who used rigorous methods to solve somatic mysteries.[47]

Pittsburgh workers' bodies filled the pages of the survey as the most tangible evidence of industrial negligence. The survey writers exposed the weaknesses of workers' bodies to a degree that had not been attempted. Two main types of bodily evidence are apparent in the survey: narratives of lives punctuated by physical trauma and images of broken, exhausted bodies. In both forms of representation, the writers scrutinized the individual as a way to illustrate statistical conclusions. Crystal Eastman opened her volume with three brief narratives of men involved in accidents between 1906 and 1907. Her descriptions of crushed hands caught in machinery and the meager financial compensations they brought to workers' families introduced a dual focus repeated throughout the survey. In a recurring series of individual cases that detailed the moment of accident for workers, the survey writers emphasized immediate causes of accidents and their economic effects on families. Caught between the cause-and-effect model of analysis was the violence of the accident itself and its somatic results. Though the survey was not silent about accidents as personal tragedies, the writers were more concerned with the larger consequences of accidents, the "permanent loss of health and power" that was ultimately another form of urban inefficiency. As Eastman declared, "If it is merely an inevitable loss in the course of industry, then it is something to grieve over and forget. If it is largely, or half, or partly unnecessary,—a waste of youth and skill and strength,— then it is something to fight about and not forget."[48]

Images of men with missing arms and legs told tales of continuous contests between workers and machines in a way that was difficult to dismiss as mere rhetoric. As a strategy to translate individual pain and loss to the reader, photographs of dismembered workers complemented texts that often failed to convey more than the economic losses that accompanied a crushed foot or an amputated arm. As the literary critic Elaine Scarry has stressed, "A great deal . . . is at stake in the attempt to invent linguistic structures that will reach and accommodate this area of experience normally so inaccessible to language." The creative act— inventing an approach to bodily suffering that would make it representative of *something*—took the form of collage in the survey. Written accounts of accidents had perhaps lost their power to move readers in Pittsburgh after years of newspaper articles detailing catastrophes and recurring lists of deaths from mundane mishaps. The survey's focus on injury reemphasized the problem in two ways. On the one hand, through biographical sketches and statistical summaries, the survey writers established a theory of accidents that explained their causes and their cost for both employers and employees. Through a series of drawings and photographs, on the other hand, the survey imparted a sense of physical catastrophe otherwise inexpressible. Eastman stated candidly the blending of the two, noting that the "steady march of injury and death means suffering, grief, bitterness, thwarted hopes incalculable. These things cannot be reckoned, they must be felt. But the loss of youth and strength and wealth-producing power . . . can be set forth to some extent in figures." Though statistics could often be "wearisome and confusing," the survey staff arranged its images to be exceptionally compelling.[49]

The survey explained loss via a Progressive reform ideology targeting businesses that failed to improve their workers' lives. According to this reasoning, Pittsburgh's industries injured workers because they treated bodies as one of many raw materials converted for use in production. The city and its industrial firms drove relentlessly for growth and increased output. The owners and managers of such firms as U.S. Steel denied the humanity of their workers, making them literally expendable. In attributing to industry the concept of the working body as resource, however, survey writers adopted it themselves as a central part of their understanding of the interaction between human and machine. Viewed in terms of James Scott's categories of social interaction—the public transcripts created when interaction is staged and "polite" versus the hidden transcripts whispered behind the scenes and out of earshot—the survey staff's argument was an attempt to attack industrialists' public transcript by claiming to reveal how they thought when they were not giving toasts at banquets or leading parades. Scott's theory insightfully places the burden of public camouflage not only on the subordinate but on the dominant as well. Those who control the "material basis of production, allowing them to extract practical conformity, and . . . the means of symbolic production, thereby ensuring that their power and control are legitimized," still need to manage appearances and couch their worldview in appropriate ways. Kellogg's researchers exposed the disparity between what industrialists said about work and the ways in which they debased it, thereby framing the laws of the labor market not as workers' economic and moral choices but as a series of callous manipulations from above.[50]

In the logic of the accusation that the worker's body was a raw material carelessly used up by industry, the "rawness" of the material mattered most. If the survey's industry was one that quickly converted human specimens into damaged goods, it was the goods' physical innocence that made the exchange so lamentable. To Kellogg and his fellow writers, rural bodies and urban, industrial bodies were fundamentally different: rural bodies were cultivated through the strenuous but invigorating rhythms of farm labor, while urban bodies were manipulated by the artificial discipline of mechanized production; rural bodies were healthy; industrial bodies slid down a steep slope of injury. The perceived division allowed Kellogg's researchers to locate machinery as the specific site at which healthy, well-functioning men became waste products. This categorization also complicated the interpretation of physical tasks, making the observation of bodies at work an assignment for specialists. Workers were no longer just native-born or foreign-born, male or female, skilled or unskilled. They also belonged to physical types that social researchers created and catalogued through extensive survey work. The social science historian Stephen Turner emphasizes the survey's understanding of the industrial environment as constructed, an insight that seems simple enough but that becomes crucial to an analysis of working bodies in the writing of John Fitch and Eastman. Turner notes that "the fact that no single person had made these environments . . . did not make these social institutions any less 'made'" to the survey staff. Their suggested reforms, then, became a "to do" list that would remake the world. The body of work was both participant in making the environment and itself made.[51]

Peter Roberts's article in the survey's final volume, *Wage-Earning Pittsburgh*, exemplified the way in which writers created a vocabulary of raw material around the worker's body. In "Immigrant Wage Earners," Roberts noted the influx of workers from agricultural districts of southern and eastern Europe, casting the range of employment opportunities as a hotly contested market of bodies. The writer stressed that local industries needed "strong manual laborers as do no others. The Slavs have brawn for sale." But if it was their brawn that made them attractive to industry, it was also their particular type of brawn that made immigrants seemingly ideal for heavy labor. Their physical abilities had been cultivated not in other steel mills but in fields and forests. By luring these country folk into the heart of the industrial city, Roberts argued, steel magnates set in motion a pattern of migration that had filled cities in the nineteenth century and threatened to overwhelm them in the twentieth century. Survey staff echoed journalists who described immigrant workers as invading hordes, yet Roberts and his fellow writers blamed employers for degrading industrial work to the extent that immigrants could gain access to it. This slap at bosses certainly delivered a backhand to immigrants as well. McClymer notes of the survey's treatment of foreign-born workers, "Immigrants, taken as individuals, were victims of industrial conditions and were to be commiserated with. Taken together, however, they assumed monstrous proportions in Kellogg's mind; they held the labor market in their 'great, untrained, earth-bred hand.'" The process was not random but dictated by the demand for raw strength. Roberts detailed the selection system that brought "the best of the agricultural population" to the city and provided "a body of men physically most fit for the heaviest demands made by our industries." Pittsburgh's steel mills exerted a magnetic pull, ultimately concentrating thousands of able bodies in a few square miles devoted to heavy production.[52]

Roberts then used Pittsburgh workers' agricultural background to suggest the disorientation caused by mill technology. Men who were familiar with the relatively simple work of farms suddenly stood among hulking furnaces and overhead cranes that produced steel. Roberts estimated that "ninety-five per cent have no knowledge of modern machinery or methods of modern production; they are children in factory training." Mills placed a new regimen of control and constraint upon workers who had to fit themselves into a designed production process. They commanded their own bodies only as far as the mechanical pace allowed. The "special posture" and "special routine" of steelmaking made the survey writers nostalgic for a lost system of labor in which people set their own pace. As the heart of their argument against industry, Roberts and his fellow writers placed mill laborers within a context of bewildering machinery whose power was only partially understood.[53]

Just as the scientific theory of recapitulation in the late nineteenth century turned evolutionary biology into an explanation of "advanced" and "primitive" cultures around the world, the survey's researchers produced a hierarchy of sorts between the technologically initiated and uninitiated ("genuine Americans" vs. "children in factory training"). The initiation process that all new workers must endure took the form of a high-stakes struggle. Workers battled machines to gain the upper hand and make it safely through the day. This view of steelmaking was not unique to the survey writers. During the survey's year of intensive research in Pittsburgh, the journalist William Hard published a series of articles in *Everybody's Magazine* about Chicago's steel industry. Hard presented a picture of a day's work on a mill floor, claiming that most steelworkers were all too familiar with "flaming streams of angry metal [and] red-hot writhing steel snakes that hiss." After observing workers' attempts to dodge constant dangers, Hard concluded, "Steel is war." The survey echoed this proclamation, suggesting that bodies arriving in Pittsburgh, though equipped with great strength and endurance, were virtually powerless against the onslaught of mechanization and accidents. In their repeated juxtaposition of individuals and masses, survey staff presented the industrial "child" as a sympathetic figure and industrial "children" as unruly, unthinking figures who contributed to their own ruin. In a combination of enticement and battle, Pittsburgh's industry filled its working ranks with potential victims. Exposing the before-and-after effect of steelmaking was crucial to the survey's goal of awakening the city's middle class; if there was no action, the process would continue. According to one survey writer, Pittsburgh "beckons, uses up, and beckons to more."[54]

This narrative of immigration, employment, and injury in Pittsburgh provided the interpretive foundation of the survey's most comprehensive descriptions of workers' bodies. Fitch's *The Steel Workers* and Eastman's *Work-Accidents and the Law* combined text and image to place bodies in the foreground of an indictment against employers. Although their investigative emphases and professional backgrounds differed greatly, Fitch and Eastman together produced a dual understanding of the industrial body. A clear pattern can be read in their accounts, one in which the body of the Pittsburgh worker appeared either in the mill and mired in a process of destruction or outside of the mill, maimed by an accident on the job. The writers implied that these were the best- and worst-case scenarios for steelworkers. The most that men in mills could hope for was an exhausted body. The nightmare they tried to avoid was death or permanent injury.[55]

The working body in Fitch's report was simultaneously powerful and weak. Because it existed only in relation to the machines around it, the body at work exuded imagery of both valiant struggle and futile effort. The worker entered "his daily fight with modern machinery" as an "industrial soldier" but invariably lost. Fitch admired steelworkers' bodies as raw expressions of elemental force; within mills, amid the roar and glare of open furnaces, he could not distinguish workers as individuals with their own identities and histories. Instead, he rendered them into a series of images representing the process through which rural bodies became industrial bodies. Their bodies were physically and symbolically enmeshed in an anonymous work environment; communicating with hand signals, barks, and whistles, steelworkers lived in a strange world with rules of its own.[56]

What could the social researcher learn from a trip to the mill floor? Fitch's initial view of the mill found "faces reddened by the glare of fire and hot steel, muscles standing out in knots and bands on bare arms, clothing frayed with usage and begrimed by machinery." Struck by the figures at work before him, Fitch declared that the world of mechanized industry was "full of men in greasy overalls." The descriptive traits Fitch mentioned

—glowing face, straining muscles, and ruined clothing—referred to the power of the production process to mark the body and the worker's ability to assert his own strength within an overwhelming mechanical system. The world may have been full of men in greasy overalls, but they all wielded their own reserve of physical power that gave them dignity in their otherwise begrimed lives. Fitch's descriptions centered on parts of an unassembled whole. Faces, muscles, and clothes hardly made for real persons, but they could serve as sensory cues of the meaning of hard work. Fitch's method of providing staccato images—a glimpse of color here, a shred of cloth there—typified the data collection of the survey as a whole. The researchers favored the amassing of data as an end in itself, expecting the data to reveal truths via their immensity and serial presentation.[57]

As Fitch moved further into the mill, he came across another scene of work. He saw a man "dressed only in trousers and a flannel shirt with sleeves cut off at the shoulder, the sweat was pouring from his body and his muscles stood out in knots." Again, Fitch's emphasis on the worker's exertion made the scene something to admire, allowing perspiration and muscle to tell a tale of effort. Joseph Stella, an Italian-American artist brought to Pittsburgh to provide drawings for the survey, made a similar observation about the spectacle of mill bodies. A "naked, perspiring shining torso in dramatic agitation against the glare of the ovens" epitomized the body at work for Stella. The sweat covering workers' bodies stood as vivid proof of harsh working conditions and sustained effort. Stella saw a torso, not a person. Fitch saw faces, arms, and clothing, not people. Painter and reformer experienced industrial work as scenes; their eagerness to use workers as specimens merged uneasily with their sympathy for them.[58]

Stella's drawings amplified an image of mill men as spectacles to be decoded. The art historian Rina Youngner notes that Stella's drawings of steelworkers responded to John White Alexander's Carnegie Institute murals and contested the representation of work in Pittsburgh. In Fitch's volume, three of Stella's drawings were reproduced in the text to complement the author's mill journey. The first, "A Breathing Spell," showed a worker sitting down and leaning on a tall stoker for support. Although the worker returned the viewer's gaze, Stella positioned him away from his work for a moment and thus away from the glow of ingots and ovens. His face was obscured in shadows and barely visible. Stella made the worker's clothing dark and grimy despite the light that bathed his body from the neck down, perhaps to suggest that workers' faces could be lit by ovens, but their clothing was so soiled by the production process that it resisted all attempts at illumination. The second drawing, "In the Glare of the Converter," depicted a worker staring into the very heart of the steelmaking process. His shirt was ripped open at the neck, exposing his broad shoulders. The way in which the worker faced the "glare of the converter" suggested an ability to meet the challenge of modern industry. He dared the converter to blink first. Stella's third drawing, "In the Light of a Five-Ton Ingot," captured a similar scene: a worker's face emerged from shadows as it was flashed by light and heat from below. The man held two wooden poles, presumably ends of a stoker or pincher. He returned the gaze of the viewer, but again, his eyes blended into the murkiness behind him. His shoulders spanned the width of the drawing and even pushed past its outer edges. Here was a man who could barely be contained by an artist. Stella's three images revealed strong, able men in the workplace who, although they displayed command of their own physical power, were framed by the elements of production that sur- rounded them. Each also exhibited glimpses of the fatigue that physiolo- gists had quantified in the working body. The figures' drooping eyelids or fixed stares could seem powerful one minute and feeble the next.[59]

Drawings served as representations that were also evidence. Wanting to produce an all-encompassing survey, Kellogg and his team collected impressions, statistics, and scattered anecdotes and then presented them in a way that did not privilege one over the others. Images and written scenes performed the same duty, alerting the reader to the body as the irreducible unit of the industrial system. In *The Steel Workers* descrip- tions and drawings of workers accompanied written and photographic accounts of mill architecture and machinery. Fitch admitted the appeal of the mill landscape, noting both the "glamour about the making of steel" and the "overwhelming sense of power" produced by the "very size of things—the immensity of the tools, the scale of production." Blast furnaces seemed to rise endlessly, pushing limits of human measure as they stood "eighty, ninety, one hundred feet tall." Yet Fitch's admiration of the mill's spectacular scale was fleeting. Most of his narrative pre- sented brittle lives hidden under the structure. The survey's juxtaposition of man and machine was a prelude to the discovery of men weakened and harassed by machinery towering over them. Turn-of-the-century image makers used the visual technique of technological gigantism to represent

Drawn by Joseph Stella

J. Stella
Pittsburg, 1908

Joseph Stella

16. *A Breathing Spell.*
17. *In the Glare of the Converter.*
18. *In the Light of a Five-Ton Ingot.*

the position of the workingman in the midst of immense machinery. The technique played upon the fear and attraction that machines evoked in American culture throughout the nineteenth century. The psychologist Gerald Stanley Lee referred to it in 1913 as "terrible and strange beauty," a way to capture the combination of fright and appeal that he experienced in the presence of heavy machinery. Fitch and Stella used this weird beauty, placing the body at work in the oven's glare and in machinery's shadows. Bodies were strong and capable, but their power was always positional. In Stella's sketches, the strong workers were tired and distracted. Years of work produced muscular strength and exhaustion, as inseparable in the workplace as terror and beauty. Amid cavernous vistas filled with massive devices, workers' bodies appeared vulnerable. The difference in scale between workers and machines helped Fitch make the point that workers were overshadowed and eventually overpowered.[60]

Photographs of production in Fitch's volume gave added evidentiary weight to the dimensional relationship between men and machines. Images presented workers standing before or beside electric cranes, rollers, ladles of molten metal, and cutting machines. Workers in these photographs were almost a means of gauging the machines' size; taken from the ground level, at which workers spent their days, the photographs framed men against massive gears and pistons that reached beyond the images' upper borders. While the steelworkers pictured did not show signs of being disturbed by the surrounding machinery, their relative weakness in terms of scale problematized the notion that workers controlled the tools around them. Their daily combatants enjoyed a size advantage that became extremely dangerous when the two collided. The survey presented mills as menacing environments in which the size of machinery signaled impending trouble. Drawings and photographs demonstrated the incongruity in a more immediate way than by merely noting that blast furnaces were ninety feet taller than humans. Fitch tried to capture the sensations of making steel because it was the sensations, he argued, that wore bodies down to the point of collapse. Machinery was impressive, but it took its toll. "With such men in mind," Fitch noted, "the elemental forces, the heat, the speed, the hugeness of the appliances for reducing, melting, lifting, and rolling out the tonnage of steel and iron . . . will be of more than technical interest. They react powerfully on human nature." Machines pushed workers to their physical limits (producing fatigue) and attacked their bodily integrity (producing injury). In building their narrative toward the moment of accidental injury, Fitch and Eastman stressed the exhausting nature of work in mills. Fatigue led to accidents, making the final outcome of employment in steel mills a life-changing mishap or a near miss. Eastman wrote of steelmaking that it "demands so much of the eyes and nerves and muscles, and is done in such intense heat," that it necessarily had to be endured in short shifts and with frequent breaks.[61]

Strains of work were tied to the insatiability of modern machinery, but they were also effects of industrial capitalism. Managers and owners of steel companies introduced machinery to transform the work floor. In calling for a shorter workday in steel mills, Eastman critiqued the system of production that placed efficiency and output figures above workers' physical welfare: "There can be no doubt that the unrelaxing tension and speed in the American steel mill make for danger. To go slower would be to go backward in industry, and that is more than can be expected of America. But by shortening hours of work the dangers of speed can be lessened; the minds and bodies of the men can be kept up to the pace of the mill. Greater intensity of work necessitates longer periods of relaxation. If the strain of the work cannot be lessened the duration must be." Tired minds and tired bodies increased the risk of accidents, as momentary lapses in caution allowed machinery to strike down workers. Eastman's call for a shorter workday followed the argumentation method used throughout the survey: a physical given (bodies unable to cope with pace) could be explained by the mind-set of industrialists (profit seeking) and could be mitigated only by specific reform (less work per day). Of the three elements of this reasoning, Eastman, Fitch, and the survey team excelled at the first—establishing a known fact about bodies and machines through the collection of data. The survey's arguments about Pittsburgh were not distinctive in the reform world, but these writers' success at using bodies as variables in their equations offered a method that promised to at least sort out massive problems and make their solution the province of professionals.[62]

Stella's drawings depicted bodies in a gradual process of deterioration. In "At the Base of the Blast Furnace," the artist depicted a group of five workers shoveling coal in a dark atmosphere of smoke and sizzle. Three of the workers stooped over their shovels, one of them almost leaning on

19. Joseph Stella, *At the Base of the Blast Furnace.*

his for support. Light shone on their straining backs, drawing the viewer to the place of utmost burden: backs forced to bend and lift each day, backs that carried the city's industry. Two workers stood apart from the rest and watched their fellow workmen, yet their postures and drooping eyes suggested that they stopped shoveling from exhaustion rather than curiosity. The men at each end of the group stole a brief break from the monotony of their work, shovels still in hand but minds elsewhere. Stella described his drawings of heavy work as expressions of pain that emphasized "the spasm and the pathos of those workers condemned to a very strenuous life, exposed to the constant MENACE OF DEATH." The workers' stooping posture at the base of the blast furnace mirrored the posture of a miner presented in a photograph from Eastman's volume. In the image, a miner slumped toward a mine exit at the end of his workday. Years of working underground in low chambers inflicted their toll on his frame, bending his back into a permanent bow. Just as too many hours of

20. Slumping miner, from *Work-Accidents and the Law.*

strenuous work sapped the miner's body of its vitality and drowned his muscles in waste products, so, too, did they etch their mark on his figure. As he walked home, the miner in Eastman's photograph carried with him the disfiguring effects of work that Stella's figures eventually displayed as well. Both images leaned heavily toward the dramatic, capturing bent frames that seemed posed for the viewer's attention.[63]

Fitch's and Eastman's body at work, tired, stooped, and overwhelmed, was transformed further by personal and social catastrophes. Eastman dedicated her research to the problem of accidents in Pittsburgh's mills and factories, painting a picture of frequent and indiscriminate injury. By compiling coroners' reports, hospital records, and company reports, Eastman found that 526 men had died in industrial accidents between 1 July 1906 and 30 June 1907. Trying to refute the notion that only unskilled immigrant workers were struck down by accidents, Eastman noted that 42.5 percent of those killed were American-born workers and roughly 70 percent made the weekly wages of skilled workers. The yearly death count, while substantial, paled in comparison to nonfatal accident tallies. In the three-month period between April and June 1907, 509 men were injured in Pittsburgh industries. Eastman unearthed descriptive information for the "wrecks of 294 hospital cases" and labeled 167 of them as permanent injuries. Approximately one-quarter of the injuries were amputations of arms, legs, feet, hands, and fingers. Workers lost a total of thirty body parts in the three months of 1907, an average of ten each month or one every three days. Eastman put these figures in an unsettling perspective, thinking of all the injured workers as members of a visible community haunting Steel City streets: "In five years there would be 2,500. Ten years would make 5,000, enough to people a little city of cripples, a number noticeable even among Greater Pittsburgh's 600,000. It is no wonder that to a stranger Pittsburgh's streets are sad." The transition from the loss of individual lives and limbs to the aggregate spectacle of industry's toll was necessary for any given datum to make sense.[64]

Sad streets became one of two locations in which Fitch and Eastman presented the wounded worker's body. The body away from work—injured and tossed aside by industry and the city—appeared in the pages of the survey as either alone on the streets of Pittsburgh or in the context of a dependent family. The first type highlighted the personal, physical pain of amputation, while the second transformed the industrial accident into a severe blow against working-class family structure. The survey writers offered both images as the expected result of Pittsburgh's rapid conversion of bodies from health to frailty. Eastman's objective was to quantify Pittsburgh's annual accidents and to "see strong men just learning to face life maimed." To aid the reader in seeing scenes of physical catastrophe, Kellogg enlisted Lewis Hine to photograph amputees. Images of limblessness possessed certain rhetorical powers that survey researchers wielded as complements to their statistical presentations—the power to evoke sympathy from the viewer, the power to tarnish civic pride, and the power to exert pressure on local and national legislators. As the literary critic William Solomon notes, depictions of shattered bodies can make or break the "representational enterprise aimed at disclosing the devastating effects on human beings of participating in mechanized warfare." If the survey's war metaphor made men and machines combatants, then Hine's imagery presented wounded veterans as new models of the Pittsburgh workingman.[65]

The photographs captured workers away from their places of work and explored unseen consequences of injury by making amputated stumps the objects of both sentimental and realistic scrutiny. Hine's use of photography in the name of social reform has been discussed by many historians as a significant contribution to the way in which middle-class audiences conceptualized working conditions, poverty, and ethnicity in America's cities in the early twentieth century. He viewed his role in the survey as that of a provider of indisputable evidence. In May 1910, Hine wrote to a friend, "I have had, all along as you know, a conviction, that my own demonstration of the value of the photographic appeal, can find its real fruition best if it helps the workers realize that they themselves can use it as a lever." Unlike Stella's art, the chemical process of photography gave Hine the added claim that the injured men he depicted in the survey were real, that they lived and breathed on the streets of Pittsburgh for anyone to see. Hine hinted that his work could help the reform effort if workers themselves—"those who are in the thick of the battle"—adopted staff photographers of their own for the visual documentation of their lives. Distributing photographic duties in this way would undercut Kellogg's preference for well-placed experts cataloging and interpreting information. Notably, the survey writers did not echo Hine's appeal for a democratization of the survey process.[66]

Hine's images of injury were a far cry from his celebratory photographs of men at work in the 1930s; these pictures were meant to undermine confidence in workingmen's ability. In "The Wounds of Work" and "The Crippled Watchman—A Type" the photographer presented two men alone in injury's aftermath. Hine's caption for "The Wounds of Work" read, "When a man's hand is mutilated he keeps it out of sight." The worker in the photograph hid his left arm in the folds of his overalls, while displaying his healthy right arm prominently. The photograph's purpose was to highlight the injury; hence, Hine's caption provided an explanation for the maimed hand's invisibility. The fact that the man was forced to hide his injury in order to stand a chance at reemployment was meant to enlighten the reader about industrial employers' mercenary practices and make the worker an appropriate subject of pity. In "The Crippled Watchman—A Type," the worker's lost leg was clearly visible. Both his pinned-up pant leg and his position as a watchman at a steel plant referred to practical methods of coping with such a serious injury. Workers who lost limbs and could not continue working in mills and factories were frequently given jobs as watchmen and inspectors, jobs that paid less than skilled positions but were commensurate with common laborers' wages. The watchman in Hine's photograph leaned against the supports of a railroad trestle in a steel mill stockyard. The industrial background of tracks, barrels, and towers loomed over him in much the same way that production machinery towered over laborers on the work floor. For the watchman, however, such structures now provided the support that was taken away with the amputation of his leg. The title's description of the man as "a type" suggested that the specific details of his injury and life were less significant than his symbolic function. Hine propped the worker up against a fence, placing him before the lens to narrate a tale of loss and commiseration that was difficult to relate otherwise.

Hine's most compelling images were those that brought industrial imagery into the realm of workers' families. He accomplished this displacement by showing families explicitly or by referring to them as off-camera victims. In "One Arm and Four Children," a one-armed man posed in front of his house with his wife and children. The man stood slightly apart from his family, his link to them—his role as wage earner—compromised by his missing limb. The man's young son stood directly to his right, his right arm and feet positioned identically to his father's. The similarity of the two bodies drew a disheartening parallel between their lives; would the boy search for a way to support his family and find dangerous work in industry as well? The woman held one of her children, but her burden was certainly greater than could be depicted in a photograph. Hine suggested further the ultimate obscurity of the family trauma of industrial accidents in his photograph "Wife and Six Children in the Old Country." While the photograph showed a one-legged man on a bench with crutches next to him, the title of the work stressed the unseen family that relied on his physical well-being. In both photographs, Hine used the ordinary nature of the settings—a front porch, a nondescript bench—to normalize the fact of injury. The photographer's implication was that in any random corner of the Steel City, one could glimpse tangible effects of unseen industrial accidents. Like Eastman's imagery of a city full of limbless men, Hine's snapshots of ruined family men formed a disturbing view of Pittsburgh, but one that had to be recorded systematically for it to be useful to reformers.

Lewis Hine
21. *The Wounds of Work.*
22. *The Crippled Watchman—A Type.*

Lewis Hine
23. *One Arm and Four Children.*
24. *Wife and Six Children in
the Old Country.*

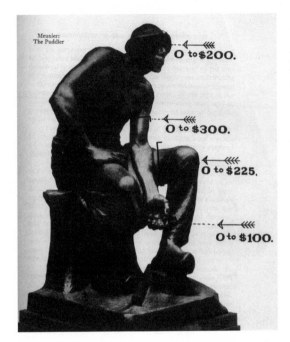

Meunier:
The Puddler

O to $200.

O to $300.

O to $225.

O to $100.

25. "Valuations Put on Men in Pittsburgh in 1907."

In what was perhaps the most provocative image in *Work-Accidents and the Law*, Eastman mapped monetary values onto a reproduction of Constantin Meunier's sculpture *The Puddler* and titled the piece "Valuations Put on Men in Pittsburgh in 1907." The amounts came from twenty-seven accident cases in which Eastman could find figures for the compensation paid by employers. The set of body parts lost and paid for included eyes, arms, legs, and fingers. The diagram argued Eastman's case that in Pittsburgh body parts and whole bodies were commodities like any other, valued according to an arithmetic of injury. Eastman's use of Meunier's sculpture radically altered the meaning of the piece. Art critics in the United States had long praised Meunier's work as an exaltation of the dignity and subtle power of modern labor. Eastman converted this icon of the enduring work ethic into an indictment of Steel City employers. The image also revealed something notable about Eastman's understanding of the problem. In presenting such a display of body parts and their values, Eastman moved beyond the language of sentimentality and the campaign to render the worker's loss comprehensible. Now the problem was a rather simple matter of economics in which workers were not receiving a fair price for their arms and legs. Like the personal accounts that opened her study, which moved quickly from moments of injury to the dollar amounts paid for them, Eastman's use of *The Puddler* accented the link between the body and money. Eastman argued that a solution to the problem of industrial injury in Pittsburgh could not focus solely on efforts to stop accidents. Instead, a better system for the "distribution of the burden of income loss" was also needed.[67]

Decades later, Eastman's way of conceiving calculations of industrial injury had become commonplace; in the 1930s workers' newspapers frequently published compensation charts that delineated the exact amount paid for eyes, legs, and fingers. Yet in the first decade of the twentieth century, Eastman's focus on the financial equation of damaged bodies represented a novel way of framing the problem of industrial accidents. While accusing employers of treating their workers like any raw material shipped into the Steel City, Eastman herself explained the dilemma in terms of cost and waste, where "every work-accident leaves a problem of poverty behind." Her fellow writers followed her lead, indicting Pittsburgh's businesses for their wasteful practices and the municipal government for its lack of oversight, all of which hindered male workers from staying on the job and providing for their wives and children. Eastman's *Puddler* illustration stated explicitly what was implicit in the rest of her presentation—that the human figure in industry was constantly fragmented and quantified and thus best understood by the researcher if further fragmented and quantified.[68]

The survey used the working body as evidence of something greater than itself, an industrial system made conspicuous by its inefficient treatment of its workers. Accidents could be reduced by isolating their causes and taking remedial action, yet the survey team had little faith that they could be prevented altogether. Eastman ultimately conceded to the prevailing belief about accidents in Pittsburgh, reporting that "danger is inherent in modern methods of production" and "men are bound to be killed and injured." If employers could not be expected to eliminate risk from the workplace, they could be held accountable for the way in which they compensated workers after risk turned into injury. The survey highlighted the distinct connection between the body of work and its economic value for employers and Pittsburgh families.[69]

CONCLUSION

The industrial worker's body became a vehicle through which the survey writers recast the nation's experience with industrial mechanization as a simple relationship between innocent bodies and indifferent machines. Workers' backgrounds allowed the survey team to make the workplace experience of Croatians, Hungarians, and Lithuanians a microcosm of America's struggle to come to terms with the machine age. Injuries that resulted from the marriage of worker and machine certainly caused physical suffering and family distress, but they were all the more troubling as the product of a bewildering introduction to a world that begged the question of whether workers guided machines or machines guided workers. The wage structure of mill work revealed that the line between the two had blurred. As a mill foreman remarked, "If the machine depends upon the man for speed, we put him on piece work; if the machine drives the man, we pay him by the day." The difference between the two systems of pay marked both workers' budgets and their sense of self. As machines and workers became cooperative partners in the policies of foremen and owners, they became bitter contestants in reform literature.[70]

Kellogg hoped to take advantage of the anxiety over the mechanization of urban life in America, writing that the survey aimed at "the human equation in our audience." When the survey staff publicized its findings in an exhibit at Pittsburgh's Carnegie Institute in November 1908, the goal was to make the results of collecting and interpreting data "intensive, graphic, educational, and suggestive" of the nature of industrial life. The exhibit featured maps, population charts, and Stella's drawings of "types of workers" from the steel industry. The exhibit publicized the findings of a year's worth of research, but it was also a representational form indicative of the survey's higher goals. Various forms of illustration made the city's failings visible, pushing visitors to recognize the ambiguity inherent in Pittsburgh's progress. Stella glimpsed it, praising the "beauty lying in the arabesques of form given by the structures of these huge volcano-like steel mills," but also noting that "God had pity on the poor muddy dark city." Before the Pittsburgh Survey, apologists for the city seemed to embrace such contradictions, imagining pollution as wealth and injury as a matter of course. The interwoven promises and threats of the Steel City were not local, according to Kellogg and his team of researchers. The assumed typicality of Pittsburgh meant that the city's narratives were also national. Eastman described *personal* catastrophes that were not immediate national catastrophes but became generalized through argumentation. Kellogg's faith in surveying as a method was that it could publicize facts about the world without waiting for "some great disaster to sensationalize the plight of the downtrodden." Truths about Pittsburgh, seemingly local and contingent, were embodied on a scale that defied civic boundaries.[71]

The city's Chamber of Commerce responded to this vision with a mix of optimism and blame, couched in a similar language of nationalizing local findings. President Lee Smith admitted that the survey revealed "the dark side of the housing conditions" but noted that these were conditions typical of "great industrial centers" rather than problems particular to Pittsburgh. Likewise, Smith explained the city government's experience with immigrants as overcoming "the difficulties in dealing with the large foreign population" that, despite its inadequate housing, profited greatly from its labor. "It is really a wonder," Smith noted, "that things are not worse than they are," given the rapid demographic shifts of the past decades. Both the chamber president and the survey staff viewed the workingman in the context of the city and the city in the context of the industrial nation. Boosters took the individual, "old-stock" worker, transformed him into an abstract image of muscle and artistry, and labeled him "Pittsburgh." Social researchers took the individual, "new-stock" worker, transformed him into a statistical profile or spectacular scene, and labeled him "Pittsburgh." Their methods of extrapolation were similar, but their results were irreconcilable.[72]

The effort to publicize the enormity of industrial waste and wreckage produced scripts and images that steered back and forth between the measurable and the boundless. The socialist paper *Justice* printed weekly tolls of fatalities caused by work accidents in the 1910s under the heading "Industrial Deaths." The editors listed accident victims' names, ages, employers, and causes of death in brief, unembellished notes. The entries for one week, published 18 October 1913, say much about the state of work in Pittsburgh's heavy industries:

Frank Barberi, 27, Pittsburg Coal, crushed by slate
John Masinik, 22, Frick Coal Company, crushed in mine
Louis Hiathi, 28, McKees Rocks Steel Car Company, electrocuted

Anton Kopp, Jones and Laughlin, burns on entire body
Louis Koenig, 14, Jones and Laughlin, burns from explosion
Frank Miller, 54, Jones and Laughlin, burns from explosion

Here were six workers, crushed, electrocuted, and burned to death in a single week, listed one after another without editorial comment. The weekly routine of the "Industrial Deaths" column in *Justice* suggests an accommodation to the violence of the local workplace. By 1913, accidents were accepted, if not expected, as a normal facet of work in Pittsburgh. A member of the AAISW wrote in the *Amalgamated Journal* that the city's road to industrial progress had been "paved with skulls and walled with corpses." For Pittsburgh's critics, workers' bodies, dead and fragmented, became the shattered stepping-stones upon which a century of industrial development and accumulated wealth had traveled.[73]

Woman's work WAS in the Home. MODERN INDUSTRY
took away her work and she FOLLOWED IT into the Factories and Workshops.

—NATIONAL CONSUMERS' LEAGUE,

"The Waste of Industry," 1915

5

"DELICATELY BUILT"

THE "PROBLEM" OF WORKING WOMEN

IN PITTSBURGH

✳ If city boosters and social reformers fought to represent Pittsburgh's workers in diametrically opposed ways, those workers who made it into celebratory events and the most spectacular of critiques were invariably men. Boosters perceived the Steel City through a manly image, leaving women's contributions to the growth of local industries unheralded on the festive streets and in the halls of high culture. Reformers, too, devoted much of their effort to chronicling the failures of local industry and government to protect male wage earners. Insofar as they uncovered the plight of working women, Progressive writers established as fact the notion that women in the workplace were a problem. Both groups perceived women to be losing a physical battle on the job. For promoters of the city in particular, this was a counterproductive tale. Women failed, unlike the mythical men of steel who seemingly enjoyed everyday victories. Women worked in suffocating workshops, places that boosters claimed to be inimical to the city's "eminent place in the field of labor or with its progressive commercial spirit and humanitarian impulse." Women's working lives were governed by the demands of machinery; their pace, their ability to repeat small movements, and their physical endurance had to be accommodated to mechanical rhythms. Assumptions about the harmful effects of modern work on female bodies and minds rendered the working woman an impossibly dismal figure for public display.[1]

The historian Joan Scott has noted that the marginalization of working women was a central historical effect of the nineteenth century. Scott's claim that historians' treatment of women as minor figures in the workplace was a direct result of persistent campaigns to push them to the industrial boundaries is well illustrated in turn-of-the-century Pittsburgh. It was not merely a celebration or criticism of manly workers that characterized the city's image but a consistent exclusion of women's work as trivial, aberrant, or unappealing. In this sense, city celebrants bought into the arguments about working women in Pittsburgh that accompanied Progressive exposés of the working man. There were no historical models of laboring women to counteract the image of the female machine tender who was gradually damaged by her job. Boosters and reformers constructed the much-noted manliness of industrial Pittsburgh through the omission of women from public displays and the presentation of working women as dependent and unprotected. Bodily spectacles in Pittsburgh defined gender with respect not only to the material realities of the workplace but also to the political dilemma signaled by the presence of working women.[2]

The American press had long marveled at and recoiled from the spectacle of women—especially foreign women—engaged in manual labor. Decades earlier, a writer for *Frank Leslie's Popular Monthly* had reviewed the state of work "among half-civilized or savage tribes or nations" to find evidence of the mistreatment of women. The result was a brief examination of the "benighted position of patriarchal people," including Turks, Indians, the "native tribes of Siberia," and inhabitants of the "Dark Continent." Although none of the tasks surveyed (cooking, curing animal skins, hunting, and grinding corn) were industrial, the association of daily work and savagery was clear. It coarsened women and was thus suited to coarse women. When average working hours for female employees began decreasing after 1900, critics worried about working women's use of free time and their boorish behavior learned on the job. Such behavior was troubling enough when confined to the factory or work-shop but became particularly alarming when transferred to the city's streets and commercial establishments. For many middle-class writers, the (presumed) economic independence of working women suggested a sexual independence that ruined reputations and destroyed families. In addition to perceptions of working women as indelicate, proponents of protective legislation argued that working women were, in fact, *too deli-cate* to survive the same hours and conditions as men. Efforts to shorten the workday and ban night work were meant to keep women's bodies healthy enough to conceive and nurture children.[3]

The most pronounced narrative of working women in Pittsburgh at the turn of the century came in Elizabeth Beardsley Butler's *Women and the Trades*. As the first volume of the Pittsburgh Survey, *Women and the Trades* trained the social reform community's lens on the other half of the "other half"—women who toiled in the city's industrial workforce. Butler's study of the women of steel (and tin, glass, garments, and crack-ers, to name a few) unintentionally expressed an argument that could be made to keep women out of not only labor spectacles but also the work-place. In a key passage from *Women and the Trades*, Butler surveyed the work of women in Pittsburgh: "Two-thirds of the women in the metal trades are Slavic,—Hungarian, Polish and Croatian. They are women of recent immigration, raw from their peasant earth, unacquainted with the language and ignorant of the ways of this country. They live in colonies of their own people. They accept the work and conditions that go with it which more often than not are unnecessarily degrading. Except where the nervous speed of American girls is in demand, these foreign women who ask neither for comfort nor for cleanliness nor higher wages, form the group characteristic of the trade." In these five sentences, Butler summarized the threefold problem of working women in Pittsburgh as she saw it. First, rationalized work tended to divide the workforce—both male and female—into groups isolated by language and culture. One of Butler's central tasks was to chart the ethnic distributions of industries, which seemingly indicated the status of each occupation in the grand scheme of Pittsburgh labor. Second, Butler alluded to physical obstacles related to work in mechanized industry, specifically its need for "nervous speed." Interpreting the pace and monotony of industrial work as a strain that only a certain type of woman could withstand, Butler argued that Americans' "success" in industrial employment was a Pyrrhic victory indeed. Finally, the work itself was designed to be as demanding on the worker as possible ("*unnecessarily* degrading") and thus stunted women's ability to reproduce in such a way as to benefit industrial society.[4]

The critique of female industrial employment in Pittsburgh found in *Women and the Trades* reiterated the survey staff's treatment of recent immigrants, especially in terms of the threat they represented to native-born or "old stock" workingmen. Paul Kellogg introduced Butler's volume with a synopsis of the ways in which Pittsburgh's working women "complicate[d] every industrial question." Kellogg described industrial payrolls as ledgers on which "the names of girls and immigrant women are entered beside those of boys and men, or are crowding them out entirely." Reviews of women's labor at the turn of the century often blamed greedy families that selfishly sent their daughters out to work. Clara E. Laughlin, for example, a Chicago-based reformer devoted to the protection and limitation of women's work in the 1910s, criticized a man who expected his daughter to go to work at sixteen because he had "been investing, as it were, in a family . . . and hoped to realize on his invest-ment." Although Butler expressed sympathy with Pittsburgh's working families, she noted that "these newcomers, sometimes by sheer physical strength, sometimes by personal indifference and a low standard, com-pete . . . on the basis of lower wages for men's work which otherwise would never have been given to girls to do." It was not coincidental that Kellogg's researchers classified both women in general and immigrant men in particular as newcomers; implicit in their designs for systems and new management techniques was a nostalgic vision of simpler times before "industrial questions" had become "complicated." Boosters and reformers shared this general orientation, both claiming the male work-ing body as the site for representing the city.[5]

It is not surprising, then, that working women did not figure promi-nently in civic parades and murals of heavy industry. What is less ob-vious, however, is why the woman at work was not useful to the survey's researchers in their critique of the workplace (as opposed to a critique of industrial society writ large). The survey's discussion of women margin-alized them as both economic agents and spectacular performers. What one reformer noted as "the constant reference to women as a 'cheap grade' of labor" became Butler's primary analytical frame in *Women and the Trades:* women undercut the bargaining power of male workers and drove wages down to crisis levels. Yet Butler's innovation was to take the analysis further, subdividing the female working population in order to detail the process through which women became this "cheap grade." The keys to this transformation were the ethnic stratification and mechanization of work tasks, trends that affected men and women equally. Women's daily tasks were just as mundane and subdivided as men's under a mechanical production regime, so Butler returned to the contention that women were incompatible with the industrial workplace. The survey staff drew on tales of women injured or worn down on the job to show the necessity for a family wage, the economic tool by which women would remain out of factories and sweatshops. Likewise, Kellogg's writers used statistical summaries of women in the workforce to suggest the dangers faced by children born into homes with enervated mothers and little supervision. Their reluctance to use either device as a means of assessing work itself signified their broader concern with production removed from the home. The problem was not that work was too hard for women, but that women had "followed" it even when it led them to economic and moral dead ends.[6]

"SOMETHING NEAR THE SOIL"
THE ETHNIC STRATIFICATION OF WORK

Massive immigration at the turn of the century turned the city's residential patterns into a subject of frequent comment and worry. Pittsburgh's topography affected neighborhood formation just as it channeled industrial growth along the area's rivers and creeks. As employers organized the workforce according to nationality, Pittsburghers of the working class lived in enclaves determined by a confluence of such factors as proximity to the workplace, ethnic composition, and terrain. The spatial layout of Pittsburgh's neighborhoods alarmed Butler:

> On the South Side are numbers of Polish families; but across the river, at the
> north of Pittsburgh, the working districts are harder to characterize. Large
> sections of the town are filling up with Slavic people. Foreign districts are
> thus gradually set off chaotically, with the streets of Americans straggling
> along the edge of them. These English-speaking families are often those who
> by reason of poor physique, or lack of ambition, or the cumulative effect of
> bad environment, have been left behind when their neighbors have climbed

away from what was not then a slum. . . . The majority are of low grade, physically, mentally, industrially; the home environment has clamped within narrow limits the developing faculties of the child.[7]

Here, Butler echoed Jacob Riis's ethnic mapping of New York in 1890. Whereas Riis used such terms as "crazy-quilt," "black mark," and "dirty stain" to depict the complexity of the urban population and the emergence of ethnic enclaves, Butler focused on the residential disorder that accompanied recent immigration. This translated for the researcher as a model of the inefficient and exploitative workplace. Particular neighborhoods exhibited a heterogeneous mixture of ethnicities, yet the work crews deployed in individual departments throughout the city were, by contrast, strictly divided along lines of national origin. In the workshops where women made clothing, Butler concluded that the "type" was initially "fundamentally good" with regard to physical stamina and ability. The starting point for female employees who were "sifted out for speed and endurance" was a life outside the workroom "in part determined by nationality." The sifting process within the industrial workplace—a combination of managerial selection and employee turnover—corresponded to the "sorting out" that occurred in many industrialized urban areas with large populations of unskilled workers. What mattered to Butler was that the internal sifting relied primarily on ethnically based perceptions of physical ability. Herein lay the root of the problem of the working woman.[8]

A focus on the physical demands and effects of work infused Butler's presentation. To depict the workforce of the mattress and awning industries, for example, she turned to the physiques required of the work, "heavy work" that attracted "a lower grade of worker—the woman of coarser physique, less industrial stability, and a lower wage-value." Most female industrial workers in Pittsburgh did not work in steel, glass, or coal. Even in the glass industry, the leading employer of women among the three, women worked jobs that writers consistently marginalized as "ancillary." Given the gender stratification of the workplace, Butler's work on female employees delved into industries that rarely served as civic symbols. It is noteworthy that she wrote a separate volume within the survey series, one demarcated along gender lines more than by the specific occupations covered or the recommendations offered. Butler studied areas that Fitch and Eastman could not because her narrative was less about industry's effects on women than about why women were in industry to begin with. Scenes of physical difficulty still featured prominently in *Women and the Trades;* Butler shared her fellow researchers' fervor for professional data collection as a revelatory act. Her claim to expertise was her ability to forge causal links between individual cases of injury or exhaustion and reproductive profiles of Pittsburgh's "chaotic" neighborhoods.[9]

The work of ironing in the garment industry, Butler explained, required "a continuous muscular exertion." Foremen hired only women who weighed 180 pounds or more, justifying their selectivity as a matter of economics—women without the necessary bulk tended to perform poorly or weaken quickly. The sheer size of such women complemented their "stolid physical poise" that foremen could not harness and drive at the speed of Anglo-American women. Butler blamed Slavic women for accepting "positions that girls of other races regard[ed] as socially inferior." The phrase "socially inferior" connected the variety of jobs within the workplace and the world beyond the factory gates. Jobs that were *socially* inferior were not just physically disagreeable, but corrosive to one's life and livelihood. When the damage was done—when the work resulted in a "coarsening of fibre and a final break in strength"—immigrant women moved to occupations that were even lower in wage and appeal. This "irresponsibility," as Butler viewed it, was less working women's economic strategy than an instinct cultivated through generations of foreign revolutions and struggle. Immigrant women were mercenaries on the job market.[10]

Butler categorized women within the larger heading of "Slavic girls" by size and appearance. She distinguished between the typical woman engaged in the relatively light yet monotonous work of canning food and the one working in the final stages of tin sheet production. The former, "the child of the city," was smaller in stature and able to move quickly. The latter was rural, "rough-skinned" peasant stock, "the life of whose parents has been close to earth." These were the women with raw muscular strength, lumbering movements, and a "readiness to do disagreeable things." Further inspection of the metals industries uncovered the types of women who produced the cores used in casting metals, both "Polish girls, round featured, with high foreheads and fair hair" and "peasant women of the Hungarian type, strong and mature." The gulf between northern and southern Europe produced Poles (with their "delicacy of feature" and "slenderness of build") and Slavs (with their "large features, eyes wide apart, coarse hands and muscular arms"). Butler focused most on the second group as a troubling spectacle of muscle and swarthiness, figures who embodied "the activities of smoking ovens, boiling crucibles and iron soft with fierce heat." These women were as marked by their work as Joseph Stella's male workers. Yet their grimy, dull appearance did not translate into the inspiration of toil. Their clothing, "stained brown from the oil of the machine," and their bodies, "bound with dirty rags," spoke only of ruin. These were broken women, soiled by their work yet also built for it. This was, after all, what they had been conditioned to do for a living.[11]

The "violence" required to sort six-pound plates of steel for ten hours each day demanded, according to Butler, "all the strength of even the earth-toughened peasant women who have followed their husbands from Poland to the mill country in America." The notion of particular women being "earth-toughened" and others being city-bred formed the core of ethnic stratification. Employers saved work that involved heavy lifting, extreme temperatures, and an ability to withstand constant moisture for women of those ethnic groups with the most prominent agricultural background. In a local laundry workshop, a manager informed Butler, "No American can stand this. We have to use Hungarians or other foreigners. It seems to be unhealthful, but I don't know. The girls don't stay long enough for us to tell." After enough experience with employees of various ethnicities, Pittsburgh's employers interpreted capability not as individual strength and stamina, but as a group characteristic. The most favored characteristics were docility and endurance. An employer in the food industry informed Butler that Poles, Hungarians, and Croatians with "a dull patient look" made the best workers because of their ability to "keep at it just like horses." Thus, women who exhibited a "peasant look about their faces, a something near the soil and the growing of dark leaves" testified to their group's ability to endure hard work.[12]

And hard work it was. From the frequent fainting spells that struck women who polished glass to the "steamy or gaseous atmosphere in laundries" that made breathing difficult, the physical conditions of Pittsburgh's workplaces distressed even the most robust employees. At a convention of the National Women's Trade Union League (NWTUL), a representative described the plight of laundry workers: "They are standing ten, twelve, fourteen, and seventeen hours a day in intense heat, breathing air laden with particles of soda, ammonia, and other chemicals. Is it any wonder that these workers become physical wrecks in a very short time, just because you and I never count the costs?" The survey team believed that its task was to count these costs and present the tabulations to the public. In addition to tallying and packaging, Butler presented an interpretation of these physical wrecks that avoided sentimental elaborations of personal tragedy. Instead, she made misfortune *productive* by compiling enough of it to establish industrial work as an unfit pursuit for those with child-rearing duties.[13]

The survey writers inadvertently distanced readers from immigrant working women by portraying them as inscrutable. Butler admitted that the "inability to share the sensations of a foreigner" was a key to the problem of the working poor. This inability manifested itself as an obsession with the color of faces, the softness of hands, the contours of limbs, and the shapes of backs. Laughlin used a narrative strategy in *The Work-A-Day Girl* that spoke to this inability to get beneath immigrants' surface. Laughlin's chapter on prostitution as the scourge of working women presented a legal scene centered on the visual disparity between Americans and immigrants. As two American parents and a foreign-born mother stood side by side in a courtroom waiting to institutionalize their daughters in order to save them from prostitution, the narrator's gaze focused on the exotic and unappealing features of the immigrant. Although Laughlin described the native-born couple briefly as "well-educated, well mannered, well dressed," she gave the foreign-born woman much more than a cursory glance: "The mother was a beak-faced, thin woman, with a curiously crooked, thin-lipped mouth, and small, bead-like eyes. Her head was wrapped in a dirty veil that had once been white. Her hands, gripping the rail beside those of the other mother, were toil-roughened and looked as if they had not been washed in a week. . . . This woman's sagging, dragging clothes exhibited not one last, lingering trace of that feminine pride of appearance which dies so late and so hard; they covered her nakedness and therewith they served their sole purpose."[14]

Butler similarly presented working-class immigrant women after years of manual labor as observable but ultimately unknowable. Just as their work appeared "rough and unpleasant," so, too, did they. Contrast that image with those native-born "girls of good appearance" whom Butler also found in Pittsburgh. That local writers found Anglo-American women to be more aesthetically pleasing is perhaps no surprise. Editors in Pittsburgh occasionally used visions of beautiful young women as a means of prettifying the dismal winter cityscape or of defending attacks on the local population as parochial. They also pressed the argument that attractive features should, in effect, disqualify women from industrial work—that pretty women were wasted in lives of behind-the-scenes wage earning. The *Bulletin* offered this sarcastic warning about the fate of an attractive female workforce: "There are more pretty girls in the world than ever before, perhaps because they know how to dress becomingly, but at all events, there is no room for the ugly girls. Factory-owners and school boards ought to bare [*sic*] in mind this fact. A body of ugly teachers would be safely permanent." The *Bulletin* also editorialized that the "best type of the American girl [was] beautiful and good and waiting to be admired of all men." The "best type[s]" would not be found in industrial work. Candy making, for example, was monopolized by native-born women whom Butler classified as "girls of good appearance, of quiet ways, usually of good physical development." Yet manufacturing confections involved excessive heat and constant contact with raw materials, conditions that could render workers unacceptable for beauty pageants. The historian S. J. Kleinberg has noted that "appearance, the ability to speak English, and a reasonable level of education" were crucial for women looking for jobs in the city's retail and clerical fields. These characteristics applied as well to women in search of manual jobs in manufacturing. Thus women who looked the part of an "American girl" were more likely to find work in service industries or performing manual tasks requiring speed.[15]

"THIN AND NERVOUS"

THE MECHANICALIZATION OF WORKERS

The heaviest of women's work in Pittsburgh required physical strength that only a few could manage for long. Butler referred to the "strong-armed women who fashion sand cores in foundries" as aberrations—women who brought muscle rather than speed to the labor market. More typical were frail but fast workers who suffered greatly as they adapted themselves to industrial demands. This "human machinery, more delicate, more sensitive, of finer metal" than Pittsburgh manufacturing devices, had to be toughened for quick and monotonous daily work over weeks or months. Butler divided speed (or "nervous") workers from strength workers according to what they offered employers. The speed women were as lamentable as the strength women, but here the problem centered on the power of machinery to mold workers into frenetic figures.[16]

Women and the Trades argued that particular women accepted unpleasant tasks like stripping tobacco in the cigar industry because it was the only work available to them. They also arrived there because of their physical inadequacy in other realms of industry. Butler explained that some were "a little stupid, a little inefficient" or possessed "a defect of sight" or a "slightly deformed body," precluding them from employment in jobs that required speed and coordination rather than muscular strength. Women who were "physically below the standard strength that keeps pace with a machine" tended to be east and south Europeans or native-born workers who had suffered injury. The speed workers, on the other hand, those forced to work up to the pace of machinery, tended to be native-born or from western and northern Europe. Butler noted that the physical standard necessary to cope with jobs in coil winding, cracker making, and canning was a combination of dexterity, speed, and the ability to reproduce small movements thousands of times a day.[17]

Seemingly oblivious to the ethnic and spatial arrangements of modern industry, national experts in work and health counseled women to choose the career path that maximized natural rhythms and movements. Anna Galbraith of the Neurological Department at the New York Orthopedic Hospital encouraged women to "choose some active occupation that will call you out of doors as much as possible" as a way to develop healthy bodies. Such advice ignored the constraints within which most working women found themselves. Active occupations abounded in Pittsburgh, but the type of activity common to jobs not requiring heavy lifting alarmed the survey team. "Nervous work" demanded that women be taught how to adapt to the appliances of modern industry, a training period which Kellogg described as "the articulation of this group of human beings to the processes, buildings, tools, wages, hours and health environment of modern industrial plants." This articulation—a human/machine coupling that served as a "compensatory action" to counteract bodily fatigue—brought women to the brink of physical collapse, according to *Women and the Trades*. Despite Galbraith's dream of vigorous outdoor work, speed women in Pittsburgh stayed inside with the machines.[18]

Women in the metal trades, according to Butler, tended devices that they did not "control or understand." An adjustment process was necessary, one that struck Butler not as an education or a cultivation but as a horrific submission to a mechanical regime. New workers took what they could get as the "industrially unadjusted," yet becoming adjusted was not necessarily an improvement. The advantages of adjusting in order to secure a higher status position were solely economic, not physical. The training process relied upon the worker's body becoming accustomed to the rigors of work, yet it also blunted her reactions and senses. In the cracker industry, Butler noted that once workers were assigned to a particular department, they could expect to work the same job for the rest of their tenure. This was a case not of workers being provided with a trade of their own, but of efficiency standards demanding "physical and mental concentration on doing one thing, the repetition of one operation a thousand times in a day, ten thousand times in a week, and that over and over again from month to month." Even if a new employee was able to "do the thing as she is told" after an hour of training, Butler estimated that cracker making required at least a month's practice to match the pace of the "experienced girl." Muscles had to be trained to perform rapidly, skin needed time to adjust to temperatures, and eyes slowly learned to follow the movements of swiftly moving chains and conveyors. When the NWTUL complained in 1909 that industrial employers were adept at "improving machinery—not eyes!" it was echoing Butler's critique of nervous work as something that women's bodies simply could not handle, even if workers learned to adapt temporarily to the demands of the job.[19]

Butler used machine imagery to describe many of the women she found in tasks requiring mechanical paces. Moving from the outside of a garment factory to the murky interior, Butler set a scene of increasing rigidity: "Outside are brick walls. Inside are two double rows of tense women, facing each other, and bending forward over their machines with eyes fixed on the glint and flash of the needle and the dark seam of the cloth. No girl who is incapable of concentration can stay in a garment factory." Here, women became stiff and agitated through the buildup of pressure on the job. The mechanized environment of "unreality and remoteness" in which many women spent their days contributed to a further distancing of women from their inherent human qualities. Instead, they turned into machinelike drones. Butler criticized the "blind haste" that gave workers in the food industry no time "to look up or away" and drove the "nerves of the workers from early morning until night." In the factories where women made metal coils, the investigator discovered a "ceaseless whirr of a thousand wheels," a cacophony within which "girls' arms keep pace with the power." For Butler, women working in the food industry served merely "as an extra arm of the machine."[20]

Ethnic stratification and mechanization of work went hand in hand. Galbraith directed Anglo-American women to study their "slow-plodding, sturdy-bodied European cousins" in order to learn techniques of working slowly but methodically. Galbraith declared that no one could replicate the working pace of "the ambitious American." Employers' and reformers' underlying belief that native-born women were more ambitious in their industrial labor than foreign-born women led to the shared assumption that American women were willing to attempt the "speed mania" that Slavic women rejected. "American girls are preferred," wrote Butler, "because they have nervous strength that can be lifted to a high pitch of speed." Ambition was to be admired as a prerequisite for economic success in industrial labor, but it was also to be condemned, given its counterproductive tendency to result in physical ruin. While accepting the experts' claims that the ideal specimen of woman was engaged in "some definite work" that resulted in ambition and personal pleasure, it was difficult for the Progressive observer to see much good coming from workshops and factories.[21]

When, at the end of the day, coil makers appeared "pale and a little tired" as they walked home, Butler glimpsed lifelong physical debilities resulting from the daily routine of working with swiftly spinning wires. Butler highlighted the "droop of the shoulders" and the "lines about the mouth" as clear markers of bodies influenced directly by the posture required of machine tenders. Stooped backs, shaking hands, wandering eyes, and facial wrinkles were the principal physical criteria in Butler's overall assessment of speed workers as "thin and nervous." This diagnosis matched the observations of work scientists in Europe who studied the first generation of female telephone exchange workers. As the historian Laura Levine Frader has explained about French women in swift mechanical trades in the early twentieth century, their ability to move quickly and coordinate their movements ultimately brought on physical impairment. Doctors reported on *nervose de la téléphoniste*, "a catch-all term for the nervous exhaustion and multiple auditory and psychological problems operators experienced." American labor reformers emphasized "strain on the nervous system" as a facet of work requiring speed or involving the constant noise of machinery. When the National Consumers' League (NCL) declared in 1915 that women's industrial work was performed more often than not in environments that were "nerve wracking and deafening," the organization meant it quite literally.[22]

Butler used the concept of nervous work to establish further that industrial employment was inherently unsuitable for women. The survey staff urged employers to guard against deplorable, traumatic accidents by changing the physical interaction between men and machines. They urged women to guard against assaults on their "nervous" systems by not allowing themselves to be used in occupations that could only damage them. Machinery in Pittsburgh coil factories produced vibrations and jolts that seemed to punish workers incessantly. Butler chronicled the intensity of mechanical work, writing that the "power action" of machinery was enough to force women to move with it, swaying back and forth while being "forced to exert considerable physical strength to keep the tape in place." After several years of such labor, women became "white and tired and drawn of face." The paleness of women involved in speed work was a mixed blessing, representing an ethnic identity that won them favorable positions but eventually signaling the strain of nerves and muscles. Labor activists agreed that it was the need to conform to mechanical paces while also mastering the levers, conveyor belts, chains, and switches that made it seem "as if the machine were running away from you, and your effort to control it makes your whole body ache."[23]

A particular worker in a cracker factory struck Butler as the epitome of how work could effect decay and strain: "I noticed especially one small girl with flushed cheeks and white lips who was folding the ends of soda cracker boxes and putting on each end a red stamp ... Her teeth were set, and her breath came hard, like that of an overspent runner at the end of a race; yet it was only ten o'clock in the morning. Her arms moved irregularly, jerkily, as if she were spurring her nervous energy to its limit." This shell of a girl was but one of thousands of victims of processes that tended to "handicap heavily the development of both body and mind." According to the labor activist Rheta Childe Dorr, women were ill prepared physically to handle the strains of modern industry, possessing "lesser power" than men and a "heightened susceptibility" to harmful conditions. Supporting such claims, the labor reformer Louis Brandeis synthesized decades of scientific study of women at work in defense of Oregon's ten-hour workday in 1908. In 1875 the Massachusetts Bureau of Labor Statistics quoted a "lady operator" who admitted that women "must have vacations, and they break down in health rapidly." In 1888 the Maine Bureau of Industrial and Labor Statistics referred to medical evidence that "woman is badly constructed for the purposes of standing eight or ten hours upon her feet" owing to "the peculiar construction of the knee," "the shallowness of the pelvis," and "the delicate nature of the foot." Four years later, the same bureau reported that "constant nervous tension from continued exertion in a modern factory or workshop, for a period of ten hours, [was] a severe strain upon the physical system." In 1901 the U.S. Industrial Commission concluded that a "long workday with the machine, especially where work is greatly specialized, in many cases reduces the grade of intelligence. . . . Long workdays under such conditions tend to inertia and dissipation when the day's work is done."[24]

The NCL joined Butler in attempting to represent the damage done to women's bodies. The league produced a series of equations to reveal the calculations that affected workers' lives most:

LONG HOURS = OVERWORK

OVERWORK = FATIGUE POISON

LOW WAGES = POOR FOOD

OVERWORK +

FATIGUE POISON +

POOR FOOD =

DISEASE AND DEATH

The signs of overwork were not just those compiled by physicians— "sleepless nights, ringing in the ears, heart palpitations, frequent urination, feverish anxiety"—but also disease and death. Late nineteenth-century doctors' assertion of a "physical bank account" to which working women added and subtracted "physiological capital" posited that physical ruin could be reckoned like financial debt. Galbraith foresaw only pathetic futures for the working woman who withdrew more than she deposited: "She may continue to exist bedridden for many years, or perhaps just be able to drag around, or her last years may be spent in an insane asylum." None of these outcomes promised a healthy civic life.[25]

THE POINT OF DIMINISHING RETURNS
SOCIAL RAMIFICATIONS

When social scientists and reformers surveyed industrial society in the United States in the first years of the twentieth century they found disturbing generational trends at work. Samuel Smith, a professor of sociology at the University of Minnesota, announced in 1912 that "the pinched and pale-faced boy in the arms of a ragged woman are the new Madonna and Child of our generation." The icons of urban life had become emblems of a type of poverty that centered on the relationship between one generation and the next. Specifically, the working-class Madonna and Child image underscored concern about women's physical ability to produce children who would be healthy enough to survive and fit enough to contribute to their own maintenance. Butler's final blow to working women's public legitimacy in Pittsburgh between 1900 and 1915 was her argument that their status as workers robbed them of their social function as mothers. In a confluence of discussions about work, exercise, prostitution, venereal disease, and birthrates, observers in Pittsburgh argued that working women doomed the future city.[26]

The historian Allison Hepler has noted that campaigns for improved working lives for women "took place within the context of women's social roles—their ability to maintain family, household, and community relations." Those interested in this topic ("workers, reformers, and factory inspectors") posited "a relationship between factory conditions and female reproductive problems." No wonder, then, that prostitution appeared so frequently in social scientists' reviews of working-class wages. Mayor William Magee convened a Morals Efficiency Commission in 1913 to measure the effects of vice in the Steel City. The commission's report declared that the local prostitution industry was "a supply of human flesh" brought to market by "procurers and white-slavers," much in the same way that raw materials arrived in the city to serve the needs of manufacturers. The commission suggested that industrial establishments relying upon women for cheap labor were also in the business of exploiting human flesh. The commission concluded that Pittsburgh was home to "the growth of the social evil, of divorce, and of race suicide," in addition to "venereal disease, insanity, graft, and crime." The report's hyperbole aided its mission; Magee charged his commission with the task of exposure, a reverse-muckraking exercise whose revelations he could then translate into feasible reform goals. Such exposure of the plight of working women brought the physical dangers of work alongside the seemingly obvious moral dangers.[27]

Deterioration at work translated into an economic problem for working women—women who were working in the first place, Butler assumed, because their income was essential to the survival of a family. In the cigar industry, where Butler found the quick work "tense and exhausting," a manager admitted that no workers could maintain the necessary pace for more than six years. Most cigar employers reckoned that "except for girls of the most robust physique, the tension seldom can be maintained." Following her pattern of highlighting individuals as illustrative cases, Butler presented a biographical sketch of the twenty-one-year-old tobacco stripper Sarah Cohen: "I should have thought her a woman of thirty-five. The first break in her strength came from typhoid, four years ago, but she never has been able to regain the speed which she had at sixteen. With overtime rolling, she was able at one time to earn $12 a week. She has to-day dropped behind into the stripping room of an alley sweatshop where she cannot finish in a day over fourteen pounds, at $.05 a pound. This means an income of $4.20 a week." Cohen's meager pay meant that even less enticing occupations awaited her in the streets and boardinghouses of Pittsburgh. Butler's brief outline—as a literary connection between physical strength, declining income, and what came after—was consonant with the survey's broader method of conflating bodies, time, and dollar amounts. Several years later, the activist Annie MacLean stated the case plainly: "There is always social wastage in overwork, and there is always the hideous haven of prostitution menacing girls who are underpaid." The story of Sarah Cohen suggested the same thing by inviting the reader to join the author as she looked at an aged figure that could no longer support itself industrially.[28]

Beyond the cigar industry, other workers were also limited by the number of years for which they could be physically productive on the job. Butler estimated that a woman could make awnings and tarps for a maximum of three or four years, while mattress manufacturing offered a decade of employment before physical disability hampered productivity. The "nervous loss" of a woman who could no longer maintain a swift pace was troubling because it represented a social burden. She and her children would become financial costs to state and local governments charged with taking care of the poor. Butler encapsulated the long-term dilemma for working women and the cities in which they lived: "Most of the girls marry at twenty or twenty-one, just at the time when their speed breaks. Some of the cost is borne by the homes into which they go. This social waste, more serious by far than the destruction of the individual, we have not yet the means of estimating. Those who know these factory workers intimately know only that in case after case the industry is taking undeveloped girls, lifting their speed to its highest pitch, and wearing them out. They know, too, after the gap of a few years, their unfit homes and undervitalized children." Butler focused on the next generation's workforce, "undervitalized" by the strains of its mothers, to accentuate an equation that social reformers could actually solve.[29]

Her argument built upon scattered findings from across the United States by professionals charged with the same task of data collection. Just as they had produced evidence of the tendency of industrial work to harm women's bodies, state labor bureaus and federal investigative bodies claimed a strong link between such injuries and women's reproductive capabilities. The 1884 annual report by the Maine Bureau of Industrial and Labor Statistics conveyed concern about "a predisposition to pelvic disease among the female factory operatives, producing difficulty in parturition." In 1896 the secretary of the Maryland Bureau of Industrial Statistics presented the state's working women as "future wives and mothers" who were destroying their bodies through work. The implication was clear: working in an industrial occupation was a choice for which "future generations [would] answer." After the turn of the century, the U.S. Industrial Commission concluded that the lack of protective legislation for female employees had "weakened the physical and moral strength of the new generation of working people." In 1902 the Nebraska Bureau of Labor and Industrial Statistics declared that "certain kinds of work . . . render [women] incapable of bearing their share of the burdens of the family and the home." This vague language presumably referred to conception, childbirth, child rearing, and domestic work. Such was the array of functions as wives and mothers expected of women that it is no wonder the Supreme Court ruled in early 1908 that "the physical well-being of woman becomes an object of public interest and care in order to preserve the strength and vigor of the race."[30]

Most often, Butler encouraged drastic curtailment of women's work as a remedy to such threats. At the same time, however, she argued that women could offset the effects of the workday through a physical culture regimen of muscular development and fortification. This proposal reiterated journalists' appeals that women, especially women who did not work for wages, engage in playful outdoor pastimes that were also character building. In 1905 the editors of the *Bulletin* observed that middle-class women throughout the city aspired to be "open-air, oxygen-loving girl[s]" who combined traditional femininity with physical activity. "This is the age of feminine muscle and of lung cultivation," declared the *Bulletin*, a time for "swimming, boating, bathing, walking, golfing, tennis-playing, riding, and camping out." Like most bourgeois trappings, however, the world of leisurely afternoons in the park or boating excursions was inaccessible to tobacco strippers and mattress makers. As she toured the city over successive evenings, Butler found enervated and idling young women whose "lack of vitality [and] animal energy" kept them from participating in beneficial recreation after work. Even if they had wanted to be active, their options in a city devoted to labor were "roller-skating rinks, picture shows and dance halls," all, in Butler's opinion, less than adequate because they promoted physical promiscuity and indolence. Butler encouraged playground associations in the area to organize gymnastic training, dance lessons, and athletic games to help working women "counteract the effects of long sitting or standing in one position."[31]

Success or failure in bringing working women into physical health depended, according to Butler, "on the choice of the working women and the character of their industrial life, and in part on the social foresight of the community." Social workers designed summer settlement houses outside the city to offer working women an environmental break that could begin the process of physical healing. The *Bulletin* noted that one of these establishments, Lillian Home, was filled in the summer of 1904 with "mothers and children taken from the crowded sections of the city." Lillian Home offered a respite that was meant to recharge working women physically, if temporarily. "Tired mothers, in many cases the bread winners for their families," noted the *Bulletin* editors, "returned to take up their work with new strength and courage. To them the two weeks of absolute rest meant much." Butler's concern for the suffering children of Pittsburgh's working women also fit squarely in the context of the "social hygiene" movement that became quite vocal in American cities after 1900. The movement gained national publicity in the 1910s with its focus on prostitution, although leaders of groups like the American Social Hygiene Association positioned themselves as activists with multiple concerns. The association defined its field as an inclusive one, "covering activities of which the campaigns against venereal diseases and prostitution are only a part, but necessarily at the present time the more generally recognized part." Its goal was to "protect the family as a social institution and secure to the individuals of each generation a rational sex life." By focusing on the family as a threatened unit, social hygiene reformers linked men's inability to support their wives and children economically to the inferior physical condition of working-class youth. If women were forced to work outside the home to supplement the family income, reformers warned, it was only a matter of time before their low wages and exhausting labor pushed them into the life of the prostitute. Prostitution led to venereal disease, which compromised the health of the offspring.[32]

By the time the NCL launched a massive campaign for the reduction of women's hours in the 1910s, the protection of the home was front and center in their rhetorical assault. The league created an exhibit for the Panama Pacific Exposition in San Francisco that stressed working women's fatigue and its relationship to their families' well-being. A threefold emphasis on damaging body posture, nervous exhaustion, and neglected children pervaded their visual materials. The exhibit proclaimed,

FOR LOW WAGES. Some sit all day in a stooping position.
FOR LOW WAGES. Some are speeded by machines.
FOR LOW WAGES. Some sacrifice home and children.

When Magee's Morals Efficiency Commission stressed in 1913 that "family life and home joys [were] the preventives of illicit passion and roving pleasure," it made the case that only a good home life—especially at night—could keep young women from being drawn into the underworld of prostitution. Night work struck NCL leaders as a form of torture that affected more than the workers themselves. The effects of night work on women amounted to a list of losses: "loss of sunlight . . . loss of normal sleep . . . loss of home life . . . loss of social life and recreation." The NCL's vocabulary approximated Butler's in viewing women's work as a wasteful system that had to be reengineered. Two of the most tangible effects of labor, according to the league, were "neglected children" and "premature old age." Working women's labor after dark placed them in the company of a host of other city dwellers who took part in increasingly active nighttime industries. They became part of a nocturnal population, as did their children if they were able to escape from the home. The historian Peter Baldwin has argued that the modern urban night represented a "liminal new world in which conflicting moral values mingled uneasily," a time when the work ethic and the profit motive flirted dangerously with sensational aspects of the urban netherworld. The NCL created the figure of the "Mother Nightworker" to explain various problems in American cities, from bowlegged children and juvenile delinquency to dramatic differences in regional birthrates. The league noted that the "welfare of the nation depends upon the health of its mothers."[33]

The anecdotes, quantifications, and scenes that Butler assembled spoke to the Progressive project of framing women's civic burdens as future-looking. Using the pseudonym Gordon Hart, the writer Sophia Margaretta Hensley proposed in 1911 a measurement of women's contributions to the modern world: "Upon her rests the inalienable responsibility of motherhood; her life should be shaped, her thoughts held in check, her physical needs supplied, her soul developed in the light of this one great fact.... To be great for the sake of womanhood and through womanhood, to be great because only a great woman can give to the world great sons, to be great because of the recognition of the inherent godliness of the individual—this is the true ambition of woman." MacLean noted that of all the working women in industrial cities, "the overwhelming majority are young, and are destined to be the mothers of the next generation of workers." Like Hensley's fear (evident in the question, "What kind of bodies are we preparing for the next generation?"), Butler's concern for Pittsburgh's women was fed by the neo-Lamarckian belief that children could inherit physical and mental characteristics that mothers acquired over their lifetimes. As Hepler has noted, these traits could be positive or negative, but reformers in industrial cities pointed out time and again that female workers risked transmitting to their sons and daughters the debilities caused by their dangerous workplaces. Butler demonstrated alarming links between occupations and families to convince Pittsburgh's reform community that the "evils" of hard work had begun to "manifest themselves in concrete physical results," suggesting that the city's women had reached the "point of diminishing returns."[34]

CONCLUSION

The problem of industrial women, like that of mechanicalized working men, was larger than the individual worker or firm; as Kellogg noted, "The conditions and tendencies affecting their employment cannot adequately be dealt with apart from the general problems of the community." Like Fitch and Eastman in their treatment of male workers, Butler adopted Kellogg's belief that problems in industrial life were comprehensive; charting the connections between seemingly unrelated phenomena, though difficult, was crucial to making business and government efficient and to legitimizing the privileged position of social researchers in the process of setting policy. This assumption was not unique to the staff of the Pittsburgh Survey but paralleled the standard Progressive pronouncement on social engineering in general and legislation regarding working women in particular. Sophonisba Breckinridge of the Chicago School of Civics and Philanthropy noted in 1909 that the length of the working day, the issue of night work, the "provision of certain decencies in working conditions, the relation of marriage to work, [and] the relation of work of mothers to the life of children" were "questions of vital concern to the community." The stakes were incredibly high, as critics warned that women's "invasion of the fields of work outside the home" could only lead to a "marked decline in fecundity." Reformers fighting for improvements in women's workdays presented a bleak picture in which the "fierce struggle to make a living" resulted in the weakest members of the workforce becoming a "serious burden to society."[35]

MacLean wrote in 1916 that American society could not pay the bill for the damage done to women when "reduced to economic terms." She implied that reducing human misery and waste to financial calculations was unseemly yet essential to reformers' goal of improving the state of the American poor. Indeed, this type of translation from the physical to the economic and social served as the primary lens through which Butler viewed Pittsburgh's working women. Thirty-five years later, the writer Henry Miller traveled through Pittsburgh on a transcontinental trip and described it as the "crucible where all values are reduced to slag." Miller's dreadful memories of the cold heart of heavy manufacturing would have fit quite well in *Women and the Trades*. The terms may have changed, but the authors' horror at employers' ability to manipulate laborers remained constant. Butler's presentation also echoed reporters' visual descriptions of Homestead workers during the violence of July 1892. Her tendency to describe immigrant working women as dark and hulking produced a different effect than the earlier coverage, however. Butler consistently moved from the individual to the abstract population group; she extrapolated from viewing bodies to calculating broad economic conditions without imagining a physical manifestation of the immigrant horde. Observers in Homestead depicted the immigrant mass as a literal entity that moved through the streets to impose its will on civic life. Butler's horde was, in some sense, working women as a whole—*they* invaded the workplace, degraded the labor market, and made the future population suffer. Writers on the scene in 1892 kept mechanization and ethnic stratification within the workplace invisible because they were less interested in explaining how immigrants had come to Homestead than in documenting the threat they now posed to public order. Butler stressed the two developments as instruments for understanding employers' manipulation of women. Experts should still read bodies as a means of defining the problem, she argued, but the problems of male and female work in Pittsburgh were fundamentally different.[36]

In Butler's appraisal, the products resulting from manufacturers' economic experiments were weak mothers who raised weak children. The Charities Publication Committee published her research just as reform journals began stressing "disquieting evidence . . . of the decline of the North-of-Europe stock" in the United States. Laughlin found a similar trend in Chicago among working-class immigrants. She joined Butler in recasting the family itself as a factory: "Homes now have but one product: citizens! And every year, the State has to take more and more spoiled and spoiling products out of slipshod, ignorant, ill-governed homes, and try to repair or reform them in citizenship factories: industrial and parental schools, asylums, refuges, and prisons." Laughlin called upon social workers to confront those women who were "unloading spoiled human product on the nation." Butler's 1909 volume of the Pittsburgh Survey presented a Progressive exposé in which the decay of family life was rooted in women's inability to measure up physically to the demands of the modern workplace. Although it would have been an afterthought at best for the survey staff, her vivid descriptions of women's work confirmed the worst assumptions that barred women from contending with men for honors in civic spectacles. More relevant to the discourse on the nature of work in Pittsburgh at the turn of the century were her conclusions about what she recorded inside mills and factories. Simply put, Butler arranged her findings to advocate the restriction of women's presence in the industrial workplace. Her emphasis on the "nervous energy" of working women, meanwhile, reinforced prevailing notions of gender difference as manifested in physical rhythms and abilities. Both city boosters and social reformers created the rhetorical power of the male working body in part through a concerted exclusion of women. Critics' selective use of female imagery was an attempt to refocus the debate away from the heroic and toward the vulnerable. As one historian has explained it, the survey writers' claims to clinical detachment were "best served by picturing the local industrial population as helpless victims in need of expert political intervention." Heroes did not require rescue. The vulnerable did, and their salvation could not be found in the workplace.[37]

6

HIDING AND

DISPLAYING THE BROKEN BODY

✴   Paul Kellogg wrote in his introduction to Crystal Eastman's volume
of the Pittsburgh Survey about the chaotic, insufficient system designed
to deal with the effects of industrial accidents in the United States. In
terms of prevention, compensation, and medical care, workers in American industries suffered severe neglect. Kellogg noted that immigrants
came "from a region of law and order to a region of law-made anarchy
so far as the hazards of industry are concerned." The American system's
anarchy resulted in injured men, unemployed, penniless, and missing
the strength or body parts necessary for heavy industrial work. Kellogg's solution to the problem was a balance between "civil rights, human
needs, and the ceaseless operations in which groups of men and powerful appliances are joined in producing what the world wants." In other
words, social scientists should isolate the sources of anarchy through
exhaustive observation and develop means to control them.[1]

Taking Kellogg's statement as a prescription for the problems of industrial society in general and of Pittsburgh in particular, one sees that the

reformer's course of action would have first reconciled two facts—that men were compelled to work amid powerful machinery and that machinery was intrinsically dangerous—by attempting to make machines safer. Second, Kellogg wanted to reimburse the injured worker for physical and economic loss, providing the money owed by the system that crushed and afflicted him. Finally, the survey's solution called for a consideration of the broken body, with special attention to its needs and inadequacies after life-altering calamities. The balance between these three phases of action—neutralizing the threat of accidents at the workplace, paying the worker automatically for his injury, and providing for his physical needs—was too much for any one program or law to accomplish in turn-of-the-century Pittsburgh, but Kellogg hoped that coordinated effort could bring the American system in line with those established in Europe. Although professional researchers could offer general guidelines for these efforts, they would not directly implement them.

In the aftermath of the survey, three groups with clear investments in Pittsburgh industry developed distinct methods of relief to answer Kellogg's concerns. In the mills and mines of southwestern Pennsylvania, safety engineers and medical directors installed mechanical safeguards and first aid departments to protect life and limb from trauma and to respond to emergencies. In labor organizations, corporate boardrooms, and the state legislature, a momentous discussion continued about the best way to remunerate injured workers. The discussion culminated in 1915 in a legislative act that did away with common-law standards that had frustrated workers' attempts at compensation. Finally, artificial limb manufacturers refined their marketing techniques to convince the dismembered worker that he could rebuild his life by rebuilding his body. All three coalitions played the role of ameliorators, assuming first and foremost that workingmen should be approached as victims and that their bodies begged for intervention. At first glance, these efforts suggest that the survey changed the symbolic landscape in Pittsburgh so that imagery of unbroken men of steel no longer resonated. A closer look, however, shows that they created new celebratory narratives of tenacious working figures while concealing that which was disturbing and unsolvable. For safety engineers, lawmakers, and limb makers appearances mattered.

Though Kellogg did not address it as such, his idea of a comprehensive response to industrial accidents answered the question of what to do with the body of work in Pittsburgh, now exposed as frail and distressed. Should activists expose the broken body further, holding case studies and statistics before the public until an appropriate reform agenda had been satisfied? Or should they strategically withdraw images of damaged working bodies, offering a more positive vision of work in a scientifically managed future? Each of the projects to aid the injured, vulnerable worker incorporated a powerful tension between displaying and hiding his body. Survey staff turned the display of the body into a central vehicle for publicity of and justification for social engineers' approach to phenomena that they had defined as problems. The displayed body had the power to get things done if its impotence and disability were prominent enough to offend or anger. Conversely, a central theme of the institutional process of recovery involved masking the injured body, denying its existence in a postsurvey city that claimed to be home to an active government and responsive industry.

Industrial employers, the state legislature, and prosthesis companies all believed that the problem of the working body could be solved; therefore, they were all invested in the disappearance of troubling bodies as a fulfillment of their professional promise. First, in the campaign for workplace reform, the tension revealed itself in heightened efforts to prevent the occurrence of injury and subsequently to treat injuries within industrial establishments rather than in public hospitals. Safety engineers tried to eradicate accidents (and their most conspicuous form of evidence, the injured body) in an attempt to improve workers' morale, reduce workforce waste, and lessen the public stigma of mills and mines as slaughterhouses. When it came to publicizing their emergency medical innovations, however, employers needed visible proof of the injured body in order to show how well they could treat it. Safety and medical programs offer a vivid example of an alignment between groups that more often competed for control of working lives. Industrialists and labor reformers eventually agreed that safety devices and first aid programs produced a better workplace, even if they disagreed on what "better" actually meant.

Second, the legislative push toward a state workmen's compensation law hinged upon taking the contest for reimbursement out of the public eye of the courthouse and into the predictable, unseen realm of bureaucracy. Workers' largely unsuccessful lawsuits in the period between 1880 and 1915 were a form of public display in which the injured presented themselves as victims of irresponsible employers and offered their injuries as evidence of the wrongs companies had committed. Workmen's compensation operated in an antithetical fashion, making the question of fault irrelevant and removing the injured body from the scrutiny of the legal system. Again, the solution posed its own ambiguities; once industry and government incorporated a no-fault process that converted injury into a dollar value, employers could expect workers and lawmakers to agree on the inevitability of accidents. Injury became part of the workday, something for which managers could account but not a disruption with which they should preoccupy themselves.

Finally, the marketing of artificial limbs in turn-of-the-century Pittsburgh relied upon the display of physical loss and the illusion of bodily integrity as reasons to purchase technical, state-of-the-art goods. In their attempts to persuade amputees that dismemberment was unflattering but that artificial limbs could get them working again, limb makers relied upon visual exposure of injury as a motivational force. At the same time, manufacturers explained how easy it would be for the injured man with a prosthesis to slip unnoticed into the ranks of the able-bodied. Consumer prosthetics were perhaps the most telling example of the flexibility of bodily imagery at a time when doctors and salesmen argued that traumatic injury could be constructive. The eternal optimism of the advertiser matched the confidence of the city booster in its creative interpretation of the tragic and unappealing.

The three campaigns suggest the power of professional discourses to render the body invisible even as they organized themselves around its weaknesses. The politics of visibility in Pittsburgh dictated that Eastman's imaginary streets full of the dismembered should not exist. Institutional responses to accidents and injury essentially agreed with boosters' notion that the appropriate body to display was one of ability and power. Labor organizations, for their part, recognized the significance of displaying bodies as signs of strength in industry. The sense of manhood with which the performance of heavy, dangerous work in Pittsburgh was imbued could become a rallying point for workers' resistance to the state of industrial labor. The *Amalgamated Journal* called on workers in 1910 to "show your manhood by raising your strong voice in a mighty protest. Raise your mighty arm to give battle to your enemy who is drunk with lust. He believes you are a weakling and will not fight. He believes you do not possess the red corpuscles of a virile man." The rhetoric of this challenge to labor blended the imagery of physical strength with the antagonism of class struggle. If workers used their strong voices, mighty arms, and virile red corpuscles, they could wage a triumphant battle against the employer, who placed profits above safety. The call for working bodies to engage in a class war was not conducive to corporate, legislative, and commercial visions of a viable solution, however; industrial employers who sought to improve their accident statistics, lawmakers who wished to systematize the reparation process, and limb makers who pursued customers all preferred workers' bodies to be passive and untroubling when exhibited. The body of work persisted as an emblem to be manipulated in the name of institutional goals.[2]

SAFETY AND MEDICAL PROGRAMS

When the results of the Pittsburgh Survey began appearing in the national press in 1909, notes the historian Maurine Greenwald, the establishment press responded swiftly and defensively. The journalist Robert Jones wrote a four-part series of articles in the winter of 1909–10 to contest the survey's claims against industrial employers and the city government. Jones's "Pittsburgh, A City to be Proud Of" series in the *Gazette Times* narrated a new tale about the city, one in which employers wrapped machinery in layers of safety devices (only to be thwarted by the nonchalance of experienced workers); funded modern emergency medical care departments within their workplaces (only to be ignored by survey investigators); and aided injured workers financially (only to be accused of ruthless business calculations). Jones's articles centered on the nature of injuries in steel mills and the procedures employers used to prevent accidents and treat injured workers. The reporter provided a model of civic and industrial defense against the survey's charges that alternately addressed them as legitimate and discounted them as unfair. The articles also were a blueprint of the way in which employers' safety and medical campaigns treated the injured body as a visible sign.[3]

In his article of 26 December, Jones first presented the safety devices in Pittsburgh mills that tamed machinery. To counteract claims that the Steel City was "a sort of industrial inferno" in which a man's physical health was regarded as "the cheapest of commodities," Jones tried to repair employers' image by presenting them as world leaders in industrial safety technology. Arguing that "every large industrial plant in the Pittsburgh district" had a team of safety experts to check and ameliorate the hazards of each work routine, Jones implied that modern machinery was manageable. Among the seventeen photographs included in the first article, were six of safety shields, caution signs, and cutoff switches in U.S. Steel plants, offered by the *Gazette Times* as tangible evidence of employers' caution. Jones viewed the widespread discovery of accidents in Pittsburgh as a presurvey achievement of manufacturers unaided by such "hostile critics." The U.S. Steel Committee of Safety, Jones noted, was composed of high corporate officials who were "enthusiasts in the work of accident prevention" and spared "neither energy nor expense."[4]

Echoing the view of foremen and managers whom Fitch and Eastman interviewed, Jones argued that a great percentage of industrial accidents were the result of worker negligence. Industry could not protect workers from themselves, he worried, for they often took an indifferent approach to potential dangers. Jones argued the case for human error, noting that "machines can be 'checked for safety,' but the same process cannot be applied to human beings. The mechanical engineer can guarantee the strength and efficiency of his devices, but he cannot guarantee that the men for whose protection they are designed will do their share." To Jones, workers not only displayed indifference to safety measures, but often resisted them outright. Mill machines struck down workers only when men allowed them to. Every pay envelope they received from their company included a general statement encouraging safety—"Be careful in doing your work to avoid accidents to yourself and fellow workmen" or "Carelessness as to the safety of yourself or others will be sufficient cause for dismissal"—yet Jones claimed that the threat to their health and their job was not enough to keep many men from behaving recklessly. Jones's counternarrative suggested that the danger of industry lay not in working with machines but in taking them for granted. He struck at the very foundation of the survey writers' argument that the raw material of human beings was quickly converted into scrap by machinery. Those who began work in healthy and able condition, Jones stressed, were the ones who could cope most effectively.[5]

When accidents occurred (Jones stressed that they were bound to occur until workers took their safety more seriously), employers utilized an array of medical devices and procedures to care for the injured body. Jones detailed the process through which mill managers cared for their injured workers and described the infrastructure of the workplace, including emergency hospitals, first aid boxes, and dressing stations, designed to address emergency needs. The writer noted the significance of medical departments in management's concept of a well-running operation: "Ask the superintendent of any big plant what he is proudest of and he will lead you to the miniature hospital with its nurse in spotless uniform, its immaculate tiled walls and floor, the countless devices for saving life and easing pain, and he will call attention to the perfection of arrangements unexcelled by those of any large hospital in the land." In this account, the medical department rivaled the Bessemer converter and the open-hearth furnace as a dazzling mill spectacle. The miniature hospital was a significant sight for the visitor to see, but only if it was unoccupied; Jones did not describe medical departments in action but instead took his readers through the personnel and equipment that stood by, ready to take care of any medical emergency.[6]

The *Gazette Times* writer saved his most detailed attack for the argument built into Eastman's *Puddler* diagram. He opened his third article by questioning Eastman's evidence, noting that although the twenty-seven compensation figures listed may have been accurate, "perhaps ten times as many received much more generous treatment. The illustration and the table, therefore, are not what they purport to be." Eastman's image and statistics were not evidence of Pittsburgh's exploitation of workers, Jones argued, but a symptom of survey writers' misunderstanding of modern industry. Jones presented himself as deeply offended by the very notion of dollar values attached to body parts and unchecked risks accepted for their lack of expense. He noted the inherent danger of the survey's position: "The idea that human life here is rated as a crude commodity, a sort of raw material to be used or sacrificed ruthlessly to tonnage and profits is utterly absurd. The truth is just the other way about. Every possible precaution in the way of safety device, rules, shop arrangement, etc., is taken to protect life and limb." Jones confronted the survey's narrative of injury and work, asking if Pittsburgh could have reached its level of industrial dominance if it had been ruled by "a policy of blood and iron which starved the soul, crushed the spirit, stunted the body, and brutalized the manhood." Pittsburgh employers recognized that their interests and those of industrial workers were one and the same, the health and wealth of bodies and markets.[7]

In dismissing the survey as a figment of hostile imaginations, Jones revealed a central concern of the various safety programs that began in

Pittsburgh's industries after the turn of the century. The central objective of safety campaigns was accident prevention, the elimination of the injured worker's body as a problem of civic image and scientific scrutiny. Jones's photographs of safety devices represented the analytical shift that his argument favored: the injured worker's torn limbs need not be depicted by artists and photographers if there were safety devices on the scene that stopped accidents from occurring and were themselves subjects of graphic interest. Jones took the survey writers to task, arguing that their reliance on individual biographies, or "concrete instances," was a deceitful means of drawing conclusions from atypical cases. The city boosters' solution was to expose investigators' questionable use of biographies and statistics; the employers' solution was to make their work places safer, to deprive investigators of such concrete instances. Safety campaigns fit into what the historian Gerald Eggert termed the first phase of labor reform, when employers sought to change the physical surroundings of the workplace as an initial way to satisfy workers and reformers. Eggert attributed the formation of U.S. Steel's national safety program to the public disclosure of accident figures and anecdotes that accompanied William Hard's article of November 1907, "Making Steel and Killing Men." The bad public images of Chicago and Pittsburgh industry presented by Hard and Eastman had the power to spawn safety committees and programs precisely because they relied upon the Progressive assumption of a strong connection between an individual case of physical suffering and a citywide problem of neglected workers. By attacking the method, Jones attacked the legitimacy of the survey's brand of social science.[8]

Safety programs were meant to improve industrial manufacturers' public image by overcoming workers' belief that accidents were inevitable. Programs emphasized the idea that accidents were unnecessary and could be prevented through employees' constant vigilance. The Carnegie Steel Company informed its employees in the 1910s that the "best safety device known" was a careful and conscientious worker. Workers' key to mill safety, according to the company's General Safety Committee, was to avoid "cylinder heads, belts, gears, shears, scrap drops, saws, flying shears, and any kind of moving machinery" unless necessitated by the "nature of their occupation." Few jobs inside or outside Pittsburgh steel mills afforded workers the opportunity to keep away from such hazards, yet the spirit of comprehensive vigilance remained on the top of safety engineers' list of effective practices. The engineer Stephen Tener of the American Steel and Wire Company concluded that "lives are saved and accidents prevented—and this is being accomplished by the application of common-sense methods, teaching the foremen safe methods and safe practices, and through them, drilling the workmen in man-saving operations." The safety committee of the Carnegie Steel Company hoped that Pittsburgh industry would stop producing its most ghastly by-product, the "crippled and helpless wrecks who were once strong men."[9]

If efforts at work safety were obsessed with eliminating injured workers' bodies from snapshots of industry, care of workers in medical departments was more concerned with displaying injured bodies as salvageable entities. When Jones took his readers through a quick tour of mill emergency departments, he underscored the belief that those areas of the industrial workplace were spectacles, places in which one should pay close attention to the order and cleanliness of emergency equipment and the bodily care they represented. Although Jones saw no patients recovering in the medical wards of steel mills, he implied that their treatment would also be important to see. The injured body in the process of being saved was an instructive and inspiring spectacle. Two public events from 1911 illustrate this point. The Bureau of Mines held a "first aid field meet" in Pittsburgh's Arsenal Park that summer designed to instruct miners (and crowds of local journalists) on steps that area coal companies had taken to care for injured workers in times of catastrophe. Between twenty and thirty thousand miners gathered in the park to watch teams from local mines compete in rescue drills. The *Iron City Trades Journal* reported that the park exhibit also featured a "temporary gallery" erected to resemble a mine interior. The bureau placed the faux mine at the bottom of a natural amphitheater, creating a stage show in which injured miners and their rescuers provided the entertainment. The writer for the *Iron City Trades Journal* explained, "There will be a gas explosion in this play mine; miners will be 'entombed' and one of the Government rescue corps in oxygen helmets will enter and save the men. One side of the miniature mine will be open its entire length in order that the onlookers may witness everything that happens in an underground horror except the loss of life." By staging a disaster and rescue operation for a large crowd of workers, the Bureau of Mines made explicit the fact that emergency medical programs relied upon a measure of physical display that safety programs avoided. Here, the injured body was not a sight to eradicate, but one to publicize as a problem that could be solved by medical experts.[10]

Four months later, an even more visible exhibition of mine safety maneuvers occurred in Pittsburgh. On October 30–31, the Bureau of Mines staged the first national mine safety contest. The event featured rescue crews marching formally into the entrance of an artificial mine to begin drills and "trotting" one hundred yards in formation to prove respiratory stamina. James Paul of the bureau advised rescue crews to think of the audience when competing in such events: "Contests and demonstrations are usually given in the presence of spectators, and every facility should be provided that will admit of the spectators seeing the treatment given, and the events should be disposed of in such manner that time is not lost or wasted, to the annoyance of the spectators and the teams. . . . In dressing a wound or injury the work should be performed in such manner as to permit the spectators to see the treatment." Contests like this were as much symbolic events for the education of the public as they were training for the teams themselves. Treatment could be visually pleasing if it remained hypothetical. Winners and losers alike in safety competitions promoted the vision of industrial employers as diligently focused on workers' well-being. Paul's advice introduced a second layer of effort to the proceedings: workers had to perform but also had to be conscious of the fact that they were performing.[11]

A question remained of where to solve the problematic body, in the workplace or in public hospitals. Pittsburgh's medical community had concerned itself with workers' health ever since the massive growth of local industry in the mid–nineteenth century. Disease control was a daily operation for health officials, yet the treatment of industrial injuries occupied just as much of doctors' time. In 1905, for example, the Western Pennsylvania Hospital gave 560 "gratuitous dressings" for emergency cases brought from the "Mill districts." The hospitals of Pittsburgh, where cots were "never unoccupied," were sad scenes for local writers, who could not ignore the tale they told of dangerous work in the city. One writer reported that sunny days brought "dozens of men" out to the courtyards of the Western Pennsylvania Hospital, where they spent the day "hobbling along on crutches" and affecting passersby with the sight of amassed casualties. The problem of the body of work in the public hospital, it seemed, was that it was never alone; crowds of dismembered and hobbled workers lingered in the halls and on the patios of Western Penn, positioning themselves directly before onlookers. Journalists imagined a "human stream" or a "gory grist of broken, burned, and shattered mortality" making its way to hospital emergency rooms from mills and mines. Novelists depicted the end of a shift at a Pittsburgh steel mill as a daily routine in which a loaded ambulance bore the dead and wounded to the nearest hospital.[12]

After the turn of the century, medical departments within industrial establishments became increasingly common as employers sought to counteract this troubling imagery. Employers traditionally dealt with trauma in mills and mines by hiring doctors-on-call. Many mills established long-term relationships with individual physicians who responded to emergency cases exclusively. Dr. H. H. Clark, who advertised his services widely in city directories and industrial almanacs, served as the official surgeon for Carnegie Steel Company's Upper and Lower Union mills and Lucy blast furnaces in the early 1880s. Although Clark continued his private practice in downtown Pittsburgh, the company expected him to tend immediately to accidents that required medical care. The practice of founding makeshift medical departments soon followed, as employers acted on the notion that the speed of first aid was crucial to recovery rates. As early as 1890, Carnegie's Lower Union mill featured a "Red Cross department" that combined basic first aid services with a doctor on telephone call. When the United States Steel Company formed after the turn of the century, it established a more formal emergency medical ward in its Homestead Steel Works in 1908. By 1909, Dr. William Estes declared that "nearly every large mining company" in Pennsylvania had an attending surgical team to care for wounded miners. Jones claimed that the medical services offered by employers in the area had reached such a level of perfection by 1910 that inspectors from the Red Cross and army medical corps declared they had never seen a better system.[13]

William O'Neill Sherman, chief surgeon of the Carnegie Steel Company, described the duty as well as the indispensability of the Pittsburgh industrial surgeon in 1914: "Where safety and preventive measures have not been entirely effective, the physician or surgeon steps in. . . . The failure to properly administer first aid, and the subsequent lack of effective surgical attention, has in the past added to the death list many whose lives might have been saved, and has steadily recruited the army of the maimed and crippled, with which the streets of our large cities are so familiar." The charge for the company surgeon was to recruit another

26. Homestead Steel Works first aid class.

type of army, one in which workers learned how to provide emergency care for each other and transport accident victims quickly to medical wards. Sherman offered a photograph from the Homestead Steel Works that showed an employee serving as an accident victim while a surgeon lectured to a group of managers and workers about the fundamentals of first aid. The photograph's point of view showed the audience of workers looking back at the camera, as the "patient," too, turned from the doctor to stare at the photographer. The viewer of the image thus watched the first aid class as it watched the viewer; only the doctor and a few of the dozen workers looked elsewhere. The effect of the image was that one had disrupted a private assembly; presumably, in the absence of the camera, all eyes in the room would have been focused on the body of the patient as the surgeon wrapped him in bandages and splints. In mobilizing the corps of workers to become partners in first aid, the Homestead Steel Works' medical staff turned the injured worker's body into the subject of observation and instruction.[14]

THE ROAD TO WORKMEN'S COMPENSATION

In a vein similar to that of mechanical and medical solutions, financial solutions to accidents in Pittsburgh's workplaces played upon a dynamic of alternately concealing and exposing the injured body. Rather than expose injuries to prove how well they could be fixed, labor groups and companies seeking to establish benefit programs for workers brought the vulnerable body to the fore as a way of selling the notion of risk. After all, disability plans and insurance schemes were viable only if large numbers of workers believed their bodies were subject to the ubiquitous threats. Yet the culmination of accident remuneration in the early twentieth century, the workmen's compensation law, relied upon a decidedly different strategy. As a systematized, no-fault program of payment, the workmen's compensation process did not need to mobilize the broken body. Instead, workmen's compensation rendered the worker's body much less visible, as its evidence of suffering and blame became less legally significant. The standardized, predictable nature of Pennsylvania's workmen's compensation law transformed the body of work from a physical reality in the workplace and the courtroom into a subject of largely bureaucratic scrutiny.

Before the era of workmen's compensation, injured workers struggled to extract money from employers through the court system. As many historians have shown, however, their chances of mounting successful litigation were slim. An array of legal defenses derived from common law traditionally protected employers from liability. The laws of fellow servant, assumed risk, and contributory negligence made it difficult for workers to win. The fellow servant doctrine held that an injury to a worker caused by the direct or indirect action of another worker could not be attributed to the employer. If a worker tipped a pile of scrap onto a fellow worker or made any action that in any way caused the pile of scrap to fall, their employer could not be held liable. The assumed risk doctrine stated that once a worker had been informed that a particular job involved certain dangers, it was his responsibility to refuse the job or assume the risk (and financial burden) of future accidents. A coal miner whose legs were crushed in a roof-fall had little chance of winning a liability case because his job had an inherent, assumed risk of such an accident. The doctrine of contributory negligence maintained that if a worker's actions contributed to his accident in the slightest degree, the employer could not be held responsible. Any variation from normal procedure (if there was such a thing) could be interpreted as a contributory factor in the courtroom. These three legal defenses were formidable —as David Brody noted, U.S. Steel lost only six liability cases to employees between 1906 and 1912.[15]

This dismal record for litigious workers contrasts with Jones's claim that workers in Pittsburgh routinely received adequate settlements from their employers without any of the parties undergoing the disagreeable features of a trial. There was very little encouraging news for workers who wished to sue their bosses or managers for liability. The *Amalgamated Journal* criticized laws that thwarted workers' efforts to survive after injury. In 1901, the journal published "Man's Inhumanity to Man," a poem about the plight of an armless beggar thrown from the ranks of the employed after an industrial accident. The worker who spoke in "Man's Inhumanity to Man" regretted the fact that he was not a soldier, for a soldier would have been compensated adequately for his disability. Instead, he wandered the streets penniless, a mere worker who was found to have assumed the risk that eventually took his limbs. The poem ended with a call to his union brethren to take action:

Such laws as these, and laws they are
    (But alter them **you** can)
Very plainly do they go to show
    Man's inhumanity to man.[16]

Labor organizations answered the call by constructing a narrative of loss and wrongdoing. Beginning in the last decades of the nineteenth century, organized labor explained the difficulties of accident litigation in terms of a lopsided contest between perpetrator-employers and victim-employees. Labor's repeated appeals for employer liability laws at the turn of the century targeted legislators' sympathy by emphasizing the physical and economic hardships created by accidents. These appeals certainly complemented the glut of labor reform writing after the turn of the century, which stressed the humanistic and economic effects of anonymous, unseen industrial accidents. Yet workers did not depend entirely on rhetoric in their attempts to make their lives less precarious after injury. Rather than wait for state legislators to pass more stringent employer liability laws (or a comprehensive workmen's compensation law), industrial workers in Pittsburgh turned to several options of emergency relief before 1915.[17]

The first was life insurance. During the first decade of the twentieth century, labor organizations focused increasingly on workplace trauma, emphasizing both the "vast amount of human suffering and sorrow" caused by injury and financial effects that could "materially curtail the normal longevity" of Pittsburgh industrial workers. A heightened emphasis on life insurance as a requisite for upstanding union members accompanied this focus. In 1908, the *Amalgamated Journal* began a campaign to promote workers' life insurance options as a way of protecting families and making physical strain worth more than wages. The AAISW argued that life insurance was a commonsense approach to the problem of potential death or injury, an investment upon which many workers' families would unfortunately have to rely. Part of the union's message to workers was that they should invest in the bodies that allowed them to earn a wage, taking pride in the fact that their lives and limbs, if damaged in an accident, were worth a tangible amount of money.[18]

Campaigns to encourage workers to purchase life insurance were notoriously unsuccessful before the turn of the century, and few industrial workers actually held such policies by 1900. In 1890, the commissioner of labor reported that only 29 percent of Pennsylvania steelworkers had life insurance. The numbers were even lower for other major industries; 13 percent of blast furnace workers and 3 percent of bituminous coal miners held life insurance policies. Although more than three million Americans owned life insurance by 1900, it is difficult to estimate how many of them were industrial workers. The persistence with which the labor press appealed to its readers to consider life insurance suggests that such promotions were daunting tasks. The traditional popularity of fraternal and benevolent associations in Pittsburgh's working-class neighborhoods meant that policies from insurance firms were often viewed as unnecessary expenditures or outright scams. Yet by 1908, the *Amalgamated Journal* presented insurance as a prudent way in which a worker could provide for his family beyond the aid of unions and social clubs.[19]

When unions broached the subject of insurance, they did so in graphic terms that exposed the injured body or shattered corpse as a potential liability for a worker's wife and children. One such piece, "Thirty-cent Husbands," which appeared in the *Amalgamated Journal* in February

1909, epitomized the paper's plea to workers to make their vulnerability on the mill floors a financial safeguard through life insurance. In the story, a steelworker's wife woke suddenly in the middle of the night, startled by bad dreams that had plagued her since her husband had had a minor work accident. Her husband, "a man who had been deaf to all appeals that he should insure his life," tried to calm her fragile nerves as she told him the details of her nightmare. She had dreamed of making a trip to town, where local merchants advertised "Husbands for Sale" from stalls and shop windows. Although some of the model husbands sold for as much as five thousand dollars, the types that most resembled her husband were "done up in bunches like radishes and marked 30 cents." In this story of bodily appraisal and spousal disappointment, the industrial worker who failed to insure his body from the ravages of the production process devalued himself in his wife's eyes.[20]

The mill wife's nightmare upended Eastman's mental arithmetic of measuring bodies in terms of compensatory value, turning it instead into a purchasing decision for women. Here, women of the steel town wandered through the market, eyeing potential husbands and judging their worth on the basis of merchants' prices. Better models made better husbands because they were better men. Their claims to masculinity were based upon their insurance portfolios, which discerning wives recognized as important corollaries to strong bodies. Women in this tale quickly calculated the worth of a steelworker's body, derived from the value he placed upon it when he accepted or refused insurance. The writer of the piece effectively emphasized the practice of displaying the worker's body as a motivational device. The Pittsburgh worker who could envision himself strung up with other men like a bunch of radishes and placed in a bargain bin of unmanly physical specimens was meant to fear the public revelation of his lack of insurance. The humiliation of such a disclosure took the form of an unflattering bodily display in "Thirty-cent Husbands," which effectively imagined the body of work as a figure that needed protection and codified value. The *Amalgamated Journal* suggested that in an age of cold calculations, only the ignorant worker resisted the necessity of measuring his physique on a financial scale.

If the market drama of "Thirty-cent Husbands" was not enough to make AAISW members dwell on their vulnerability, union writers also stressed the probability of injury for bodies caught in the industrial trap. The Insurance Department of the *Amalgamated Journal* asked workers directly, "What are your chances of living twenty years?" and "Can you afford to tempt fate?" Answers were discouraging, yet the Insurance Department dangled the carrot of insurance as the bright side of the sorry state of industrial safety. Labor writers used more aggressive selling techniques as well, noting that the workingman who died without leaving insurance money should be buried as a pauper, "shoved into a hole and left to rot." Unlike mythical tales of workers gathering to bury their dead in solemn and respectful ceremonies in the shadow of the mill, the interment of the uninsured, the writer stressed, should be as contemptible as possible. His body was worthless and should be discarded accordingly.[21]

AAISW leaders hoped that workers would also take advantage of a second option for financial relief, not in lieu of but in addition to life insurance. In the last decades of the nineteenth century, the local labor press regularly solicited donations from readers for families of workers who died in work accidents. The union benefit plan formalized the process, paying members for the loss of work due to injury or disease and paying members' families in the case of death. The *Amalgamated Journal* shows that by the spring of 1900, AAISW members debated among themselves the merits of a benefit program. Two positions emerged: those who believed that the financial security of a program made it a crucial step toward a stronger union and those who resented any increase in monthly dues that might not translate into tangible rewards or, worse yet, might drive members away from the association. After years of consideration, the union decided in favor of taking action. The AAISW convention of 1906 created a committee to analyze the pros and cons of a benefit plan, and two years later the program began. Every member of the union paid three dollars annually to maintain the fund. In return, a member in good standing who was injured to the extent that he could not work received five dollars a week for a maximum of thirteen weeks. Although the temporarily disabled worker could theoretically receive a total of sixty-five dollars for an injury, from the last quarter of 1908 to the second quarter of 1911, the AAISW benefit fund paid on average between twenty-four and twenty-five dollars. This would suggest that the average temporary disability kept a worker from his job for just over a month, enough time for sprains and fractures to heal. The AAISW's death benefit program paid workers' families between one hundred and five hundred dollars, depending on how long the deceased had been in good standing with the union. Permanent disability entitled a member to half the amount of the death benefit for which he qualified. The union benefit program, then, was designed as a stopgap measure meant to prevent the collapse of a worker's family in the immediate aftermath of a work accident. The payments of five dollars a week or a lump sum between fifty and two hundred fifty dollars offered some immediate relief, but an injured worker had to seek other income quickly.[22]

A similar scheme of payment came from company benefit plans, the third option for workers seeking money to cover injuries or deaths. U.S. Steel's company benefit plan, established in January 1910, funded medical treatment for injured workers, a death compensation equal to eighteen months' wages, permanent disability compensation equal to six to eighteen months' wages, and temporary compensation during an injured worker's recovery. Between 1911 and 1915, the U.S. Steel plan paid a yearly average of three hundred to four hundred dollars to employees who had sustained permanent disabilities from work accidents. The accident benefit plan for the American Sheet and Tin Plate Company itemized physical losses suffered by men at work and paid accident victims particular sums for particular body parts. The company's plan placed the highest value on a worker's arm, paying eighteen months' wages for the loss of one arm. An amputated leg or hand brought the worker a year's wages, while an eye equaled six months' wages. Across the nation, company benefit programs created detailed schedules and classifications of payment for specific body parts.[23]

Organized labor was often wary of employers' benefit plans, however. When the American Sheet and Tin Plate Company announced its accident and death benefit plan in 1910, the *Amalgamated Journal* explained that the company was merely trying to evade lawsuits and divide unionized and nonunionized workers. Labor writers emphasized that employers undervalued their workers in physical and financial terms; thus, their benefit plans could never compensate workers adequately for the damage that manufacturers wreaked upon them. A story in the *Iron City Trades Journal* described a worker who, when his arm was cut off at the elbow by a machine, "sacrificed on the wheel of modern commerce," received only $127 for his lost limb, enough to buy an artificial replacement but hardly enough to repay such permanent disability. The historian Stuart Brandes noted that two of the most egregious shortcomings of company benefit plans at the turn of the century were that they were largely funded by workers themselves, making accident prevention less urgent for management, and that their payments were simply too small to cover medical expenses and lost wages.[24]

Appeals for life insurance agencies and union and company benefit plans undermined the booster narrative of healthy pace and mechanical harmony in the Steel City. Inducing workers to trade a portion of their income for a potential payout required admitting, even emphasizing, the nature of physical damage in Pittsburgh's industrial workplaces. Insurance promoters' motivations were varied: insurance companies profited as their rolls of policyholders grew; unions secured the membership of men who paid into a system from which they could withdraw only in times of misfortune; and employers improved their public profile while possibly dulling the sharp edges of labor unrest. Each scheme emerged in the context of a legal environment in which workers struggled to prove employer liability for accidents or chronic hazards. Employer responsibility for accident compensation gave way by the 1910s to a Progressive solution: "community responsibility" in the form of automatic compensation paid by state governments. The social scientists who promoted the passage of workmen's compensation stressed its distinct advantages over litigation, namely, its predictability, its avoidance of placing blame, and its power to harmonize class relations. Workmen's compensation also served another purpose, however; within Pittsburgh's arena of frequent accidents and contested causes, workmen's compensation fit well with both industry's conception of accidents as inevitable features of innovative production and Eastman's theory of accidents as social and economic crises. The historian Roy Lubove argued that Eastman's survey work anticipated the logic of the state's workmen's compensation law by "linking equity, social expediency, and prevention." It also fit well with a legal redefinition of accidents that occurred in the United States during the mid- to late nineteenth century. The literary critic Nan Goodman has traced the process through which the mechanization of work revolutionized American literary and legal perceptions of personal responsibility. Machines produced a sense of "action-at-a-distance," which complicated an accident's chain of causation. Whereas the trio of legal defenses employers used before 1915 attempted to fix blame and deflect it away from the employer, the workmen's compensation model acknowledged that blame was a difficult fact to establish and could always be broadened further from the employee to the employer and ultimately to society at large. The National Association of Manufacturers approved of workmen's compensation because of its central concept of liability without fault. Here was a compensation plan that acknowledged the damaged body of work but did not dwell upon it or ask it to prove itself as the result of individual or corporate culpability.[25]

The statistician Frederick Hoffman predicted in 1909 that when the American middle class was awakened fully to the startling tallies of accidental death in the nation's industries and realized the "social necessity of reasonable and rational compensation of injured workmen as a right," the United States would place itself "on par with the other civilized nations of the world." Montana's legislature was the first to adopt a workmen's compensation law, in 1909. In the next seven years, thirty-one other state bodies passed such laws. The historian Robert Asher attributes the passage of the New York workmen's compensation law in 1909 to the increased public knowledge of industrial accidents generated by such investigations as the Pittsburgh Survey. Interestingly, the Pennsylvania legislature was not similarly moved by the findings of accidents in its own state to act quickly. When Asher referred to the "glacial pace" of reform in New York in the late nineteenth century and early twentieth, he could easily have been speaking of Pennsylvania in the 1910s. Only when mounting pressure from reform groups and labor representatives formed after 1910 did legislators take action on workmen's compensation.[26]

Pennsylvania's lawmakers found themselves in a regional reference group, including their counterparts in New York, New Jersey, Ohio, and West Virginia, that passed workmen's compensation laws between 1910 and 1913. Although this alone was not enough to force Pennsylvania's hand, surrounding states' passage gave the idea a stamp of legitimacy that was difficult to ignore. The city's labor press had long applauded government compensation plans established in European nations around the turn of the century. The *Iron City Trades Journal* published an article in the autumn of 1910 that praised the Danish system of workmen's compensation for its absolute protection of workers and its economic reliability for both workers and employers. Within the politics of the regional reference group, reformers could also turn to neighboring states as examples that placed Pennsylvania in a bad light. Eastman championed the work of New York's liability commission as a good model for Pennsylvania, showing that the catalysts of their reforms—uncertainty, waste, delay, and class antagonism—were also evident in Pittsburgh. The *Pitts-*

burgh Post reviewed West Virginia's compensation law in the winter of 1913, noting that it was successful in paying workers for their injuries and generating a feeling of harmony between labor and capital. With both labor critics and the establishment press lauding surrounding states for their management of industrial accidents, state legislators were faced with a problem of public image. Though few Americans ever read labor leaders' critiques, the staff of the Pittsburgh Survey managed to generate enough publicity for their findings to drive home the point that the injured, neglected worker was a common sight on Pittsburgh streets. Moreover, as the sociologist Eliza Pavalko has noted, the court system was home to a "very visible and direct form of the employer-worker struggle," creating sharp fracture lines that could be smoothed only through legislative reform. Workmen's compensation offered a way to deflect such criticism and problematic imagery, to bring the state up to par with its neighbors, and, at the same time, to please employers who wanted a predictable system of compensation. By 1914, the state's commissioner of labor and industry reported that the "people of Pennsylvania have reached the point where they demand that aid be given those injured in employment."[27]

Pennsylvania's state government had, in fact, already taken action. In 1912, Governor John Tener convened a committee of seven to draft a compensation law for legislative debate. The committee was composed of two eastern Pennsylvania attorneys, two Philadelphia manufacturers, a law professor from the University of Pennsylvania, the president of the Pittsburgh district miners, and a skilled steelworker from Monessen, a mill town south of Pittsburgh along the Monongahela River. Pittsburgh's labor press ran a series of articles in the spring of 1912 that offered readers biographical sketches of the two labor representatives and assured area workers that they would fight for their best interests in Harrisburg. The committee's resulting draft was based largely on the New Jersey law passed the previous year. In July of 1912, labor representatives from across the state gathered in Harrisburg to address the committee and promote the New Jersey model of automatic, no-fault payments dispensed by a central government body.[28]

When, in the spring of 1913, the state House passed a compensation bill that incorporated much of the committee's draft, observers warned that it could potentially die in the Senate, where "a large number of its body [were] employers of labor." Although they supported workmen's compensation as a solution to the problem of accidents, many industrialists worried that passage of the bill would mark the first step toward a compensation system in which individual employers became financially responsible for the accidents that occurred in their plants. Some businessmen feared that state compensation was an intermediary step toward codified employer liability. Accordingly, some employers sought to sway the legislature away from compensation even as they prepared for its passage by selecting their workforces more methodically. An unexpected result of the drive toward a compensation law in Pennsylvania was employers' new interest in physical tests as a measuring device in the hiring process. *Iron Age* reported in 1915 that a "great many" manufacturers in the region were considering adopting formal physical examinations in anticipation of the more rigorous compensation laws they feared would come. If compensation laws became a financial burden for companies, they needed a set of guidelines by which the man who was "physically unfit for the work" could be "weeded out." Thus, while workmen's compensation promised to remove the spectacle of injury from the courtroom, it inadvertently vaulted the healthy body into an even more intense spotlight, as men vying for jobs had to display their physical capabilities and prove themselves superior to their fellow applicants.[29]

For decades, workers in the city's heavy industries had expected to be sized up physically before they were hired. Men who were "large, strong, active, and willing" had always had an advantage in the Pittsburgh job market, especially in steel, glass, and coal. With the growth of scientific management principles after 1910, however, labor complained that employers tried to quantify not only their "length, breadth, and thickness as a machine," but also their "grade of hardness, malleability, tractability, general serviceability." The object of the industrial employer seemed to be the construction of an ideal worker-machine through a process of "molding, hammering, filing, and polishing" that fit him into his assigned job. This attention to the varieties of physical measurement also extended to a worker's ability to withstand a hypothetical accident. Villain overseers who yelled, "Get to work, you damned lazy cattle!" in labor novels revealed workers' recognition that their bodies were used as a raw material to attain a desired result, but hiring agents and managers who found an applicant's breaking point by injuring him on the job line were a different type of beast altogether. A fictional account of a physical examination at the door of an employment office illustrated the concern about the objectification of workers in Pittsburgh in the limbo before work-men's compensation: "The muscles of all applicants for jobs were tested for their strength, and hammers, sometimes the handles, quite often the steel heads, rapped and stung bared arms. A sickly grin, or forced laugh-ter, was the only acknowledgement of the blow. The bare chest was hammered with a clenched fist, or even with thumb-knuckles, as if a pugilist were to be hardened to meet the blows of his opponent. Woe to him . . . who failed to grin when his arm or chest was being pounded with a hammer—he went to the scrap heap without mercy." W. E. Trautmann and Peter Hagboldt's words echoed the critiques of labor reformers, who worried that the legal system's inequities levied more pressure on the body of work to prove itself invincible.[30]

Architects of workmen's compensation in Pennsylvania counseled that this type of overt scrutiny would be eliminated by a rational state law that removed all onus from employers. Harry Mackey, the chairman of the state compensation board, wrote in the *Amalgamated Journal* that his goal was to eliminate waste from all phases of the accident process. Mackey targeted institutional waste in such forms as accidents that went uncompensated, money spent to win compensation in court, court fees that reduced the occasional verdict in favor of the worker, and money paid to insurance companies. The chairman stressed that "certainty must be established" in order to eliminate the guesswork of litigation. In-stead of companies paying for their workers' injuries, the loss would be "charged to production," with consumers ultimately supporting the com-pensation program. By passing the Workmen's Compensation Act of 1915 the General Assembly nullified the fellow servant, assumed risk, and contributory negligence defenses and established a state board to monitor compensation claims. The act defined injury to a worker as "violence to the physical structure of the body and such disease or infec-tion as naturally results from them." For total disability, the state com-pensated workers with half of their wages for the first 500 weeks after the accident. Following the model of company benefit plans, the act also supplied varying levels of compensation for specific injuries. The loss of an arm or a leg (amputated above the elbow or knee) brought a compen-sation of a half wage for 215 weeks, whereas the loss of a hand or a foot brought the same amount for 175 weeks. If a worker lost both arms, both legs, or both eyes, the board considered him totally disabled and com-pensated him accordingly.[31]

Workmen's compensation brought a single, standardized means of remuneration for industrial accidents that promised to eliminate the most glaring problems of inequity and inefficiency facing workers. In passing the law, the state legislature also managed to eliminate the most glaring evidence of accidents, removing the injured body from the public arena of the legal system and ushering it into the shadowy halls of bureaucracy. The automatic, prescribed nature of workmen's compensation, combined with its procedural routine and lack of contestation, amounted to a reversal of the legal system's exhibitionary qualities; no longer would the broken body stand as a public spectacle upon which a judicial verdict rested. Furthermore, the sweeping reach of workmen's compensation precluded much of the advertising copy displayed after the turn of the century to sell insurance and benefit plans by exposing the body of the steelworker or coal miner as a figure that could easily be damaged and devalued at any minute. That is not to say, however, that advertising based on the injured body vanished from Pittsburgh in the 1910s with the advent of workmen's compensation. On the contrary, advertising for a different solution to the injured body emerged in the postsurvey Steel City, one that promised even more to the damaged body of work than reimbursement.

"HUMAN-REPAIR SHOPS"
THE ART OF ARTIFICIAL LIMBS

While employers and legislators organized methods to prevent accidents, treat their effects, and reimburse workers for lost wages, a third approach to the problem of the injured working body also gained momentum after the turn of the century. Artificial limbs were as tentative a solution to the problem of vulnerable working bodies as safety, medical, and financial programs, but, more than other institutional remedies, they addressed the physical effects of accidental injury. Safety and medical programs emerged as compromises between labor reformers, who publicized the ugly fact of accidents, and employers, who longed for efficient production and less negative publicity. Workmen's compensation came about as the culmination of decades of labor grievances and a state legislature pressured by reformers and the actions of neighboring state governments. The artificial limbs industry, on the other hand, had existed in the United States for more than half a century by the time the survey publicized the problem of dismemberment. The push for a prosthetic solution was not so much a response to the survey's display of vulnerable bodies as an amplification of selling practices that limb makers had successfully employed to attract military clientele before the turn of the century.

Manufacturers of artificial limbs found that the key to marketing their products in Pittsburgh in the first two decades of the twentieth century was frequently shifting between displaying the injured body as a motivational force for consumption and hiding the injured body by making it a walking illusion of integrity. To persuade the injured worker to purchase a prosthetic device, limb makers were careful to show the debilitating physical, social, and economic effects of amputation in their advertising; their catalogues became showcases for human wrecks made new through the proper use of their products. Moreover, limb makers' other critical message, conveyed in dozens of catalogues distributed throughout the country, was that the artificial limb provided a measure of concealment that rendered the injured body invisible to prying eyes and thereby allowed the user to avoid feeling the shame of physical abnormality. The amputee's use of a prosthesis depended upon a desire to hide the vulnerability of his body while in public and display his body as a reconstructed tool in the workplace. The double logic of prosthesis—in which artificial limbs reminded all who saw them of violent dismemberment but also suggested its mechanical transcendence—focused on the injured body's equal evidence of weakness and strength. Both visual cues were valuable in the limbs market.[32]

The artificial limbs industry in survey-era Pittsburgh was a combination of local manufacturers with small workshops and national firms with large distribution offices. The late nineteenth century saw the emergence of a fledgling prosthesis industry in the Steel City when the area's leading company, the Artificial Limb Manufacturing Company (ALMC), formed in 1869. By the mid-1880s, Pittsburgh's commercial directories heralded the company as "widely known and deservedly popular" throughout Pennsylvania and applauded its dedication to producing new types of limbs to enhance the comfort and mobility of its clients. ALMC advertisements from the 1870s and 1880s intimated that the company's staff, composed entirely of amputees, was especially sensitive to the needs of the injured and the intricacies of wearing a limb. From this first prominent manufacturer in the city, the scale of Pittsburgh's artificial limbs industry grew steadily until the prospective limb purchaser had many options from which to choose. The prosthetic boom in Pittsburgh came during the first decade of the twentieth century, when widely advertised national manufacturers began opening sales offices in the city. Local branch offices of national firms connected the major marketing campaigns launched from such manufacturing centers as New York, Chicago, and Minneapolis with the burgeoning limbs market in the Steel City. In 1900, four firms sold artificial limbs in Pittsburgh—ALMC, Feick Brothers, Neubert and Sons, and Otto Helmond, an individual craftsman. By 1910, six more companies had come to Pittsburgh, including the national distributors American Artificial Limbs, Doerflinger Artificial Limb Company, National Artificial Limb and Brace Manufacturing Company, and J. F. Rowley. Advertisements for these companies appeared frequently in both the establishment press and the labor press from the 1890s through the 1910s and invariably promised the best-made, least expensive, and most comfortable limb available on the market.[33]

But newspaper advertisements were not the primary means by which limb makers sought to entice injured workers to purchase their products. Manufacturers' product catalogues promoted an array of prosthetic devices by creating dreamworlds of bodily integrity and pride in which accidents were the beginning of fantastic journeys for working bodies. Limb manufacturers used their catalogues to promise injured workers both renewed physical capabilities and social reintegration; the man who lost his job when he lost his arm or leg, catalogues claimed, did not have to spend the rest of his days out of work and feeling useless. With the aid of a well-made artificial limb, the former industrial worker could once again fulfill his role as wage earner.

Images of men wearing artificial limbs, structured displays of the various components of prosthetic devices, and testimonials from customers thriving with their new arms or legs conveyed three distinct visions of the prosthetic consumer: the consumer as a man whose body appeared to be whole; as a product of American technological power; and as a body that worked once again and earned a wage. Catalogues employed a symbolic repertoire that offered a vision not only of the best products on the market, but also of the ideal, reconstructed consumer. Artificial limb companies were in the business of selling both body parts and self-image. Limb makers thus encouraged injured workers to hide the wounds of work from public view to conserve their manhood and normalcy and, conversely, to display the mechanical remedy with pride to enhance their claims to physical ability and technological wonder. The dual strategies of emphasis and elision centered on the injured body itself. Limb makers instructed the injured worker to present his reconstituted body to the world with the logic of the salesman, accentuating the pleasant and impressive qualities of prosthetic reconstruction and masking its limitations.[34]

Limb makers' first concern was to persuade the prospective client that artificial limbs made it possible for a man with a glaring disability to slip back into the crowd of the able-bodied, unblemished and undetected. A. A. Marks, a national distributor whose catalogues were widely available in the Pittsburgh region and who did most of its business through the mail, claimed there were "many thousands of people" who could "mingle with other people without disclosing their loss" because they had used the company's prostheses. The problem of visible disability, according to limb makers, was that it branded the accident victim as both unsightly and unemployable. The "sudden, alarming" ubiquity of the amputee that characterized the post–Civil War United States was mirrored after the turn of the century by the prevalence of the industrial walking wounded —men who had lost their arms, legs, fingers, and eyes and subsequently their jobs. The editors of the Pittsburgh Survey used Lewis Hine's photographs of such men to shock the reader into civic action. Limb catalogues used the power of the stare to make a purchase seem inevitable. The scrutiny that catalogues turned on the exposed stump was not a spontaneous or disinterested glance at injury, but the stare that the disability theorist Rosemarie Thomson argues "estranges and discomforts" both the viewer and the viewed. The public disclosure of limblessness became an unpardonable decision for the injured man, an act that set him apart from the passerby, invited unwelcome inquiries, and made public life generally unpleasant. Limb makers argued that dismemberment suffered in the course of doing industrial work was a reality that could be acknowledged within the fraternity of the wounded but should be hidden elsewhere. The prospective purchaser who suddenly saw himself as the subject of countless double takes and whispered conversations would, presumably, be more inclined to solve the problem once and for all.[35]

A central continuity between artificial limb companies' appeals to Civil War veterans in the late nineteenth century and industrial workers in the early twentieth century was an emphasis on the ease with which the injured could mask the loss of a limb and conceal the embarrassing fact of dismemberment. Manufacturers stressed the aesthetic perfection of limbs that only experts trained in their science and manufacture could detect as artificial. The local manufacturer Feick Brothers noted that "those who wear artificial limbs seldom wish to expose their misfortune"; thus the key to a comfortable life after dismemberment was careful concealment of the stump and the artificial limb. A. A. Marks stressed a similar point, declaring that "no person who maintains his self-respect, no matter what his disability may be, cares to be constantly reminded of it, and the commiseration of others, above all things, is the most abhorrent." Limblessness was strange, but it was also pitiful and worrisome. According to limb makers, the loss of an arm or a leg produced psychological burdens for the man who had constantly to fret about his public appearance, lest he become a childlike or feminized subject of general sympathy. The Chicago-based producer J. F. Rowley addressed the injured worker's need directly, stating that "one of your reasons for buying an artificial leg is to disguise or hide your loss from the public; you want to appear as a man, and you can do this only by learning to use the leg perfectly. . . . the man who hitches, limps, or swings while walking, deceives no one, for all know he has an artificial leg." As much as conspicuity, manhood was at stake. Those who lost a limb should be prepared to forget their loss and move on without harboring the persistent memory of their dismemberment. Because accident victims' "minds and dispositions" gradually became "prepared by Nature to bear their misfortunes," it was essential that they stop others from reminding them of the freakish nature of dismemberment. A. A. Marks concluded that only an artificial limb could "conceal the loss, restore a natural appearance to the person, avoid observation and comment, and . . . become companionable and necessary to the wearer's mental comfort." The "annoying and odious" attention of strangers was the first affliction of dismemberment that could be solved by prostheses.[36]

To deflect such scrutiny, limb makers modeled their products after the appearance of Anglo-American arms and legs and the mechanics of experimental test subjects. Manufacturers stressed that they had devoted much thought and observation to the design of their limbs. An ALMC newspaper advertisement that ran in the late nineteenth century promised that its newest artificial leg offered the "nearest approach to the natural member of any invention of the age." Feick Brothers, too, chose the phrase "nearest approach to the natural member" to suggest that its limbs came as close to human anatomy as was technologically possible at the turn of the century. Though artificial limbs could not be perfect substitutes for lost body parts—Feick Brothers stressed that "there is no perfect limb"—they could be made to such a degree of sophistication that the wearer's body and the stranger's eye could be easily tricked. The natural appearance of a covered prosthesis, stressed limb makers, produced situations in which only the manufacturer himself could distinguish those with disabilities from the able-bodied. Because firms studied the motion of the human body in minute detail, they claimed to be able to approximate the body's functions with wood, metal, and rubber. A. A. Marks produced a series of drawings of a man walking that, much like the work of the era's chronophotographers and scientific managers, broke the body's movements into discrete stages. Marks's image was meant to convince the reader that their craftsmen and designers had mastered the mechanics of walking; all that was left was to engineer a suitable simulation. The artificial limb that "represented the natural movement" of a man in motion was designed to work smoothly by obeying the "laws governing locomotion"; it turned a progression of poses into a smooth, continuous performance. J. F. Rowley noted that most artificial legs allowed a man who walked slowly to "make a fair appearance," yet when he quickened his pace to three miles per hour, his motion became "awkward and ungainly," making him "the observed of all observers." The best legs, therefore, were those to which the amputee could easily acclimate himself. The pinnacle of prosthetic engineering re-created the walk, the balance, and the complete repertoire of common motions that enabled the uninjured body to perform without conscious thought.[37]

The J. F. Rowley Company informed the readers of its advertising copy that "to see is to be convinced" of the quality and authenticity of its artificial legs. Evidence of the prostheses' illusory authenticity was crucial to the marketing narratives of the manufacturers. The disability scholar Harlan Hahn noted that representations used in bodily advertisements "may have been even more important than their content," for they forged a direct, tactile connection between marketing image and bodily image that was otherwise clouded by technical claims and copy clichés. J. F. Rowley adopted this visual premise as the central marketing device of its 1911 catalogue; the volume was meant to "encourage the unfortunate by placing photographic reproductions of men showing the extent of their

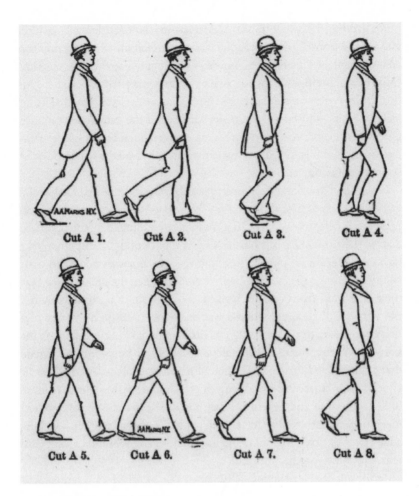

27. A. A. Marks walking diagram.

loss and restoration." Manufacturers used the before-and-after technique rampantly as a means of convincing the amputee of the tricks he could accomplish. The first image in these series showed a man, often seated, with his stump or stumps exposed in an overt presentation of his injury. The second image typically depicted the same man standing, fully clothed, the sleeves or legs of his suit filled with unseen artificial limbs. Drawings presented in all catalogues showed men in the process of dressing themselves and putting on their artificial limbs. When limbless, the men appeared stiff and uncomfortable; yet when standing with their limbs in place, they were transformed into models of gentlemanly fashion and ease. A contrasting technique was the revelation of injury after the achievement of illusion. J. F. Rowley's catalogue featured an image of three men standing side by side, one of whom wore two artificial legs. All three men were of a similar height and build, and each dressed alike, in jackets, pants, and bow ties. Rowley challenged the catalogue reader to detect the illusion. A second photograph revealed the bearer of the artificial limbs, holding the other two men on his shoulders to prove the strength of the devices.[38]

In addition to marketing messages that stressed the artificial limb's power to let its wearer slip into the obscurity of somatic normalcy, limb makers provided two contrasting messages that encouraged workers to display their prostheses as objects of pride and utility. Invisibility might have been desired in public, but if injured workers were to regain their ability to earn a wage in a competitive labor market, they must show that their new limbs functioned as well as the originals. In order to convince the amputee that his prosthesis was a device worth revealing in certain contexts, manufacturers tied its production and performance to the ever-increasing potential of machine technology. Limb makers argued that artificial body parts were the culmination of decades of scientific effort. Limbs conceived by inventive craftsmen were brought to fruition by the precision and repetition that could be offered only by modern machinery. Wearing an artificial limb made the injured worker a walking advertisement for American engineers' lofty achievements, a billboard for mechanized production.

As the J. F. Rowley catalogue explained, "An artificial leg is a mechanical device, a machine if you will, pure and simple. As in all other machines an artificial leg consists of parts, and . . . the whole leg . . . represents the parts assembled or combined." A prosthetic device was both an effective replacement for the natural limb and an amalgam of screws, bolts, hinges, and clamps. The essence of human motion could be mimicked by bringing various parts together in a mechanical system. However powerful and precise the machinery, limb manufacturers still required skilled men to work the machines and produce the best prosthesis technology could afford. Therefore, man and machine worked side by side to combine the craftsman's skill with the machine's precision. Entrepreneurs' vision of cooperation is astounding because they offered it to workers who had suffered greatly from the apparent incompatibility of man and machine. Here was a therapeutic narrative of machinery—machinery that attempted to mitigate the damage it had done. Machinery removed workers' limbs, but it also provided them with replacements, which were compact machines themselves. The Rowley catalogue revealed the extent to which artificial limbs were marketed as machines in their own right. Rowley explained, "You will have the further advantage of wearing an artificial leg, every part of which is standardized . . . therefore all parts are interchangeable and easily replaced without interference or delay should you meet with an accident." Turn-of-the-century industrial workers were well acquainted with the concept of interchangeable parts, and their own precarious position in the largely unskilled Pittsburgh workforce cast a dire meaning on the phrase "easily replaced without interference or delay."[39]

The function of limb catalogues, then, was to make favorable and inspiring the image of interchangeable parts and the machines that produced them. Images of artificial limb components revealed the technical precision that formed the foundation of prosthetic reconstruction. The sharp edges, smooth lines, and polished surfaces displayed in catalogues suggested that machines could make wonderfully intricate and beautiful products. The internal anatomy of limbs was equally intricate, connecting dozens of parts into a sophisticated mechanical system. The standardization of parts was essential, for it made limb repair a simple task. The artificial limb was the sum of its parts, a fully functioning machine built from precise and wondrous gadgets. Images also reemphasized the point that human motion was fundamentally a mechanical process. With the help of the body-as-machine metaphor, images of mechanical joints could make the argument that steel and aluminum couplings were not mere imitations of human tissue, but rather imitations that, in terms of performance, were so close to the real thing that such distinctions mattered little. Limb catalogues stressed that machines and machine-made parts were not to be feared or loathed. Instead, they gave the injured worker the opportunity to recapture the spirit of wholeness and ability that had been taken from him.

The significance of the limb machine was that it gave the amputee working power once again. Limb makers presented the dismembered body as a source of both wonder and pity; men who had lost limbs were visually exotic but also deprived of social utility. A central purpose of the artificial limb, then, was to return the accident victim to his rightful position as a wage earner by allowing him to perform work again. The assertion of the literary critic Erin O'Connor that dismemberment "unmanned" male workers, giving their bodies a "distinctly feminine side," suggests that late nineteenth-century American workers centered their conception of manliness on bodily integrity. The "theatrical malingering" of the amputee's stump—its phantom pains, its reluctance to heal, its sensitivity—raised concerns about the ability of workingmen to return to the workforce. Limb manufacturers, on the other hand, defined the worker's body in terms of what it could do. A. A. Marks promised that "persons wearing two artificial legs are so thoroughly in control of their means of locomotion that they go about much as other people. They readily resume their former occupations, no matter how arduous they may have been."[40]

After dismemberment, the industrial worker's body became a tool in the hands of the limbs maker, the focus of a process in which "a helpless member of society" became "a useful one." J. F. Rowley noted that by using their products "helpless cripples [had] become useful members of society" once again. Limb makers presented the accident victim as a man whose work ethic was as strong as ever, but whose body needed to be reworked to satisfy that ethic. Physical ability after prosthetic reconstruction was a matter of overall balance, ease of movement, and dexterity. Limb makers used rather outlandish means to show that men with artificial limbs could use their bodies in a variety of physical situations. J. F. Rowley's catalogue suggested the range of physical movements offered by artificial legs with images of men walking tightropes and riding bicycles. Both acts required a fine sense of balance and the ability to coordinate the movement of artificial legs with the rest of the body. Although the worker-amputee would never have to balance on a tightrope or ride a bicycle to prove his social utility, limb makers presented these images as proof that artificial legs would provide a sturdy base upon which men could work. Catalogues were, after all, a subtle form of entertainment in which the amputee could imagine his possibilities after being remade. The tightrope and the bicycle introduced a sense of wonder into the narrative of physical renewal, posing a challenge to hybrids of the body and the machine that were always up to the task.[41]

Like the American surgical community of the early twentieth century, limb manufacturers believed that the primary value of an amputation stump was its ability to accommodate a prosthetic device and reestablish normal function. This utilitarian view of stumps extended to the limb itself when limb makers considered industrial work as the goal of artificial arms and legs. Limbs meant to facilitate industrial work, as opposed to those meant to give the amputee a natural appearance in public, were not made with aesthetics in mind. Instead, limb makers produced working limbs with an eye toward cost and basic function. Although a middle-class accident victim or a skilled worker with ample compensation might seek an attractive, realistic limb, doctors and manufacturers alike stressed that for many workers it was "better to sacrifice appearance to strength and utility." The needs of the industrial workplace determined the design of an industrial worker's artificial limb, an appendage that could be "laid aside as a mere tool" at the end of the workday. The cheap, useful artificial limb, "a perpetual reminder of the wearer's bereft condition," gave no illusion of bodily integrity but allowed the accident victim an opportunity to balance himself on the mill floor or the mine chamber and even manipulate tools with a mechanical hand or attachment. Peg legs and hook arms served the most basic functions of supporting weight and lifting objects without any pretense of anatomical authenticity. The difference between "elegance and utility" in artificial limbs translated into a matter of cost for the amputee. Feick Brothers' peg leg, the company noted, was "intended for laboring men, and others whose means will not permit the purchase of an expensive artificial limb." Though a full-model limb for an amputation between the knee and the ankle cost seventy dollars, Feick Brothers' peg leg cost only ten dollars. A. A. Marks peg legs started at fifteen dollars.[42]

The most advertised type of practical artificial limb in the early 1910s was the artificial arm that accommodated a variety of working implements for a variety of tasks. Feick Brothers sold two versions of artificial arms that came with detachable hands, allowing the injured worker to attach an array of tools for different types of work. This "very useful tool for laborers, farmers, and railroad employes" was the ultimate expression of prosthetic utility; the manufacturer made no attempt to produce a lifelike limb, for the purpose of the device was not illusion but work. The artificial arm here became a workbench, a platform for any type of tool that an industrial worker could use. Armed with such a device, a worker could swap hooks, pinchers, files, or clasps (in addition to knives, forks, and spoons) at will. A. A. Marks also sold artificial arms with interchangeable tools and presented a drawing of such tools at work in a

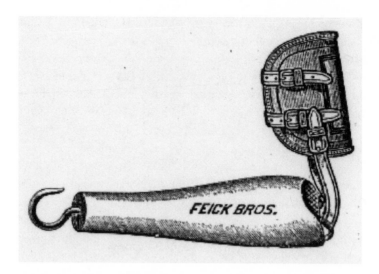

28. Feick Brothers artificial limb.
29. A. A. Marks artificial limb.

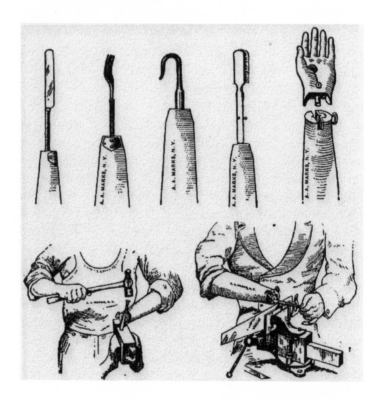

workshop. The images cropped the workers' bodies, focusing on artificial limbs at work without attempting to incorporate them into the men's entire somatic ensembles. Here mechanical arms and their deserved presence in the workplace filled the artist's frame; for each illustrated worker, a natural arm worked in tandem with an artificial arm to show how one complemented the other.[43]

The promise of artificial limb catalogues, as the medical historian Lisa Herschbach has noted, was that "loss was constructive; that amputation in particular could lay out new paths, voyages of discovery, and that science and technology would show the way." Manufacturers employed symbols in their catalogues to sell products and secure a place in American techno-medical history. They did so also to establish a community of consumers around the use of prosthetic devices, a group of people with the same problem following the same path toward solution. In the 1870s, the writer William Rideing noted a new trend in the marketing of artificial limbs to Civil War amputees. Manufacturers began including testimonial sections in their catalogues as another way to impress upon prospective customers the quality of their products. Rideing noted that testimonials expressed the "experiences of crippled men whose infirmities have been relieved . . . by the dexterity of artisans in human-repair shops." When limb makers turned their attention to industrial workers after the turn of the century, the use of testimonials and correspondence networks became even more prominent. Part of the objective of letter writing was to make consumers believe they had access to every scrap of information available on artificial limbs. Feick Brothers noted that there had been "entirely too much mystery thrown about the making of artificial limbs." Equipped with lengthy lists of actual amputees who wore artificial limbs, limb makers stressed, the prospective customer could have all his questions answered and never feel alone in dismemberment.[44]

Limb makers capitalized upon the isolating effect of injury to make themselves seem essential for the amputee. Entrepreneurs attempted to unite the atomized mass of the industrial limbless into a cohesive network of savvy consumers. Most catalogues ended with lengthy collections of customer commendations that followed a standard sequence: a brief account of the dismembering accident, a favorable review of the prosthesis's performance, and an affirmation of the manufacturer's supremacy. Many letters from grateful customers ended by welcoming correspondence. A steamboat worker from Kentucky declared himself "ready and willing to give any information . . . to anyone in need." A man from New Jersey encouraged "everybody that has need of a leg" to visit him and observe him in action. Testimonials were meant to establish letter-writing networks in which amputees could exchange information about the best models, the most comfortable techniques, and shared experiences. Pittsburgh's injured workers were promised a close and meaningful connection with amputees across the country who understood the hopelessness, indignity, and poverty of dismemberment. A. A. Marks encouraged prospective buyers to send the company a list of the men with whom they wished to correspond; Marks would provide the list of addresses upon receipt. J. F. Rowley went even further, establishing a "Ten Year Club" for individuals who had worn a Rowley leg for ten years or more and wanted to correspond with both veterans and newcomers to the world of artificial limbs. In its 1911 catalogue, the company supplied one hundred letters from satisfied customers, including their addresses.[45]

Questions remain: How did Pittsburgh workers respond to these prosthetic narratives? and how many of them actually purchased artificial limbs after suffering permanent injury in the workplace? One thing is certain: the cost of the most sophisticated prostheses put them out of reach for the majority of accident victims. Limbs with movable joints, cushioned sockets, and a smooth, tan complexion cost between seventy and one hundred and fifty dollars. The least elaborate prostheses on the market cost between ten and thirty dollars. At a time when average yearly incomes for workers in Pittsburgh's major industries ranged from five hundred to eight hundred dollars, the cost of a "special" artificial limb, as J. F. Rowley described its top model, was prohibitive for many. The compensation amounts offered to workers under existing accident relief programs were notoriously uneven. Though some iron and steel manufacturers paid workers as much as eight hundred dollars for the loss of a limb, many firms offered only fifty. Several industrial employers in Pittsburgh offered workers artificial limbs as part of their compensation for work-related injuries. The U.S. Steel Corporation's accident relief plan of 1910, gave amputees, in addition to twelve to eighteen months' wages, artificial limbs. U.S. Steel's goal, however, was to assist workers in regaining their working ability; peg legs and hook arms sufficed for the work positions available to the injured. Several coal company programs reviewed by the commissioner of labor in 1909 provided workers with seventy-five dollars explicitly for the purchase of an artificial limb. Coupled with the unemployment that immediately followed the loss of a limb, the compensation paid to injured workers from companies meant that "working limbs" were the only option for the vast majority of Pittsburgh industrial amputees. The appeals of bodily disguise and social emulation must have been subordinated to the appeals of display and reconstructed ability.[46]

Injured workers in Pittsburgh and industrial America might have shared a sense of physical and economic loss, but they needed new cues to think of themselves as members of a distinct group, the prosthetically reconstructed. Although artificial limbs had been readily available on the American market since the 1840s, the turn-of-the-century limb industry made the first attempt to mobilize the industrial wounded into their own subculture. As injured workers pondered the possibility of prosthetic augmentation, they entered an ambiguous era in the Steel City, one in which their bodies were further converted into commodities, discarded and replaced when damaged. Limb makers' advertising claims created long lists of new capabilities for amputees to desire as their own, incorporated into the privacy of their bodies. Yet their photographs and illustrations reinforced the notion that the body of work was a public asset, belonging to industries as useful tools and to cities as models of perfection. Workers might hide their stumps to avoid personal discomfort, but what they displayed in lieu of disability was a facade of able-bodied normalcy. Catalogue images produced new therapeutic narratives for the type of men whom Lewis Hine posed on Pittsburgh's streets and framed as helpless, futureless victims. Limb makers promised help and a future by encouraging workers to think of their bodies before accidents as merely the original versions of works in progress. Bodies could be disfigured, but they could also be transfigured, updated, and reworked in a process limited only by technical innovation and the size of amputees' pocketbooks.[47]

CONCLUSION

For limb-making companies, a cohesive community of reconstructed workers was an appealing vision of group affinity based on a belief in a better industrial future. With a happy ending that combined physical ability and psychological ease, the prosthetic narrative was a marketable alternative to Eastman's "little city of cripples." Limb makers' efforts, like those of safety engineers, industrial surgeons, and state legislators, were meant to restore the body of work to some degree of grandeur by vesting it with renewed power and value. In the case of workmen's compensation, this effort was a program to value the body literally, with exact dollar amounts distributed to injured workers over specific time periods. For safety engineers, the key was to convince the individual worker that his body was valuable enough to warrant safeguarding, teaching the allegedly indifferent employee that he alone could stop accidents. Company doctors and first-aid teams deemed that workers' lives were worth saving, stressing that even a broken body held more value than a dead one. Through the efforts of these groups, moreover, another type of value emerged from broken bodies: individuals could make careers for themselves by providing forms of relief. Like the social researchers of the Pittsburgh Survey, they turned the act of dealing with the problematic working body into a professional rallying point. Researchers amassed bodily evidence to prove, first, that there was a problem involving working bodies and, second, that a trained attention to detail and an ability to tease out underlying connections were essential to future resolution. Each of the groups discussed in this chapter presented themselves as students of the crisis and the key to a solution.

In addition to their determination to revive the healthy body of work, these institutional responses also labored to charge it with a sense of longevity. City boosters' image of the body of work around the turn of the century had a timeless quality to it, suggesting that even in a time of rampant technological and demographic change, the distinctive figure of the Steel City remained as powerful as ever. The Pittsburgh Survey refuted this notion, arguing that the body of work was undergoing profound change and, in fact, might disappear entirely under the weight and menace of mechanical work. Various responses to the problem of accidents in the 1910s sought to restore the body, rescuing it from the swift decline that trauma and injury seemed to portend. Although they depended on various degrees of injury's exposure and concealment, medical, governmental, and commercial figures all vowed that the able, working body would persist. This pledge could be equally philanthropic and self-serving, geared as much toward justice and assistance as toward profit and image. Yet it also struck a chord with boosters, workers, and the Pittsburgh middle class, all of whom longed for relief from the trouble highlighted in the survey. The image of industrial work put forth in limb catalogues and safety contests acknowledged weaknesses and ugliness that the Chamber of Commerce's pamphlets avoided altogether. But as long as limb makers exhibited satisfied, productive customers and safety officials awarded teams for rescuing workers from imaginary accidents, their scripts also offered a triumphant endpoint that Progressive writers did not echo. The prosthetic promise diverged significantly from the survey's narrative, not in its optimistic forecast, but in its implication that the process of solving the problem was straightforward. Unlike Fitch, Eastman, and Butler, each of whom stressed the complexity of dealing with the body of work, limb makers made speed and convenience their stock-in-trade.

The persistence of the working body that was an article of faith for many Pittsburghers was a hollow claim for others. Yet even those who criticized industry for its crimes and indignities were roused by the belief that the body could withstand the worst that modern work had to offer. Before the turn of the century, this notion was best expressed by yet another item that appeared in the city's labor press to offer workers a way of thinking about their bodies. In 1896, the *National Labor Tribune* printed Ella Wheeler Wilcox's "Endurance," a poem that traveled the treacherous path of a worker's life. Wilcox's words took the reader through successive acts of survival, from one trauma to another, and ended with a body eager to assert its evidence. Wilcox did not describe a triumph over industrial life, but a slow, halting endurance; the body's persistence came as a surprise to both the poet and the reader. In adopting that stance, the poem spoke well to the institutional remedies of the 1910s, framing them not as complete solutions to the problem body but as partial amends, schemes to aid it in its stubborn refusal to collapse. Whether encouraging or disheartening, the endurance of the working body in Pittsburgh seemed evident on the eve of the First World War:

How much the heart may bear and yet not break!
How much the flesh may suffer, yet not die!
I question much if any pain or ache
Of soul or body brings our end more nigh;
Death chooses his own time; till that is sworn,
All evils may be borne.

We shrink and shudder at the surgeon's knife,
Each nerve recoiling from the cruel steel,
Whose edge seems searching for the quivering life.
Yet to our sense the bitter pangs reveal,
That still, although the trembling flesh be torn,
This also can be borne.

We see a sorrow rising in our way
And try to flee from the approaching ill;
We seek some small escape, we weep and pray;
But when the blow falls, then our hearts are still.
Not that the pain is of its sharpest shorn,
But that it can be borne.

We wind our life about another life.
We hold it closer, dearer than our own;
Anon it faints and falls in deathly strife,
Leaving us stunned and stricken and alone.
But, ah! we do not die with those we mourn;
This also can be borne.

Behold, we live through all things—famine, thirst,
Bereavement, pain, all grief and misery,
All woe and sorrow; life inflicts its worst
On soul and body, but we cannot die,
Though we may be sick and tired and faint and worn,
Let all things be borne.[48]

Justice, even scant justice, has never been done to the picturesque features of Pittsburg by either poet or artist.

—*Bulletin*, 6 May 1905

EPILOGUE

"THAT'S WORK, AND THAT'S WHAT

PEOPLE LIKE TO WATCH"

✳ Few observers questioned the appeal of the male working body in Pittsburgh in the late nineteenth century and early twentieth. The *nature* of that appeal was a constant matter of debate. For the Chamber of Commerce member William Scaife, the grandeur of working bodies formed the common thread of civilizations past and present. For the Pittsburgh Survey writer Crystal Eastman, the condition of working bodies exemplified in eloquent fashion the reckless logic of industrial capitalism. For the artificial leg manufacturer John Rowley, the mechanics of working bodies made them conveniently adjustable. The Pittsburgh worker's body was both text and spectacle at the turn of the century, used alternately to offer instruction and pleasure, polemic and horror to the city's residents, visitors, and observers. The male worker's body provided a series of narratives during this time of jarring transformation, suggesting ways of finding continuity amid change, addressing dire problems of life and death, and reasserting progress as the hallmark of the dominant civic culture. When the body became a highly portable symbol of the status of the city, however, it also became divorced from the people whose work remained hidden in mills and mines. Writers and researchers, manufacturers and legislators all searched the worker's body for clues about its trials and triumphs in the mechanized workplace, but each increasingly ignored the possibility that Pittsburgh workers' lives could be defined by anything other than their work.

In the city known for steel, work and the bodies that performed it continued to command center stage in the stories that people told of themselves and each other. Symbol makers seized upon the body as a way of defining order, yet, as Dominick LaCapra reminds us, one person's order is another person's "contestatory other." Progressives' designs for a controlled future posited little more than chaos in a present that boosters argued was hectic but rewarding. What employers viewed as the carelessness and unruliness of experienced workers was, to workers, a means of putting ideals of independence and citizenship into practice. Homesteaders' assault on Pinkerton guards was both the workers' systematic defense of rights and reporters' horde run amok. Three parting glimpses of Pittsburgh work spectacles end this study of the industrial working body. Each suggested a return to form in the 1910s, mirroring boosters' confident representations of the body before the turn of the century. Yet each was also complicated by labor critics' and social reformers' discourses on injury and physical inadequacy. The trio showed, moreover, that a different kind of production continued unabated in Pittsburgh, one that was independent of booms and busts in steel, glass, and coal.

First, a failure. In the autumn of 1909, the Pittsburgh Chamber of Commerce and city council contracted the nationally renowned pageant designer Percy MacKaye to produce two civic celebrations for the summers of 1910 and 1911. The first was to be a Fourth of July patriotic pageant, and the other a community-building display based on local industry. MacKaye wrote his drama for the summer of 1911, titled the "Masque of Labor," to boost civic pride by personifying the spirit of labor and exhibiting its positive effects for the Steel City. MacKaye collaborated with John White Alexander in deciding which features of industry to emphasize in the "Masque of Labor." The pair worked in the winter of 1909 and 1910 to provide the city with a series of "practical symbolic forms" that would allow Pittsburghers to share in the same ideas and images about themselves. These images stressed the central spectacle of men at work as the epitome of the "riches of history, folk-lore, tradition, and contemporary American life." MacKaye and Alexander built a historical pageant that combined feats of strength, chronicles of industrial milestones, and details of production processes from raw materials to finished products. MacKaye reasoned that as a practical symbolic form, the sight of a man hard at work would resonate with a Pittsburgh audience that had been repeatedly schooled in the significance of this common figure.[1]

MacKaye believed that the people "most authentically responsive" to the messages conveyed in civic dramas were industrial workers themselves, men "amid smoke and molten ore" who built the city into a modern marvel. Accordingly, he wanted Pittsburgh's workers to see themselves in the "Masque of Labor" as figures whose physical perfection inspired the rest of the city and the nation to new heights. MacKaye planned to use "splendid expert wrestlers" in scenes involving men at work and "thousands" of steel, glass, and coal workers in chorus and nonspeaking roles. The wrestlers would supply the physiques and movements necessary for the dramatic presentation of work, while the ranks of workers would offer some suggestion of the magnitude of the Pittsburgh workforce as it assembled itself on stage. Moreover, the inclusion of workers around the periphery of highlighted work spectacles would create the union of "high standards in art with democratic sympathies" that MacKaye held as crucial to civic pageants. If Pittsburgh workers were not present in the audience *and onstage*, he believed his drama would be virtually powerless. MacKaye wanted his pageant to do more than offer representations of workers; he believed he could use such representations to dissect modern industrial life. He preferred the title "masque" over "pageant" because it connoted an interpretation of society and life rather than a mere exhibition. The "Masque of Labor" would offer Pittsburghers both a narrative of their own lives and a historical explanation of how their city reached its current state. Furthermore, MacKaye hoped, it would give them a clear rationale to reinforce their sense of community around the displayed figure of the industrial worker. It would have been hard for boosters to find a better vehicle for their sympathies than the "Masque of Labor."[2]

MacKaye's civic celebrations, however, were not to be. Three months before the 1910 pageant was to begin, a government bribery scandal swept through the pages of the local press and brought an immediate halt to city spending. In the last weeks of March, dozens of city councilmen admitted to accepting money in exchange for votes. The council canceled MacKaye's pair of pageants quietly, incurring little notice from a local press eager to publish the latest details of municipal deceit. When Pittsburgh celebrated the Fourth of July in 1910 and 1911, it did so without the benefit of MacKaye's and Alexander's vision of festivities revolving around the body of work.[3]

Second, a triumph. Despite the setback of 1910, a "gigantic drama" involving workers' bodies finally came to Pittsburgh three years later. In the winter of 1913–14, the Carnegie Institute presented a three-week public exhibition of the sculptures of Constantin Meunier. The collection consisted of ten plasters, seventy-seven bronze sculptures, fourteen watercolors, thirteen pastels, and thirty sketches, all of which took work and industry as their subjects. The collection's special emphasis on the "valiant puddlers and foundrymen" was meant to strike a nostalgic chord for Pittsburghers. Meunier's works graced the institute's galleries as a reminder of the city on the rise, enmeshed in the growth of the nineteenth century and still known more for its iron than its steel. Meunier had stripped many of the exhibited figures to the waist, reminiscent of the focus on naked torsos that had epitomized the iconography of work in Pittsburgh since the 1880s. Sculptures such as *Miner Working at Vein*, *Puddlers at the Furnace*, and *Glassblowers* showed premechanized workers, artisans with tools as they manipulated raw materials with only their muscles and skills to aid them. Puddlers appeared in six sculptures and paintings, miners in twelve works, and glassworkers in five. Individual bronze reliefs showed glassworkers repairing a broken melting pot and miners using picks and shovels to break and load coal. Also in tow was Meunier's *The Puddler*, restored to its original form and stripped of the dollar amounts added by Eastman four years earlier. With the taint of accidental dismemberment removed, Meunier's puddler regained his power to epitomize "official" Pittsburgh, and exhibitors hoped that his muscular frame would bear the weight of history and civic pride.[4]

A contemporary expert on Meunier's work, Christian Brinton, assured the public that the collection met those expectations. Brinton noted that Meunier's sculptures stripped "every vestige of extraneous appeal" from the workers, focusing the viewer on the abstract relationship between bodies and work. Although the static sculptures and drawings could show only snapshots of labor, art critics agreed that the figures welcomed the viewer into a world of work that could not otherwise be known by the average Pittsburgher. The *Pittsburgh Sun* marveled at Meunier's technique of capturing the worker "in the very instant of action." The sculptures that came to Pittsburgh in 1913 showed virile men "for whom no task [was] too difficult, no burden too heavy." The action—the work—implied by the sculptures gave the half-clad figures a set of positive meanings for art critics; a *Pittsburgh Sun* writer concluded that the collection exhibited Meunier's talent for finding "the beautiful in the life of toil." The *Gazette Times* noted that Meunier's work was especially appropriate for Pittsburgh. His celebration of labor fit well with the interests of those who staged beauty and civic identity through myriad work spectacles in Pittsburgh over the past twenty-five years.[5]

The Meunier exhibit was well attended during its three-week run at the Carnegie Institute. The *New York Times* reported that "men from the mines and factories of Pittsburgh" showed the "keenest appreciation" of Meunier's work, although no local newspapers reported similar working-class attendance. Appreciative workers may have been the "very prototypes of the laborers depicted by Meunier," but it is impossible to judge whether praise from workers was an actual reaction recorded by reporters or merely the wishful thinking of the institute's staff. Either way, the goal of attracting workers to the exhibit was clear. Brinton remarked that the exhibition was "most significant" as an example of labor given a positive image of itself. The educational role of art persisted in Pittsburgh, but now it could also be used to help the industrial worker understand himself and the importance of his work. Brinton, local art critics, and the staff of the institute hoped the Meunier exhibit served as a mirror to reflect the dignity and power of local labor.[6]

Finally, a stalemate. At some point between the turn of the century and 1920, a local legend is said to have emerged in immigrant working-class neighborhoods of southwestern Pennsylvania. The myth of Joe Magarac told the tale of a "superworker," inhuman yet seemingly likeable and inspirational, who transcended the demands of the workplace and won a dubious victory over industry. Magarac was actually made of steel, molded from the material that gave Pittsburgh its claim to fame for much of the twentieth century. Towering above his fellow workers and wielding arms the size of smokestacks, Magarac worked twenty-four hours a day and called his beloved mill home. He was able to load open-hearth furnaces, stir molten steel, and make finished rails by hand. As a result of his relentless work ethic, Magarac eventually overproduced; the excess of metal he made with his own steel hands forced his employers to shut down the mill and fire their employees. Barred from his only passion in life, Magarac melted himself down in a furnace, providing enough steel for the construction of a new mill and thus ensuring that production would continue in Pittsburgh. Embodying both the problem of and solution to work in the mechanized steel mill of the early twentieth century, Magarac destroyed himself yet lived on in the architecture of industry.[7]

Folklorists and historians have attributed Magarac's tale alternately to Pittsburgh's unskilled east European workers and U.S. Steel's public relations department. Whether Magarac was created in the immigrant steelworking communities of Pittsburgh around the turn of the century, developed as a corporate fairy tale in the 1930s, or popularized in the national media as a patriotic fable in the 1940s, the appeal of an ideal steelworker whose body defined and defied the inhuman conditions of the industrial workplace was apparent. Magarac beat the industrial system doubly, through tireless labor and self-sacrifice. His ability to withstand the dangers and pressures of the workplace—so much so that he made the mill his home—made Magarac an embodiment of a work ethic and a level of physical stamina that were elusive for mortal workers. His cheerful sacrifice in the name of production was that of the ideal worker, sensitive to the needs of employers and devoted to work. Finally, he embodied one of those "powerfully mammoth figures" that William Solomon has argued gave workers a "reassuring sense of wholeness, totality, and even indestructibility."[8]

Yet the myth of Joe Magarac offers an antithetical reading as well, one that places him in the realm of working-class satire rather than reverence. Despite *Life* magazine's contention that he stood as the "god of all steelworkers," Magarac, if created by workers at all, could very well have been imagined as a critique of the industrial regime, pieced together as the perfect worker management had envisioned but could not quite form from the men of Pittsburgh. In Croatian the word *magarac* means "donkey" or "jackass," suggesting that the heroic figure of the unrelenting worker may have been ridiculed for his unthinking acceptance of millwork. As Jennifer Gilley and Stephen Burnett have noted in their history of the myth, "Magarac's cheerfulness mocks the struggles and tragedies of his contemporaries." His delight in melting himself for the company, his willingness to stay in the mill eternally, and his machinelike body were all reasons for workers to fear and resent him rather than applaud his efforts. U.S. Steel's liberal use of Magarac in promotional materials and newsletters showed that these qualities were corporately accessible, but the notion that workers bought into them as well has yet to be demonstrated.[9]

Like Joe Magarac, MacKaye's abortive attempt at an industrial pageant and Meunier's collection of labor sculptures can also be read in less civic-minded ways. When MacKaye planned to hire wrestlers to play the role of workers in his "Masque of Labor," he decided not to allow workers to perform their own work spectacles. If wrestlers could be better representations of manly physiques and work skills, then it was because the symbols that MacKaye wanted for the Steel City were too much to ask of actual workers, who would instead fill the choral ranks. Wrestlers put to work on stage highlighted the physical act of work to a degree that workers themselves could no longer accomplish. Pittsburgh's industrial employees were to take part, of course, but as a faceless mass whose combined voice was a surrogate for their individual abilities and histories. For MacKaye, work was emblematic of Pittsburgh but in a way that revealed further abstraction between work and the body of work.

Meunier's representations of premechanized labor were fine pieces of nostalgia, yet the intervening years had brought to Pittsburgh frequent charges of deskilling, long rosters of the dead and injured, and major conflicts between labor and capital. In the context of the Pittsburgh of 1913, the art historian Melissa Dabakis has argued, Meunier's collection was "notable for that which it denied and concealed." The sculptures "offered relief from the stereotyped picture of radicalized and militant strikers dominating current political debates," eliminating a political edge that would devalue the artworks for the custodians of Pittsburgh's public image. Meunier had stressed that his art was concerned with workers who were not enemies of society, but active members, participants in the pursuit of a better world. Any notion of class conflict in the sculptures was incidental, an interpretation the artist himself did not acknowledge. Though a tenacious critic might find evidence of struggle or subversion in sculpted faces and muscles, adherents to the celebratory culture of Pittsburgh in the early twentieth century chose to emphasize the more pleasant symbols of exhilarating work and rugged physiques. One visitor to the collection concluded that Meunier's lasting effect was a single image of a worker composed of dozens of faces and bodies, "confused in the remembrance" because of their ubiquity.[10]

In the twenty-first century, Pittsburghers continue to create images of their city. With the collapse of the local steel and coal industries in the 1970s and 1980s, the body marked by heavy industrial work has largely faded from public view. Today, marketers, real estate developers, and city officials present Pittsburgh as a corporate and technological hub, a product of the ketchup bottle and the computer as much as of the world of Bessemer converters and mine shafts. Glimpses of powerful bodies certainly persist, however. City leaders routinely evoke the brawn of the Pittsburgh Steelers football team as an identifiable vision of local toughness. The train ride at the Kennywood amusement park carries riders past displays of the Battle of Homestead and Joe Magarac. The city's Steel Industry Heritage Corporation sells mugs, clocks, and T-shirts featuring a generic, muscled steelworker staring into the glowing distance. These examples of popular entertainment and education spectacles threaten to become caricatures of olden days but also serve a political function in the postindustrial city. Such imagery is evidence of a "Pittsburghness" that requires determined remembering in order to unsilence the past. Current symbol makers who use industrial figures to remind the public of manufacturing history's human face have their work cut out for them. This was vividly demonstrated when developers opened the Waterfront shopping center on the former site of the Homestead Steel Works in 1999. The site retained architectural reminders of an industrial past, including picturesque smokestacks and the mill's pump house, but it replaced production with consumption (and retail employment) as what people do on that particular stretch of the Monongahela River.[11]

The blend of entertainment, commerce, and history that exudes from such figures is telling, for the body of work imagined a century ago by the city's boosters was more proximate to actual working bodies but just as dependent upon a sense of enjoyment and nostalgia. Take the *Bulletin's* whimsical call in 1905 for work spectacles staged formally in city streets:

> The world never tires of a lover. It also never tires of a worker. . . . Walk along Fifth Avenue any hour of the day—or of the night, for that matter—and you will see a crowd clustered along one side of the street with eyes intently fixed on the other side. A theatre is being erected there, and a small army of workmen are rushing to and fro, carrying mortar and bricks and timbers, and hoisting great beams of steel to their places. It is a veritable bee-hive of activity, and that's why people gather on the other side of the street to look,

with riveted eyes and gaping mouths, very often—for they're beholding the miracle of human toil. It is a pity Mr. Davis cannot turn this wonderful sight into some financial remuneration. Why not have the workmen enclosed in some way and charge admission to see them work? There surely would be few empty seats. Or, better still, why does not some enterprising manager put on a "stunt" in which some mason comes on the stage and builds a brick wall? That's work, and that's what people like to watch.[12]

Compare this 1905 vision of a city rooted in work with a version from 2007, courtesy of the Tourism Office of the Pennsylvania Department of Community and Economic Development: "The Waterfront location is as exciting as it is historic—a towering line of smoke stacks represents the legacy of the former Homestead Steel Mill, where the Homestead Steel Strike of 1892 took place, a labor riot between the military and the steelworkers of Andrew Carnegie. In the summer, visit Kennywood, a historical landmark and one of 'America's Finest Traditional Amusement Parks,' and Sandcastle Water Park, once a railroad yard. Seven miles of railroad track were removed to make way for the waterpark."[13] The tourism board's juxtaposition of the exciting present and *significant* past speaks volumes about the lasting appeal of work as a useful tool in creating a sense of place. In the logic of the state's Website, the notion that people once made something in this particular locale means that today's shoppers should want to spend their money there. What connects this twenty-first-century marketing device to the symbolic contest a century before is the assumption that work is not only something that one does, but also something that one should imagine others doing, as a way to simplify complex experiences or to discover hidden details.

It is impossible to determine what Pittsburgh workers made of the Meunier exhibit or the Magarac legend on the eve of the First World War, just as their impressions of earlier civic parades, city guidebooks, artificial limb catalogues, and the Pittsburgh Survey remain obscured by lack of evidence and the privileges of business and civic leaders. In their critique of the celebratory body of work Progressive reformers spoke of Pittsburgh's workers, but they also tried to speak *for* them in tangible, though imperfect, ways. Efforts to lower the number of accidents in local industrial establishments, reduce the length of the workday, and bring about a better system of compensation after injury or death all sought improvements in the lives of Pittsburgh's industrial workforce. While

30. Detail from *Life* magazine cover, 16 May 1912.

instituting these changes, reformers made the body of work their clinical focus and rendered it a piece of evidence to be placed on public exhibit. Artificial limb makers adopted a similar strategy, deploying the dismembered body as a vehicle for the supply-and-demand process of the market. What all such efforts at representation in Pittsburgh shared, whether elevating the body as the pinnacle of strength or exposing the weaknesses it harbored, was the power and prevalence to make the figure of the Pittsburgh worker a generic one. When Pittsburgh's marketers sell the region today as the home of innovation, they extend this process. Viewing the open-hearth furnace as the heir of the puddling furnace or framing biotechnology as a worthy successor to heavy manufacturing presents a heartening, if teleological, connection between now and then, but it cleanses local narratives of messy things like conflict, failure, and suffering and the people who experienced them.[14]

The cover of *Life*'s issue of 16 May 1912 may be the best illustration. Captioned "So now we come to Pittsburgh," the cover image presented characters that symbolized the city in the 1910s. Sharing the stage with a pollution reformer, a couple embracing amid bags of money, and a child tour guide was the industrial worker. Broad-shouldered, muscular, pale, and wearing far fewer clothes than his fellow symbols, the Pittsburgh worker was the heart of the city, whose smokestacks still belched clouds of dark fumes into the night. Pittsburgh's cast of stock characters, a cliché by 1912, had been developed decades before through boosters' efforts to narrate a simple version of a growing, pulsing, clanging modern industrial city. Examining representations of workers' bodies a century later, however, reveals the complexity of the figures that met such demands. The appeal of the body of work in 1912 was the belief that it helped the uninitiated understand Pittsburgh on a more profound level. The promise of the body of work today is that it helps one understand such beliefs and the methods used to realize them.

NOTES

INTRODUCTION

1 *Bulletin*, 11 November 1905.

2 Keith Gandal, *The Virtues of the Vicious*, 13.

3 Carl Sandburg, *Chicago Poems*; Henry James, *The American Scene*; Linda Tomko, *Dancing Class*, xvi.

4 D. C. Ripley, quoted in *Toasts and Responses at the Banquet Given by the Chamber of Commerce of Pittsburgh, 27 May 1892*, 69.

5 Barbara Melosh, *Engendering Culture*, 84; Gandal, *The Virtues of the Vicious*, 71. Over two decades ago, Daniel Rodgers, in *The Work Ethic in Industrial America, 1850–1920*, xii, asked, "What happened to work values when work itself was radically remade?" Rodgers's answer, that work values persisted with renewed potency in the United States yet became increasingly abstract and removed from the realities of the workplace, underscored the social and political usefulness of anachronism.

6 William H. Sewell Jr., "The Concept(s) of Culture," 51; Elizabeth Faue, *Community of Suffering and Struggle*, 74–75; Roy Rosenzweig, *Eight Hours for What We Will*, 75.

7 Sewell Jr., *Logics of History*, 172.

8 Lincoln Steffens, *The Shame of the Cities*, 1.

9 James C. Scott, *Domination and the Arts of Resistance*, 92.

10 For a particularly strong statement of the possibilities and restrictions that

audiences impose on authors, see Lawrence W. Levine, "The Folklore of Industrial Society: Popular Culture and Its Audiences," 1398–99.

11 Dominick LaCapra, *Rethinking Intellectual History*, 31, 34 n. 9; William H. Sewell Jr., "Geertz, Cultural Systems, and History," 41–49.

12 Anthony N. Penna, "Changing Images of Twentieth-Century Pittsburgh," 49; *Bulletin*, 11 November 1905.

13 Elizabeth Beardsley Butler, *Women and the Trades*, 17; Waldon Fawcett, "The Center of the World of Steel," 190.

14 Francis Couvares, *The Remaking of Pittsburgh*, 19.

15 David Montgomery, *The Fall of the House of Labor*, 58.

16 Harry Braverman, *Work and Monopoly Capital*; Melvin Dubofsky, "Technological Change and American Worker Movements, 1870–1970," in *Hard Work*, 181; Michael Nuwer, "From Batch to Flow"; Dave Jardini, "From Iron to Steel"; Claudia Goldin and Lawrence F. Katz, "Technology, Skill, and the Wage Structure," 252.

17 Henry Gourley, quoted in *Toasts and Responses at the Banquet Given by the Chamber of Commerce of Pittsburgh, 27 May 1892*, 20.

18 Randolph E. Bergstrom, *Courting Danger*, 21. Alan Derickson observed in *Workers' Health, Workers' Democracy*, xiii, that historians had "virtually ignored workers' resistance to victimization by industrial illness and injury" prior to the late 1980s. Sarah F. Rose similarly notes in " 'Crippled' Hands," 29, that "disabled workers appear so frequently as passive victims—whose lives testify to everyday dangers of work, the nature of class conflict, and the rise of working-class mutuality—but so rarely as agents." On the mixed implications of cross-class representations of workers, see John Pultz, *The Body and the Lens*, 80.

1. INDUSTRIAL CHANGE AND WORK IN PITTSBURGH

1 Seelye A. Willson, "The Growth of Pittsburgh Iron and Steel," 540; William Lucien Scaife, "Pittsburg—A New Great City," 57; "Pittsburgh, the Giant Industrial City of the World," 841. Other nicknames given to Pittsburgh during this period were the Smoky City, the Workshop of the World, the City of Brains and Brawn, and Pittsburgh the Powerful.

2 Francis Couvares, in *The Remaking of Pittsburgh*, focused on the switch from the Iron City to the Steel City as a harbinger of the metalworker's reduced status. Richard Oestreicher explained the transition in this way: "In the Iron City, most people were either wage earners or bosses. As the Iron City became the Steel City, the bosses became corporate executives. As the executives decided to invest their capital elsewhere, their employees, the 'mill hunks,' became unemployed." See Richard Oestreicher, "Working-Class Formation, Development, and Consciousness in Pittsburgh, 1790–1960," in *City at the Point,* 111. For an excellent overview of Pittsburgh's immigration patterns in the nineteenth century, see Nora Faires, "Immigrants and Industry: Peopling the 'Iron City,'" in *City at the Point,* 3–31.

 3 On the city's glass industry in the late nineteenth century, see Anne Madarasz, *Glass,* 45–61. Two of the best works that place the regional coal industry in its larger industrial context are Carmen DiCiccio, *Coal and Coke in Pennsylvania,* and Andrew Roy, *A History of the Coal Miners of the United States.* The connection between coal mining and the steel industry in Pittsburgh was summarized well by Muriel Sheppard: "The steel mills must have pig iron to make steel and the blast furnaces must have coke to make pig iron, so that if anything happens to shut off the coke supply it is a case of 'Stick won't beat dog, dog won't bite pig, pig won't jump over the stile.'" See Muriel Sheppard, *Cloud by Day,* 21.

 4 James Kitson, "The Iron and Steel Industries of America," 631; *Souvenir Handbook: Some Things of Interest in and about Pittsburgh, to be Visited by the Iron and Steel Institute of Great Britain; Year Book and Directory of the Chamber of Commerce of Pittsburgh, PA* (1903), 46.

 5 Lillian W. Betts, "Pittsburg: A City of Brain and Brawn," 17. The Chamber of Commerce's effort to publicize the physiques of Pittsburgh industry coincided with its efforts to establish a "Greater Pittsburgh," a geographical and industrial unit that would reveal statistically the area's true commercial and manufacturing power. Beginning in 1894, the Chamber of Commerce urged the annexation of Allegheny City to the north and various smaller towns surrounding the city center. The Chamber of Commerce reasoned that "in all public and official statements of population, commerce, and industrial production, Pittsburgh [was] dwarfed" when compared to major cities that had annexed "outlying but dependent suburbs." Whereas New York thrived on ocean commerce, Chicago took advantage of its westward position, and San Francisco and New Orleans enjoyed international traffic, Pittsburgh relied only on "her own brain, her own energy, and her own industry." In December 1907, Pittsburgh annexed Allegheny City, and a Greater Pittsburgh was born.

 When I refer to Pittsburgh, I refer more broadly to the industrial region of southwestern Pennsylvania that radiated outward from Pittsburgh along the Ohio, Allegheny, Monongahela, and Youghiogheny rivers. Whether designated as the "Pittsburgh District" (the Pittsburgh Survey's circular region measuring forty to fifty miles from downtown Pittsburgh), the "Pittsburgh Metropolitan District" (a Census Bureau term to designate Pittsburgh and all incorporated towns within the same circular region), or the "Pittsburgh region" (the historian Roy Lubove's term for six counties in southwestern Pennsylvania), the city's surrounding industrial region encompassed more than the city limits. The difficulty of finding a standard reveals the complex process through which city boosters, census workers, and reformers sought a vocabulary to describe the effect of Pittsburgh on other cities and towns. The Chamber of Commerce envisioned "the mighty arms of Pittsburgh's industries" as they reached into neighboring counties. Simply referring to "Pittsburgh" was not enough when the industrial influence of the city seemed to defy its own borders. In 1901, the *Pittsburg Leader* claimed that the "universal understanding is that Pittsburg includes all that territory in Eastern Ohio, West Virginia, and Western Pennsylvania."

On these concepts, see Edward K. Muller, "Industrial Suburbs and the Growth of Metropolitan Pittsburgh, 1870–1920," 58–73; Roy Lubove, *Twentieth-Century Pittsburgh*, 3, 27; Pittsburgh Chamber of Commerce, *Greater Pittsburgh*; John Newton Boucher, *A Century and a Half of Pittsburg and Her People*, 519; *Pittsburg at the Dawn of the 20th Century*; and Sarah H. Killikelly, *The History of Pittsburgh*, 244.

6 Jones and Laughlin's American Iron and Steel Works employed thirty-two hundred workers in 1890 and over five thousand at the turn of the century. Carnegie Steel's Homestead Works employed three thousand workers in the early 1890s and over ten thousand in 1910. John A. Fitch, *The Steel Workers*, 22; U.S. Census Bureau, *Thirteenth Census: 1910*, 10:930–31; *Annual Report of the Factory Inspector of the Commonwealth of Pennsylvania*; Couvares, *The Remaking of Pittsburgh*, 11; Erasmus Wilson, ed., *Standard History of Pittsburg, Pennsylvania*, 945; Carnegie Steel Company, *General Statistics and Special Treatise on the Homestead Steel Works*, 14.

7 Warren C. Scoville, *Revolution in Glassmaking*, 44; *All About Pittsburgh and Allegheny*, 132, 162; *Some Things of Interest in and about Pittsburgh*. Madarasz, *Glass*, 50, includes a discussion of the industry's growth in relation to that of other American cities at the turn of the century.

8 Carmen P. DiCiccio, "The Rise and Fall of King Coal," 143.

9 Mary Heaton Vorse, *Men and Steel*, 13. For a vivid example of the planning behind a "model" mill town, see Anne E. Mosher, *Capital's Utopia*.

10 Population figures are from U.S. Bureau of the Census, *Tenth Census: 1880*, *Eleventh Census: 1890*, *Twelfth Census: 1900*, and *Thirteenth Census: 1910*. On the growth of Monessen, see Matthew S. Magda, *Monessen*, 4–9.

11 Census figures are from *Tenth Census: 1880*, 1:861; *Eleventh Census: 1890*, 2:632; *Thirteenth Census: 1910*, 10:931; *Annual Report of the Factory Inspector of the Commonwealth of Pennsylvania*. The Chamber of Commerce's numbers are from J. Morton Hall, *America's Industrial Centre*, 38; Pittsburgh Chamber of Commerce, *Pittsburgh the Powerful*, 85.

12 *Tenth Census: 1880*, 1:338; *Thirteenth Census: 1910*, 10:931.

13 Coal mining figures are from U.S. Congress, *Reports of the Immigration Commission*, 18; W. Jett Lauck, "The Bituminous Coal Miner and Coke Worker of Western Pennsylvania," 34; and DiCiccio, "The Rise and Fall of King Coal," 144.

14 "Pittsburgh, the Giant Industrial City of the World," 841; *The Story of Pittsburgh and Vicinity Illustrated*; Theodore W. Nevin, *Pittsburg and the Men Who Made It*, 24.

15 Scaife, "Pittsburg—A New Great City," 53. See also Arthur Hiorns, *Iron and Steel Manufacture*, 151, which attributes the success of steel over iron to three factors: the greater speed, expanded scope, and lesser reliance on human labor that distinguished the Bessemer process from puddling.

16 Percival Roberts Jr., "The Puddling Process, Past and Present," 356; Jardini, "From Iron to Steel," 285; Hiorns, *Iron and Steel Manufacture*, 89; Brody, *Steelworkers in America*, 8. A modified form of puddling known as "boiling" was also used in iron and steel production in the late nineteenth century. Because the variations in the two processes were minor, I use the term *puddling* throughout to refer to both puddling and boiling.

17 Couvares, *The Remaking of Pittsburgh*, 14.

18 Jardini, "From Iron to Steel," 275; *Directory of Pittsburgh and Allegheny Cities*. On the culture of skilled workers in nineteenth-century Pittsburgh, see Couvares, *The Remaking of Pittsburgh*, 21–40. My treatment of skilled workers' double defense of their rights as both men and workers is informed by Gregory L. Kaster, "Labour's True Man," 24–64.

19 Killikelly, *The History of Pittsburgh*, 250–51. Peter Temin, *Iron and Steel in Nineteenth-Century America*, 125, describes the production of crucible steel before the introduction of the Bessemer process.

20 W. David Lewis, *Iron and Steel in America*, 40; Swank, *Statistics of the Iron and Steel Production of the United States*, 128; "Homestead as Seen by One of its Workmen," 167; Scaife, "Pittsburg—A New Great City," 56; "Pittsburgh, the Giant Industrial City of the World," 846. On the importance of continuous processes in late nineteenth-century industry, see Alfred D. Chandler Jr., *The Visible Hand*, esp. chap. 8.

21 Hiorns, *Iron and Steel Manufacture*, 65–66; Scaife, "Pittsburg—A New Great City," 51; Montgomery, *The Fall of the House of Labor*, 58; Fitch, *The Steel Workers*, 29. Specific blast furnace dimensions and production figures are collected in Swank, *Statistics of the Iron and Steel Production of the United States*, 145.

22 John Porter, "Manufacture of Pig Iron," in *The ABC of Iron and Steel*, 80; Scaife, "Pittsburg—A New Great City," 51, 55; Fitch, *The Steel Workers*, 27–30.

23 Brody, *Steelworkers in America*, 36; Fitch, *The Steel Workers*, 29.

24 This description of puddling is based on Fitch, *The Steel Workers*, 33; Temin, *Iron and Steel in Nineteenth-Century America*, 17; Jardini, "From Iron to Steel," 277; Hiorns, *Iron and Steel Manufacture*, 88–89; Ralph Keeler and Harry Fenn, "The Taking of Pittsburgh, III," 262; James Davis, *The Iron Puddler*, 93, 98–113; "The American Iron and Steel Works of the Jones and Laughlin Company" (1867), in Jones and Laughlin Company manuscript collection, HSWP, 5.

25 This description of the Bessemer process is based on "Making Bessemer Rails," 238; Jardini, "From Iron to Steel," 277; Lewis, *Iron and Steel in America*, 36; Hiorns, *Iron and Steel Manufacture*, 144–47; Scaife, "Pittsburg—A New Great City," 54, 57; and *Bulletin*, 22 November 1890. Fitch, *The Steel Workers*, 40, describes the Bessemer converter as an "immense egg-shaped barrel hung on axles."

26 This description of the open-hearth process is based on Temin, *Iron and Steel in Nineteenth-Century America*, 139; Lewis, *Iron and Steel in America*, 40; Swank, "Statistics of the Iron and Steel Production," 127; "Pittsburgh, the Giant Industrial City of the World," 845; Fitch, *The Steel Workers*, 44; and "Homestead as Seen by One of its Workmen," 167.

27 "Homestead as Seen by One of its Workmen," 166.

28 Hamlin Garland, "Homestead and its Perilous Trades," 6.

29 Temin, *Iron and Steel in Nineteenth-Century America*, 165; Katherine Stone, "The Origins of Job Structures in the Steel Industry," 66; Fawcett, "The Center of the World of Steel," 201.

30 Daniel Nelson, *Managers and Workers*, 28; Roberts, "The Puddling Process, Past and Present," 357, 362; Scaife, "Pittsburg—A New Great City," 53; Henry M. Howe, "Notes on the Bessemer Process," 1138.

31 Brody, *Steelworkers in America*, 8; Paul Krause, *The Battle for Homestead, 1880–1892*, 288; Fitch, *The Steel Workers*, 33, 51; *Amalgamated Journal*, 10 July 1902. As I show in chapter 3, nostalgia for the spectacle of puddling formed a substantial part of the booster campaigns around the turn of the century that described Pittsburgh in terms of its workers and their bodies.

32 U.S. Congress, Industrial Commission, *Report of the Industrial Commission on the Relations and Conditions of Capital and Labor*, 98.

33 Pearce Davis, *The Development of the American Glass Industry*, 30; *Souvenir of the Allegheny County Centennial*, 123; Keeler and Fenn, "The Taking of Pittsburgh, III," 262; Madarasz, *Glass*, 2.

34 Davis, *The Development of the American Glass Industry*, 84; Dennis Zembala, "Machines in the Glasshouse," 91, 92, 102; Couvares, *The Remaking of Pittsburgh*, 25–27. On the mechanization of all sectors of the glass industry in the nineteenth century, see Zembala, "Machines in the Glasshouse."

35 Scoville, *Revolution in Glassmaking*, 78; *Bulletin*, 23 December 1893; Robert Schwartz, quoted in Richard John O'Connor, "Cinderheads and Iron Lungs," 28, 31; "A Piece of Glass," 248; Zembala, "Machines in the Glasshouse," 27, 94, 333.

36 O'Connor, "Cinderheads and Iron Lungs," 30, 46; Mary E. Bakewell, *Of Long Ago*, 28. Zembala finds that wages for double-thickness workers were not always as high as O'Connor states. Statistics for the Pennsylvania window glass industry in the early 1880s suggest that the wages were not necessarily as disparate for single- and double-thickness blowers. The average daily wages for three years in the 1880s as determined by the state's Bureau of Industrial Statistics appear in the following table.

Average Daily Wages of Window Glass Workers, 1880, 1881, 1883

Occupation	1880	1881	1883
Double-thickness blowers	$7.15	$6.41	$9.75
Single-thickness blowers	$4.74	$4.31	$6.00
Double-thickness gatherers	$3.49	$3.52	$5.22
Single-thickness gatherers	$2.77	$2.86	$3.75

Source: Pennsylvania Bureau of Industrial Statistics, *Annual Report*, 1883, 102–3

For a complete list of average wages for all typed of window glass workers, see Pennsylvania Bureau of Industrial Statistics, *Annual Report*, 1883, 102–3.

37 Davis, *The Development of the American Glass Industry*, 175, 180.

38 *Report of the Industrial Commission*, 7:47; Davis, *The Development of the American Glass Industry*, 189; *National Glass Budget*, 21 March 1903, quoted in Scoville, *Revolution in Glassmaking*, 191.

39 Zembala, "Machines in the Glasshouse," 194–201.

40 "Manufacture of Window Glass with Natural Gas," 183; "The City of Pittsburgh," 64. *Scientific American*'s description of the handblown process was based upon a visit to the Pittsburgh works of S. McKee & Co. in the autumn of 1885.

41 Zembala, "Machines in the Glasshouse," 64; "Manufacture of Window Glass with Natural Gas," 183, estimates that the average window glass blower produced nine to ten cylinders an hour for eight and a half hours each day.

42 O'Connor, "Cinderheads and Iron Lungs," 262; Davis, *The Development of the American Glass Industry*, 183.

43 O'Connor, "Cinderheads and Iron Lungs," 17. The transformation of the gatherer's and blower's tasks illustrates vividly a key characteristic of mechanization in the steel, glass, and coal industries. Machines did not simply displace and deskill workers but produced new sets of skills and positions for the workers who remained in mechanized production. Moreover, while such occupational labels as roller, blower, and miner did not change, the tasks which they denoted changed drastically. See Nuwer, "From Batch to Flow," 808–12.

44 On flattening and cutting, see O'Connor, "Cinderheads and Iron Lungs," 36–38.

45 Davis, *The Development of the American Glass Industry,* 180; Madarasz, *Glass,* 61. The factory that Davis examined, the Chambers Glass Company, was located in New Kensington, sixteen miles northeast of Pittsburgh.

46 Willard Glazier, *Peculiarities of American Cities,* 338; Keeler and Fenn, "The Taking of Pittsburgh, III," 262. Keeler and Fenn elaborated upon the importance of coal to the city's growth by referring to it as both a "swarthy Atlas" and the "smoking Santa Claus" of Pittsburgh's gifts to the world. Their imagery of exchanging gifts would be repeated twenty years later in John White Alexander's mural "The Crowning of Labor" at the Carnegie Institute. See chapter 3.

47 *Bulletin,* 13 September 1890, 1 November 1890, 8 November 1890. In 1913, J. E. Wallin of the city's Mellon Institute of Industrial Research noted that "cities befouled with murky smoke are at a decided disadvantage as tourist or residential places. Wealthy tourists and globe-trotters go to the brilliant, resplendent, ornate, clean cities—the show places—and not to the nasty, pungent smoke producers. Even if the tourist perchance does come to a dirty town he will rarely tarry there for any length of time. Few towns which tolerate the smoke nuisance can hope to compete for tourist trade." See J. E. Wallin, "Psychological Aspects of the Problem of Atmospheric Smoke Pollution," 8–9, 40.

48 Scaife, "Pittsburg—A New Great City," 51.

49 James M'Killop, *Coal and American Coal Mining,* 112; DiCiccio, "The Rise and Fall of King Coal," 114.

50 Keith Dix, *Work Relations in the Coal Industry,* 31. On the terminology and job descriptions of the four types of tonnage workers, see DiCiccio, "The Rise and Fall of King Coal," 266–67.

51 This description of mechanized mining is based on Homer Greene, *Coal and the Coal Mines,* 197, 198; Edward W. Parker, "Coal-Cutting Machinery," 415–22; and DiCiccio, "The Rise and Fall of King Coal," 283–85. The total number of machines used to mine coal in southwestern Pennsylvania increased steadily in the late nineteenth century. In the early 1890s, only seven mining operations in the Pittsburgh district used a total of seventy-two machines for coal extraction. By 1898, ninety-nine coal companies were operating over one thousand machines to mine a quarter of their total output. The Bureau of Mines estimated that by 1907, 40 percent of the bituminous coal mined in the Pittsburgh region was mined by machine. By 1914, coal companies in the area extracted more coal by machine than by the hand method. These figures suggest a slow onslaught of mechanization in regional mining; however, the transition from manual to machine undercutting was gradual and sporadic until the 1920s, when mining in the region was made semiautomatic and continuous. Many miners in the Pittsburgh area continued to use the simple tools of previous generations to cut and load coal after the turn of the century. See U.S. Department of the Interior, Bureau of Mines, *Coal-Mine Fatalities in the United States, 1870–1914,* 108, 295; *Reports of the Immigration Commission,* 424; Parker, "Coal-Cutting Machinery," 410.

52 This description of undercutting and blasting is based on Howard N. Eavenson, *The First Century and a Quarter of American Coal Industry,* 204; Greene, *Coal and the Coal Mines,* 196–97; Dix, *Work Relations in the Coal Industry,* 8–12; and Dix, *What's a Miner to Do?,* 5–14.

53 Dix, *What's a Miner to Do?,* 32–46.

54 Lauck, "The Bituminous Coal Miner," 49.

55 John Bodnar's *The Transplanted* remains the most insightful study of immigration to American cities during this period. The most rigorous works on immigration to Pittsburgh during this period are John Bodnar, Roger Simon, and Michael P. Weber, *Lives of Their Own;* S. J. Kleinberg, *The Shadow of the Mills;* and Frank Serene, "Immigrant Steelworkers in the Mon Valley."

56 Faires, "Immigrants and Industry," 5–8; *Tenth Census: 1880,* 1:895; DiCiccio, "The Rise and Fall of King Coal," 203. Census figures show that almost half (48 percent) of the ironworkers living within the city limits in 1880 were native-born. Irish workers accounted for 20 percent of the total, while English and German immigrants represented 16 and 13 percent, respectively. Approximately 69 percent of the city's glassworkers in 1880 were native-born. The rest of the workforce was 18 percent German, 7 percent English, and 4 percent French. See O'Connor, "Cinderheads and Iron Lungs," 57.

57 *Tenth Census: 1880,* 1:671; *Thirteenth Census: 1910,* 3:572; Percy MacKaye, *The Civic Theater in Relation to the Redemption of Leisure,* 45. On migration networks and the nature of family relocation, see Bodnar, *The Transplanted,* 57–76 passim; June Granatir Alexander, "Moving into and out of Pittsburgh," in *A Century of European Migrations, 1830–1930,* 200–220; and Oestreicher,

"Working-Class Formation," 130–31. On the use of the term *new immigration* in the late nineteenth century, see Josephine Wtulich, *American Xenophobia and the Slav Immigrant*, 8.

58 *Reports of the Immigration Commission*, 6:35, 248; Oestreicher, "Working-Class Formation," 130; Serene, "Immigrant Steelworkers in the Mon Valley," 99.

59 Board of Directors Minutes, 28 March 1876, Records of the Greater Pittsburgh Chamber of Commerce; Scaife, "Pittsburg—A New Great City," 49; H. C. Stiefel, *Slices from a Long Loaf,* 169.

60 *Bulletin,* 7 December 1895; Wtulich, *American Xenophobia,* 7; Chamber of Commerce of Pittsburgh, "Report of the Committee on Housing Conditions on Workman's Dwellings," *Year Book and Directory of the Chamber of Commerce of Pittsburgh, PA* (1903), 46. In her *Outlook* article on Pittsburgh, Lillian Betts noted the "sections of the city and through its suburbs where foreigners have brought conditions that inevitably result in degradation. These are race quite as much as local conditions; they are found in every city to which these races emigrate."

61 Joseph S. Roucek, "The Image of the Slav in U.S. History and in Immigration Policy," 32; Alexander Irvine, *The Magyar,* 51; *Bulletin,* 4 February 1905. The Immigration Commission noted that the Slav was "sometimes wrongly called in the United States 'Hun.'" A good overview of the stereotypes surrounding Slavic immigrants is Karel D. Bicha, "Hunkies," 16–38.

62 *Commoner and American Glass Worker,* 22 December 1888; U.S. Congress, Senate, Committee Upon the Relations Between Labor and Capital, *Report of the Committee of the Senate Upon the Relations Between Labor and Capital,* 7.

63 U.S. Congress, Senate, *Investigation of Labor Troubles,* 209; Fitch, *The Steel Workers,* 31; *Amalgamated Journal,* 4 July 1912; DiCiccio, "The Rise and Fall of King Coal," 203, 266. Edwin Bjorkman, "What Industrial Civilization May Do To Men," 11490–1, reported that of the population of "Southerners" living in Pittsburgh, 82 percent were unskilled. Bjorkman compared this figure to the "Northerners" of the Steel City, 32 percent of whom were unskilled. "Southerners" were Austrians, Hungarians, Italians, and Russians, and "Northerners" were British, Irish, German, Swedish, and French residents. Bjorkman also observed that to English-speaking Pittsburghers, "these men with unpronounceable names and strange ways are just 'Hunkies'—dumb, dull, driven brutes, so utterly beneath contempt that even competition with them is out of the question."

64 "The Iron Industry's Labor Supply," 91; interview with Willard Smith, series 1, tape 10, Pittsburgh Oral History Project; *Reports of the Immigration Commission,* 6:66.

65 Nevin, *Pittsburg and the Men Who Made It,* 64; Wtulich, *American Xenophobia,* 15; Henry Rood, *The Company Doctor,* 225; *Reports of the Immigration Commission,* 6:417. A manager for a Pittsburgh steel company asked James Oppenheim, "What can we do for them? These Hunkies are animals." See James Oppenheim, "The Hired City," 38.

66 *Reports of the Immigration Commission,* 8:434.

67 Leon Mioduski, 4 December 1890, letter 215 in Witold Kula, Nina Assorodobraj-Kula, and Marcin Kula, *Writing Home,* 357; Julian Krzeszewski, 10 February 1891, letter 177 ibid., 315.

68 "The City of Pittsburgh," 63; "Pittsburgh, the Giant Industrial City of the World," 842; Scaife, "Pittsburg—A New Great City," 51.

69 "Pittsburgh, the Giant Industrial City of the World," 845.

70 Scaife, "Pittsburg—A New Great City," 55; Andrea Graziosi, "Common Laborers, Unskilled Workers, 1880–1915," 542; Fitch, *The Steel Workers,* 39. Unions in each industry attempted to control the implementation of new technologies that displaced and deskilled workers. Ralph Helstein, "Reaction of American Labor to Technological Change," in *Labor in a Changing America,* 70, described the ambivalence of the industrial worker who "may embrace the results of the new technology, [but] does not embrace the role assigned to him in the factory system." Helstein argued that after the extreme mechanization of the second industrial revolution, the worker "must be completely responsive to the repetitive demands of a machine whose sole function is to produce the goods which make it possible for him . . . to achieve a better standard of living."

71 Fitch, *The Steel Workers,* 33–34, 47; "Pittsburgh, the Giant Industrial City of the World," 853; Secretary of Internal Affairs of the Commonwealth of Pennsylvania Annual Report (1885), 45; Oppenheim, "The Hired City," 38. Another view of steelmaking, from "The City of Pittsburgh," 62, described a "boy, far off in a corner set apart for bright levers." John Hobson, "The Influence of Machinery upon Employment," 118, reminded readers that machine tending was not automatic work but engaged the worker "in seeing that his portion of the machine works in accurate adjustment to the rest."

72 Brody, *Steelworkers in America,* 31; Fitch, *The Steel Workers;* Graziosi, "Common Laborers, Unskilled Workers, 1880–1915," 516; interview with Reuben Sayles, series 1, tape 8, Pittsburgh Oral History Project.

73 *Commoner and American Glass Worker,* 12 January 1889; Antoine Joseph, *Skilled Workers' Solidarity,* 130. On the intellectual reaction to mechanization and immigration, see James B. Gilbert, *Work without Salvation.*

74 Faires, "Immigrants and Industry," 23; Wtulich, *American Xenophobia,* 19;

Bulletin, 9 August 1890. On the "ethnic invisibility" of whiteness, see Richard Dyer, "White," 44–65; and Uli Linke, "White Skin, Aryan Aesthetics," in *German Bodies,* 32.

75 Scaife, "Pittsburg—A New Great City," 50; *Amalgamated Journal,* 17 August 1911; "Homestead as Seen by One of its Workmen," 169.

2. THE BATTLE OF HOMESTEAD

1 Robert Cornell diary, 6 July 1892. For historical analysis of the Homestead strike, see Krause, *The Battle for Homestead, 1880–1892;* David P. Demarest, ed., *"The River Ran Red": Homestead 1892;* Leon Wolff, *Lockout, the Story of the Homestead Strike of 1892;* and J. Bernard Hogg, "The Homestead Strike." Placing the lockout at Cornell's intersection of chaos and physiques emphasizes two themes that are central to the historiography of late nineteenth-century industrial labor: immigration and industrial masculinity. Dale Knobel and Matthew Frye Jacobson have examined nativist writers' and lawmakers' equation of immigrants' appearance with their supposed inability to function in the American political and economic system. Such physiognomic scrutiny worked to classify both individual subjects encountered directly in daily life and masses of immigrants glimpsed in newspaper articles, magazine editorials, and census reports. Jacobson, especially, saw "moments of violence and civic unrest" such as riots and lynchings as a key opportunity for nativist marginalization of immigrants. Civic crises allowed journalists and politicians to establish a correlation between ethnic diversity and disorder. Moreover, historians of science and public health in the late nineteenth century have found a similar sense of alarm about alien physical attributes in the discourses of municipal engineers and municipal health departments. Ultimately, immigration historians have provided vivid case studies of Americans' ability to translate the visual cues of ethnic identity into signs of bodily danger. See Dale T. Knobel, *"America for the Americans,"* 219–34; Matthew Frye Jacobson, *Whiteness of a Different Color,* 39–68; Alan M. Kraut, "Plagues and Prejudice: Nativism's Construction of Disease in Nineteenth- and Twentieth-Century New York City," in *Hives of Sickness,* 69; Amy L. Fairchild, *Science at the Borders.* See also John Duffy, *The Sanitarians,* 178–83; and Alan M. Kraut, *Silent Travelers.* Second, historians' attention to the versions of masculinity adopted by (or attributed to) late nineteenth-century workers has revealed the visual and rhetorical cues that made gender just as prominent as ethnicity in working-class identity. Tension between the models of "rough" and "respectable" manhood emerging from Gilded Age factories and mines paralleled middle-class men's fears of emasculation at the hands of muscular, belligerent, unskilled workers and admiration for physically capable, upstanding, skilled workers. The boundaries between the two archetypes were porous. Indeed, as Mary Blewett showed in her study of Massachusetts textile workers, a prevailing version of industrial manhood stressed "skill and physical strength, along with respectability and law-abiding sobriety." These attributes, combined with what another historian has termed a "manly stance" against employers, formed an environment in which aggressive labor strikes seemingly balanced roughness and respectability. Thus, for a middle-class audience, both standards of masculinity were troubling because they emphasized economic and political conflicts manifested in decidedly physical ways. The close connection between a "sturdy," bodily definition of manliness and workers' claims to an increased share of industrial profits emerged most prominently during work stoppages. See Mary H. Blewett, "Masculinity and Mobility," 165; Gregory L. Kaster, "Labour's True Man," 25–27; E. Anthony Rotundo, "Body and Soul," 28–29. See also Joseph P. Cosco, *Imagining Italians;* Stephen H. Norwood, *Strikebreaking and Intimidation,* 21–26, 34–64; Ruth Oldenziel, *Making Technology Masculine;* and Paul Michel Taillon, "What We Want Is Good, Sober Men," 319–38.

2 Russell W. Gibbons, "Dateline Homestead," in Demarest, *"The River Ran Red,"* 158–59.

3 Krause argues persuasively for the need to place the events of 6 July into a broader context of the labor movement in Pittsburgh and a tradition of working-class republicanism. Although the direct cause of the lockout was the disputed wage reduction, this dispute can be seen as a product of workers' belief in the republican values of independence and the common good, two concepts threatened by the company's decision to lower the minimum tonnage rate. See Krause, *The Battle for Homestead,* 5–15. Much study of Homestead has focused on the death of steel industry unionism in 1892 as a devastating moment for generations of townspeople. For narratives that suggest the short- and long-term effects of the lockout, see, in addition to Krause's study, Garland, "Homestead and its Perilous Trades," 2–20; Margaret Byington, *Homestead;* Thomas Bell, *Out of this Furnace;* and Judith Modell, *A Town Without Steel.*

4 *The World* [New York], 2 July 1892; *The Local News* [Homestead], 2 July 1892; *Pittsburgh Dispatch,* 4 July 1892.

5 *Pittsburgh Times,* 1 June 1892.

6 *Pittsburgh Dispatch,* 6 July 1892; Krause, "East-Europeans in Homestead," in Demarest, *"The River Ran Red,"* 63–65; Krause, *The Battle for Homestead,* 220. Historians of American crowd behavior have demonstrated the central place of the crowd in political, racial, and economic conflicts. Their project in recent

decades has been to resurrect the political and economic aims of street action, contextualizing mass disorder by positioning it along a continuum of public efforts to defend neighborhoods, ostracize individuals, or assert social equality. Less attention has been paid to the spectacle of the aggressive crowd and the ways in which this spectacle became the keystone of journalists' reports. In particular, pictorial newspapers and illustrated journals argued for the volatility of labor conflicts as measured by the strikers' appearance. Joshua Brown noted that "in physiognomy and costume," immigrants from eastern Europe became a primary symbol of social instability in the pages of *Frank Leslie's Illustrated Newspaper.* The visual techniques of presenting crowds became, like the words *riot* and *mob* themselves, "rhetorical bludgeons, handy for discrediting working-class organizations and justifying attacks on them." See William Pencak, "Introduction," in *Riot and Revelry in Early America,* 15; Eugene E. Leach, "The Literature of Riot Duty," 25, 39; Joshua Brown, *Beyond the Lines,* 186. American studies that stress the political and economic underpinnings of crowd action include Paul A. Gilje, *The Road to Mobocracy* and *Rioting in America;* Iver Bernstein, *The New York City Draft Riots;* David Grimsted, *American Mobbing, 1828–1861;* and David O. Stowell, *Streets, Railroads, and the Great Strike of 1877.*

   7 *Pittsburgh Dispatch,* 6 July 1892.

   8 *St. Louis Post-Dispatch,* 6 July 1892, excerpted in Demarest, *"The River Ran Red,"* 75; Krause, *The Battle for Homestead,* 14.

   9 J. J. McIlyer, quoted in Samuel A. Schreiner, *Henry Clay Frick,* 87; *New York Herald,* 7 July 1892; Myron Stowell, *"Fort Frick," or the Siege of Homestead,* 40.

   10 "The Homestead Strike," *North American Review,* 374; Arthur Burgoyne, *Homestead,* 56; *New York Times,* 7 July 1892; *New York Herald,* 7 July 1892.

   11 *St. Louis Post-Dispatch,* 6 July 1892, excerpted in Demarest, *"The River Ran Red,"* 75; *New York Herald,* 7 July 1892; James Weir Jr., "The Methods of the Rioting Striker as Evidence of Degeneration," 952–54; Gregory M. Pfitzer, *Picturing the American Past,* 227–28. Weir, a doctor from Owensboro, Kentucky, concluded that bad nutrition, intemperance, and "sexual perversion" were three sure signs of a potentially savage workforce.

   12 *The World* [New York], 7 July 1892; *New York Herald,* 7 July 1892.

   13 Burgoyne, *Homestead,* 58; *New York Herald,* 7 July 1892. On the Pinkerton Detective Agency, see Frank Morn, *The Eye that Never Sleeps;* and Robert Michael Smith, *From Blackjacks to Briefcases,* 4–21.

   14 On the science of savagery, see Steven Jay Gould, "Measuring Bodies: Two Case Studies on the Apishness of Undesirables," chap. in *The Mismeasure of Man,* 113–45. On the popularity of wildness in the United States at the turn of the century, see Christopher A. Vaughan, "Ogling Igorots," 219–20. Such a narrative strategy also suggested workers' inability to function as a responsible citizenry. Following Jacobson's positioning of turn-of-the-century racial discourse in the United States as a tension between the demands of capitalism and republicanism, one must note the deep political implications of the language of savagery. Reporters recast the initial appearance of Homestead workers on the morning of the battle in light of their actions later in the day. Behavior interpreted by the press as riot, defiance, and mob violence delegitimized workers' moral and political claims against their employer. The portrayal of Homesteaders as a threatening, primitive tribe effectively defined their capacity for self-government as that of the "heathen" or the cannibal. See Jacobson, *Whiteness of a Different Color*, 13–14, 73, 166–68. For comparison to news reports on the massive railroad strike of 1877 in Pittsburgh, see Richard Slotkin, *The Fatal Environment*, 480–89. A key difference between the two events, as Slotkin notes, is that the local workforce of 1877 was "predominantly white and largely American-born."

15 *New York Herald*, 7 July 1892; Stowell, *"Fort Frick,"* 46; Burgoyne, *Homestead*, 60.

16 U.S. Congress, House, *Investigation of the Employment of Pinkerton Detectives in Connection with the Labor Troubles at Homestead, Pennsylvania*, 52; *New York Herald*, 7 July 1892.

17 Stowell, *"Fort Frick,"* 51.

18 Ibid., 52.

19 *The World*, 7 July 1892; *New York Herald*, 7 July 1892. The phrase "eloquent with the effects of battle" is from Alan Trachtenberg, *Reading American Photographs*, 116.

20 Stowell, *"Fort Frick,"* 52; *The World* [New York], 7 July 1892.

21 Stowell, *"Fort Frick,"* 59; *New York Herald*, 7 July 1892; "The Homestead Riots," *Harper's Weekly* 36 (16 July 1892): 678.

22 *New York Times*, 7 July 1892; Stowell, *"Fort Frick,"* 55. When Weihe testified before a Senate committee in 1883 on the state of immigrant labor in the Pittsburgh region, he referred to immigrant steelworkers as "the scuff, the bad specimens of the working classes." Weihe's experiences in Homestead in the late 1880s, the period in which immigrant workers supported the union's demands, had eased his disdain somewhat. When he testified about the lockout in November 1892, Weihe referred to the "certain class of foreigners . . . who very often have their own ideas of what has taken place in the country they have come from, and would perhaps feel like doing in this country things that are not particularly American." See U.S. Congress, Senate, *Report on Labor and Capital*, 7; and U.S. Congress, Senate, *Investigation of Labor Troubles*, 199.

23 Burgoyne, *Homestead*, 82; U.S. Congress, House, *Investigation of the Employment of Pinkerton Detectives*, ix.

24 *The World* [New York], 7 July 1892; Burgoyne, *Homestead*, 84; "The Homestead Riots," 678.

25 Theodore Roosevelt, *The Winning of the West*, 27–29; Sherry Smith, *Reimagining Indians*, 8–11.

26 Burgoyne, *Homestead*, 83; *Army and Navy Register* editorial quoted in Jerry M. Cooper, *The Army and Civil Disorder*, 254–55.

27 *Pittsburgh Dispatch*, 6 July 1892.

28 *Bulletin* [Pittsburgh], 23 July 1892.

29 *New York Times*, 10 July 1892; *St. Louis Post-Dispatch*, 12 July 1892, excerpted in Demarest, *"The River Ran Red,"* 131.

30 Stowell, *"Fort Frick,"* 96, *The World* [New York], 8 July 1892. The meeting of the funeral processions was also described in the *Pittsburgh Commercial Gazette*, 8 July 1892.

31 Burgoyne, *Homestead*, 72; *New York Times*, 11 July 1892; *Pittsburgh Press*, 9 December 1892.

32 Howells, introduction to Garland, *Main-Travelled Roads*, 4; Garland, "Homestead and its Perilous Trades," 2–20.

33 Hamlin Garland, quoted in Larzer Ziff, *The American 1890s*, 102; Garland, "Homestead and its Perilous Trades," 3.

34 James M. Martin, *Which Way, Sirs, the Better?*, 17, 98; *New York Times*, 9 July 1892; Burgoyne, *Homestead*, 60. O'Donnell was a heater in the Homestead works' 119-inch plate mill, in charge of keeping slabs of steel at the correct temperature between various stages of rolling. On the use of "types" in images of striking workers, see Pfitzer, *Picturing the American* Past, 227–28.

35 Rina C. Youngner, *Industry in Art*, 93, 104–12; Leach, "The Literature of Riot Duty," 26.

36 *Bulletin*, 11 November 1905.

37 *Pittsburgh Illustrated* (Pittsburgh, 1892), 26.

3. THE WORKING BODY AS A CIVIC IMAGE

1 Tony Bennett, "The Exhibitionary Complex," in Nicholas Dirks, Geoff Eley, and Sherry Ortner, *Culture/Power/History: A Reader in Contemporary Social Theory*, 124; Joseph D. Weeks, quoted in *Toasts and Responses at the Banquet Given by the Chamber of Commerce of Pittsburgh, 27 May 1892*, 85.

2 Report of the Superintendent to the Board of Directors of the Chamber of

Commerce of Pittsburgh, 27 March 1882. On boosterism in northern cities, see Sally F. Griffith, "Order, Discipline, and a Few Cannon," 131–55; L. Diane Barnes, "Booster Ethos," 27–42; Jean Spraker, "Come to the Carnival at Old St. Paul," 233–46; and Sally F. Griffith, *Home Town News.* The role of boosterism in the growth of western and southern cities has been the focus of much scholarly study, including Carl Abbott, *Boosters and Businessmen;* Don H. Doyle, *New Men, New Cities, New South;* David Hamer, *New Towns in the New World;* and Timothy R. Mahoney, "A Common Bond of Brotherhood," 619–46. Two insightful works on Canadian cities are Paul-Andre Linteau, *The Promoter's City,* and Dominic T. Alessio, "Capitalist Realist Art," 442–69. A broad comparative study of civic boosterism in the United States, Canada, and Great Britain is Stephen V. Ward, *Selling Places.*

3 T. J. Keenan Jr., quoted in *Toasts and Responses at the Banquet Given by the Chamber of Commerce of Pittsburgh, 27 May 1892,* 74. The visit of the Crown Prince of Siam to Pittsburgh in 1902 is a good example of the social interaction of the press with the business and cultural elite. Newspapermen, industry executives, social club officers, and arts patrons comprised the vast majority of attendees at the formal luncheon held at the city's Duquesne Club. See "Table Arrangement at Luncheon Given by Mr. J. Francis Torrance in honor of HRH The Crown Prince of Siam," box 1, folder 1, Albert J. Logan papers. Edward White, in *150 Years of Unparalleled Thrift,* noted that "Pittsburgh's principal development has been within the life of the Chamber." For more on the professional organizations to which the Chamber of Commerce sent invitations, see the Board of Directors Minutes, Records of the Greater Pittsburgh Chamber of Commerce. Scholars studying the ways in which civic leaders have presented their cities through public spectacles have considered similar issues of social control. David Glassberg's seminal work on turn-of-the-century civic pageantry emphasized the struggle to "forge a united community of believers out of residents with diverse ethnic, class, and regional backgrounds." Glassberg argued that public displays merged the goals of boosters—comprised of the "economic, educational, and hereditary elite" of towns across the nation—with the goals of the artists and coordinators who carried out the performances. Whereas the latter sought a communal emotional experience to bolster individuals' sense of citizenship, the former hoped to build a spirit of social and political cooperation that would make urban industry and infrastructure more efficient. Bennett's concept of an "exhibitionary complex" is most useful in understanding the relationship between display and power in industrial cities such as Pittsburgh. Bennett explained the exhibitionary complex as a technique of urban display that sought the public's self-identification with the power of the capitalist. "Subjugated by flattery," city residents sided with the donors and directors of museums and exposition halls that offered the public an opportunity for participation and a sense of civic encouragement. See David Glassberg, *American Historical Pageantry*, 14, 31, 162, 284; Bennett, "The Exhibitionary Complex," 124, 130.

4 Sherry Lee Linkon and John Russo, *Steeltown U.S.A.*, 69, 89. Linkon and Russo write that in civic representations work "could be seen as beneficial to body and spirit, yet such images could also serve to distract workers from concerns about safety or wages." Historians' attention to the nexus of masculinity and the body at the turn of the century has provided an analytical frame in which to consider these displays. Gail Bederman's *Manliness and Civilization* succeeded in showing that American middle-class manhood at the turn of the century was not a finite collection of attitudes and traits, but an ongoing process dependent upon men's public performances in both extraordinary and habitual contexts. Bederman's theory of a dynamic masculinity posited that class and racial identity were so invested in competing versions of what made a man "manly," that to study any of the three aspects in isolation missed the crucial connections between them. Other historians have shown how concern about the male body during this period resulted in new popular models of manhood that stressed the physical conditioning of the body as an antidote to the increasingly sedentary life of the urban middle classes. See Gail Bederman, *Manliness and Civilization*; Melissa Dabakis, *Visualizing Labor in American Sculpture*; Rotundo, "Body and Soul," 28–29; John F. Kasson, *Houdini, Tarzan, and the Perfect Man*. Bederman builds upon a performative model of gender developed in Judith Butler, *Gender Trouble*, 24–25. Butler writes, "There is no gender identity behind the expressions of gender; that identity is performatively constituted by the very 'expressions' that are said to be its results." On the working lives of Pittsburgh's turn-of-the-century middle classes, see Ethel Spencer, *The Spencers of Amberson Avenue*, and Ileen A. DeVault, *Sons and Daughters of Labor*.

5 Matthew Riddle, quoted in *Toasts and Responses at the Banquet Given by the Chamber of Commerce of Pittsburgh, 27 May 1892*, 38.

6 "The City of Pittsburgh," 50; Keeler and Fenn, "The Taking of Pittsburgh," 262.

7 Wilson, ed., *Standard History of Pittsburg*, 971; Scaife, "A Glimpse of Pittsburg," 83; "The City of Pittsburg," 202; *Bulletin*, 20 November 1890.

8 *Bulletin*, 22 November 1890, 12 June 1897; "Pittsburgh, the Giant Industrial City of the World," 844; Carnegie Steel Company, "General Plan of Works Showing Course for Visitors to Follow through the Mill"; *Pittsburgh Sun*, 21 March 1910; *Year Book and Directory of the Chamber of Commerce of Pittsburgh, PA*

(1905), 68. Nancy Koehn notes that tours of the city's Heinz food factory began in the 1890s and featured company guides, lectures, and souvenirs. See Nancy F. Koehn, "Henry Heinz and Brand Creation in the Late Nineteenth Century," 349–93. Tours of the Carnegie Steel Works in Homestead occurred before the company produced the 1907 plans. Members of the British Iron and Steel Institute made frequent trips to the mills, including a large gathering in early 1905. See *Year Book and Directory of the Chamber of Commerce of Pittsburgh, PA* (1905), 72. When members of the International Association for Testing Materials convened in Pittsburgh in the summer of 1912, they also spent two hours touring the Homestead works. See "Program of Entertainment of 300 Delegates to the International Association for Testing Materials," William Stevenson papers, box 4, folder 1.

9 *Bulletin,* 12 June 1897; *Illustrated Guide and Handbook of Pittsburgh and Allegheny,* 31; "Pittsburgh, the Giant Industrial City of the World," 844. One mill tourist was the writer Willa Cather, who, during her few years in Pittsburgh around the turn of the century, toured the Homestead Steel Works. Along with the grimy aura of a city of industry, Cather appreciated the sight of "workers moving like ants in a clanging inferno" as they made steel. See E. K. Brown, *Willa Cather,* 81.

10 "Pittsburgh, the Giant Industrial City of the World," 845; *Bulletin,* 11 November 1905; "The City of Pittsburgh," 57, 63.

11 *Pittsburgh Sun,* 21 October 1908.

12 *Guide to all Points of Interest in and about Pittsburgh;* Henry Gourley, quoted in *Toasts and Responses at the Banquet Given by the Chamber of Commerce of Pittsburgh,* 27 May 1892, 20; Board of Directors Minutes, 6 February 1893, 22 May 1893, 19 June 1893, Records of the Greater Pittsburgh Chamber of Commerce. See also J. Morton Hall, *America's Industrial Centre.*

13 "Pittsburg's Praises," biographical clipping file, box 1, folder 1, Albert J. Logan papers; *Bulletin,* 25 February 1893, 22 July 1893.

14 Burd Shippen Patterson, "The Aesthetic and Intellectual Side of Pittsburg," 67; "Pittsburgh, the Giant Industrial City of the World," 844; Scaife, "A Glimpse of Pittsburg," 83. Pittsburgh boosters shared with their counterparts in Chicago the ability to manipulate any piece of economic or geographic information to help predict the continued success of the city. See Carl S. Smith, *Urban Disorder and the Shape of Belief,* 47.

15 George E. McNeill, ed., *The Labor Movement,* 477; "The City of Pittsburgh," 57, 64; Davis, *The Iron Puddler,* 92; Keeler and Fenn, "The Taking of Pittsburgh, III," 262.

16 Michael Santos, "Between Hegemony and Autonomy," 403. On the masculinization of work in the late nineteenth century, see commentary in Dee Garceau, *The Important Things of Life.*

17 Board of Directors minutes, 6 February 1908, Records of the Greater Pittsburgh Chamber of Commerce; *Amalgamated Journal,* 4 December 1902.

18 William Blaikie, "Is American Stamina Declining?" 242; Bederman, *Manliness and Civilization,* 185. The turn-of-the-century preoccupation with sports and primitivism in America depended upon the hope that such practices might build the body and the character in a way previously ascribed to work. See Rotundo, "Body and Soul," 28–29.

19 Henry Childs Merwin, "On Being Civilized Too Much," 838; Davis, *The Iron Puddler,* 97–98; Gilbert, *Work without Salvation,* 67. The link between physical strength and imperialist power was perhaps best illustrated by the tenets of Theodore Roosevelt's "strenuous life." On Roosevelt's conception of strenuous imperialism, see Bederman, *Manliness and Civilization,* 184–96. See also T. J. Jackson Lears's notion of the hard side of antimodernism in *No Place of Grace,* 301–5. In Lears's description, the hard side of the disquiet about overcivilization manifested itself in groups devoted to "risk-taking and physical exertion" as a way to experience the authentic in a world that seemed increasingly manufactured and mediated.

20 Oestreicher, "Working-Class Formation, Development, and Consciousness in Pittsburgh, 1790–1960," in *City at the Point,* 121. During the five-month period of March–July 1896, the *National Labor Tribune* printed fictional tales that involved the skill of lion tamers, the bravery of hunters on the trail of tigers and panthers, and the violent experiences of Civil War soldiers. See *National Labor Tribune,* 5 March 1896, 12 March 1896, 30 April 1896, and 9 July 1896.

21 *Bulletin,* 29 November 1890; Scaife, "A Glimpse of Pittsburg," 85; Report of the Superintendent to the Board of Directors of the Chamber of Commerce of Pittsburgh, 27 March 1882; "The City of Pittsburgh," 57; Union Trust Company, *Industrial Pittsburgh;* Betts, "Pittsburg: A City of Brain and Brawn," 17; J. William Pope, "Pittsburgh," printed in *Illustrated Guide and Handbook of Pittsburgh and Allegheny,* 13. Anthony Penna has suggested that the emphasis on the vigorous pace of work in Pittsburgh was meant to impart a human quality to a city that had been known for decades for its inanimate products. Iron, steel, glass, and coal had defined the city since the mid–nineteenth century, but the scrutiny on persistent, healthy work brought the body more in focus than the products. See Penna, "Changing Images of Twentieth-Century Pittsburgh," 52.

22 Reuben Miller, quoted in *Toasts and Responses at the Banquet Given by the Chamber of Commerce of Pittsburgh, 27 May 1892,* 25.

23 The phrase is Mark Seltzer's, in *Bodies and Machines*, 13. "The City of Pittsburgh," 59, 64; *All About Pittsburgh and Allegheny*, 113; James Bridge, *The Inside History of the Carnegie Steel Company*, 164.

24 "The City of Pittsburgh," 58; Garland, "Homestead and its Perilous Trades," 6, 8.

25 James P. Roe, "Manufacture of Wrought Iron," in *The ABC of Iron and Steel*, 98; Davis, *The Iron Puddler*, 85; "The City of Pittsburgh," 58. Public displays of naked whiteness have certainly not been limited to the iconography of work in Pittsburgh. Uli Linke, in "White Skin, Aryan Aesthetics," in *German Bodies*, 31, suggests an "intertwining of whiteness and nakedness" as a recurring theme in twentieth-century German culture.

26 *Bulletin*, 19 May 1894.

27 "The American Iron and Steel Works of the Jones and Laughlin Company" (1867); "Homestead as Seen by One of its Workmen," 164, 169; *Bulletin*, 16 May 1896; Davis, *The Iron Puddler*, 87.

28 Frank Popplewell, *Some Modern Conditions and Recent Developments in Iron and Steel Production in America*, 107; *J. M. Kelly's Handbook of Greater Pittsburg*; Rood, *The Company Doctor*, 225; W. E. Trautmann and Peter Hagboldt, *Hammers of Hell*, 60; Edwin Bjorkman, "What Industrial Civilization May Do To Men," 11491.

29 Popplewell, *Some Modern Conditions*, 110.

30 George N. McCain, *A Sketch of the Celebration of Allegheny County*; George H. Thurston, *Allegheny County's Hundred Years*. There was much overlap between the membership of the Chamber of Commerce and the membership of the centennial organizing committee. See Pittsburgh Chamber of Commerce, *Fifty Years of the Chamber of Commerce of Pittsburgh, 1874–1924*, 110.

31 Mary P. Ryan, "The American Parade: Representations of the Nineteenth-Century Social Order," in *The New Cultural History*, 132–33, 152. See also Susan G. Davis, *Parades and Power*. The similarities between urban celebrations and urban architecture as vehicles of civic pride are illustrated in Mary P. Ryan, "A Laudable Pride in the Whole of Us," 1131–70. The two often went hand in hand—cornerstone laying and opening rituals celebrated both the buildings themselves and the act of celebration. On similar symbolic considerations in workers' parades in Canada, see Craig Heron and Steve Penfold, "The Craftmen's Spectacle," 363.

32 *Pittsburgh Commercial Gazette*, 25 September 1888, 26 September 1888.

33 Michael Kazin and Steven J. Ross, "America's Labor Day," 1296–1300.

34 Krause, *The Battle for Homestead*, 195; *Pittsburgh Telegraph*, 17 June 1882.

35 Board of Directors Minutes, 3 October 1887, 17 October 1887, Records of the Greater Pittsburgh Chamber of Commerce; *Bulletin,* 29 September 1888; *Commoner and Labor Herald,* 23 October 1887. The Chamber of Commerce eventually spent $19,375 on the Centennial, certainly its largest expenditure on a promotional event in the late nineteenth century.

36 *Commoner and American Glass Worker,* 22 September 1888; "Souvenir of the Allegheny County Centennial," 118–23; Heron and Penfold, "The Craftmen's Spectacle," 365.

37 *Pittsburgh Commercial Gazette,* 26 September 1888; *Commoner and American Glass Worker,* 29 September 1888; *Pittsburgh Post,* 26 September 1888.

38 *Pittsburgh Commercial Gazette,* 20 September 1888, 21 September 1888.

39 Susan G. Davis, *Parades and Power,* 113, 157.

40 *Pittsburgh Post,* 22 September 1888; *Amalgamated Journal,* 22 January 1903. The poem, titled "Papa on Parade," was told from the viewpoint of a worker's child, who felt proud as his or her father went by in a labor parade.

41 *Bulletin,* 26 August 1905.

42 Leland D. Baldwin, *Pittsburgh,* 342; Wilson, *Standard History of Pittsburg,* 956; Board of Directors Minutes, 1 September 1879, 18 October 1880, 5 September 1881, Records of the Greater Pittsburgh Chamber of Commerce.

43 Baldwin, *Pittsburgh,* 342; *Bulletin,* 8 December 1888, 25 October 1890; Western Pennsylvania Exposition Society (WPES), *Pittsburg and its Exposition,* 5; *Pittsburgh Commercial Gazette,* 6 September 1889; WPES, *Pittsburg and its Fifth Annual Exposition,* 7; Dravo quoted in Board of Directors Minutes, 7 May 1888, Records of the Greater Pittsburgh Chamber of Commerce. All of Pittsburgh's major steel, glass, and coal companies funded the annual event and took part in its planning throughout the year. For a list of firms involved, see Pittsburg Exposition Society, "Partial List of Citizens, Firms, and Corporations, All Eligible to Life Membership in the Pittsburg Exposition Society," (n.d.), HSWP.

44 WPES, *Exposition Handbook and Guide,* 40; *Bulletin,* 22 November 1890, 25 October 1890; Secretary of Internal Affairs of the Commonwealth of Pennsylvania, *Annual Report, Part III: Industrial Statistics,* 22; Bakewell, *Of Long Ago,* 59; John Ryckman, quoted in *Pittsburgh Commercial Gazette,* 13 September 1889, 6 September 1890. On contemporary industrial exhibitions, see Keith Walden, *Becoming Modern in Toronto,* 160; and Steven Conn, "The Philadelphia Commercial Museum: A Museum to Conquer the World," in *Museums and American Intellectual Life, 1876–1926,* 117–18. A simulated glass factory also appeared in the city's Luna Park when it opened in 1905. Workers in the small glassworks produced ornamental jewelry and novelties for amusement park visitors. See *Bulletin,* 8 July 1905.

45 *Pittsburgh Commercial Gazette,* 6 September 1890, 7 September 1891;

WPES (1890), 40. Mechanical Hall was alternatively called Machinery Hall, although that label was used much less frequently by the press.

46 Walden, *Becoming Modern in Toronto*, 15; Bennett, "The Exhibitionary Complex," 128; Peter H. Hoffenberg, *An Empire on Display*, 27; WPES, *Report of the President and Treasurer for the Year 1897; Bulletin*, 13 September 1890. Participation in the glass display extended to a sense of camaraderie and equality with the workers. The *Bulletin* joked that "about a thousand persons a day are convinced that they could make a lamp chimney or a tumbler if they had half a chance." Hoffenberg writes that imperial exhibitions in England in the late nineteenth century "offered living pictures of the nation and empire." Each Saturday was "People's Day" at the exposition, during which free admittance was offered to the public; these were intended as an opportunity for the WPES to teach working-class Pittsburghers the meaning of their city with similar living pictures. Bennett, "The Exhibitionary Complex," 137, refers to the "techniques and rhetorics" of display and pedagogy as the exhibitionary complex's primary devices for the "moral and cultural regulation of the working classes." At the same time, the power of the Pittsburgh Exposition's spectacle was in its seeming spontaneity, stripped of any pretense of heavy-handed teaching. The *Commercial Gazette* noted on the eve of the first exposition in 1889 that seven out of ten Pittsburghers were unaware that the WPES even existed, let alone orchestrated the array of processes and products.

47 WPES, Greater Pittsburgh Exposition.

48 *Bulletin*, 25 October 1890, 29 October 1892, 12 June 1897; Smith, *Urban Disorder and the Shape of Belief*, 85; Board of Directors Minutes, 7 May 1888, Records of the Greater Pittsburgh Chamber of Commerce.

49 Joseph D. Weeks, quoted in *Toasts and Responses at the Banquet Given by the Chamber of Commerce of Pittsburgh*, 27 May 1892, 86. Edwin Howland Blashfield, *Mural Painting in America*, 24; Board of Directors minutes, 4 June 1908, Records of the Greater Pittsburgh Chamber of Commerce; Trudy Baltz, "Pageantry and Mural Painting," 220. On the bodily conventions of late nineteenth-century American art, see David Bjelajac, "Art and Commerce in the Gilded Age, 1865–1905," in *American Art*, esp. 256.

50 See Pauline King's critique of the mural in *American Mural Painting*, 252–53.

51 On Blashfield's earlier work in the context of the beaux arts mural movement, see Bailey Van Hook, *The Virgin and the Dynamo*; Leonard Amico, *The Mural Decorations of Edwin Howland Blashfield*; and King, *American Mural Painting*, 72, 198.

52 Blashfield, *Mural Painting in America*, 199.

53 Ibid., 45.

54 Blashfield, *Mural Painting in America,* chap. 4 passim; Union Trust Company, *Industrial Pittsburgh,* 20, 56; King, *American Mural Painting,* 255. For a similar emphasis on rapport between building and mural, see "Mural Paintings in American Cities," 125–28.

55 Vernon Gay and Marilyn Evert, *Discovering Pittsburgh's Sculpture,* 4; Adeline Adams, *Daniel Chester French,* 58; *Pittsburgh Dispatch,* 16 June 1904. On the dedication ceremony, see "Official Souvenir Program of the Exercises attending the Unveiling of the Monument Erected to the Memory of Col. James Anderson by Andrew Carnegie."

56 Adams, *Daniel Chester French,* 112. See also Michael Richman, *Daniel Chester French;* and Charles H. Caffin, *American Masters of Sculpture,* 58, 70.

57 Adams, *Daniel Chester French,* 58.

58 *Pittsburgh Post,* 2 June 1904; *Pittsburgh Dispatch,* 2 June 1904.

59 *Pittsburgh Dispatch,* 7 April 1907; Charles H. Caffin, "The New Mural Decorations of John W. Alexander," 847. The most thorough analyses of Alexander's murals are Sarah J. Moore, "John White Alexander (1856–1915)," 309–25; and Van Hook, *The Virgin and the Dynamo,* 50–52, 159–60.

60 "The Crowning of Labor: The John White Alexander Mural Paintings in the Carnegie Institute, Pittsburgh," 32; *Memorial of the Celebration of the Carnegie Institute at Pittsburgh, P.A.,* 399.

61 *Memorial of the Celebration of the Carnegie Institute at Pittsburgh, P.A.,* 407; *Pittsburgh Dispatch,* 7 April 1907; *Gazette Times,* 7 April 1907; Caspar Purdon Clarke, "Study in Black and Green," 425.

62 *Gazette Times,* 7 April 1907; *Pittsburgh Dispatch,* 7 April 1907; *Pittsburgh Post,* 7 April 1907; Caffin, "The New Mural Decorations of John W. Alexander," 848; Clarke, "Study in Black and Green," 425. In an interview with the *Dispatch,* 10 April 1907, Alexander stressed that he wanted to exhibit the "spirit of force and the nobility of labor" in his work.

63 Caffin, "The New Mural Decorations of John W. Alexander," 848; Moore, "John White Alexander (1856–1915)," 316; Bailey Van Hook, "From the Lyrical to the Epic," 79. On the manliness of Alexander's mural, see also Martha Banta, *Imaging American Women,* 672–77; and Janet Cecelia Marstine, "Working History," 397.

64 *Pittsburgh Dispatch,* 7 April 1907; "The Crowning of Labor," 32; Clarke, "Study in Black and Green," 425.

65 *Pittsburgh Dispatch,* 20 September 1908.

66 Sidney A. King, W. H. Stevenson, and R. W. Johnston, *The Story of the Sesqui-Centennial Celebration of Pittsburgh,* 156; *Pittsburgh Sun,* 13 June 1906;

Pittsburgh Dispatch, 27 September 1908; *Official Municipal Program of the Sesqui-Centennial Celebration of the City of Pittsburgh; Pittsburgh Post,* 2 October 1908.

67 David Glassberg, *American Historical Pageantry,* 1, 43–47, 126; *Bulletin,* 9 September 1893, 8 September 1894, 2 September 1905. Philadelphia's celebration of its 225th anniversary, also held in October 1908, presented a seven-day itinerary that divided each day into a themed ceremony, much like Pittsburgh's sesquicentennial. Philadelphia's organizational plan, featuring Church Day, Military Day, Municipal Day, Industrial Day, Children's Day, a historical pageant, and Athletics Day, was essentially an expanded version of the celebration discussed here. The "pageantry craze" that swept the United States in the early twentieth century borrowed conventions of historical commemoration and fascination with arts and crafts displayed in England at the turn of the century to make local history and antiquated craftsmanship the twin pillars of civic identity. In Pittsburgh, simple displays of handicrafts were mimicked on trade floats and carried to a new level of sophistication and mechanization in manufacturers' floats that followed. The sesquicentennial provided a timeline of "mighty and wonderful achievements," from the rough work of "hardy pioneers" in the eighteenth century to the physical feats of industrial laborers of the twentieth century. The "vast panorama of magnificence and splendor" made man and machine coworkers, pushing each other to new levels of achievement. See *Pittsburgh Sun,* 29 September 1908, 1 October 1908.

68 *Pittsburgh Dispatch,* 27 September 1908, 2 October 1908; King et al., *The Story of the Sesqui-Centennial Celebration,* 12.

69 *Pittsburgh Dispatch,* 1 October 1908.

70 *Pittsburgh Dispatch,* 2 October 1908; King et al., *The Story of the Sesqui-Centennial Celebration,* 161.

71 *Pittsburgh Dispatch,* 2 October 1908; King et al., *The Story of the Sesqui-Centennial Celebration,* 161. See the *Pittsburgh Chronicle-Telegraph* series on Sundays in the summer of 1908.

72 *Souvenir of Pittsburg.* The bottom-left and top images are typical of many photographs taken by manufacturers between 1880 and 1920 as a means of documenting their workforces and establishments. The Jones and Laughlin photograph collection at the HSWP is the most comprehensive, containing many images of workers posed with their tools and machines at work without human input.

73 WPES, Pittsburgh Exposition; SIACP (1880), 195; Mellon Bank, *Pittsburgh: 1758–1908.*

74 Carol Wolkowitz, "The Working Body as a Sign: Historical Snapshots," in

Kathryn Backett-Milburn and Linda Mckie, *Constructing Gendered Bodies*, 87; Dana Brand, *The Spectator and the City in Nineteenth-Century American Literature*, 2; *Pittsburgh Sun*, 21 October 1908; Scaife, "A Glimpse of Pittsburg," 87. Sharon Corwin has argued that an "effacement of labor" such as the one I describe is indicative of representations of labor in the era of scientific management. See Sharon Corwin, "Picturing Efficiency," 140.

75 Smith, *Urban Disorder and the Shape of Belief*, 96; *Year Book and Directory of the Chamber of Commerce of Pittsburgh, PA* (1903), 68.

4. THE PITTSBURGH SURVEY

1 Oppenheim, "The Hired City," 36; *Bulletin*, 28 January 1905; Trautmann and Hagboldt, *Hammers of Hell*, 60.

2 Carroll Wright, *Some Ethical Phases of the Labor Question*, 99; Gilbert, *Work without Salvation*, 5–6; Upton Sinclair, *The Industrial Republic*, 128.

3 Josephine Goldmark, *Fatigue and Efficiency*, 75; *Engineers' Society of Western Pennsylvania*, 334. On the Pittsburgh Survey, see Maurine W. Greenwald and Margo Anderson, eds., *Pittsburgh Surveyed*, and Clarke A. Chambers, *Paul U. Kellogg and the Survey*.

4 John F. McClymer, *War and Welfare*, 6, 32.

5 Kleinberg, *The Shadow of the Mills*, 28, 31. Hamlin Garland's 1894 article on Homestead steelmaking was one of the first national chronicles of local industrial hazards. See Garland, "Homestead and its Perilous Trades," 2–20.

6 Figures are based on an analysis of the *Annual Report of the Factory Inspector of the Commonwealth of Pennsylvania*; and Allegheny County, Office of the Coroner, "Record of Inquests Held," 1899–1915.

7 This analysis of steel industry accidents is based on *First Annual Report of the Commissioner of Labor and Industry, 1913–14*, part II, 15. The commissioner's report examined 18,931 accidents reported in 1914.

8 *Annual Report of the Factory Inspector of the Commonwealth of Pennsylvania*, 291–92. During the 1910s, the socialist weekly *Justice* published such brief descriptions of deaths in Pittsburgh workplaces as a standard feature of its call for industrial reforms.

9 The relative safety of work in the glass industry was mirrored in other countries as well. In the United Kingdom, for instance, the glass industry in the last two decades of the nineteenth century had yearly accident rates that were almost four times lower than those of the metals industry. See John Calder, *The*

Prevention of Factory Accidents, 69. On the failures of the Lubbers machine, see Scoville, *Revolution in Glassmaking,* 192.

10 U.S. Congress, Senate, Committee Upon the Relations Between Labor and Capital, *Report of the Committee of the Senate Upon the Relations Between Labor and Capital,* 1:30; U.S. Congress, Senate, *Reports of the Immigration Commission,* 14:173.

11 U.S. Department of the Interior, Bureau of Mines, *Coal-Mine Fatalities in the United States, 1870–1914,* 8. These figures represent only those accidents that were reported officially to the state's mine inspectors; thus, they probably underreport deaths in mines during these thirty-four years. The inspectors themselves were skeptical about the accuracy of their statistics, noting that they were dependent upon the honesty of coal companies. See *Annual Report of the Factory Inspector of the Commonwealth of Pennsylvania,* 4.

12 Muriel Sheppard, *Cloud by Day,* 154; *Annual Report of the Secretary of Internal Affairs of the Commonwealth of Pennsylvania,* 289; Frederick L. Hoffman, "Accidents in Bituminous (Pennsylvania) Mines," 120–21.

13 Roy, *A History of the Coal Miners of the United States,* 303–4.

14 Ibid., 120–21.

15 William Gibbons, *Those Black Diamond Men,* 141.

16 Dix, *Work Relations in the Coal Industry,* 25.

17 Copeland and Blair advertisement in *Pittsburgh Commercial Gazette,* 18 September 1889; SIACP (1883), 155. The problem of internal health was certainly not ignored by the state's industry-monitoring officials. At a convention of the International Association of Factory Inspectors of North America in 1894, Pennsylvania's chief factory inspector stated that legislative efforts "that strive only to avoid the danger of the elevator, the molten metal, the vats, pans, and cauldrons . . . and other dangerous elements in the mechanical world" would do little to help the state's industrial workers if they did not also address "the vastly more important fields of ventilation and sanitation." The inspector continued, "Dangerous machinery has slain its thousands, but a defective sanitary system, together with an insufficient supply of ventilation has slain its tens of thousands." See the *Annual Report of the Factory Inspector of the Commonwealth of Pennsylvania,* 455.

18 Gibbons, *Those Black Diamond Men,* 158.

19 Robert Watchorn, "The Cost of Coal in Human Life," 176; interview with Ignacy Mendyk, series 2, tape 13, Pittsburgh Oral History Project; *Amalgamated Journal,* 20 October 1910.

20 Lauck, "The Bituminous Coal Miner and Coke Worker of Western Pennsylvania," 38, 49; *Reports of the Immigration Commission,* Vol. 6, 511.

21 Fawcett, "The Center of the World of Steel," 192.

22 John Williams-Searle, "Courting Risk," 40–41.

23 *Bulletin*, 10 November 1888, 4 March 1893; *Amalgamated Journal*, 29 April 1909, 4 January 1912; *Report of the Committee of the Senate Upon the Relations Between Labor and Capital*, 1:31; Trautmann and Hagboldt, *Hammers of Hell*, 111.

24 Christopher C. Sellers, *Hazards on the Job*, 35–36; *Bulletin*, 4 March 1893, 26 July 1890; *Pittsburgh Sun*, 31 December 1909. The prevalence of injury in Pittsburgh's industries also generated literary images of disability. A novelist writing about the bituminous mines of southwestern Pennsylvania introduced his tale with a crowd of fifty miners, many of whom were disabled by work accidents: "This lad, hobbling around with a crutch, has lost his leg; so has that man yonder, and that other one leaning against the telegraph-pole. . . . Mike Boyle, striding up and down the track, had an arm mashed three years ago next month, and it had to come off." See Rood, *The Company Doctor*, 6.

25 U.S. Congress, House, *Investigation of the Employment of Pinkerton Detectives in Connection with the Labor Troubles at Homestead, Pennsylvania*, 96; Watchorn, "The Cost of Coal in Human Life," 176; *Amalgamated Journal*, 1 May 1902.

26 *Amalgamated Journal*, 2 December 1909; *National Labor Tribune*, 5 March 1896.

27 Terence Powderly, "The Army of Unemployed," in McNeill, ed., *The Labor Movement*, 581.

28 *Amalgamated Journal*, 14 June 1900.

29 SIACP (1885), 163; *Pittsburgh Telegraph*, 17 June 1882; Harvey A. Levenstein, *Revolution at the Table*, 23–26, 101; Elaine N. McIntosh, *American Food Habits in Historical Perspective*, 102–5. See also Mary H. Blewett, "Masculinity and Mobility," 170, for a similar description of industrial workers' reliance on meat as a prerequisite for physical ability.

30 *Amalgamated Journal*, 6 September 1900, 17 February 1916; *Iron City Trades Journal*, 24 June 1910.

31 Elliott Gorn, *The Manly Art*, 141–42; *Amalgamated Journal*, 12 March 1903; *Pittsburgh Dispatch*, 6 September 1908; *Iron City Trades Journal*, 4 September 1908; McNeill, *The Labor Movement*, 477. The *Dispatch* reported that workers found a street parade in the downtown area too strenuous in the heat of the day but responded enthusiastically to the athletic competitions in the amusement parks surrounding the city. Exercise, of course, was only one leisure activity that could improve the worker's body. In an interesting twist on the middle-class

condemnation of working-class alcohol consumption, Pittsburgh's Independent Brewing Company urged workers to "Guard Your Health" by using only beer with the purest ingredients. See the *Iron City Trades Journal*, 2 September 1910.

32 *Amalgamated Journal*, 14 June 1900. On the political use of athletics within the working class, see W. L. Guttsman, *Workers' Culture in Weimar Germany*, 136. Guttsman writes, "The strengthening of the body was seen not only as a valuable correction to the general strains and the debilitating influences of heavy physical work. Its body-building function was also regarded as a valuable preparation for the class struggle."

33 Shoshana Zuboff, "The Laboring Body: Suffering and Skill in Production Work," in *In the Age of the Smart Machine*, 36.

34 Anson Rabinbach, *The Human Motor*, 6, 38, 231.

35 Seltzer, *Bodies and Machines*, 100, 113; Pultz, *The Body and the Lens*, 30; Marta Brown, "Marey and the Organization of Work," in *Picturing Time*, 324, 348.

36 Martha Banta, *Taylored Lives*, 26–27; Thomas Oliver, "The Physiology and Pathology of Work and Fatigue," in *Dangerous Trades*, 106–9; Goldmark, *Fatigue and Efficiency*, vi, 12–13; Emory Bogardus, "The Relation of Fatigue to Industrial Accidents, Part I," 214; Wallin, "Psychological Aspects of the Problem of Atmospheric Smoke Pollution," 23. Frederic S. Lee, a New York physiologist who wrote the introduction to Goldmark's volume on fatigue, noted that while machinery demanded more and more from workers, their "fundamental physiological needs" had not changed since the building of the pyramids. On Lee and the activism of physiologists, see Derickson, "Physiological Science and Scientific Management in the Progressive Era," 485.

37 Oliver, "The Physiology and Pathology of Work and Fatigue," 104–5, 117; *Amalgamated Journal*, 15 October 1908; Trautmann and Hagboldt, *Hammers of Hell*, 117; Richard Gillespie, "Industrial Fatigue and the Discipline of Physiology," in *Physiology in the American Context, 1850–1940*, 238.

38 Bogardus, "The Relation of Fatigue to Industrial Accidents, Part I," 209, 355–57; Oliver, "The Physiology and Pathology of Work and Fatigue," 113; Goldmark, *Fatigue and Efficiency*, 79; Henry C. Potter, "Man and the Machine," 386, 392; Fawcett, "The Center of the World of Steel," 203. On the notion of "mechanicalized men," see Rodgers, *The Work Ethic in Industrial America, 1850–1920*, esp. chap. 3.

39 Goldmark, *Fatigue and Efficiency*, 72; Bogardus, "The Relation of Fatigue to Industrial Accidents, Part I," 355.

40 "Homestead as Seen by One of its Workmen," 169; Oliver, "The Physiology and Pathology of Work and Fatigue," 104; Simon Sosienski, 15 January 1891, letter 259 in Kula et al., *Writing Home*, 413; Trautmann and Hagboldt, *Hammers of Hell*, 13.

41 *National Labor Tribune*, 20 February 1896; *Amalgamated Journal*, 25 September 1913, 15 July 1915, 10 December 1908.

42 *Amalgamated Journal*, 27 February 1902, 13 November 1902, 9 January 1904, 2 January 1913; Trautmann and Hagboldt, *Hammers of Hell*, 118.

43 Kitson, "The Iron and Steel Industries of America," 629; Kleinberg, *The Shadow of the Mills* 237–8; Rodgers, *The Work Ethic in Industrial America*, 181.

44 McClymer, *War and Welfare*, 32. On social narrative strategies at the turn of the century, see Tony Higbie, "Crossing Class Boundaries," 559–92.

45 Oppenheim, "The Hired City," 34; Chamber of Commerce of Pittsburgh, Annual Report, 1909, 47; Joan Waugh, *Unsentimental Reformer*, 12. On the role of the Russell Sage Foundation in funding the survey, see David C. Hammack and Stanton Wheeler, *Social Science in the Making*.

46 Robert W. DeForest, in National Municipal League, *Proceedings of the Pittsburgh Conference for Good City Government*, 5, 22; McClymer, *War and Welfare*, 22; Chambers, *Paul U. Kellogg and the Survey*, 33–35; Lubove, *Twentieth-Century Pittsburgh*, 6–9.

47 Kellogg, "Field Work of the Pittsburgh Survey," in *The Pittsburgh District: Civic Frontage*, 492; Chambers, *Paul U. Kellogg and the Survey*, 33–35.

48 Crystal Eastman, *Work-Accidents and the Law*, 3–4, 11, 15.

49 Elaine Scarry, *The Body in Pain*, 6; Eastman, *Work-Accidents and the Law*, 13. Eastman related a conversation she overheard between a coroner's deputy and a journalist looking for a good story. The official informed the reporter, "There's a man killed by a fall of slate out at Thom's Run. You don't want that, do you?" The reporter declined, suggesting to Eastman that accidental deaths had become so commonplace by 1907 that they were no longer newsworthy. See Eastman, *Work-Accidents and the Law*, 34.

50 Scott, *Domination and the Arts of Resistance*, 78.

51 Stephen Turner, "The Pittsburgh Survey and the Survey Moment: An Episode in the History of Expertise," in Greenwald and Anderson, *Pittsburgh Surveyed*, 37. The appeal of rural bodies for the American middle class around the turn of the century has been noted by several scholars, among them Bedermann, *Manliness and Civilization*, and Kathryn Grover, ed., *Fitness in American Culture*.

52 Peter Roberts, "Immigrant Wage Earners," in *Wage-Earning Pittsburgh*, 37; McClymer, *War and Welfare*, 95. Bodnar, *The Transplanted*, found that the waves of European immigrants to cities such as Pittsburgh were typically craftsmen trying to avoid a drop in status in the face of the expansion of commercial agriculture. While they were new to the heavily industrialized urban area, they were not ignorant of machinery and modern production techniques.

53 Roberts, "Immigrant Wage Earners," 38. E. P. Thompson, "Time, Work-Discipline, and Industrial Capitalism," 56–97, is the seminal statement of the historical shift from task orientation to the system of clocked, regulated time in factory labor in England.

54 Hard, "Making Steel and Killing Men," 588; Wright, *Some Ethical Phases of the Labor Question,* 110. Steven Jay Gould, "Measuring Bodies: Two Case Studies on the Apishness of Undesirables," in *The Mismeasure of Man,* 113–45, writes, "Recapitulation served as a general theory of biological determinism. All 'inferior' groups—races, sexes, and classes—were compared with the children of white males." On the use of recapitulation theory in turn-of-the-century racial and sexual discourse, see Siobahn B. Somerville, "Scientific Racism and the Invention of the Homosexual Body," in *Queering the Color Line,* 15–38.

55 Kellogg recruited Eastman, a Vassar and New York University law graduate, for her familiarity with corporate compensation policies and legislation. In 1910, Eastman drafted New York's workmen's compensation law as a member of the state's Commission on Employers' Liability and Causes of Industrial Accidents. Fitch joined the survey team from the University of Wisconsin's graduate program in political economy. For more on Eastman and Fitch, see Chambers, *Paul U. Kellogg and the Survey,* 75–76; Lubove, "John A. Fitch, *The Steel Workers,* and the Crisis of Democracy," introduction to Fitch, *The Steel Workers,* vii–xiv; and Blanche Wiesen Cook, ed., *Crystal Eastman on Women and Revolution.*

56 Hard, "The Law of the Killed and the Wounded," 361–71.

57 Fitch, *The Steel Workers,* 10; McClymer, *War and Welfare,* 220.

58 Fitch, *The Steel Workers,* 51; Stella, quoted in Greenwald, "Visualizing Pittsburgh in the 1900s: Art and Photography in the Service of Social Reform," in Greenwald and Anderson, *Pittsburgh Surveyed,* 136.

59 Youngner, *Industry in Art,* 145. For brief accounts of Stella's Pittsburgh drawings, see John Baur, *Joseph Stella,* 25–26, and Irma Jaffe, *Joseph Stella,* 19–23. The effects of Stella's time in Pittsburgh on his career as an artist were noted by both Baur and Jaffe. Jaffe wrote, "The modern world, the United States, steel, and electricity were forged into a single concept then and forever in his imagination."

60 Fitch, *The Steel Workers,* 3; Gerald Stanley Lee, *Crowds,* 36; Julie Wosk, *Breaking Frame,* 67–69.

61 Greenwald, "Visualizing Pittsburgh in the 1900s," 132; Fitch., *The Steel Workers,* 21; Eastman, *Work-Accidents and the Law,* 55.

62 Eastman, *Work-Accidents and the Law,* 74.

63 Joseph Stella, quoted in Jaffe, *Joseph Stella*, 20. On the power of manual work to inscribe workers' bodies, see Douglas C. Sackman, "Nature's Workshop," 29.

64 Eastman, *Work-Accidents and the Law*, 11–13. In a similar visual strategy, Edwin Bjorkman observed that "the streets of Pittsburgh are crowded with deformed and mutilated human specimens. Rows of crippled beggars crouch near the mill entrances on pay-days." See Bjorkman, "What Industrial Civilization May Do To Men," 11494. The statistics in *Work-Accidents and the Law* applied to all major industrial firms in the Pittsburgh district, not just steel mills, glasshouses, and coal mines. Eastman's research confirmed earlier findings about accidents. In the steel industry, 22 percent of fatal injuries involved overhead cranes, 12 percent were caused by falls, 11 percent were caused by explosions, and 5 percent involved the operation of rolling machinery. In the coal mining industry, Eastman estimated that 67 percent of accidental deaths were caused by roof-falls, 13 percent by collisions with mine cars, and 8 percent from electrocution. See Eastman, *Work-Accidents and the Law*, 35, 51.

65 Eastman, *Work-Accidents and the Law*, 223; William Solomon, *Literature, Amusement, and Technology in the Great Depression*, 9. Joanna Bourke, *Dismembering the Male*, 59, notes the patriotic power of limblessness in British society in the 1920s. Bourke writes, "In the struggle for status and resources, absence could be more powerful than presence. The less visible or invisible diseases that disabled many servicemen could not compete with limblessness."

66 Lewis Hine to Frank Manny, 2 May 1910, quoted in Daile Kaplan, ed., *Photo Story*, 16; Hine, quoted in Maren Stange, "The Pittsburgh Survey: Lewis Hine and the Establishment of Documentary Style," in *Symbols of Ideal Life*, 72. On Hine's place in the development of social work in America, see especially Greenwald, "Visualizing Pittsburgh in the 1900s"; Trachtenberg, "Camera Work/ Social Work," in *Reading American Photographs*, 164–230; Susan Meyer, "In Anxious Celebration," 319–52; and Stange, "The Pittsburgh Survey," passim. Rosemarie Garland Thomson has identified four frameworks, or visual rhetorics, that have been used to view disability in American history: the wondrous mode, which juxtaposed the extraordinary disabled with the ordinary viewer; the sentimental mode, which positioned the disabled below the viewer as an object of pity; the exotic mode, which presented the disabled as an alien; and the realistic mode, which normalized and minimized the disability. See Rosemarie Garland Thomson, "Seeing the Disabled," 339, 346, 349.

67 Eastman, *Work-Accidents and the Law*, 119.

68 Janet Wells Greene, "Camera Wars," 140; Eastman, "Work-Accidents and Employers' Liability." Eastman's image of the puddler was powerful enough that the *Amalgamated Journal* reprinted it to explain accident benefits on 12 August 1909.

69 Eastman, "Work-Accidents and Employers' Liability."

70 Roberts, "Immigrant Wage Earners," 42.

71 Kellogg, "Field Work of the Pittsburgh Survey," 501; "First Civic Exhibition in Connection with the National Municipal League and the American Civic Association," 10–12; Joseph Stella, quoted in Baur, *Joseph Stella*, 26; Kellogg, quoted in Turner, "The Pittsburgh Survey and the Survey Moment: An Episode in the History of Expertise," in Greenwald and Anderson, *Pittsburgh Surveyed*, 43.

72 Chamber of Commerce of Pittsburgh, Annual Report, 1909, 40, 47.

73 *Justice* [Pittsburgh], 18 October 1913; *Amalgamated Journal*, 11 December 1902.

5. WORKING WOMEN

1 *Bulletin*, 28 January 1905.

2 Joan W. Scott, "'L'ouvrière! Mot impie, sordide . . . ,'" 119–42. Scott notes on page 142, "Historians who treat women workers as marginal to processes of urbanization and industrialization mistake historically constructed meanings for objective facts and thus miss half the story."

3 "Girls of Other Lands at Work," *Frank Leslie's Popular Monthly* 18 (August 1884): 247; Kathy Peiss, *Cheap Amusements*, 164–68, 178–84; Sharon Wood, *The Freedom of the Streets*, 16–17; Alice Kessler-Harris, *Out to Work*, 184–86; Nancy Foner, "Immigrant Women and Work in New York City, Then and Now," 95–113.

4 Elizabeth Beardsley Butler, *Women and the Trades*, 228.

5 Ibid., 3, 26; Clara E. Laughlin, *The Work-A-Day Girl*, 46. On Laughlin's emphasis on the problems of working women, see Judith Raftery, "Chicago Settlement Women in Fact and Fiction," 37–58.

6 Edith Abbott, *Women in Industry*, 212. Abbott further remarked: "It has become something of a public habit to speak of the women who work in factories to-day as if they were invaders threatening to take over work which belongs to men by custom and prior right of occupation." See Abbott, *Women in Industry*, 322.

7 Butler, *Women and the Trades*, 320.

8 Jacob A. Riis, *How the Other Half Lives*, 23–25; Butler, *Women and the Trades*, 125. On ethnic and racial "sorting out," see Thomas W. Hanchett, *Sorting Out the New South City*, and Mosher, *Capital's Utopia*.

9 Butler, *Women and the Trades,* 156.

10 Ibid., 180, 24. Rose, "'Crippled' Hands," 38, notes that even "light" work exposed women to the brunt of injuries. Rose points to chemical poisoning in shoe factories, rubber factories, and tin can factories and toxic inhalation in electrical assembly work as key examples.

11 Butler, *Women and the Trades,* 25, 210, 219.

12 Ibid., 227, 182, 33, 77.

13 Ibid., 242, 360; National Women's Trade Union League, Convention Handbook, 1909, 10. The Pennsylvania legislature first enacted in 1897 and reenacted in 1905 a maximum of sixty hours per week for women and a maximum of twelve hours per day. Noted in Louis D. Brandeis and Josephine Goldmark, *Women in Industry,* 4.

14 Butler, *Women and the Trades,* 26; Laughlin, *The Work-A-Day Girl,* 73.

15 Butler, *Women and the Trades,* 24, 57; *Bulletin,* 21 January 1905, 3 June 1905; Kleinberg, *The Shadow of the Mills,* 150. Butler added, "Perhaps the handling of sugar and the eating of it help to make so many of the girls plump and round-armed."

16 Kellogg, introduction to Butler, *Women and the Trades,* 5.

17 Ibid., 17, 5, 77.

18 Anna M. Galbraith, *Hygiene and Physical Culture for Women,* 269; Kellogg, introduction to Butler, *Women and the Trades,* 3; Tim Armstrong, *Modernism, Technology, and the Body,* 3.

19 Butler, *Women and the Trades,* 209, 23, 61; National Women's Trade Union League, Convention Handbook, 1909, 10.

20 Butler, *Women and the Trades,* 103, 210, 216, 37.

21 Galbraith, *Hygiene and Physical Culture for Women,* 274, 266; Butler, *Women and the Trades,* 238; Annie Marion MacLean, *Women Workers and Society,* 35.

22 Butler, *Women and the Trades,* 216, 125; Laura Levine Frader, "From Muscles to Nerves," 144, 141; Abbott, *Women in Industry,* 209; National Consumers' League, "The Eight Hours Day for Wage Earning Women." On the early history of the league, see Landon R. Y. Storrs, *Civilizing Capitalism,* 13–23. Frader writes of the ideal telephone worker, "In short, she needed good nerves—a quality that men did not possess and which made them less desirable as operators. So, whereas in many contexts women had been excluded from jobs because of their 'nervous qualities,' scientists now rejected 'muscles' in favor of nerves," and argued that "women's physical difference from men—their allegedly greater nervousness, their ability to move rapidly and react quickly to external stimuli, their capacity to give sustained attention to work—qualified them for the job."

23 Butler, *Women and the Trades*, 216, 238; National Women's Trade Union League, Convention Handbook, 1909, 10.

24 Butler, *Women and the Trades*, 65, 28; Rheta Childe Dorr, "Women's Demand for Humane Treatment of Women Workers in Shop and Factory"; Brandeis and Goldmark, *Women in Industry*, 19–39.

25 National Consumers' League, "The Eight Hours Day for Wage Earning Women"; Galbraith, *Hygiene and Physical Culture for Women*, 273–75.

26 *Problems in Eugenics*, 484.

27 Allison L. Hepler, *Women in Labor*, 15; "Report and Recommendations of Morals Efficiency Commission," 1, 8, 15. On the national movements to regulate, segregate, and abolish prostitution, see David J. Pivar, *Purity and Hygiene*, and Brian Donovan, *White Slave Crusades*.

28 Butler, *Women and the Trades*, 96; MacLean, *Women Workers and Society*, 8.

29 Butler, *Women and the Trades*, 156, 96.

30 Brandeis and Goldmark, *Women in Industry*, 39, 52, 20, 6.

31 *Bulletin*, 3 June 1905; Butler, *Women and the Trades*, 324, 300.

32 Butler, *Women and the Trades*, 333; *Bulletin*, 20 May 1905; American Social Hygiene Association, *The American Social Hygiene Association, 1914–1916*, 4.

33 National Consumers' League, "The Eight Hours Day for Wage Earning Women"; "Report and Recommendations of Morals Efficiency Commission," 27; Peter C. Baldwin, "Nocturnal Habits and Dark Wisdom," 596–97.

34 Gordon Hart [Sophia Margaretta Hensley], *Woman and the Race*, 15, 49, 162; MacLean, *Women Workers and Society*, preface; Hepler, *Women in Labor*, 16; Butler, *Women and the Trades*, 354.

35 Butler, *Women and the Trades*, 3; Abbott, *Women in Industry*, x; Theresa Schmid McMahon, "Women and Economic Evolution," 86; MacLean, *Women Workers and Society*, 34. In her introduction to Abbott's history of women's industrial employment, Breckinridge established their "helplessness" (in terms of bargaining power) as the primary reason that women's work had been considered a problem in American society.

36 MacLean, *Women Workers and Society*, 8; Henry Miller, *The Air-Conditioned Nightmare*, 26.

37 "Is America Changing the Physical Types of Men?," 12536; Laughlin, *The Work-A-Day Girl*, 98–99; Oestreicher, "The Spirit of '92: Popular Opposition in Homestead's Politics and Culture, 1892–1937," in Greenwald and Anderson, *Pittsburgh Surveyed*, 204.

6. HIDING AND DISPLAYING THE BROKEN BODY

1 Kellogg, introduction to Eastman, *Work-Accidents and the Law*, v.

2 Samuel Bloch, "Killing Workers a Little Detail," *Amalgamated Journal*, 20 October 1910.

3 See Greenwald, "Visualizing Pittsburgh in the 1900s: Art and Photography in the Service of Social Reform," in Greenwald and Anderson, *Pittsburgh Surveyed*, 149–51.

4 Jones, "Truth About Accidents in Pittsburgh Industries."

5 Ibid. The subtitle of Jones's article is "How Employers Guard the Lives of Their Workmen by the Most Elaborate System of Protective Devices in the World." Eastman had argued that although industry and insurance agents claimed careless workers caused accidents, employers' approach to accidents treated them as isolated incidents that were unrelated. As a result of this view, little was done to find patterns in accidents and injuries that could lead to accident prevention. Eastman, *Work-Accidents and the Law*, 84.

6 Jones, "How Pittsburgh Employers Care for the Injured."

7 Jones, "Devices for Pittsburgh Employes' Comfort and Some of Their Homes"; Jones, "How Pittsburgh Employers Care for the Injured"; Jones, "Truth About Accidents in Pittsburgh Industries."

8 Jones, "Truth About Accidents in Pittsburgh Industries"; Gerald Eggert, *Steelmasters and Labor Reform, 1886–1923*, xiv, 44.

9 Sidney J. Williams, *The Manual of Industrial Safety*, 9; Carnegie Steel Company, "General Instructions to Employees to Avoid Accidents, March 1917," William J. Gaughan collection; "Year Marks Progress in Industrial Safety," 10.

10 *Iron City Trades Journal*, 20 June 1911.

11 James W. Paul, "Rules for Mine-Rescue and First-Aid Field Contests," 5–6, 8, 10.

12 Killikelly, *The History of Pittsburgh*, 391; *Bulletin*, 4 March 1893, 7 October 1893; Trautmann and Hagboldt, *Hammers of Hell*, 25. On the disease-fighting efforts of the Allegheny County Board of Health, see Jacqueline Karnell Corn, *Environmental Health in Nineteenth-Century America*, 179–80, 238.

13 Richard Edwards, *Industries of Pennsylvania*, 160; Serene, "Immigrant Steelworkers in the Mon Valley," 109; William L. Estes, "Surgery of Accidents," in *Surgery: Its Principles and Practice*, vol. 5, ed. William Williams Keen, 916; Jones, "Truth About Accidents in Pittsburgh Industries."

14 William O'Neill Sherman, "Surgical Organization of the Carnegie Steel Company," Appendix to *Wage-Earning Pittsburgh*, 455–60.

15 Kleinberg, *The Shadow of the Mills*, 35–39; Brody, *Steelworkers in Amer-*

ica, 92. England's Workmen's Compensation Act, passed in 1897, resolved that "when a person, on his own responsibility and for his own profit, sets in motion agencies which create risks for others, he ought to be civilly responsible for the consequences of what he does." See Calder, *The Prevention of Factory Accidents,* 57. See also John Fabian Witt, *The Accidental Republic,* 41, 72.

16 *Amalgamated Journal,* 17 October 1901.

17 Julian Go, "Inventing Industrial Accidents and their Insurance," 410–11.

18 *Amalgamated Journal,* 7 January 1909; Robinson, "The Amalgamated Association of Iron, Steel and Tin Workers," 71, 75.

19 *Report of the Commissioner of Labor,* 1272, 1290, 1293; Randolph E. Bergstrom, *Courting Danger,* 156. On benevolent and fraternal societies in Pittsburgh in the late nineteenth century, see Kleinberg, *The Shadow of the Mills,* 274–76.

20 *Amalgamated Journal,* 18 February 1909.

21 *Amalgamated Journal,* 17 March 1910, 14 April 1910.

22 *Amalgamated Journal,* 16 September 1909. The average payment figures are based on the quarterly payment figures published in the *Amalgamated Journal* between 1908 and 1911. Financial institutions also courted workers. A 1915 print advertisement for the People's Savings Bank of Pittsburgh which promoted the "accident account" informed readers of the *Amalgamated Journal,* "you **cannot** prevent accidents—you **can** provide for them." See *Amalgamated Journal,* 4 March 1915. Kleinberg, *The Shadow of the Mills,* 272–73, details the informal strategies for raising money in the days before formal benefit programs. Organized labor's calls for money to pay for accidents appear frequently in the pages of the labor press in the late nineteenth century. The editors of the *Commoner and American Glass Worker,* 12 January 1889, argued that until the wages of industrial workers reflected the severe risk to life that the men faced each day, they would continue to accept monetary donations for injured men and their families.

23 Eggert, *Steelmasters and Labor Reform, 1886–1923,* 45; U.S. Steel and Carnegie Pension Fund, *Eleventh Annual Report, 1921,* 6; *Amalgamated Journal,* 30 June 1910. For itemized lists of payments in various company programs, see *Report of the Commissioner of Labor,* 517–21.

24 *Amalgamated Journal,* 30 June 1910; *Iron City Trades Journal,* 20 August 1909; Stuart D. Brandes, *American Welfare Capitalism, 1880–1940,* 96–97.

25 Go, "Inventing Industrial Accidents and their Insurance," 415; Lubove, "Workmen's Compensation and the Prerogatives of Voluntarism," 258, 266; Nan Goodman, *Shifting the Blame,* 67.

26 Frederick L. Hoffman, "Industrial Accidents and Industrial Diseases," 589; Eliza Pavalko, "State Timing of Policy Adoption," 592; Robert Asher, "Failure and Fulfillment," 202, 220.

27 Jack L. Walker, "The Diffusion of Innovations Among the American States," 890–91; *Iron City Trades Journal,* 30 September 1910; Eastman, *Work-Accidents and the Law,* 269–95; *Pittsburgh Post,* 28 December 1913; Pavalko, "State Timing of Policy Adoption," 607; *Amalgamated Journal,* 9 July 1914. Pavalko, "State Timing of Policy Adoption," 602, shows that New York adopted a workmen's compensation law in 1910, New Jersey and Ohio in 1911, and West Virginia in 1913. For more on the public image problem of liability lawsuits, see Paul Bellamy, *A History of Workmen's Compensation, 1898–1915.* Bellamy, xxiv, states that "workmen's compensation acted to 'retransform' a special type of increasingly visible and problematic 'public event'—injuries to workers—back into 'private events,' matters of contract." In a similar vein, Anthony Bale, "America's First Compensation Crisis: Conflict over the Value and Meaning of Workplace Injuries under the Employers' Liability System," in David Rosher and Gerald Markowitz, *Dying for Work,* 34, notes that "class struggle over the compensatory value of the labor power expended by workers in the form of bodily suffering and death produced in the labor process" came mainly through the vehicle of individual court cases rather than of collective action.

28 *Iron City Trades Journal,* 16 February 1912, 21 June 1912.

29 Commonwealth of Pennsylvania, *Legislative Journal,* 27 June 1913; "Physical Examination Tested," 1077. When steelworkers struck in Pittsburgh in 1919, one of their demands was the end of physical examinations of men applying for employment. See Vorse, *Men and Steel,* 50.

30 "Homestead as Seen by One of its Workmen," 164; *Amalgamated Journal,* 23 February 1911; Trautmann and Hagboldt, *Hammers of Hell,* 110–12.

31 *Amalgamated Journal,* 24 February 1916; *Laws of the General Assembly of the Commonwealth of Pennsylvania, 1915.* In the summer of 1916, Pennsylvania's supreme court declared the compensation law constitutional. By that time, the *Amalgamated Journal* noted, twenty thousand cases had already been handled by the compensation board. See *Amalgamated Journal,* 27 July 1916.

32 On the double logic of prostheses, see Seltzer, *Bodies and Machines,* 60.

33 *Cities of Pittsburgh and Allegheny,* 193; *Directory of Pittsburgh and Allegheny Cities; Pittsburgh Directory* (Pittsburgh, 1910). In 1909, the *Pittsburgh Sun* listed two other sources for artificial limbs—Forster Artificial Limb Company and Pittsburgh Physicians Supply Company. Neither were listed a year later in the city directory. A particularly consistent run of ALMC advertisements can be found in the *Commoner and Labor Herald* in the summer and autumn of 1887. For representative advertisements from other manufacturers, see *Pittsburgh Sun,* 14 December 1909; *Justice,* 11 October 1913; *Iron City Trades Journal,* 21 May 1909, 4 June 1909. Philip Wilson, "Principles of Design and Construction of Artificial

Legs," 6, dates the national prosthetic boom to the 1890s, when many original patents expired.

34 Catalogues were neither clear reflections of the aspirations of the injured, nor merely evil manipulations concocted to dupe the gullible. Instead, catalogues can best be characterized as collections of images seen through the distortions of a funhouse mirror, a metaphor used by Roland Marchand to explain American advertising's representational strategies between the First and Second World Wars. Marchand argued that American print advertisements skewed social realities, amplifying certain desires and fears while eliding any solutions to consumers' problems that did not involve a purchase. See Roland Marchand, *Advertising the American Dream*, xvi. These kinds of appeal were not new at the turn of the century; as Lisa Herschbach has shown, limb makers marketed their goods after the Civil War with similar themes of illusion, dignity, and utility. By the turn of the century, the diligent industrial worker had replaced earlier models of physical ability such as the craftsman, the farmer, and the ship captain as the main protagonist in manufacturers' tales of bodily reconstruction. See Lisa Herschbach, "Fragmentation and Reunion," 102.

35 A. A. Marks, *Manual of Artificial Limbs*, 4; David D. Yuan, "Disfigurement and Reconstruction in Oliver Wendell Holmes's 'The Human Wheel, Its Spokes and Felloes,'" 72; Thomson, "Seeing the Disabled," 347.

36 Yuan, "Disfigurement and Reconstruction," 73–75; Feick Brothers, *Illustrated Catalogue and Price List of Surgical Instruments*, 552; A. A. Marks, *Manual of Artificial Limbs*, 183, 248; J. F. Rowley, *An Illustrated Treatise on Artificial Legs*, 84.

37 ALMC advertisement, *National Labor Tribune*, 11 June 1887; Feick Brothers, *Illustrated Catalogue and Price List of Surgical Instruments*, 552; A. A. Marks, *Manual of Artificial Limbs*, 18; J. F. Rowley, *An Illustrated Treatise on Artificial Legs*, 24. Marks noted that "kinetoscopic photography affords the most valuable aid to an investigation of the knee and ankle joints when performing their functions."

38 J. F. Rowley, *An Illustrated Treatise on Artificial Legs*, 5; Harlan Hahn, "Advertising the Acceptably Employable Image: Disability and Capitalism," in *The Disability Studies Reader*, ed. Lennard J. Davis, 178. J. F. Rowley, *An Illustrated Treatise on Artificial Legs*, 94, connected its "seeing is believing" argument to the authority of photography: "The science of photography is simply holding the mirror up to nature and making permanent the reflection therein, and we may as well say here that a photograph cannot be had of a man in any condition unless the man is there identically as represented.... In order to place this matter before you so there will be no question of your understanding it thoroughly, we secured the services of one of the most expert artists with a camera in America to take photographs (snap shots), of Rowley wearers in action, running, jumping, making pedal mounts on bicycles, etc. These photographs have been made into engravings by the half-tone process and appear on the following pages, and we will pay one hundred dollars in gold to the man who will prove that they are not made from instantaneous photographs (snap shots), or that they are not an exact reproduction of the man in action."

39 J. F. Rowley, *An Illustrated Treatise on Artificial Legs,* 86, 123.

40 Erin O'Connor, "Fractions of Men," 744, 761; A. A. Marks, *Manual of Artificial Limbs,* 106. For comparison with European efforts to reconstruct the war wounded, see Seth Koven, "Remembering and Dismemberment," 1169; and Roxanne Panchasi, "Reconstructions," 110–12.

41 A. A. Marks, *Manual of Artificial Limbs,* 15; J. F. Rowley, *An Illustrated Treatise on Artificial Legs,* 12, 44. Amputees were frequently used in turn-of-the-century popular culture as a source of amusement and trickery. On the use of amputees' prosthetic feats as entertainment, see Martin F. Norden, *The Cinema of Isolation,* 8–24. Norden notes that motion pictures such as *Don't Pull My Leg* (1908), *The Empty Sleeve* (1909), and *Story of a Leg* (1910) turned amputees into comic characters and their artificial limbs into props. The films managed to normalize the spectacle of amputees in public but also marginalized them as victims or con artists.

42 Warren Stone Bickham, "Amputations," in *Surgery: Its Principles and Practice,* vol. 5, ed. William Williams Keen, 805; E. Muirhead Little, *Artificial Limbs and Amputation Stumps: A Practical Handbook,* 97; William Rideing, "Patched Up Humanity," 783; Panchasi, "Reconstructions," 122; Feick Brothers, *Illustrated Catalogue and Price List of Surgical Instruments,* 556; A. A. Marks, *Manual of Artificial Limbs,* 176, 267. The division of artificial limbs in terms of elegance and utility was formalized in the British military distribution system. By the 1910s, England's Ministry of Pensions had divided the artificial arms it provided to accident victims into three categories: heavy workers' arms, light workers' arms, and light dress arms. See Little, *Artificial Limbs and Amputation Stumps,* 86, 122.

43 Feick Brothers, *Illustrated Catalogue and Price List of Surgical Instruments,* 558; A. A. Marks, *Manual of Artificial Limbs,* 224.

44 Herschbach, "Fragmentation and Reunion," 92; Rideing, "Patched Up Humanity," 784; Feick Brothers, *Illustrated Catalogue and Price List of Surgical Instruments,* 552.

45 A. A. Marks, *Manual of Artificial Limbs,* 257; J. F. Rowley, *An Illustrated Treatise on Artificial Legs,* 123–24.

46 *Report of the Commissioner of Labor* (1890), 1272–93; J. F. Rowley, *An*

Illustrated Treatise on Artificial Legs, 80; Eastman, *Work-Accidents and the Law,* 301–2; *Report of the Commissioner of Labor* (1909), 518

47 In a much more indirect way than limb catalogues, the labor press also encouraged a sense of prosthetic affinity. Labor journals in Pittsburgh tried to foster a grim feeling of camaraderie around the prevalence of amputation and prostheses in working communities. In the autumn of 1913 the *Amalgamated Journal* half-joked that the nation's supply of wood for artificial limbs was running low. "Save your legs!" the editorial board told its readers. The *Amalgamated Journal* also acted as a cheerleader of sorts, presenting its readers with tales of amputees who had overcome their disabilities to make themselves useful again. The journal told readers of a Long Island artist who, after losing both arms, painted with his mouth. The title of the article, "Works Without Hands," suggested the possibility of social utility even after dismemberment. Like the tightrope walker and the bicycle rider, the armless artist transcended his dismemberment to matter once again. See *Amalgamated Journal,* 6 October 1904, 9 October 1913.

48 *National Labor Tribune,* 23 April 1896.

EPILOGUE

1 MacKaye, *The Civic Theater in Relation to the Redemption of Leisure,* 254–55; MacKaye, "The New Fourth of July," 394.

2 Kenneth G. Bryant, "Percy MacKaye and the Drama of Democracy," 71–73; MacKaye, *The Civic Theater in Relation to the Redemption of Leisure,* 45, 71, 288; MacKaye, "The New Fourth of July," 394, 396. On historical pageantry of the early twentieth century and MacKaye's place within it, see also Glassberg, *American Historical Pageantry,* and Duncan James Rollo, "Percy MacKaye's Vision of the National Drama as an Expression of the American Identity." This was not the first time Pittsburghers prepared to watch a dramatic production involving the city's laborers. In the 1870s, several plays written for the local theater brought workers in during half-price "people's nights." Following the success of "The Workmen of Pittsburgh" in 1877, the Pittsburgh Opera House staged in October 1878 a fictionalized account of the 1877 railroad strike titled "The Lower Million." A group of 150 workers from the area played the roles of "rioters," bringing praise from the local press for the authenticity of the re-creation. See James Allison Lowrie, "A History of the Pittsburgh Stage, 1861–1891," 134–38.

3 Glassberg, *American Historical Pageantry,* 172. The story of the city council bribery affair was reported in the *Sun,* 21 March 1910 through 24 March 1910.

4 Cornelia Sage, "Constantin Meunier—An Appreciation," 536; Christian Brinton, "Constantin Meunier's Message to America," 152. The exhibition at the Carnegie Institute was part of a six-city tour from November 1913 to April 1914. The collection was also displayed in Buffalo, New York, Chicago, Detroit, and St. Louis. A complete list of the pieces exhibited can be found in Christian Brinton, *Catalogue of an Exhibition of the Works of Constantin Meunier*, 65–80.

5 Brinton, *Catalogue of an Exhibition of the Works of Constantin Meunier*, 50; *Pittsburgh Sun*, 30 December 1913; Brinton, "Constantin Meunier's Message to America," 154; *Gazette Times*, 20 December 1913.

6 *Bulletin*, 3 January 1914; *New York Times*, 18 January 1914; Brinton, "Constantin Meunier's Message to America," 149.

7 My understanding of the Magarac legend is greatly indebted to Jennifer Gilley and Stephen Burnett, "Deconstructing and Reconstructing Pittsburgh's Man of Steel." The authors' discussion of the multiple contexts and political uses of Magarac in twentieth-century Pittsburgh is a model work that explores the close relationship between representation and civic history. See also Owen Francis, "The Saga of Joe Magarac: Steelman," 505–11, and George Carver, "Legend in Steel," 129–36.

8 Solomon, *Literature, Amusement, and Technology in the Great Depression*, 11.

9 *The Life Treasury of American Folklore*; Gilley and Burnett, "Deconstructing and Reconstructing Pittsburgh's Man of Steel," 400.

10 Dabakis, *Visualizing Labor in American Sculpture*, 105, 113–17; Sage, "Constantin Meunier—An Appreciation," 536.

11 For an example of a scholarly effort to use remembrance as a means of picturing a postindustrial future, see Modell, *A Town Without Steel: Envisioning Homestead*.

12 *Bulletin*, 11 November 1905.

13 Pennsylvania Department of Community and Economic Development, "Shopping in PA" Website, http://www.shoppinginpa.com/shoppinginpa/ City Experience.do?page=waterfront.

14 The Allegheny Conference on Community Development, the Greater Pittsburgh Convention and Visitors Bureau, and the Senator John Heinz Pittsburgh Regional History Center are particularly enthusiastic proponents of regional innovation as a marketing theme. See their joint Website to celebrate Pittsburgh's 250th anniversary at http://www.imaginepittsburgh.com/index.aspx.

BIBLIOGRAPHY

PRIMARY SOURCES

Abbott, Edith. *Women in Industry: A Study in American Economic History*. New York: D. Appleton, 1909.

Albert J. Logan papers. MSS 96. Library and Archives Division. Historical Society of Western Pennsylvania. Pittsburgh.

All About Pittsburgh and Allegheny. Pittsburgh, 1876.

Allegheny County. Office of the Coroner. Record of Inquests Held, 1899–1915. Pennsylvania State Archives. Harrisburg.

Amalgamated Journal [Pittsburgh].

American Social Hygiene Association. *The American Social Hygiene Association, 1914–1916*. New York, 1916.

Backert, A. O., ed. *The ABC of Iron and Steel*. 5th ed. Cleveland: Penton, 1925.

Bakewell, Mary E. *Of Long Ago: The Children and the City*. Pittsburgh: University of Pittsburgh Press, 1949.

Baldwin, Leland D. *Pittsburgh: The Story of a City*. Pittsburgh: University of Pittsburgh, 1938.

Bemis, Edward W. "The Homestead Strike." *Journal of Political Economy* 2 (January 1894): 369–96.

Betts, Lillian W. "Pittsburg: A City of Brain and Brawn." *Outlook* 69 (7 September 1901): 17–33.

Bjorkman, Edwin. "What Industrial Civilization May Do To Men." *World's Work* 17 (April 1909): 11479–98.

Blaikie, William. "Is American Stamina Declining?" *Harper's Monthly* 79 (July 1889): 241–44.

Blashfield, Edwin Howland. *Mural Painting in America*. New York: C. Scribner's Sons, 1913.

Bogardus, Emory. "The Relation of Fatigue to Industrial Accidents, Part I." *American Journal of Sociology* 17 (September 1911): 206–22.

Boucher, John Newton. *A Century and a Half of Pittsburg and Her People*. New York: Lewis Publishing, 1908.

Bourne, Randolph. "In the Mind of the Worker." *Atlantic Monthly* 113 (1914): 375–82.

Brandeis, Louis D., and Josephine Goldmark. *Women in Industry*. New York: National Consumers' League, 1908.

Bridge, James. *The Inside History of the Carnegie Steel Company: A Romance of Millions*. New York: Aldine, 1903.

Brinton, Christian. "Constantin Meunier's Message to America." *International Studio* 51 (January 1914): 149–57.

——. *Catalogue of an Exhibition of the Works of Constantin Meunier*. New York: Redfield Brothers, 1914.

Bulletin [Pittsburgh].

Burgoyne, Arthur. *Homestead: A Complete History of the Struggle of July, 1892, between the Carnegie Steel Company, Limited, and the Amalgamated Association of Iron and Steel Workers*. Pittsburgh: Rawsthorne Engraving and Printing, 1893.

Butler, Elizabeth Beardsley. *Women and the Trades: Pittsburgh, 1907–1908*. New York: Charities Publication Committee, 1909.

Byington, Margaret. *Homestead: The Households of a Mill Town*. New York: Charities Publication Committee, 1910.

Caffin, Charles H. "The New Mural Decorations of John W. Alexander." *Harper's Monthly* 114 (May 1907): 845–56.

——. *American Masters of Sculpture*. New York: Doubleday, Page, 1913.

Calder, John. *The Prevention of Factory Accidents*. New York: Longman's, Green, 1899.

Carnegie Steel Company. *General Statistics and Special Treatise on the Homestead Steel Works*. Pittsburgh: Carnegie Steel Company, 1912.

Carver, T. N. "Machinery and the Laborers." *Quarterly Journal of Economics* 22 (1908): 210–32.

Chamber of Commerce of Pittsburgh. Annual Reports. Library and Archives Division. Historical Society of Western Pennsylvania. Pittsburgh.

———. "Report of the Committee on Housing Conditions on Workman's Dwellings." Pittsburgh: Chamber of Commerce, 1911.

———. *Toasts and Responses at the Banquet Given by the Chamber of Commerce of Pittsburgh, 27 May 1892.* Library and Archives Division. Historical Society of Western Pennsylvania. Pittsburgh.

Cities of Pittsburgh and Allegheny: Leading Merchants and Manufacturers. New York: Historical, 1886.

"The City of Pittsburgh." *Harper's New Monthly* 62 (December 1880): 49–68.

Clarke, Caspar Purdon. "Study in Black and Green." *Everybody's* 21 (September 1909): 424–25.

Commoner and American Glass Worker [Pittsburgh].

Commonwealth of Pennsylvania. Annual Report of the Factory Inspector of the Commonwealth of Pennsylvania.

———. Bureau of Industrial Statistics. Annual Report.

———. First Annual Report of the Commissioner of Labor and Industry, 1913–14.

———. *Laws of the General Assembly of the Commonwealth of Pennsylvania, 1915.*

———. *Legislative Journal.* 27 June 1913.

———. Secretary of Internal Affairs of the Commonwealth of Pennsylvania. Annual Report.

Cornell, Robert. Diary. MSS 159, box 2. Library and Archives Division. Historical Society of Western Pennsylvania. Pittsburgh.

"The Crowning of Labor: The John White Alexander Mural Paintings in the Carnegie Institute, Pittsburgh." *Mentor* 13 (May 1925): 32.

Davis, James. *The Iron Puddler: My Life in the Rolling Mills.* New York: Grosset and Dunlap, 1922.

Directory of Pittsburgh and Allegheny Cities. Pittsburgh: J. F. Diffenbacher, 1880–1900.

Dorr, Rheta Childe. "Women's Demand for Humane Treatment of Women Workers in Shop and Factory." *Hampton's Magazine* (December 1909).

Eastman, Crystal. "Work-Accidents and Employers' Liability." *The Survey* (3 September 1910).

———. *Work-Accidents and the Law.* New York: Charities Publication Committee, 1910.

Edwards, Richard. *Industries of Pennsylvania.* Philadelphia, 1881.

Engineers' Society of Western Pennsylvania. Pittsburgh, 1930.

Fawcett, Waldon. "The Center of the World of Steel." *Century* 62 (June 1901): 190–202.

Feick Brothers. *Illustrated Catalogue and Price List of Surgical Instruments.* 3d ed. Pittsburgh, 1896.

"First Civic Exhibition in Connection with the National Municipal League and the American Civic Association." Pittsburgh: National Municipal League, 1908.

Fitch, John A. *The Steel Workers.* New York: Charities Publication Committee, 1910.

Galbraith, Anna M. *Hygiene and Physical Culture for Women.* New York: Dodd, Mead, 1895.

Garland, Hamlin. "Homestead and its Perilous Trades." *McClure's* 3 (June 1894): 2–20.

——. *Main-Travelled Roads.* 1891; reprint, New York: Harper and Brothers, 1922.

Gibbons, William. *Those Black Diamond Men: A Tale of the Anthrax Valley.* New York: F. H. Revell, 1902.

"Girls of Other Lands at Work." *Frank Leslie's Popular Monthly* 18 (August 1884): 247.

Glazier, Willard. *Peculiarities of American Cities.* Philadelphia: Hubbard Brothers, 1885.

Goldmark, Josephine. *Fatigue and Efficiency: A Study in Industry.* New York: Russell Sage Foundation, 1912.

Greene, Homer. *Coal and the Coal Mines.* Boston: Houghton Mifflin, 1889.

Guide to all Points of Interest in and about Pittsburgh. Pittsburgh: Chamber of Commerce, 1893.

Hall, J. Morton. *America's Industrial Centre.* Pittsburgh: Chamber of Commerce, 1891.

Hard, William. "Making Steel and Killing Men." *Everybody's* 17 (November 1907): 580–91.

——. "The Law of the Killed and the Wounded." *Everybody's* 19 (September 1908), 361–71.

Hart, Gordon [Sophia Margaretta Hensley]. *Woman and the Race.* Westwood, Mass.: Ariel Press, 1911.

Hiorns, Arthur. *Iron and Steel Manufacture.* New York: Macmillan, 1889.

Hobson, John. "The Influence of Machinery upon Employment." *Political Science Quarterly* 8 (March 1893): 97–123.

Hoffman, Frederick L. "Accidents in Bituminous (Pennsylvania) Mines." *Coal Age* 27 (July 1912): 119–21.

——. "Industrial Accidents and Industrial Diseases." *Publications of the American Statistical Association* 11 (December 1909): 567–603.

"Homestead as Seen by One of its Workmen." *McClure's* 3 (July 1894): 163–69.

"The Homestead Riots." *Harper's Weekly* 36 (16 July 1892): 678.

"The Homestead Strike." *North American Review* 155 (September 1892): 355–75.

Howe, Henry M. "Notes on the Bessemer Process." *Transactions of the American Institute of Mining Engineers* 19 (1890–91): 1138.

Illustrated Guide and Handbook of Pittsburgh and Allegheny. Pittsburgh: Fisher and Stewart, 1887.

Iron City Trades Journal [Pittsburgh].

"The Iron Industry's Labor Supply." *Iron Age* 96 (8 July 1915): 91–92.

Irvine, Alexander. *The Magyar: A Story of the Social Revolution*. Girard, Kan.: Socialist Publishing, 1911.

"Is America Changing the Physical Types of Men?" *World's Work* 19 (February 1910): 12536.

J. M. Kelly's Handbook of Greater Pittsburg. Pittsburgh: J. M. Kelly, 1895.

James, Henry. *The American Scene*. New York: Harper and Brothers, 1907.

Jones, Robert W. "Devices for Pittsburgh Employees' Comfort and Some of their Homes." *Pittsburgh Gazette Times*, 9 January 1910.

——. "How Pittsburgh Employers Care for the Injured." *Pittsburgh Gazette Times*, 2 January 1910.

——"Truth About Accidents in Pittsburgh Industries." *Pittsburgh Gazette Times*, 26 December 1909.

Jones and Laughlin Company. Manuscript collection. Library and Archives Division. Historical Society of Western Pennsylvania (HSWP). Pittsburgh.

Keeler, Ralph, and Harry Fenn. "The Taking of Pittsburgh, III." *Every Saturday*. 18 March 1871.

Keen, William Williams, ed. *Surgery: Its Principles and Practice*. Volume 5. Philadelphia: W. B. Saunders, 1909.

Killikelly, Sarah H. *The History of Pittsburgh: Its Rise and Progress*. Pittsburgh: B. C. Gordon Montgomery, 1906.

King, Pauline. *American Mural Painting*. Boston: Noyes, Platt, 1902.

King, Sidney A., W. H. Stevenson, and R. W. Johnston. *The Story of the Sesqui-Centennial Celebration of Pittsburgh*. Pittsburgh: R. W. Johnston Studios, 1910.

Kitson, James. "The Iron and Steel Industries of America." *Contemporary Review* 59 (May 1891): 625–41.

Kling, Peter M. *Why a Boy Should Learn a Trade*. Pittsburgh: P. F. Smith, 1906.

Lauck, W. Jett. "The Bituminous Coal Miner and Coke Worker of Western Pennsylvania." *Survey* 26 (1 April 1911): 34–51.

Laughlin, Clara E. *The Work-A-Day Girl: A Study of Some Present-Day Conditions*. New York: Fleming H. Revell, 1913.

Lee, Gerald Stanley. *Crowds: A Moving Picture of Democracy*. New York: Doubleday, Page, 1913.

Little, E. Muirhead. *Artificial Limbs and Amputation Stumps: A Practical Handbook*. Philadelphia: Blakiston, 1922.

Local News [Homestead, Penn.].

MacKaye, Percy. "The New Fourth of July." *Century* 80 (July 1910): 394.

——. *The Civic Theater in Relation to the Redemption of Leisure*. New York: Mitchell Kennerley, 1912.

MacLean, Annie Marion. *Women Workers and Society*. Chicago: A. C. McClurg, 1916.

"Making Bessemer Rails." *Harper's Weekly* 30 (10 April 1886): 238.

"Manufacture of Window Glass with Natural Gas." *Scientific American* 54 (20 March 1886): 183–84.

Marks, A. A. *Manual of Artificial Limbs—Copiously Illustrated—An Exhaustive Exposition of Prosthesis*. New York, 1914.

"Marks' Improvements on Artificial Limbs." *Journal of the Franklin Institute* 136 (July 1893): 70–75.

Martin, James M. *Which Way, Sirs, the Better? A Story of Our Toilers*. Boston: Arena Publishing, 1895.

McCain, George N. *A Sketch of the Celebration of Allegheny County*. Pittsburgh: Snowden and Peterson, 1888.

McMahon, Theresa Schmid. "Women and Economic Evolution: The Effects of Industrial Changes Upon the Status of Women." Ph.D. diss., University of Wisconsin, 1912.

McNeill, George E., ed. *The Labor Movement: The Problem of To-Day*. Boston: M. W. Hazer, 1887.

Mellon Bank. *Pittsburgh: 1758–1908*. Pittsburgh, 1908.

Memorial of the Celebration of the Carnegie Institute at Pittsburgh, P.A. Pittsburgh: Board of Trustees of the Carnegie Institute, 1907.

Merwin, Henry Childs. "On Being Civilized Too Much." *Atlantic Monthly* 79 (June 1897): 838–46.

Miller, Henry. *The Air-Conditioned Nightmare*. New York: New Directions, 1945.

M'Killop, James. *Coal and American Coal Mining*. Airdrie, Scotland: Baird and Hamilton, 1876.

"Mural Paintings in American Cities." *Scribner's* 25 (1899): 125–28.

National Consumers' League. "The Eight Hours Day for Wage Earning Women." New York, 1916.

———. "The Waste of Industry." New York, 1915.

National Labor Tribune [Pittsburgh].

National Municipal League. *Proceedings of the Pittsburgh Conference for Good City Government*. New York, 1908.

National Women's Trade Union League. Convention Handbook, 1909. Chicago, 1909.

Nevin, Theodore W. *Pittsburg and the Men Who Made It*. Pittsburgh: Burton Press, 1904.

New York Herald.

New York Times.

Nichols, Starr Hoyt. "Men and Machinery." *North American Review* 166 (May 1898): 602–11.

Official Municipal Program of the Sesqui-Centennial Celebration of the City of Pittsburgh. Pittsburgh: Sesquicentennial Committee, 1908.

"Official Souvenir Program of the Exercises attending the Unveiling of the Monument Erected to the Memory of Col. James Anderson by Andrew Carnegie." Pittsburgh, 1904.

Oliver, Thomas. *Dangerous Trades: The Historical, Social, and Legal Aspects of Industrial Occupations as Affecting Health*. New York: E. P. Dutton, 1902.

"On Marks' Artificial Limbs." *Journal of the Franklin Institute* 127 (May 1889): 329–36.

Oppenheim, James. "The Hired City." *American Magazine* 70 (May 1910): 33–40.

Outerbridge, Alexander E. "Machinery and the Man." *Journal of the Franklin Institute* 151 (June 1901): 464–68.

Parker, Edward W. "Coal-Cutting Machinery." *Transactions of the American Institute of Mining Engineers* 29 (1899): 405–59.

Patterson, Burd Shippen. "The Aesthetic and Intellectual Side of Pittsburg." *Review of Reviews* 31 (January 1905): 6.

Paul, James W. "Rules for Mine-Rescue and First-Aid Field Contests." *Miners' Circular* 13 (1913).

Pennsylvania State Archives. Harrisburg.

"Physical Examination Tested." *Iron Age* 95 (13 May 1915): 1077–78.

"A Piece of Glass." *Harper's Monthly* 79 (July 1889): 245–64.

Pinkerton, Allan. *Strikers, Communists, Tramps, and Detectives*. New York: G. W. Carleton, 1878.

"Pittsburgh, the Giant Industrial City of the World." *Harper's Weekly* 47 (23 May 1903): 841–53.

"Pittsburg, Pennsylvania." *North American Review* 156 (June 1893): 17–22.

Pittsburgh Chamber of Commerce. *Fifty Years of the Chamber of Commerce of Pittsburgh, 1874–1924.* Pittsburgh: Murdoch, Kerr, 1924.

——. *Greater Pittsburgh: The Rise, Progress, and Triumph of an Imperial City.* Pittsburgh: Charles E. Lipscomb, 1904.

——. *Pittsburgh the Powerful.* Pittsburgh: Industry Publishing Co., 1907.

Pittsburg at the Dawn of the 20th Century: The Busiest City in the World. Pittsburgh: Pittsburg Leader, 1901.

Pittsburgh Directory. 1910.

Pittsburgh Dispatch.

The Pittsburgh District: Civic Frontage. New York: Survey Associates, 1914.

Pittsburg Exposition Society. "Partial List of Citizens, Firms, and Corporations, All Eligible to Life Membership in the Pittsburg Exposition Society." (n.d.) Library and Archives Division. Historical Society of Western Pennsylvania. Pittsburgh.

Pittsburgh Oral History Project. Library and Archives Division. Historical Society of Western Pennsylvania. Pittsburgh.

Pittsburgh Post.

Pittsburgh Telegraph.

Pittsburgh Times.

Popplewell, Frank. *Some Modern Conditions and Recent Developments in Iron and Steel Production in America.* Manchester: University Press, 1906.

Potter, Henry C. "Man and the Machine." *North American Review* 165 (October 1897): 385–92.

Problems in Eugenics: Papers Communicated to the First International Eugenics Congress held at the University of London, July 24th to 30th, 1912. London: Eugenics Education Society, 1912.

"The Proletarian Art of Constantin Meunier." *Current Literature* 39 (September 1905): 271–74.

Records of the Greater Pittsburgh Chamber of Commerce. MSS 284. Library and Archives Division. Historical Society of Western Pennsylvania. Pittsburgh.

"Report and Recommendations of Morals Efficiency Commission." Pittsburgh, 1913.

Report of the Commissioner of Labor. Washington, D.C.: Government Printing Office, 1890.

Rideing, William. "Patched Up Humanity." *Appletons' Journal* 13 (19 June 1875): 783–84.

Riis, Jacob A. *How the Other Half Lives.* 1890; reprint, New York: Penguin, 1997.

Roberts, Percival, Jr. "The Puddling Process, Past and Present." *Transactions of the American Institute of Mining Engineers* 8 (1879–80): 355–62.

Rood, Henry. *The Company Doctor: An American Story.* New York: Merriam, 1895.

Roosevelt, Theodore. *The Winning of the West.* Volume 2. New York: Putnam's, 1889.

Rowley, J. F. *An Illustrated Treatise on Artificial Legs.* Chicago, 1911.

Roy, Andrew. *A History of the Coal Miners of the United States.* Columbus: J. L. Trauger, 1907.

Sage, Cornelia. "Constantin Meunier—An Appreciation." *Scribner's* 55 (April 1914): 535–38.

Sandburg, Carl. *Chicago Poems.* New York: H. Holt, 1916.

Scaife, William Lucien. "Pittsburg—A New Great City." *American Monthly Review of Reviews* 31 (January 1905): 48–76.

Simons, A. M. "Wasting Human Life." *Intercollegiate Socialist* 2 (February/March 1914): 13.

Sinclair, Upton. *The Industrial Republic: A Study of the America of Ten Years Hence.* New York: Doubleday, Page, 1907.

Souvenir Handbook: Some Things of Interest in and about Pittsburgh, to be Visited by the Iron and Steel Institute of Great Britain. Pittsburgh: Pittsburgh Committees of Reception, 1890.

Souvenir of Pittsburg. Portland: L. H. Nelson, 1905.

Souvenir of the Allegheny County Centennial. Pittsburgh: Snowden and Peterson, 1888.

Steffens, Lincoln. *The Shame of the Cities.* New York: McClure, Phillips, 1904.

Stiefel, H. C. *Slices from a Long Loaf.* Pittsburgh: Bissell Block, 1905.

Stowell, Myron. *"Fort Frick," or the Siege of Homestead.* Pittsburgh: Pittsburg Printing, 1893.

Swank, James Moore. *Statistics of the Iron and Steel Production of the United States.* Washington, D.C.: Government Printing Office, 1881.

The Story of Pittsburgh and Vicinity Illustrated. Pittsburgh: Gazette Times, 1908.

Thurston, George H. *Allegheny County's Hundred Years.* Pittsburgh: A. A. Anderson and Son, 1888.

Trautmann, W. E., and Peter Hagboldt. *Hammers of Hell.* Chicago: New World, 1921.

Union Trust Company. *Industrial Pittsburgh*. Pittsburgh, 1908.

U.S. Census Bureau. Tenth Census: 1880. Eleventh Census: 1890. Twelfth Census: 1900. Thirteenth Census: 1910. Washington, D.C.: Government Printing Office.

U.S. Congress. House of Representatives. *Investigation of the Employment of Pinkerton Detectives in Connection with the Labor Troubles at Homestead, Pennsylvania*. Washington, D.C.: Government Printing Office, 1893.

U.S. Congress. Immigration Commission. *Reports of the Immigration Commission*. Volume 6, Immigrants in Industries. Washington, D.C.: Government Printing Office, 1911.

U.S. Congress. Industrial Commission. *Report of the Industrial Commission on the Relations and Conditions of Capital and Labor*. Volume 7. Washington, D.C.: Government Printing Office, 1901.

U.S. Congress. Senate. Committee upon the Relations Between Labor and Capital. *Report of the Committee of the Senate upon the Relations Between Labor and Capital*. Volume 2. Washington, D.C.: Government Printing Office, 1885.

——. *Investigation of Labor Troubles*. Washington, D.C.: Government Printing Office, 1893.

U.S. Department of the Interior. Bureau of Mines. *Coal-Mine Fatalities in the United States, 1870–1914*. by Albert H. Fay, Bulletin 115. Washington, D.C.: Government Printing Office, 1916.

U.S. Steel and Carnegie Pension Fund. Eleventh Annual Report, 1921.

Vorse, Mary Heaton. *Men and Steel*. New York: Boni and Liveright, 1920.

Wage-Earning Pittsburgh. New York: Survey Associates, 1914.

Wallin, J. E. "Psychological Aspects of the Problem of Atmospheric Smoke Pollution." *Mellon Institute of Industrial Research Bulletin* 3 (1913): 3–40.

Watchorn, Robert. "The Cost of Coal in Human Life." *Outlook* 92 (22 May 1909): 171–83.

Weir, James, Jr. "The Methods of the Rioting Striker as Evidence of Degeneration." *Century* 48 (October 1894): 952–54.

Western Pennsylvania Exposition Society. *Exposition Handbook and Guide*. Pittsburgh, 1890.

——. *Greater Pittsburgh Exposition*. Pittsburgh, 1895.

——. *Pittsburg and its Exposition*. Pittsburgh, 1889.

——. *Pittsburg and its Fifth Annual Exposition*. Pittsburgh, 1893.

——. *Pittsburgh Exposition*. Pittsburgh, 1899.

——. Report of the President and Treasurer. 1897–1908.

White, Henry. "Machinery and Labor." *Annals of the American Academy of Political and Social Science* 20 (July 1902): 223–31.

William J. Gaughan Collection. Archives of Industrial Society. Archives Service Center. University of Pittsburgh. Pittsburgh.

William Stevenson Papers. MSS 71. Library and Archives Division. Historical Society of Western Pennsylvania. Pittsburgh.

Williams, Sidney J. *The Manual of Industrial Safety*. Chicago: A. W. Shaw, 1927.

Willson, Seelye A. "The Growth of Pittsburgh Iron and Steel." *Magazine of Western History* 2 (October 1885): 540–71.

Wilson, Erasmus, ed. *Standard History of Pittsburg, Pennsylvania*. Chicago: H. R. Cornell, 1898.

Wilson, Philip. "Principles of Design and Construction of Artificial Legs." *Publications of the Red Cross Institution for Crippled and Disabled Men* 2 (10 July 1918): 6–11.

World [New York].

Wright, Carroll. *Some Ethical Phases of the Labor Question*. Boston: American Unitarian Association, 1903.

"Year Marks Progress in Industrial Safety." *Blast Furnace and Steel Plant* 6 (January 1918): 10.

SECONDARY SOURCES

Abbott, Carl. *Boosters and Businessmen: Popular Economic Thought and Urban Growth in the Antebellum Middle West*. Westport, Conn.: Greenwood Press, 1981.

Adams, Adeline. *Daniel Chester French*. New York: Houghton Mifflin, 1932.

Alessio, Dominic T. "Capitalist Realist Art: Industrial Images of Hamilton, Ontario, 1884–1910." *Journal of Urban History* 18 (August 1992): 442–69.

Alexander, June Granatir. "Moving into and out of Pittsburgh: Ongoing Chain Migration." In *A Century of European Migrations, 1830–1930*, edited by Rudolph J. Vecoli and Suzanne M. Sinke. Urbana: University of Illinois Press, 1991.

Amico, Leonard. *The Mural Decorations of Edwin Howland Blashfield*. Williamstown, Mass.: Sterling and Francine Clark Art Institute, 1978.

Armstrong, Tim. *Modernism, Technology, and the Body: A Cultural Study*. New York: Cambridge University Press, 1998.

Asher, Robert. "Failure and Fulfillment: Agitation for Employers' Liability Legislation and the Origins of Workmen's Compensation in New York State, 1876–1910." *Labor History* 24 (1983): 198–222.

Backett-Milburn, Kathryn, and Linda Mckie, eds. *Constructing Gendered Bodies*. New York: Palgrave, 2001.

Baldwin, Peter C. " 'Nocturnal Habits and Dark Wisdom': The American Response to Children in the Streets at Night, 1880–1930." *Journal of Social History* 35 (Spring 2002): 593–611.

Baltz, Trudy. "Pageantry and Mural Painting: Community Rituals in Allegorical Form." *Winterthur Portfolio* 15 (Autumn 1980): 211–28.

Banta, Martha. *Imaging American Women: Idea and Ideals in Cultural History*. New York: Columbia University Press, 1987.

——. *Taylored Lives: Narrative Productions in the Age of Taylor, Veblen, and Ford*. Chicago: University of Chicago Press, 1993.

Barnes, L. Diane. "Booster Ethos: Community, Image, and Profit in Early Clarksburg." *West Virginia History* 56 (1997): 27–42.

Baron, Ava. "Masculinity, the Embodied Male Worker, and the Historian's Gaze." *International Labor and Working-Class History* 69 (Spring 2006): 143–60.

Baur, John. *Joseph Stella*. New York: Praeger, 1971.

Bederman, Gail. *Manliness and Civilization: A Cultural History of Gender and Race in the United States, 1880–1917*. Chicago: University of Chicago Press, 1995.

Bell, Thomas. *Out of this Furnace*. Boston: Little, Brown, 1941.

Bellamy, Paul. *A History of Workmen's Compensation, 1898–1915: From Courtroom to Boardroom*. New York: Garland, 1997.

Bergstrom, Randolph E. *Courting Danger: Injury and Law in New York City, 1870–1910*. Ithaca, N.Y.: Cornell University Press, 1997.

Bernstein, Iver. *The New York City Draft Riots: Their Significance for American Society and Politics in the Age of the Civil War*. New York: Oxford University Press, 1990.

Bicha, Karel D. "Hunkies: Stereotyping the Slavic Immigrants, 1890–1920." *Journal of American Ethnic History* 2 (Fall 1982): 16–38.

Bjelajac, David. *American Art: A Cultural History*. New York: Harry N. Abrams, 2001.

Blewett, Mary H. "Masculinity and Mobility: The Dilemma of Lancashire Weavers and Spinners in Late-Nineteenth-Century Fall River, Massachusetts." In *Meanings for Manhood: Constructions of Masculinity in Victorian America*, edited by Mark C. Carnes and Clyde Griffen. Chicago: University of Chicago Press, 1990.

Bodnar, John, Roger Simon, and Michael P. Weber. *Lives of their Own: Blacks,*

Italians, and Poles in Pittsburgh, 1900–1960. Urbana: University of Illinois
Press, 1982.

———. *The Transplanted: A History of Immigrants in Urban America.* Bloomington: Indiana University Press, 1985.

Bourke, Joanna. *Dismembering the Male: Men's Bodies, Britain, and the Great
War.* Chicago: University of Chicago Press, 1996.

Brand, Dana. *The Spectator and the City in Nineteenth-Century American Literature.* New York: Cambridge University Press, 1991.

Brandes, Stuart D. *American Welfare Capitalism, 1880–1940.* Chicago: University of Chicago Press, 1970.

Braverman, Harry. *Work and Monopoly Capital: The Degradation of Work in
the Twentieth Century.* New York: Monthly Review Press, 1974.

Brody, David. *Steelworkers in America: The Nonunion Era.* Cambridge, Mass.:
Harvard University Press, 1960.

Brown, E. K. *Willa Cather: A Critical Biography.* New York: Knopf, 1953.

Brown, Joshua. *Beyond the Lines: Pictorial Reporting, Everyday Life, and the Crisis of Gilded Age America.* Berkeley: University of California Press, 2002.

Brown, Marta. *Picturing Time: The Work of Etienne-Jules Marey (1830–1904).*
Chicago: University of Chicago Press, 1992.

Bryant, Kenneth G. "Percy MacKaye and the Drama of Democracy." Ph.D. diss.,
University of Nebraska, 1991.

Butler, Judith. *Gender Trouble: Feminism and the Subversion of Identity.* New
York: Routledge, 1990.

Carver, George. "Legend in Steel." *Western Pennsylvania Historical Magazine* 27
(September 1944): 129–36.

Chambers, Clarke A. *Paul U. Kellogg and the Survey: Voices for Social Welfare
and Social Justice.* Minneapolis: University of Minnesota Press, 1971.

Chandler, Alfred D., Jr. *The Visible Hand: The Managerial Revolution in American Business.* Cambridge, Mass.: Harvard University Press, 1977.

Collomp, Catherine. "Unions, Civics, and National Identity: Organized Labor's
Reaction to Immigration, 1881–1897." *Labor History* 29 (Fall 1988): 450–74.

Conn, Steven. *Museums and American Intellectual Life, 1876–1926.* Chicago:
University of Chicago Press, 1998.

Cook, Blanche Wiesen, ed. *Crystal Eastman on Women and Revolution.* New
York: Oxford University Press, 1978.

Cook, Peter. *The Industrial Craftsworker: Skill, Managerial Strategies, and
Workplace Relationships.* London: Mansell, 1996.

Cooper, Jerry M. *The Army and Civil Disorder: Federal Military Intervention in
Labor Disputes, 1877–1900.* Westport, Conn.: Greenwood Press, 1980.

Corn, Jacqueline Karnell. *Environmental Health in Nineteenth-Century America*. New York: Peter Lang, 1989.

Corwin, Sharon. "Picturing Efficiency: Precisionism, Scientific Management, and the Effacement of Labor." *Representations* 84 (Fall 2003): 139–65.

Cosco, Joseph P. *Imagining Italians: The Clash of Romance and Race in American Perspectives, 1880–1910*. Albany: State University of New York Press, 2003.

Couvares, Francis. *The Remaking of Pittsburgh: Class and Culture in an Industrializing City, 1877–1919*. Albany: State University of New York Press, 1984.

Dabakis, Melissa. *Visualizing Labor in American Sculpture: Monuments, Manliness, and the Work Ethic, 1880–1935*. New York: Cambridge University Press, 1999.

Davis, Natalie Zemon. "The Reasons of Misrule: Youth Groups and Charivaris in Sixteenth-Century France." *Past and Present* 50 (February 1971): 41–75.

Davis, Pearce. *The Development of the American Glass Industry*. Cambridge, Mass.: Harvard University Press, 1949.

Davis, Susan G. *Parades and Power: Street Theater in Nineteenth-Century Philadelphia*. Philadelphia: Temple University Press, 1986.

Demarest, David P., ed. *"The River Ran Red": Homestead 1892*. Pittsburgh: University of Pittsburgh Press, 1992.

Derickson, Alan. "Physiological Science and Scientific Management in the Progressive Era: Frederic S. Lee and the Committee on Industrial Fatigue." *Business History Review* 68 (Winter 1994): 483–514.

——. *Workers' Health, Workers' Democracy: The Western Miners' Struggle, 1891–1925*. Ithaca, N.Y.: Cornell University Press, 1988.

DeVault, Ileen A. *Sons and Daughters of Labor: Class and Clerical Work in Turn-of-the-Century Pittsburgh*. Ithaca, N.Y.: Cornell University Press, 1990.

DiCiccio, Carmen. "The Rise and Fall of King Coal: A History of the Bituminous Coal and Coke Industry of Pennsylvania from 1740–1945." Ph.D. diss., University of Pittsburgh, 1996.

——. *Coal and Coke in Pennsylvania*. Harrisburg: Pennsylvania Historical and Museum Commission, 1996.

Dirks, Nicholas B., Geoff Eley, and Sherry B. Ortner, eds. *Culture/Power/History: A Reader in Contemporary Social Theory*. Princeton: Princeton University Press, 1994.

Dix, Keith. *What's a Miner to Do?: The Mechanization of Coal Mining*. Pittsburgh: University of Pittsburgh Press, 1988.

——. *Work Relations in the Coal Industry: The Hand-Loading Era, 1880–1930*. Morgantown: West Virginia University Press, 1977.

Donovan, Brian. *White Slave Crusades: Race, Gender, and Anti-vice Activism, 1887–1917*. Urbana: University of Illinois Press, 2006.

Doyle, Don H. *New Men, New Cities, New South: Atlanta, Nashville, Charleston, Mobile, 1860–1910*. Chapel Hill: University of North Carolina Press, 1990.

Dubofsky, Melvin. *Hard Work: The Making of Labor History*. Urbana: University of Illinois Press, 2000.

Duffy, John. *The Sanitarians: A History of American Public Health*. Urbana: University of Illinois Press, 1990.

Dyer, Richard. "White." *Screen* 29 (1988): 44–65.

Eavenson, Howard N. *The First Century and a Quarter of American Coal Industry*. Pittsburgh: privately printed, 1942.

Eggert, Gerald. *Steelmasters and Labor Reform, 1886–1923*. Pittsburgh: University of Pittsburgh Press, 1981.

Fairchild, Amy L. *Science at the Borders: Immigrant Medical Inspection and the Shaping of the Modern Industrial Labor Force*. Baltimore: Johns Hopkins University Press, 2003.

Faue, Elizabeth. *Community of Suffering and Struggle: Women, Men, and the Labor Movement in Minneapolis, 1915–1945*. Chapel Hill: University of North Carolina Press, 1991.

Foner, Nancy. "Immigrant Women and Work in New York City, Then and Now." *Journal of American Ethnic History* 18 (Spring 1999): 95–113.

Frader, Laura Levine. "From Muscles to Nerves: Gender, 'Race' and the Body at Work in France, 1919–1939." *International Review of Social History* 44 (1999 Supplement): 123–47.

Francis, Owen. "The Saga of Joe Magarac: Steelman." *Scribner's* 90 (November 1931): 505–11.

Gandal, Keith. *The Virtues of the Vicious: Jacob Riis, Stephen Crane, and the Spectacle of the Slum*. New York: Oxford University Press, 1997.

Garceau, Dee. *The Important Things of Life: Women, Work and Family in Sweetwater County, Wyoming, 1880–1929*. Lincoln: University of Nebraska Press, 1997.

Gay, Vernon, and Marilyn Evert. *Discovering Pittsburgh's Sculpture*. Pittsburgh: University of Pittsburgh Press, 1983.

Gilbert, James B. *Work Without Salvation: America's Intellectuals and Industrial Alienation, 1880–1910*. Baltimore: Johns Hopkins University Press, 1977.

Gilje, Paul A. *Rioting in America*. Bloomington: Indiana University Press, 1996.

———. *The Road to Mobocracy: Popular Disorder in New York City, 1763–1834*. Chapel Hill: University of North Carolina Press, 1987.

Gillespie, Richard. "Industrial Fatigue and the Discipline of Physiology." In *Physiology in the American Context, 1850–1940, edited by Gerald L. Geison. Bethesda: American Physiological Society, 1987.

Gilley, Jennifer, and Stephen Burnett. "Deconstructing and Reconstructing Pittsburgh's Man of Steel: Reading Joe Magarac against the Context of the 20th-Century Steel Industry." *Journal of American Folklore* 111 (Fall 1998): 392–408.

Glassberg, David. *American Historical Pageantry: The Uses of Tradition in the Early Twentieth Century*. Chapel Hill: University of North Carolina Press, 1990.

Go, Julian. "Inventing Industrial Accidents and Their Insurance." *Social Science History* 20 (Fall 1996): 401–38.

Goldin, Claudia, and Lawrence F. Katz. "Technology, Skill, and the Wage Structure: Insights from the Past." *American Economic Review* 86 (May 1996): 252–57.

Goodman, Nan. *Shifting the Blame: Literature, Law, and the Theory of Accidents in Nineteenth-Century America*. Princeton: Princeton University Press, 1998.

Gorn, Elliott. *The Manly Art: Bare-Knuckle Prize Fighting in America*. Ithaca, N.Y.: Cornell University Press, 1986.

Gould, Steven Jay. *The Mismeasure of Man*. New York: Norton, 1981.

Graziosi, Andrea. "Common Laborers, Unskilled Workers, 1880–1915." *Labor History* 22 (Fall 1981): 512–44.

Greene, Janet Wells. "Camera Wars: Images of Coal Miners and the Fragmentation of Working Class Identity, 1933–1947." Ph.D. diss., New York University, 2000.

Greenwald, Maurine W., and Margo Anderson, eds. *Pittsburgh Surveyed: Social Science and Social Reform in the Early Twentieth Century*. Pittsburgh: University of Pittsburgh Press, 1996.

Griffith, Sally F. "'Order, Discipline, and a few Cannon': Benjamin Franklin, the Association, and the Rhetoric and Practice of Boosterism." *Pennsylvania Magazine of History and Biography* 116 (April 1997): 131–55.

——. *Home Town News: William Allen White and the Emporia Gazette*. New York: Oxford University Press, 1989.

Grimsted, David. *American Mobbing, 1828–1861: Toward Civil War*. New York: Oxford University Press, 1998.

Grover, Kathryn, ed. *Fitness in American Culture: Images of Health, Sport, and the Body, 1830–1940*. Amherst: University of Massachusetts Press, 1989.

Guttsman, W. L. *Workers' Culture in Weimar Germany: Between Tradition and Commitment*. New York: Berg, 1990.

Hahn, Harlan. "Advertising the Acceptably Employable Image: Disability and

Capitalism." In *The Disability Studies Reader*, edited by Lennard J. Davis. New York: Routledge, 1997.

Hamer, David. *New Towns in the New World: Images and Perceptions of the Nineteenth-Century Urban Frontier*. New York: Columbia University Press, 1990.

Hammack, David C., and Stanton Wheeler. *Social Science in the Making: Essays on The Russell Sage Foundation, 1907–1971*. New York: Russell Sage Foundation, 1994.

Hanchett, Thomas W. *Sorting Out the New South City: Race, Class, and Urban Development in Charlotte, 1875–1975*. Chapel Hill: University of North Carolina Press, 1998.

Hays, Samuel P., ed. *City at the Point: Essays on the Social History of Pittsburgh*. Pittsburgh: University of Pittsburgh Press, 1989.

Helstein, Ralph. "Reaction of American Labor to Technological Change." In *Labor in a Changing America*, edited by William Haber. New York: Basic Books, 1966.

Hepler, Allison L. *Women in Labor: Mothers, Medicine, and Occupational Health in the United States, 1890–1980*. Columbus: Ohio State University Press, 2000.

Heron, Craig, and Steve Penfold. "The Craftsmen's Spectacle: The Labour Day Parades in Canada, the Early Years." *Histoire Sociale* 58 (November 1996): 357–89.

Herschbach, Lisa. "Fragmentation and Reunion: Medicine, Memory, and Body in the American Civil War." Ph.D. diss., Harvard University, 1997.

Higbie, Tony. "Crossing Class Boundaries: Tramp Ethnography and Narratives of Class in Progressive Era America." *Social Science History* 21 (Winter 1997): 559–92.

Hoffenberg, Peter H. *An Empire on Display: English, Indian, and Australian Exhibitions from the Crystal Palace to the Great War*. Berkeley: University of California Press, 2001.

Hogg, J. Bernard. "The Homestead Strike." Ph.D. diss., University of Chicago, 1943.

Jacobson, Matthew Frye. *Whiteness of a Different Color: European Immigration and the Alchemy of Race*. Cambridge, Mass.: Harvard University Press, 1998.

Jaffe, Irma. *Joseph Stella*. Cambridge, Mass.: Harvard University Press, 1970.

Jardini, Dave. "From Iron to Steel: The Recasting of the Jones and Laughlin's Workforce between 1885 and 1896." *Technology and Culture* 36 (April 1995): 271–301.

Joseph, Antoine. *Skilled Workers' Solidarity: The American Experience in Comparative Perspective*. New York: Garland, 2000.

Kaplan, Daile, ed. *Photo Story: Selected Letters and Photographs of Lewis W. Hine*. Washington: Smithsonian Institution Press, 1992.

Kasson, John F. *Houdini, Tarzan, and the Perfect Man: The White Male Body and the Challenge of Modernity in America*. New York: Hill and Wang, 2001.

Kaster, Gregory L. "Labour's True Man: Organised Workingmen and the Language of Manliness in the USA, 1827–1877." *Gender and History* 13 (April 2001): 24–64.

Kazin, Michael, and Steven J. Ross. "America's Labor Day: The Dilemma of a Worker's Celebration." *Journal of American History* 78 (March 1992): 1294–1323.

Kessler-Harris, Alice. *Out to Work: A History of Wage-Earning Women in the United States*. New York: Oxford University Press, 1982.

Kleinberg, S. J. *The Shadow of the Mills: Working-Class Families in Pittsburgh, 1870–1907*. Pittsburgh: University of Pittsburgh Press, 1989.

Knobel, Dale T. *"America for the Americans:" The Nativist Movement in the United States*. New York: Twayne, 1996.

Koehn, Nancy F. "Henry Heinz and Brand Creation in the Late Nineteenth Century: Making Markets for Processed Food." *Business History Review* 73 (Autumn 1999): 349–93.

Koven, Seth. "Remembering and Dismemberment: Crippled Children, Wounded Soldiers, and the Great War in Great Britain." *American Historical Review* 99 (October 1994): 1167–1202.

Krause, Paul. *The Battle for Homestead, 1880–1892: Politics, Culture, and Steel*. Pittsburgh: University of Pittsburgh Press, 1992.

Kraut, Alan M. "Plagues and Prejudice: Nativism's Construction of Disease in Nineteenth- and Twentieth-Century New York City." In *Hives of Sickness: Public Health and Epidemics in New York City*, edited by David Rosner. New Brunswick, N.J.: Rutgers University Press, 1995.

——. *Silent Travelers: Germs, Genes, and the "Immigrant Menace."* New York: Basic Books, 1994.

Kula, Witold, Nina Assorodobraj-Kula, and Marcin Kula. *Writing Home: Immigrants in Brazil and the United States, 1890–1891*. Translated by Josephine Wtulich. New York: Columbia University Press, 1986.

LaCapra, Dominick. *Rethinking Intellectual History: Texts, Contexts, Language*. Ithaca, N.Y.: Cornell University Press, 1983.

Leach, Eugene E. "The Literature of Riot Duty: Managing Class Conflict in the Streets, 1877–1927." *Radical History Review* 56 (Spring 1993): 23–50.

Lears, T. J. Jackson. *No Place of Grace: Antimodernism and the Transformation of American Culture, 1880–1920*. New York: Pantheon, 1981.

Levenstein, Harvey A. *Revolution at the Table: The Transformation of the American Diet*. New York: Oxford University Press, 1988.

Levine, Lawrence W. "The Folklore of Industrial Society: Popular Culture and Its Audiences." *American Historical Review* 97 (December 1992): 1369–99.

Lewis, W. David. *Iron and Steel in America*. Greenville, Del.: Eleutherian Mills-Hagley Foundation, 1976.

The Life Treasury of American Folklore. New York: Time, Inc., 1961.

Linke, Uli. "White Skin, Aryan Aesthetics." In *German Bodies: Race and Representation After Hitler*. London: Routledge, 1999.

Linkon, Sherry Lee, and John Russo. *Steeltown U.S.A.: Work and Memory in Youngstown*. Lawrence: University Press of Kansas, 2002.

Linteau, Paul-Andre. *The Promoter's City: Building the Industrial Town of Maisonneuve, 1883–1918*. Translated by Robert Chodos. Toronto: J. Lorimer, 1985.

Lowrie, James Allison. "A History of the Pittsburgh Stage, 1861–1891." Ph.D. diss., University of Pittsburgh, 1943.

Lubove, Roy. "Workmen's Compensation and the Prerogatives of Voluntarism." *Labor History* 8 (Fall 1967): 254–79.

——. *Twentieth-Century Pittsburgh: Government, Business, and Environmental Change*. New York: John Wiley and Sons, 1969.

Madarasz, Anne. *Glass: Shattering Notions*. Pittsburgh: Historical Society of Western Pennsylvania, 1998.

Magda, Matthew S. *Monessen: Industrial Boomtown and Steel Community, 1898–1980*. Harrisburg: Pennsylvania Historical and Museum Commission, 1985.

Mahoney, Timothy R. " 'A Common Bond of Brotherhood': Male Subculture, the Booster Ethos, and the Origins of Urban Social Order in the Midwest of the 1840s." *Journal of Urban History* 25 (July 1999): 619–46.

Marchand, Roland. *Advertising the American Dream: Making Way for Modernity, 1920–1940*. Berkeley: University of California Press, 1985.

Marstine, Janet Cecelia. "Working History: Images of Labor and Industry in American Mural Painting, 1893–1903." Ph.D. diss., University of Pittsburgh, 1993.

McClymer, John F. *War and Welfare: Social Engineering in America, 1890–1925*. Westport, Conn.: Greenwood Press, 1980.

McIntosh, Elaine N. *American Food Habits in Historical Perspective*. Westport, Conn: Praeger, 1995.

Melosh, Barbara. *Engendering Culture: Manhood and Womanhood in New Deal Public Art and Theater.* Washington, D.C.: Smithsonian Institution Press, 1991.

Meyer, Susan. "In Anxious Celebration: Lewis Hine's Men at Work." *Prospects* 17 (1992): 319.

Modell, Judith. *A Town Without Steel: Envisioning Homestead.* Pittsburgh: University of Pittsburgh Press, 1998.

Montgomery, David. *The Fall of the House of Labor: The Workplace, the State, and American Labor Activism, 1865–1925.* New York: Cambridge University Press, 1987.

Moore, Sarah J. "John White Alexander (1856–1915): In Search of the Decorative." Ph.D. diss., City University of New York, 1992.

Morn, Frank. *The Eye that Never Sleeps: A History of the Pinkerton National Detective Agency.* Bloomington: University of Indiana Press, 1982.

Mosher, Anne E. *Capital's Utopia: Vandergrift, Pennsylvania, 1855–1916.* Baltimore: Johns Hopkins University Press, 2004.

Muller, Edward K. "Industrial Suburbs and the Growth of Metropolitan Pittsburgh, 1870–1920." *Journal of Historical Geography* 27 (January 2001): 58–73.

Nelson, Daniel. *Managers and Workers: Origins of the Twentieth-Century Factory System in the United States, 1880–1920.* Madison: University of Wisconsin Press, 1995.

Norden, Martin F. *The Cinema of Isolation: A History of Physical Disability in the Movies.* New Brunswick, N.J.: Rutgers University Press, 1994.

Norwood, Stephen H. *Strikebreaking and Intimidation: Mercenaries and Masculinity in Twentieth-Century America.* Chapel Hill: University of North Carolina Press, 2002.

Nuwer, Michael. "From Batch to Flow: Production Technology and Work-Force Skills in the Steel Industry, 1880–1920." *Technology and Culture* 29 (October 1988): 808–38.

O'Connor, Erin. "'Fractions of Men': Engendering Amputation in Victorian Culture." *Comparative Studies in Society and History* 39 (October 1997): 742–77.

O'Connor, Richard John. "Cinderheads and Iron Lungs: Window-Glass Craftsmen and the Transformation of Workers' Control, 1880–1905." Ph.D. diss., University of Pittsburgh, 1991.

Oldenziel, Ruth. *Making Technology Masculine: Men, Women, and Modern Machines in America, 1870–1945.* Amsterdam: Amsterdam University Press, 1999.

Panchasi, Roxanne. "Reconstructions: Prosthetics and the Rehabilitation of the Male Body in World War I France." *differences* 7 (1995): 109–64.

Pavalko, Eliza. "State Timing of Policy Adoption: Workmen's Compensation in the United States, 1909–1929." *American Journal of Sociology* 95 (November 1989): 592–615.

Peiss, Kathy. *Cheap Amusements: Working Women and Leisure in Turn-of-the-Century New York.* Philadelphia: Temple University Press, 1986.

Pencak, William, Matthew Dennis, and Simon P. Newman, eds. *Riot and Revelry in Early America.* University Park: Pennsylvania State University Press, 2002.

Penna, Anthony N. "Changing Images of Twentieth-Century Pittsburgh." *Pennsylvania History* 43 (January 1976): 49–63.

Pfitzer, Gregory M. *Picturing the American Past: Illustrated Histories and the American Imagination, 1840–1900.* Washington, D.C.: Smithsonian Institution Press, 2002.

Pivar, David J. *Purity and Hygiene: Women, Prostitution, and the "American Plan," 1900–1930.* Westport, Conn.: Greenwood Press, 2002.

Pultz, John. *The Body and the Lens: Photography 1839 to the Present.* New York: Harry N. Abrams, 1995.

Rabinbach, Anson. *The Human Motor: Energy, Fatigue, and the Origins of Modernity.* New York: Basic Books, 1990.

Raftery, Judith. "Chicago Settlement Women in Fact and Fiction: Hobart Chatfield Chatfield-Taylor, Clara Elizabeth Laughlin, and Elia Wilkinson Peattie Portray the New Woman." *Illinois Historical Journal* 88 (Spring 1995): 37–58.

Richman, Michael. *Daniel Chester French: An American Sculptor.* New York: National Trust for Historic Preservation, 1976.

Robinson, Jesse S. "The Amalgamated Association of Iron, Steel and Tin Workers." *Johns Hopkins University Studies in Historical and Political Science* 38 (1920): 1–166.

Rodgers, Daniel T. *The Work Ethic in Industrial America, 1850–1920.* Chicago: University of Chicago Press, 1974.

Rollo, Duncan James. "Percy MacKaye's Vision of the National Drama as an Expression of the American Identity." Ph.D. diss., Kent State University, 1974.

Rose, Sarah F. "'Crippled' Hands: Disability in Labor and Working-Class History." *Labor* 2 (Spring 2005): 27–54.

Rosenzweig, Roy. *Eight Hours for What We Will: Workers and Leisure in an Industrial City, 1870–1920.* Cambridge: Cambridge University Press, 1983.

Rosner, David, and Gerald Markowitz, eds. *Dying for Work: Workers' Safety and Health in Twentieth-Century America.* Bloomington: Indiana University Press, 1987.

Rotundo, E. Anthony. "Body and Soul: Changing Ideals of American Middle-

Class Manhood, 1770–1920." *Journal of Social History* 16 (Summer 1983): 23–38.

Roucek, Joseph S. "The Image of the Slav in U.S. History and in Immigration Policy." *American Journal of Economics and Sociology* 28 (January 1969): 29–48.

Rudé, George. *The Crowd in History: A Study of Popular Disturbances in France and England, 1730–1848.* New York: Wiley, 1964.

Ryan, Mary P. "'A Laudable Pride in the Whole of Us': City Halls and Civic Materialism." *American Historical Review* 105 (October 2000): 1131–70.

———. "The American Parade: Representations of the Nineteenth-Century Social Order." In *The New Cultural History*, edited by Lynn Hunt. Berkeley: University of California Press, 1989.

Sackman, Douglas C. "'Nature's Workshop': The Work Environment and Workers' Bodies in California's Citrus Industry, 1900–1940." *Environmental History* 5 (January 2000): 27–53.

Santos, Michael. "Between Hegemony and Autonomy: The Skilled Iron Workers' Search for Identity, 1900–1930." *Labor History* 35 (Summer 1994): 399–423.

Scarry, Elaine. *The Body in Pain: The Making and Unmaking of the World.* New York: Oxford University Press, 1985.

Schreiner, Samuel A. *Henry Clay Frick: The Gospel of Greed.* New York: St. Martin's Press, 1995.

Scott, James C. *Domination and the Arts of Resistance: Hidden Transcripts.* New Haven: Yale University Press, 1990.

Scott, Joan W. "'L'ouvrière! Mot impie, sordide . . .': Women Workers in the Discourse of French Political Economy, 1840–1860." In *The Historical Meanings of Work*, edited by Patrick Joyce. New York: Cambridge University Press, 1987.

Scoville, Warren C. *Revolution in Glassmaking: Entrepreneurship and Technological Change in the American Industry, 1880–1920.* Cambridge, Mass.: Harvard University Press, 1948.

Scranton, Philip. "None-Too-Porous Boundaries: Labor History and the History of Technology." *Labor History* 29 (October 1988): 728–36.

Sellers, Christopher C. *Hazards on the Job: From Industrial Disease to Environmental Health Science.* Chapel Hill: University of North Carolina Press, 1997.

Seltzer, Mark. *Bodies and Machines.* New York: Routledge, 1992.

Serene, Frank. "Immigrant Steelworkers in the Mon Valley: Their Communities and the Development of a Labor Class Consciousness." Ph.D. diss., University of Pittsburgh, 1979.

Sewell, William H., Jr. "The Concept(s) of Culture." In *Beyond the Cultural*

Turn: New Directions in the Study of Society and Culture, edited by Victoria E. Bonnell and Lynn Hunt. Berkeley: University of California Press, 1999.

———. "Geertz, Cultural Systems, and History: From Synchrony to Transformation." In *The Fate of "Culture": Geertz and Beyond*, edited by Sherry B. Ortner. Berkeley: University of California Press, 1999.

———. *Logics of History: Social Theory and Social Transformation*. Chicago: University of Chicago Press, 2005.

Sheppard, Muriel. *Cloud by Day: The Story of Coal and Coke and People*. Chapel Hill: University of North Carolina Press, 1947.

Slotkin, Richard. *The Fatal Environment: The Myth of the Frontier in the Age of Industrialization, 1800–1890*. New York: Atheneum, 1985.

Smith, Carl S. *Urban Disorder and the Shape of Belief: The Great Chicago Fire, the Haymarket Bomb, and the Model Town of Pullman*. Chicago: University of Chicago Press, 1995.

Smith, Robert Michael. *From Blackjacks to Briefcases: A History of Commercialized Strikebreaking and Unionbusting in the United States*. Athens: University of Ohio Press, 2003.

Smith, Sherry. *Reimagining Indians: Native Americans through Anglo Eyes, 1880–1940*. New York: Oxford University Press, 2000.

Solomon, William. *Literature, Amusement, and Technology in the Great Depression*. New York: Cambridge University Press, 2002.

Somerville, Siobahn B. *Queering the Color Line: Race and the Invention of Homosexuality in American Culture*. Durham, N.C.: Duke University Press, 2000.

Spencer, Ethel. *The Spencers of Amberson Avenue: A Turn-of-the Century Memoir*. Pittsburgh: University of Pittsburgh Press, 1983.

Spraker, Jean. "'Come to the Carnival at Old St. Paul': Souvenirs from a Civic Ritual Interpreted." *Prospects* 11 (1987): 233–46.

Stange, Maren. *Symbols of Ideal Life: Social Documentary Photography in America, 1890–1950*. New York: Cambridge University Press, 1989.

Stone, Katherine. "The Origins of Job Structures in the Steel Industry." *Review of Radical Political Economics* 6 (Summer 1974): 61–97.

Storey, John. *Inventing Popular Culture*. Malden, Mass.: Blackwell, 2003.

Storrs, Landon R. Y. *Civilizing Capitalism: The National Consumers' League, Women's Activism, and Labor Standards in the New Deal Era*. Chapel Hill: University of North Carolina Press, 2000.

Stowell, David O. *Streets, Railroads, and the Great Strike of 1877*. Chicago: University of Chicago Press, 1999.

Taillon, Paul Michel. "'What We Want is Good, Sober Men': Masculinity,

Respectability, and Temperance in the Railroad Brotherhoods, c. 1870–
1910." *Journal of Social History* 36 (Winter 2002): 319–38.

Temin, Peter. *Iron and Steel in Nineteenth-Century America: An Economy Inquiry.* Cambridge: MIT Press, 1964.

Thompson, E. P. "The Moral Economy of the English Crowd in the Eighteenth Century." *Past and Present* 50 (February 1971): 76–136.

———. "Time, Work-Discipline, and Industrial Capitalism." *Past and Present* 38 (1967): 56–97.

Thomson, Rosemarie Garland. "Seeing the Disabled: Visual Rhetorics of Disability in Popular Photography." In *The New Disability History: American Perspectives,* edited by Paul K. Longmore and Lauri Umanksi. New York: New York University Press, 2001.

Tomko, Linda. *Dancing Class: Gender, Ethnicity, and Social Divides in American Dance, 1890–1920.* Bloomington: Indiana University Press, 1999.

Trachtenberg, Alan. *Reading American Photographs: Images as History, Mathew Brady to Walker Evans.* New York: Hill and Wang, 1989.

Van Hook, Bailey. "From the Lyrical to the Epic: Images of Women in American Murals at the Turn of the Century." *Winterthur Portfolio* 26 (Spring 1991): 63–80.

———. *The Virgin and the Dynamo: Public Murals in American Architecture, 1893–1917.* Athens: Ohio University Press, 2003.

Vaughan, Christopher A. "Ogling Igorots: The Politics and Commerce of Exhibiting Cultural Otherness, 1898–1913." In *Freakery: Cultural Spectacles of the Extraordinary Body,* edited by Rosemarie Garland Thomson. New York: New York University Press, 1996.

Walden, Keith. *Becoming Modern in Toronto: The Industrial Exhibition and the Shaping of a Late Victorian Culture.* Toronto: University of Toronto Press, 1997.

Walker, Jack L. "The Diffusion of Innovations Among the American States." *American Political Science Review* 63 (September 1969): 880–99.

Ward, Stephen V. *Selling Places: The Marketing and Promotion of Towns and Cities, 1850–2000.* New York: Routledge, 1998.

Waugh, Joan. *Unsentimental Reformer: The Life of Josephine Shaw Lowell.* Cambridge, Mass.: Harvard University Press, 1997.

Williams-Searle, John. "Courting Risk: Disability, Masculinity, and Liability on Iowa's Railroads, 1868–1900." *Annals of Iowa* 58 (Winter 1999): 27–77.

Witt, John Fabian. *The Accidental Republic: Crippled Workingmen, Destitute Widows, and the Remaking of American Law.* Cambridge, Mass.: Harvard University Press, 2004.

Wolff, Leon. *Lockout, the Story of the Homestead Strike of 1892: A Study of Violence, Unionism and the Carnegie Steel Empire*. New York: Harper and Row, 1965.

Wood, Sharon. *The Freedom of the Streets: Work, Citizenship, and Sexuality in a Gilded Age City*. Chapel Hill: University of North Carolina Press, 2005.

Wosk, Julie. *Breaking Frame: Technology and the Visual Arts in the Nineteenth Century*. New Brunswick, N.J.: Rutgers University Press, 1992.

Wtulich, Josephine. *American Xenophobia and the Slav Immigrant: A Living Legacy of Mind and Spirit*. Boulder: East European Monographs, 1994.

Youngner, Rina C. *Industry in Art: Pittsburgh, 1812 to 1920*. Pittsburgh: University of Pittsburgh Press, 2006.

Yuan, David D. "Disfigurement and Reconstruction in Oliver Wendell Holmes's 'The Human Wheel, Its Spokes and Felloes.'" In *The Body and Physical Difference: Discourses of Disability*, edited by David T. Mitchell and Sharon L. Snyder. Ann Arbor: University of Michigan Press, 1997.

Zembala, Dennis. "Machines in the Glasshouse: The Transformation in the Glass Industry, 1820–1915." Ph.D. diss., George Washington University, 1984.

Ziff, Larzer. *The American 1890s: Life and Times of a Lost Generation*. New York: Viking, 1966.

Zuboff, Shoshana. *In the Age of the Smart Machine: The Future of Work and Power*. New York: Basic Books, 1988.

INDEX

Schwartz, Robert, 38
Scientific American, 42, 283 n. 40
Scientific management, 170, 245, 302
 n. 74
Scott, James, 6, 179
Secretary of Internal Affairs of Penn-
 sylvania, 158–59
Sesquicentennial parade, 137–44, 301
 n. 67; Jones and Laughlin Steel
 Company float in, 142–44; Man-
 ufacturers Committee float in, 140;
 pageantry and, 138–39; Riter-
 Conley Manufacturing Company
 float in, 140, 142
Sewell, William, Jr., 4–5, 7, 8
Sherman, William O'Neill, 234–35
Simons, A. M., 149
Sinclair, Upton, 150
Slavs. *See* Immigrants, immigration:
 "new"
Smith, Samuel, 215
Smoke (pollution): boosters' criticism
 of, 45, 94; representations of, 124,
 131–32, 275; tourism and, 9, 58,
 284 n. 47
Social hygiene movement, 219
Social reformers, 5–6, 8, 10, 13–15,
 200–201, 203–4, 207–8, 214–23,
 224, 226, 231, 242, 243, 266; criti-
 cism of employers by, 20, 149, 172–
 73; mechanization and, 150; profes-
 sionalization and, 151–52, 221. *See
 also* Pittsburgh Survey
Sosienski, Simon, 172–73
Sotak, Joseph, 83, 87
Spectacle. *See* Work: spectacle of
"Steel City," 7, 18–19, 50, 278 n. 2
Steel industry, 27–29, 279 n. 3;
 Bessemer process in, 26, 28, 32–33,
 58, 59, 142–43, 281 n. 15, 282 n. 25;
 blast furnaces in, 30–31; electrification of, 35; growth of, 22, 24; open-

hearth process in, 28–29, 33–34;
 mechanization of, 32–37, 68–69;
 rolling process in, 34, 35; workplace
 tours of, 92, 94–96, 147
Steel Industry Heritage Corporation,
 272
Steel Workers, The (Fitch): fatigue in,
 187; machinery in, 185–86; mill
 architecture and, 184; scenic
 approach in, 183; workers' bodies
 in, 182–83. *See also* Stella, Joseph
Steffens, Lincoln, 5–6
Stella, Joseph, 183, 207, 307 n. 59; "A
 Breathing Spell," 183–84; "At the
 Base of the Blast Furnace," 187–89;
 "In the Glare of the Converter," 184;
 "In the Light of a Five-Ton Ingot,"
 184; on Pittsburgh's scenery, 197
Stiefel, H. C., 53
Stowell, Myron, 65, 83; on barbarism
 in Homestead, 76, 79; representations of workers by, 76–77; on Foy's
 challenge, 75

Taylor, Frederick Winslow, 170
Technological gigantism, 184–85
Tener, John, 244
Tener, Stephen, 232
Trautmann, W. E., 149, 173, 246

Union benefit plans, 240–41, 242,
 246
Union Trust Company, 104
United States Bureau of Mines: accident statistics of, 155; mechanization statistics of, 285 n. 51; mining
 safety competitions of, 232–33
United States Immigration Commission: on accidents, 160–61; definition of *Slav* by, 53–54, 286 n. 61;
 ethnic stratification of workforce
 and, 56; on physical effects of work,
 155

United States Industrial Commission, 214, 217

United States Steel Committee of Safety, 229

United States Steel Corporation: accident litigation of, 237; accident relief plan of, 241, 260; Joe Magarac and, 270; medical services and, 234; reaction of, to Pittsburgh Survey, 231, 260

Unskilled labor: boosters' distaste for, 11, 52, 61; ethnic divisions within, 55; ethnic nicknames for, 53, 56; in Homestead, 67, 70; mechanization and, 11, 29–30, 36, 40–41, 49, 56, 60, 62; pageantry and, 117

Wain, Silas, 77, 87

Walkley, David Birdsey, 107, 108

Watchorn, Robert, 164

Waterfront shopping center, 272, 273

Weihe, William: in Allegheny County Centennial parade, 116; in Homestead lockout, 78–79; on new immigrants, 54, 291 n. 22

Weir, James, 73, 290 n. 11

Welfare capitalism, 231

Western Pennsylvania Exposition Society, 91; aesthetics and, 120; as educator, 119; glass exhibit and, 122–23

Western Pennsylvania Hospital, 233

Wilcox, Ella Wheeler, 263–64

Willson, Seelye, 17

Women: in art, 125–25, 132; Butler's categories of, 206–7; ethnic stratification of work by, 206; insurance and, 238–39; labor legislation and, 201–2; marginalization of, 20, 200–204, 309 nn. 2, 6; mechanized work and, 210–15, 310 n. 22; physiques

of immigrant, 204–5, 208–9; prostitution and, 215–17; reproductive abilities of, 217–21; speed vs. strength of, as workers, 209–10, 212–13

Women and the Trades (Butler), 202–3, 223; "American girls" in, 209, 212; categorization of women in, 206–7; immigration in, 203, 204–5, 208, 222; mechanization in, 209–10, 211; motherhood in, 215, 217, 218, 222; "nervous work" in, 213–14, 217; women's competition with men in, 203–4; workers' deterioration in, 216–17

Work: concern about, 100–101, 149–52, 212–21; ethnic division of, 51, 55–56, 180, 202, 204–9, 210; risk and, 162–65, 196, 227, 229, 230, 231, 236, 240, 310 n. 10; spectacle of, 11, 20, 44, 59–60, 68–69, 92, 95, 98–99, 107–9, 120–22, 123, 132, 136–37, 266, 271, 287 n. 71, 295 n. 9, 317 n. 2. *See also* Mechanization; Work ethic

Work-Accidents and the Law (Eastman), 177; accident statistics in, 190, 308 n. 64; criticism of employers in, 187, 224, 312 n. 5; economic crisis in, 196, 198; *The Puddler* and, 195–96; representation of workers in, 189–90.

Work-A-Day Girl, The (Laughlin), 208

Workers: "savagery" of, 53–57, 62, 72–76, 78–80, 81, 117, 291 n. 14; skills as identity for, 99; written descriptions of, 104–6. *See also* Accidents: workers' response to; Amalgamated Association of Iron and Steel Workers; Pittsburgh Survey

EDWARD SLAVISHAK

is an assistant professor of history

at Susquehanna University.

Library of Congress Cataloging-in-Publication Data

Slavishak, Edward Steven.

Bodies of work : civic display and labor in industrial Pittsburgh / Edward Slavishak.

p. cm. — (Body, commodity, text)

Includes bibliographical references and index.

ISBN 978-0-8223-4206-9 (cloth : alk. paper)

ISBN 978-0-8223-4225-0 (pbk. : alk. paper)

1. Working class—Pennsylvania—Pittsburgh—History.

2. Industrialization—Pennsylvania—Pittsburgh—Social aspects.

3. Industries—Pennsylvania—Pittsburgh—Social aspects.

4. City promotion—Pennsylvania—Pittsburgh—History.

5. Pittsburgh (Pa.)—History. I. Title.

HD8085.P63S63 2008

305.5′62097488609034—dc22

2008013879